The Teaching c in Primary Schools

6th edition

This new edition *Teaching of Science in Primary Schools* will help all concerned with primary school education with decisions about how to select, plan, conduct and evaluate science activities. It provides a rationale for teaching that puts children at the centre of their learning and reflects the current emphasis on inquiry-based activities, formative assessment and the role of discussion, argumentation and communication in science education.

This fully revised and expanded edition explores:

- the compelling reasons for starting science in the primary school;
- within-school planning in the context of less prescriptive national requirements;
- the differences in the primary science curriculum across the countries of the UK;
- the implications of the rapid changes in opportunities for children and teachers provided by increased use of ICT and greater access to the internet;
- the role of school and teacher self-evaluation as a means of improving provision for children's learning;
- the need for dependable teacher-based summative assessment for recording and reporting children's achievements;
- the importance for both teachers and learners of reflecting on the process and content of their activities.

Other key aspects of teaching, such as questioning and strategies for helping children to develop understanding, skills, positive attitudes and enjoyment of science, are preserved. The combination of theory and practice makes this book essential reading for practising teachers, those entering the profession and those studying for further qualifications.

Wynne Harlen, OBE, PhD, has been involved in teaching and research in science education, evaluation and pupil assessment throughout her long career, during which time she has been Sidney Jones Professor of Science Education at the University of Liverpool, UK and Director of the Scottish Council for Research in Education.

Anne Qualter, PhD, has wide experience of research and professional development in science and is now Head of the Centre for Lifelong Learning at the University of Liverpool, UK.

The Teaching of Science in Primary Schools

6th edition

**Wynne Harlen
and Anne Qualter**

Routledge
Taylor & Francis Group

LONDON AND NEW YORK

Sixth edition published 2014
by Routledge
2 Park Square, Milton Park, Abingdon, Oxon OX14 4RN

and by Routledge
711 Third Avenue, New York, NY 10017

Routledge is an imprint of the Taylor & Francis Group, an informa business

First edition published by David Fulton Publishers 1992

Fifth edition published by Routledge 2009

British Library Cataloguing in Publication Data
A catalogue record for this book is available from the British Library

Library of Congress Cataloging in Publication Data
Harlen, Wynne.
The teaching of science in primary schools / Wynne Harlen and
Anne Qualter. – Sixth edition.
     pages cm
   1. Science – Study and teaching (Elementary) I. Qualter, Anne,
   1955– II. Harlen, Wynne. Teaching, learning and assessing science
   5–12. III. Title.
   LB1585.H298 2014
   372.35044–dc23   2013026063

ISBN: 978-0-415-65664-1 (hbk)
ISBN: 978-0-415-65665-8 (pbk)
ISBN: 978-1-315-85096-2 (ebk)

Typeset in Bembo
by HWA Text and Data Management, London

Printed by Bell & Bain Ltd, Glasgow

MIX
Paper from
responsible sources
FSC® C007785

We dedicate this book to the memory of Brenda Keogh,
whose creative thinking has left its mark on primary science teaching.

Contents

Acknowledgements

We would like to thank the many teachers in schools and other educators who, consciously and unconsciously, have helped us to reflect on the developments in primary science education since the fifth edition of this book. In particular, thanks are due to: Angela Bettridge and the children of Cunningham Hill Infants School; David Leigh Evans of Sarn Associates and the industries supporting his work, including E.On and BHP Bilton; Kathy Schofield, previously of St Edwards Primary School Runcorn; Lisa Fleet and her class at Claremont Community Primary School; Chris Williams for permission to reference 'Mr Andrews' primary science blog; Joanna Redzimski, Head Teacher of Ridgeway School Croydon for permission to reproduce her school curriculum policy statement; Yvonne Niescier of Sacred Heart Catholic College, Crosby; and Judith Salmon and her staff of Blackmoor Park Infants in Liverpool.

We would also like to express our gratitude to the following for permission to reproduce figures from their publications:

- The Association for Science Education for permission to reproduce material from various issues of *Primary Science Review* and from *Primary Science*.

- Sage publications for permission to reproduce material from M. Schilling, L. Hargreaves, W. Harlen, and T. Russell (1990) *Assessing Science in the Primary Classroom, Written Tasks*.

- Millgate House Publishers for permission to reproduce a concept cartoon from *Concept Cartoons in Science Education, 2000*.

- Routledge for permission to reproduce material from W. Harlen, C. Macro, K. Reed and M. Schilling (2003) *Making Progress in Primary Science Handbook* (second edition).

- Liverpool University Press for permission to reproduce various drawings from SPACE Research Reports on *'Growth'* (1990), *'Sound'* (1990), *'Processes of Life'* (1992), and *'Evaporation and Condensation'* (1990).

- Harper Collins for raising no objection to the reproduction of a drawing from Nuffield Primary Science Teachers' Guide (ages 7–12) *The Earth in Space*, second edition (1995).

- Springer for permission to reproduce an image from R. Kershner, N. Mercer, P. Warwick, and J. Staarman Kleine, (2010) Can the interactive whiteboard support young children's collaborative communication and thinking in classroom science activities? *Computer-supported Collaborative Learning*, 5, 359–383.

- NFER for permission to reproduce a diagram from C. Hague and S. Payton (2010) *Digital Literacy across the Curriculum: a Futurelab handbook*. Futurelab, Bristol www.futurelab.org.uk.

Introduction

In the 22 years since the first edition of this book there have been many undulations in the attention given to science in the primary school curriculum. In 1992, the implications of teaching science in every primary school and to every child, as required by the newly introduced National Curriculum in England and Wales, and advised by guidelines in other parts of the UK, were still being worked out. Indeed, implementation at KS2 was still a few years away. Many teachers were unsure of what science at the primary school level was all about. So it was that the 1992 edition of the book began with a chapter entitled 'Science – What is it?' Over the subsequent years, helped by experience and better preparation of teachers, the need to discuss the nature of science as such faded, enabling more attention to be given to what learning and teaching science means at the primary level: the 'what' turned into 'how'.

Coming to recent changes since the publication of the last (fifth) edition of the book in 2009, there has been a down-turn in the attention to science. Various reasons for this include the ending of national testing in science in England, a move towards cross-curricular topics and a focus on skills with too little regard to content. All of these changes could – and should – have improved the teaching of science, but circumstances (such as the retention of high stakes testing in English and mathematics in England) allowed attention to drift away, as if we had forgotten how important it is for children to be able to collect and use evidence to develop their understanding of the world around them. For that reason we begin this edition with a section titled 'Compelling reasons for teaching science in primary schools'.

Other parts of the book reflect the considerable changes in primary education in general and in the political landscape that have affected the provision for science in the primary school, particularly in England, where a number of education agencies previously providing guidance and materials for teachers no longer exist.

One of the areas that has seen the most rapid change and seems set to continue to develop more quickly than any other is the use by teachers and pupils of ICT, both in school and in everyday life. Not only have the technologies available increased but the greater confidence of teachers in using them has enabled ICT to become more integrated into teaching and learning. Teachers are also using materials and guidance from online sources and are less dependent on books and paper-based guides. Children are taking the initiative in using the internet and social networking to find information. The facility for children to submit work to the teacher and to obtain feedback on it online makes one wonder how long it may be before we see the paper-free classroom.

A further area where what was seen as innovation is now being absorbed into regular practice is the use of formative assessment, or assessment for learning (AfL). Of course, not everything described as AfL matches intentions, but the greater use of open questioning, positive feedback, sharing goals and involving pupils in self-assessment is encouraging. But as well as concern for AfL, attention has turned to assessment of learning, since the end of national testing in science created a need for 'a coherent framework for assessment designed to support learning and provide dependable information for reporting achievement at pupil, school and national levels' (Nuffield Foundation, 2012: 7). So we have proposed some procedures for moderated teacher-based assessment, in which pupils have a role, designed to help progress towards and report on achievement of the requirements of the programme of study at particular stages. This reflects a world-wide increase in interest in pupil assessment and its impact on how and what is taught in the classroom. The OECD has been conducting a long-term study of assessment and evaluation in its member countries and in its report emphasises the importance of putting the learners at the centre:

> They should be fully engaged with their learning and empowered to assess their own progress (which is also a key skill for life-long learning). It is important, too, to monitor broader learning outcomes, including the development of critical thinking, social competencies, engagement with learning and overall well-being.
>
> (OECD, 2013: 3)

The report admits that these are not easy to measure and require the collection and use of both quantitative and qualitative data.

Allied with self-assessment by pupils is self-evaluation by teachers and schools. In theory this enables schools to take responsibility for improving practice, just as children take more responsibility for improving their work. However, this process is better developed in relation to general practice than to particular subject areas and the extent to which it is being applied specifically for improving science education is as yet limited. So, in the final part of the book, we deal with the formative evaluation of practice at class and school levels. This involves identifying where progress needs to be made through the actions of the science subject leader or, more formally, through auditing the provision for science, as required when taking part in the Primary Science Quality Mark scheme. Once needs are analysed action can be taken to enhance provision for children's learning in science.

As well as addressing areas of change in primary science education, the book deals with the enduring duties and tasks of teachers and school management that are involved in planning and implementing programmes designed for children to enjoy scientific activity, to stimulate and sustain their curiosity and develop their understanding of the world around them. These include: the importance of using well-formulated questions; finding out and building from the ideas that children bring to the classroom, from what they have been told or have developed through their own thinking; the value of talk, dialogue and argumentation; learning outside the classroom; and the importance of good management and planning at school and class levels. We have provided ideas for developing children's knowledge and understanding and their inquiry skills and offered some theory to support these suggestions. As in the previous edition, we have aimed to enhance the discussion of these aspects of practice through use of examples, particularly drawing throughout the book on five case studies in Chapter 3.

The structure of the book

The 25 chapters are arranged in six parts: compelling reasons for teaching science in primary schools; how children learn; the teacher's role; assessment for and of learning; planning for progression; and formative evaluation of practice. These themes, helped by cross-referencing between chapters, make it possible to 'dip into' the book according to interest at a particular time.

The first chapter of the book begins by taking a broad view of the reasons for science education as whole and the principles that should guide decisions about what and how to teach. This is followed by looking briefly at the history of how primary science has developed since the 1960s, leading to the compelling reasons for science being included in children's education from the start. The second chapter describes how the goals of learning science at the primary school level are expressed in the curriculum requirement at the national level in the countries of the UK. We look particularly at the changes that have taken place since about 2005. At that time curriculum requirements were quite similar across the UK but now there is divergence in the requirements or guidelines in England, Northern Ireland, Scotland and Wales. Chapter 3 comprises case studies of activities in five different classes, between them covering the ages 5 to 11 years. Each account provides some background information and one or more lessons on a topic. All the examples describe real events in real classes and are not intended as models, although they reflect several features of effective practice in science education for young children. Some significant features are discussed in relation to aspects that are picked up in later chapters of the book. Chapter 4 starts this discussion by providing some criteria that can be used in evaluating and in planning and adapting activities to increase the opportunities for developing scientific understanding, skills and attitudes. It draws upon research into learning and also from what is known from neuroscience about changes in the brain that accompany learning.

Part 2 discusses various aspects of learning in science, beginning in Chapter 5 with the importance of starting from the ideas that children have formed from their experience and from what they are told and which they bring into school. Examples of children's ideas show that they are the product of reasoning, and so make sense to the children. It follows that these ideas have to be taken seriously and addressed in helping children to come to hold more scientific ideas. In Chapter 6 a model of learning through inquiry helps to identify the role of inquiry skills in the development of ideas from 'small' to 'bigger' ideas. Chapter 7 concerns various forms of talk and its importance in the development of children's understanding. The section ends with a chapter on how the use of ICT can enhance children's learning in science, pointing out that it is not a substitute for first-hand experience or talk and discussion. Examples show how ICT can support different aspects of inquiry in science, from enhancing observation, to collecting evidence, to testing ideas with models and simulations.

Part 3 complements the previous part by discussing the teacher's role in bringing about learning through inquiry. Chapter 9 focuses on learning outside the classroom, showing how to ensure that visits are not just a fun day out but an important part of learning. Chapter 10 deals with the key role in all learning of teachers' questions. This is followed by two chapters dealing with how to help development of understanding and of inquiry skills. Some key characteristics of children's own ideas, identified in Chapter 5, are revisited and strategies teachers can use to help children to develop more scientific ideas are suggested. Chapter 13 considers children's emotional response to learning activities. It looks at how teachers can help to motivate learning and encourage positive attitudes towards learning science. The section ends with a chapter concerning the range and uses of ICT tools available to the teacher, with particular attention to how the teacher uses them in advancing children's learning in science.

Part 4 is about the assessment of pupils for the two main purposes of helping learning (formative assessment) and reporting learning (summative assessment). It begins with general discussion of purposes, methods, properties and uses of assessment and a summary of the characteristics of formative and summative assessment. The next three chapters discuss key aspects of using assessment for learning: methods of gathering evidence; interpreting evidence and providing feedback that helps learning; and the role of children in assessing their work. The final chapter in this section concerns summative assessment. It discusses and illustrates three different approaches to reporting pupils' achievements at particular times and sets out some disadvantages and limitations of using tests for assessing the goals of primary science. Procedures for using teachers' judgements and which involve the formative use of evidence as well as summative reporting are outlined.

Part 5 comprises three chapters concerned with planning the provision for science. Chapter 20 discusses planning a school programme that provides for continuity and progression as children pass through the school. The science subject leader has an important role in this long-term planning and in developing a policy for science that is consistent with the philosophy of the school. The medium-term and short-term planning at the class level is the subject of Chapter 21, which includes a reminder that creative learning requires creative teaching. The section ends with a chapter on sources and resources and ways in which practical work is supported. It considers issues concerned with the selection, storage and maintenance of equipment and materials, and then matters relating to safety. It includes a list of sources of activities and materials available, often free, from the internet.

Part 6 concerns the formative evaluation of how schools provide for children's learning in science. This involves gathering and analysing data at the class level (Chapter 23) and at the school level (Chapter 24). In both cases this involves identifying standards or criteria to be used in judging performance. Action that can be taken to improve provision is suggested in Chapter 25, which includes a description of major sources and providers of continuing professional development in science for primary teachers.

This book is neither a 'how to do it' textbook nor a comprehensive account of theories of learning and of the expanding body of research in science education. Instead it describes good practice and shows how this is underpinned by relevant theories about teaching and learning. Throughout the book there are frequent references to research and sources of information which are intended to help those who wish to go further or to explore the evidence base for the practices that are suggested. Hopefully it will provide some useful ideas both for those starting on a career in primary science and for those wishing to reflect on and develop their current practice.

Wynne Harlen,
June 2013

Compelling reasons for teaching science in primary schools

1

The importance of primary school science

Introduction

If education is a preparation for life, it must prepare pupils for life in a world in which science and its applications in technology have key roles. It follows that children need to develop: some knowledge and understanding of aspects of the natural environment; a capacity to reason from evidence; an understanding of the nature of science and of how scientific knowledge is developed; and the key ideas that will help them make sensible decisions about how they live their lives and which affect the lives of others. There are several strong reasons why it cannot be adequately achieved through secondary school science alone.

The arguments for including science in the primary school curriculum are part of the larger case for teaching science to all pupils. So we begin this chapter by reviewing briefly some principles that apply to science education as a whole before turning to the question of why science should begin in the primary school. Since science has been included at the primary school level only relatively recently in the history of schooling, it is relevant to look back at how this change has come about. The reasons given have changed, or rather evolved, during the second part of the twentieth century as a result of research about children's learning and review of the goals of science education as a whole. Recognition of the importance for all young people, not just for future scientists, of developing understanding of key concepts, inquiry skills and appreciation of the nature of science – encapsulated in the notion of scientific literacy – has been accompanied by realisation that this learning cannot be achieved unless it begins in the primary school.

Principles of science education

Science is a major area of human mental and practical activity and the knowledge that it generates plays a vital part in our lives and in the lives of future generations. It is essential that the education of the whole population, not just of future scientists, provides them with a broad understanding of the status and nature of scientific knowledge, how it is created and how dependable it is. This becomes more and more important as science and technology take an expanding role in our lives. Some things that used to be accessible to anyone who was interested (for instance, what is under the bonnet of a car) are now the province of experts only. There is a general danger of a division between those with technological and scientific 'know how' and those without. This will not be avoided by making everyone into a scientist or technologist but by giving everyone an understanding of major ideas and principles of science, how these ideas were reached and how dependable they are.

Just as there are overarching powerful ideas in science that enable us to make sense of detailed facts, so in science education there are some general principles which apply across the details of different curricula and teaching approaches that are introduced from time to time. Principles express values and standards which should guide decisions. A set of such statements from an international group of science educators is given in Box 1.1.

The importance of science education for all

The science education that follows from these principles is important for all learners for reasons concerning learners both as individuals and as members of society. For learners as individuals:

- Science education helps them to develop the understanding, powers of reasoning and attitudes that enable them to lead physically and emotionally healthy and rewarding lives.

- Understanding aspects of the world around them, both the natural environment and that created through application of science, serves not only to satisfy – and at the same time to stimulate – curiosity but helps individuals in their personal choices affecting their health and enjoyment of the environment, as well as in their choice of career.

- Ways of learning science that lead to understanding can also help to develop learning skills that are needed throughout life in order to operate effectively in a world that is changing rapidly.

- The development of attitudes towards science and towards the use of evidence in making decisions helps learners become informed citizens, to reject quackery and to recognise when evidence is being used selectively to support arguments in favour of particular actions.

For society:

- Science education can help individuals and groups to make more informed choices in relation to avoiding, for instance, waste of energy and other resources, pollution and the consequences of poor diet, lack of exercise and misuse of drugs. As well as impact on their own daily lives, these things have wider implications for their and others' future lives through longer-term impact of human activity on the environment.

- Understanding how science is used in many aspects of life helps appreciation of the importance of science and the care that needs to be given to ensuring that scientific knowledge is used appropriately.

Box 1.1 Ten principles of science education

1. Throughout the years of compulsory schooling, schools should, through their science education programmes, aim systematically to develop and sustain learners' curiosity about the world, enjoyment of scientific activity and understanding of how natural phenomena can be explained.

2. The main purpose of science education should be to enable every individual to take an informed part in decisions, and to take appropriate actions, that affect their own wellbeing and the wellbeing of society and the environment.

3. Science education has multiple goals. It should aim to develop:

   ■ understanding of a set of 'big ideas' in science which include ideas *of* science and ideas *about* science and its role in society

   ■ scientific capabilities concerned with gathering and using evidence

   ■ scientific attitudes.

4. There should be a clear progression towards the goals of science education, indicating the ideas that need to be achieved at various points, based on careful analysis of concepts and on current research and understanding of how learning takes place.

5. Progression towards big ideas should result from study of topics of interest to students and relevance in their lives.

6. Learning experiences should reflect a view of scientific knowledge and scientific inquiry that is explicit and in line with current scientific and educational thinking.

7. All science curriculum activities should deepen understanding of scientific ideas as well as having other possible aims, such as fostering attitudes and capabilities.

8. Programmes of learning for students, and the initial training and professional development of teachers, should be consistent with the teaching and learning methods required to achieve the goals set out in Principle 3.

9. Assessment has a key role in science education. The formative assessment of students' learning and the summative assessment of their progress must apply to all goals.

10. In working towards these goals, schools' science programmes should promote cooperation among teachers and engagement of the community including the involvement of scientists.

(Harlen, 2010a)

■ Responsible decisions about the application of scientific knowledge in technology require understanding of how technology can impact both positively and negatively on society.

■ Stimulating interest in learning science through relating it to familiar situations and objects helps to develop realisation of the widespread consequences of its applications, locally and globally.

A greater general awareness of the role of science in daily life, and particularly the more informed attitudes that result from early science education, may well lead to more students choosing to specialise in science, but this is a secondary rather than a main aim of 'science for all'.

Why start science in the primary school?

Science does not have the long tradition of being central to the primary curriculum, as do English and mathematics. The reasons for including it have changed, or rather evolved, during the second half of the twentieth century. It is interesting, then, and hopefully useful, to begin with a brief history of how and why science has gradually gained its place and what is needed to maintain it.

Some relevant history

At the beginning of the twentieth century, the 'elementary' school was the only school attended by the vast majority of children. (Secondary schools were for those who could afford the fees and who began their education in private preparatory schools.) The curriculum was devoted to basic numeracy and literacy. The only form of teaching about the natural environment was the 'object lesson', in which teachers followed a dull routine of showing an object (which might be a piece of coal) and asked questions about it that often called for memory rather than observation (Harlen, 2001a). Several prominent scientists campaigned against the object lesson and advocated a wider range of topics and methods of teaching. H.E. Armstrong promoted the heuristic method of learning through discovery, based on a view of scientific knowledge as being developed inductively from observation and investigation. Although helping to promote a more active role for the children in their learning, heurism was not widely supported, since both its philosophical basis and its practicability made it difficult to defend.

The idea of children being more active in their learning more generally gained support from the writings of educators such as Dewey, Montessori and Homer Lane, building on the earlier ideas of Froebel and Pestalozzi. The approach to education they advanced came to be described as 'progressive'. In practice little changed for several decades due to the impact of the First World War, the depression in the early 1930s, then the Second World War and its aftermath. Indeed in England it was not until 1944 that the change from all-through 'elementary' education to all children moving from 'primary' and 'secondary', advocated in the late 1920s, was finally accomplished.

Building the case for primary science

Teaching science in primary and elementary schools has been justified in different ways. In the 1920s and 1930s science was advocated as part of the progressive movement and a response to recognising children's curiosity and interest in finding out about the world around, although with little effect in the vast majority of schools. The post-war period saw a groundswell of support for active learning and the inclusion of science in the primary curriculum. Somewhat different reasons were also being voiced, stemming from the widespread concern about the poor state of science education and its failure to keep up with the scientific and technological developments during and after the war. Attention was first given to renewing secondary science but it was soon realised that such science as there was in the primary school was failing both in developing pupils' understanding of the scientific aspects of the world and in preparing them for secondary science education.

The combination in the 1960s of recognition of the need to improve science education and at the same time to promote child-centred teaching and active learning in the primary school was expressed in several statements by individual educators and by the Association for Science Education, formed from the amalgamation of the SMA and AWST in 1963. For example, Nathan Isaacs, a leading educator, urged that science in the primary school should be seen as 'part of the very ABC of education' (Isaacs, 1962: 6). The reasons he gave were:

- the need for everyone to be able to relate to the rapid changes that science and technology were making to the world around,
- the ability to share in understanding and celebrating science as an important human achievement,
- the need for more scientists,
- the generation of a scientific approach to human problems through seeking relevant information and basing decisions on evidence.

Regarding primary science as a preparation for secondary science was not new, for T. H. Huxley had been also concerned for the education of future scientists, but the most strongly supported arguments were concerned with the benefit to the children during their primary school years. The predominance of such views can be seen later in the report of an international meeting of primary science educators held by UNESCO in 1980 which listed the main reasons for primary school science. These included:

- the development of an enquiring mind; promoting children's intellectual development, including thinking in a logical way and problem-solving;
- improving the quality of children's lives;
- assisting in other subject areas, especially language and mathematics;
- equipping children for living in an increasingly scientific and technological world;
- learning science can being 'real fun' (UNESCO, 1982).

Most of these claims were based on little more than wishful thinking or the response of enthusiasts to the novel activities in the early science projects. Even though there was hardly any research evidence to support them, such arguments were used in support of giving science a place in the primary curriculum. Indeed, a government statement of policy on science education in 1985 stated unequivocally that 'All pupils should be properly introduced to science in the primary school' (DES and WO, 1985).

Since that time, however, increasing research attention into children's conceptual development has gradually built a strong case for beginning science from the earliest years of education.

The impact of research

Such research in primary science as there was in the 1970s was mostly concerned with the impact of the new curriculum materials on teachers and teaching, revealing far lower levels of uptake than expected. With regard to impact on pupils, studies which compared different curriculum projects with each other or with traditional teaching from textbooks found no significant differences in pupils' scientific achievement, although some US studies reported an increase in questioning and process skills as a result of using new materials.

Despite the disappointing impact of early curriculum projects, Science 5/13 and the Nuffield Junior Science Project, the importance of science at the primary level was underlined by its inclusion in the Assessment of Performance (APU) surveys. These were carried out annually in English (from 1978 to 1983), mathematics (1979 to 1984) and science from 1980 to 1985, involving small samples of pupils at ages 11, 13 (science only) and 15 (Foxman et al., 1991).

Apart from the trends in pupils' performance provided by the results, the APU surveys added to our understanding of the nature of inquiry (or process) skills and their interaction with content knowledge. They also led directly to the research on children's ideas at the secondary level which revealed that pupils had ideas about scientific phenomena that quite often were not consistent with the scientific view. These ideas, sometimes held despite science teaching, are ones which seem to make more sense to the pupils than abstract scientific explanations.

Studies of the ideas that students hold about the scientific aspects of the world became a major focus of research in science education in the 1980s. Many of these ideas – at first called 'misconceptions' and later described as 'alternative frameworks' or 'children's ideas' – were in conflict with accepted scientific views. Research in many countries revealed remarkably consistent patterns in secondary students' ideas, which were the initial focus of attention. Subsequently the ideas of primary and middle school students were studied, particularly by Osborne and Freyberg (1985) in New Zealand, Vosniadou (1997) in Greece, Smith et al. (1993) in the USA and in England by the Science Processes and Concepts Exploration (SPACE) project (1990–8).

It was clear in this research that the children's ideas could not be ignored. Children had worked them out for themselves and believed them; it followed that they had to be the starting points from which more scientific ideas could be developed (see Chapter 5).

How children come to form these ideas has been suggested by the research into very young children of pre-school age and babies (Gopnik *et al.*, 1999), revealing intense mental activity in the pre-school years. So it is not surprising that children enter school with some ideas already formed about how things in the physical and biological world are explained. Thus a further argument was added to the case for science in the primary curriculum, that children's ideas about the world are developing throughout the primary years whether or not they are taught science. Without intervention to introduce a scientific approach in their exploration, many of the ideas they develop are non-scientific and may obstruct later learning.

Since then other research has added to the importance of starting science early:

■ Attitudes towards science develop in the pre-secondary years, earlier than attitudes to some other school subjects. This was first reported by Ormerod and Duckworth in 1975, but more recently research evidence reported by the Royal Society (2006, 2010) and by the French Académie des sciences (Charpak *et al.,* 2005) shows that most children develop interests and attitudes towards science well before the age of 14 and many before the age of 11.

■ Gender differences in academic performance, which continue to be of concern in science education at higher levels, have not appeared at the primary stage (Haworth *et al.,* 2008; Royal Society, 2010).

■ At the primary level there is no correlation between attitudes to science and science achievement, so primary children can feel positive about science regardless of their level of achievement (Royal Society, 2010).

■ Studies of the lives of renowned scientists or engineers have shown that their deep interest for science arose as early as age 6 or 7, and was often encouraged by parents or teachers (Guichard, 2007).

The contribution of primary science to scientific literacy

The aims of school science education as a whole are now commonly expressed in terms of developing 'scientific literacy'. This is the term used for the essential understanding that should be part of everyone's education, rather than a detailed knowledge of facts and theories as required by scientists in a particular field. Just as the term 'literacy' on its own denotes competence in using language at the level needed for functioning effectively in society, so scientific literacy indicates a similar competence in relation to science:

■ being able to function with confidence in relation to the scientific aspects of the world around one;

■ being able to look at something 'in a scientific way', seeing, for example, whether or not evidence has been taken into account in the explanation of an event or phenomenon, whether it makes sense in terms of related events or phenomena, and so on;

■ being aware of the nature (and limitations) of scientific knowledge and the role of values in its generation.

Box 1.2 The PISA definition of scientific literacy

In PISA [scientific literacy refers to] an individual's scientific knowledge and use of that knowledge to identify questions, to acquire new knowledge, to explain scientific phenomena, and to draw evidence-based conclusions about science-related issues, understanding of the characteristic features of science as a form of human knowledge and enquiry, awareness of how science and technology shape our material, intellectual, and cultural environments, and willingness to engage in science-related issues, and with the issues of science, as a reflective citizen.

(OECD, 2009: 14)

The term 'scientific literacy' is used in statements about the aim of science education in various countries and in statements of international bodies such as UNESCO and the OECD. Box 1.2 gives the definition used in the OECD Programme for International Student Achievement (PISA).

The statement in Box 1.2 is rather dense and it helps to unpack it a little. The following points are based on OECD (2006). In the definition of OECD scientific literacy:

- 'Knowledge' implies far more than the ability to recall information, facts and names. It includes knowledge *of* science (knowledge about the natural world) and knowledge *about* science itself.

- The 'questions' to be identified are those that can be answered by scientific enquiry.

- 'Drawing evidence-based conclusions' means knowing, selecting and evaluating information and data, while recognising that there is often not sufficient information to draw definite conclusions.

- 'The characteristic features of science' refers to the processes through which scientists obtain data and propose explanation (the science inquiry skills).

- 'Awareness of how science and technology shape our material, intellectual and cultural environment' means recognising that science is a human endeavour, one that influences our societies and us as individuals.

- 'Willingness to engage in science-related issues' implies having continuing interest in, having opinions about and participating in current and future science-based issues.

In the UK, an influential report (*Beyond 2000: Science Education for the Future*) on the aims of the science curriculum for all pupils from age 5 to 16 recommended that 'The science curriculum for 5 to 16 should be seen primarily as a course to enhance general scientific literacy' (Millar and Osborne, 1998: 9). What this means for the curriculum is set out in Box 1.3.

The aims of developing scientific literacy, as described in Box 1.2, may seem remote from primary science, but they are in essence easily identified as developing ideas ('understanding of important ideas and explanatory frameworks'),

---

Box 1.3 A curriculum for developing scientific literacy for ages 5–16

The science curriculum should:

- sustain and develop the curiosity of young people about the natural world around them, and build up their confidence in their ability to enquire into its behaviour. It should seek to foster a sense of wonder, enthusiasm and interest in science so that young people feel confident and competent to engage with scientific and technical matters.

- help young people acquire a broad, general understanding of the important ideas and explanatory frameworks of science, and of the procedures of scientific inquiry, which have had a major impact on our material environment and on our culture in general, so that they can:

  - appreciate why these ideas are valued;

  - appreciate the underlying rationale for decisions (e.g. about diet, or medical treatment or energy use) which they may wish, or be advised, to take in everyday contexts, both now and in later life;

  - be able to understand, and respond critically to, media reports of issues with a science component;

  - feel empowered to hold and express a personal point of view on issues with a science component which enter the arena of public debate, and perhaps to become actively involved in some of these;

  - acquire further knowledge when required, either for interest or for vocational purposes.

  (Millar and Osborne 1998: 12)

---

developing inquiry skills ('the procedures of scientific inquiry') and developing attitudes ('a sense of wonder, enthusiasm and interest'). Primary science has a contribution to make to all of these, as discussed further in Chapter 2. We just have to remember that in all cases we are talking about *development*, starting from the simple foundations which are needed for later more abstract ideas and advanced thinking.

Developing ideas

Development of understanding starts from making sense of particular events that we encounter. We might call the ideas found useful for this 'small' ideas, because they are specific to the events studied and have limited application beyond these. As experience extends it becomes possible to link together events which are explained in similar ways so that the ideas used to explain them then have wider application and can be described as 'bigger' ideas.

The ultimate aim of developing scientific literacy is to develop, and to be able to apply, the 'big', widely applicable, ideas that enable us to grasp what is going on in situations which are new to us. But clearly the 'big' ideas are too abstract and too remote from everyday experience to be a starting point for this learning. Learning has to start from the 'small' ideas and build upwards so that at each point the ideas are understood in terms of real experience. A major role of primary science is, therefore, to build a foundation of small ideas that help children to understand things in their immediate environment but, most importantly, at the same time to begin to make links between different experience and ideas to build bigger ideas.

Developing skills and attitudes

The overall aim of scientific literacy in relation to the development of skills and attitudes is the ability and willingness to recognise and use evidence in making decisions as informed citizens. Again the starting point is to become familiar with the ways of identifying, collecting and interpreting evidence in relation to answering questions about things around us. Being able to do this is an essential starting point to reflecting on the kinds of questions that science can, and cannot, answer and the kinds of conclusions that can, and cannot, be drawn from certain kinds of evidence.

Making links with the world around

The achievement of scientific literacy depends on, but is more than, the acquisition of scientific knowledge, skills, values and attitudes. It does not automatically result from learning science; it has to be a conscious goal even at the primary level, by giving attention to linking together ideas from a range of experiences of real phenomena, problems and events both within the classroom and outside it. Indeed, extending first-hand experience beyond what the school can supply, in the way that museums and science centres can do (see Chapter 9), is essential to the development of scientific literacy.

Contribution to learning how to learn

The rapid expansion of scientific knowledge and its applications in technology are making changes to our lives at an unprecedented rate. (Just think of the how access to the internet, through the mobile phone and i-pad, has released us from the need to be in particular places in order to communicate and find information.) Future citizens need to be able to adapt to change as a constant feature of their lives. The consequences for education are described by the OECD in Box 1.4.

There are implications for the curriculum, which are discussed in Chapter 2. What is relevant here is the contribution that primary school science can make in developing the ability to learn how to learn. First it might be necessary to explain why we refer to 'learning how to learn' and not just plain 'learning ability' or 'learning to learn'. The main reason is that the latter phrases suggest that there is something specific to be learned in the same way as learning a language or learning

Box 1.4 Impact of constant change

Students cannot learn in school everything they will need to know in adult life. What they must acquire is the prerequisites for successful learning in future life. ... Students must become able to organise and regulate their own learning, to learn independently and in groups, and to overcome difficulties in the learning process. This requires them to be aware of their own thinking processes and learning strategies and methods.

(OECD 1999: 9)

to play a musical instrument. Rather, what is to be learned is the practice, or a set of practices, that lead to learning. These practices are not about learning particular subject matter but about the process of learning itself. The aim of developing ability to learn how to learn is that someone with this ability will in theory be able to go about learning without help. That is, they become autonomous learners. Indeed, autonomy is seen as a key aim in education, often used interchangeably with phrases such as 'independent learning', 'taking responsibility for one's own learning', 'self-determination' and 'self-regulation' (Boud, 1988, quoted in James *et al.*, 2007). In the process of learning how to learn pupils become able to use strategies for learning new things, not just at school but in other contexts, and develop the attitudes that motive continued learning.

Reference to reflection and learning autonomy might seem more relevant at later stages of school than in the primary years. But, like many goals which seem too complex for young children, there are essential foundations to be laid in the primary school. The first step in reflecting on learning is to become aware of what one is actually learning. We can help this process by ensuring that children know what they are learning and why. In science what pupils do to find something out often involves physical actions that can be discussed, providing a good opportunity for children to begin thinking about what is involved in learning. Realising how they learned something through the simplest actions is a basis for reflecting on what has been learned in other ways. Children then gradually take more conscious control of their learning, and are able to pursue learning independently.

Summary

This chapter began by taking a broad view of the reasons for science education as a whole and the principles that should guide decisions about what and how to teach it. It has looked at how the rationale for beginning science in the primary school years has developed since the 1960s, gradually becoming more grounded in research, and argued in terms of its contribution to the overall goals of science education. Science education at the primary school level provides the opportunity for developing scientific ideas, challenging the non-scientific ideas that they are likely to form without guidance. It gives children experience of scientific activity to inform the development of attitudes towards science before gender stereotypes influence their views. It lays the foundations for the scientific literacy that is so important in a world increasingly dependent on scientific knowledge and its technological applications. Finally, we have noted its particular value in developing awareness of how to learn.

Further reading

Wellcome Trust (2008) *Perspectives on Education: Primary Science*: Available from http://www.wellcome.ac.uk/stellent/groups/corporatesite/@msh_peda/documents/web_document/wtd042076.pdf.

2

Primary school science curricula in the UK

Introduction

Chapter 1 identified reasons for the importance of teaching science in primary schools. The question we begin to address in this chapter is how to ensure that the intended benefits are realised. This requires action at a number of levels, from providing guidance at the national level to decisions about activities and interactions in the classroom. This chapter is concerned with the broad agenda set at national level. In Chapter 3 we look through the other end of the telescope, as it were, at specific learning activities.

Today no one would disagree with the view that the education of all young people should provide them with a basic understanding of scientific ideas – ideas about science and the procedures of science. There is lower consensus about just what ideas and procedures ought to be included, the relative emphasis to be given to them and how they are best taught. In theory we can consider separately the curriculum content and teaching methods: the 'what' and the 'how', leaving the 'how' to teachers to decide. But in practice, achieving understanding in science implies certain kinds of experience, with implications for teaching. However, since most of the rest of this book is concerned with 'how', here the focus is on 'what' as identified in curriculum documents, considered first in general terms and then in the curricula of the countries of the UK.

The curriculum

'Curriculum' is a word used with different meanings, some referring to a written document which sets out what is to be taught and/or what is to be learned, and some to the full range of experiences that affect pupils' learning, including 'the hidden curriculum' – what is unconsciously conveyed through schooling without being openly intended. The concern here is with the first of these, the content of documents that set out intended learning experiences and expected learning outcomes across the years of schooling, in this case the first six (in some cases seven) years of formal education.

This being so it is important to make a distinction between the documents that set out national curricula or guidelines and the documents that schools produce to describe the whole curriculum experienced by their pupils. The need for this distinction is based on the understanding that National Curriculum documents do not prescribe the whole of what pupils should learn. In the 2011 revision of the National Curriculum for England, described later, a clear distinction was made between the National Curriculum and the school curriculum so that pupils, parents, teachers and the wider public understand that the National Curriculum is not expected to be the totality of what is taught. The remit for the 2011 review stated the intention that the National Curriculum should constitute a core of essential knowledge and allow more scope for curricular provision determined at school or community level.

The knowledge explosion and 'big' ideas

The daily addition to our knowledge about the living and made world – widely accessible through television programmes and other media reports about newly explored parts of planet Earth and indeed other planets – is one sign that scientific knowledge is exponentially increasing. Other signs are in the applications of science in constantly changing technology, particularly in our modes of communication and access to information. How can science education be expected to keep up with this knowledge explosion? Is it not inevitable that what is taught in schools will be seen to be out-of-date and out of touch? That is only the case if we think of science education in terms of a collection of facts and theories. If, instead, we consider it as a progression towards the development of broad underlying ideas that have wide application, then we are less at the mercy of constantly expanding information. These are the ideas that help our understanding of familiar and new things around and enable us to take part in decisions as informed citizens of a world where science and technology are of ever increasing significance.

These ideas are described as 'big' or powerful ideas, which both explain new phenomena and help in seeking new facts and theories. 'Big' ideas, as noted briefly in Chapter 1, are ideas that can be applied to a wide range of related phenomena and are built from 'small' ideas that relate to specific objects or events. For example, the idea that earth worms have features that enable them to survive underground is a small idea. This idea gradually expands as it becomes linked to ideas from study of other organisms and is developed into a generalisation that applies to all organisms, a 'big' idea which endures no matter what new species are discovered. Later, in Chapter 6, we look at how this process happens and can be helped.

In the context of the school curriculum it is important for teachers, when helping children to develop the small ideas, to see these as steps towards the 'bigger' ones. For instance, planting seeds and stones in soil to see if they grow sets children thinking about differences between living and non-living things, eventually leading them, some years later, to recognise the cellular structure unique to living organisms. The powerful ideas can be expressed in a relatively short list – as an example, a list of ten identified by a group of international science

Box 2.1 Big ideas in science

Ideas *of* science

1. All material in the Universe is made of very small particles.

2. Objects can affect other objects at a distance.

3. Changing the movement of an object requires a net force to be acting on it.

4. The total amount of energy in the Universe is always the same but energy can be transformed when things change or are made to happen.

5. The composition of the Earth and its atmosphere and the processes occurring within them shape the Earth's surface and its climate.

6. The solar system is a very small part of one of millions of galaxies in the Universe.

7. Organisms are organised on a cellular basis.

8. Organisms require a supply of energy and materials for which they are often dependent on or in competition with other organisms.

9. Genetic information is passed down from one generation of organisms to another.

10. The diversity of organisms, living and extinct, is the result of evolution.

Ideas *about* science

■ Science assumes that for every effect there is one or more causes.

■ Scientific explanations, theories and models are those that best fit the facts known at a particular time.

■ The knowledge produced by science is used in some technologies to create products to serve human ends.

■ Applications of science often have ethical, social, economic and political implications.

(Harlen, 2010b)

educators is given in Box 2.1. These are not, of course, to be taught directly but relevance to them should be a reason for pupils spending time to study in depth related objects, events or phenomena, appropriate to their age and development. Topics of study should be selected so that they have, to the teachers and any observer, a clear relationship to one or more big ideas and enable understanding at an appropriate point in the progression to big ideas. Thus teachers ought to be able to explain how the ideas the children develop through the activities in which they are engaged relate to the overall big ideas and so justify the time they are spending on it.

Deciding what to teach

Prior to the introduction of the National Curriculum in 1989, the content of the primary curriculum was largely guided by the materials produced by local and national curriculum projects. The early primary science projects (in the

USA and in the UK) promulgated different views of science and what was to be achieved in learning science. Some gave priority to the development of an inquiring mind, to problem-solving capability and to logical thinking, promoting a view of science as a set of processes. This view was apparent in some of the early national science programmes in the 1960s, such as the Nuffield Junior Science project (1967) and the American Science: A Process Approach. The alternative approach of prioritising the development of major science ideas was taken by the Oxford Primary Science Project (Boyers, 1967) and Science Curriculum Improvement Study in the USA (SCIS, 1970). The rather extreme positions of these early projects soon gave way to more balanced views, acknowledging that both processes and conceptual learning are important. However, just how these goals are inter-related remains one of the issues debated in current developments in science education.

The diversity of content and to some extent of approaches was curtailed once national curricula were established. A curriculum document describes at a general level the intended learning across the relevant age range. There are generally two kinds of statement:

- inputs, or what experiences are to be provided – giving a broad overview of progression, set out year by year or for 'stages' of schooling;
- outcomes, or what is intended to be learned – specifying outcomes for the purpose of assessment, described in various ways, such as 'attainment targets' (in the English curriculum), 'learning outcomes' (in the Scottish Curriculum for Excellence), 'performance expectations', 'standards' (as in the USA) or 'achievement standards' (in the Australian Curriculum).

In some curricula, statements of what is to be taught are combined with learning outcome statements in one document; in others these are quite separate and often created by different agencies, concerned variously with the curriculum content and with assessing learning. There is also a considerable difference in what is included according to whether or not the implementation of curriculum is required by law or has only the status of 'guidelines'. Non-statutory documents can contain guidance and exemplars of teaching methods, without infringing the role of the schools to decide matters relating to how to teach.

Most curriculum statements cover the whole age range of compulsory schooling, primary and secondary. We now focus on what are included as the intended input and outcomes in the primary/elementary school years. The content and structure of these statements are considered in two periods, up to and 2005 and then after 2005, since it was around 2005 that the greatest changes were made in the national curricula and guidelines in the countries of the UK. The date is also close to the time when Wales began to prepare its own legislation for education and training, enabled by the Government of Wales Act of 2006. Since then, all four countries of the UK have different science curricula created by their own government departments of education.

Science curricula in the UK prior to 2005

England and Wales

When the National Curriculum was introduced in 1989, English, mathematics and science were designated as core subjects and were the first to be specified and in far greater detail than other subjects. Other subjects, including technology, were designated as 'foundation' subjects. The curriculum in Wales was the same as in England apart from the inclusion of Welsh language as an additional subject in the core and English not being a required part of the curriculum until the age of 7. The primary years were divided into two key stages, KS1 (Years 1 and 2) and KS2 (Years 3 to 6). The 'inputs' for each subject were expressed as a 'Programme of study' for each key stage and what children were expected to learn, the 'outputs', set out as 'Attainment Targets', specified initially at ten progressive 'levels' covering the age range 5 to 16. The expectations for the end of each key stage were expressed in relation to these levels, Level 2 for KS1 and Level 4 for KS4.

After its initial implementation, the curriculum was revised on several occasions. Soon after it was phased in, complaints were made about too much content and too much prescription. In 1995 a revised national curriculum was implemented with somewhat reduced curriculum content, and the detailed level specifications of the Attainment Targets for each subject changed to broader and simpler Level Descriptions, with the number of levels reduced to eight plus 'exceptional performance'. The content was further reduced in a revision carried out in 1999, and in 2002 the curriculum was extended to include the Foundation Stage.

Northern Ireland

The Northern Ireland Curriculum, introduced in 1989, had a similar structure to the National Curriculum for England and Wales in defining progression in ten levels across four key stages, but it also differed in several respects. The primary years were divided into key stages of equal span, 'science and technology' was identified as a combined subject throughout all four key stages rather than as separate compulsory subjects, and summative assessment took account of the retention of the transfer tests (11+) for selection to secondary schools. In addition to common tests at ages 8, 11, 14 and 16, teachers were asked to use moderated external assessment resources as a basis for reporting levels of attainment to parents and to school boards or governors at the end of key stages.

Inevitably there were complaints about the weight of the curriculum content, and particularly the burden of its assessment and reporting. In response the curriculum was reviewed and revised on a number of occasions. Eventually, following advice from the Northern Ireland Council for the Curriculum, Examinations and Assessment (CCEA), the Department of Education gave the go-ahead for a major review and revision of the Northern Ireland curriculum, resulting in the new arrangements for primary and post-primary schools being phased in from 2007.

Scotland

The development of national guidelines began in Scotland with the publication of a consultation paper in 1987. The work of developing the curriculum was taken forward by the Scottish Consultative Council on the Curriculum (SCCC). Guidelines were developed in five areas of the curriculum for the seven years of primary school and the first two years of secondary school and were consequently known as the 5–14 Curriculum Guidelines. These were non-statutory but were issued with the expectation that they would be followed, as in the case of previous official guidance. Environmental Studies, one of the five areas of the primary curriculum, included technology, health education and information technology as well as social subjects and science (Harlen, 1993). Attainment targets were expressed in terms of experiences at five levels, A to E, roughly two years apart, as in the numerical levels of the English National Curriculum. No key stages were identified and the term 'programme of study' did not carry the same meaning as in England and Wales and Northern Ireland. Not surprisingly, the 5–14 Environmental Studies Guidelines were found to be too complex and cumbersome to teach. In 2000 they were revised and separate guidelines in science (and other areas previous included in Environmental Studies) were produced which simplified the structure of what was taught and assessed and included more advice for teachers about possible learning activities and approaches.

The case for curriculum renewal

As this brief account shows, the first versions of the national curricula in the UK were several times revised soon after their implementation, to simplify the structure and to reduce the content. Despite the changes made, however, teachers continued to complain of an overloaded and overspecified curriculum and a lack of relevance to pupils' experience both within and outside school (see Box 2.2).

In England the problem of 'covering' content was exacerbated by the introduction of the national frameworks for teaching literacy (in 1998) and numeracy (in 1999), with revised frameworks provided in 2006. The time and even the methods to be used in teaching English and mathematics were specified and, although not statutory, schools were strongly advised to follow the frameworks and to show that they were giving priority to government targets in numeracy and literacy. The effect was not only to elevate the status of these subjects and to separate them from other subjects, but to downgrade others, including science. An ASE survey (ASE, 1999) confirmed that the time for science had declined from 1997 to 1998, that it had been put 'on the back-burner' at key stage 1 and that much professional development in science had been postponed. In addition the publication of national test results in England and the inevitable creation of 'league tables' put further pressure on teachers to teach the knowledge tested. For many this left little time to make science interesting and relevant to the pupils. These findings were underlined and elaborated by some of the results, in Box 2.2, of a wider study across the UK.

> **Box 2.2** Teachers' views of the curricula of the 1990s
>
> Key findings from a study of primary science across the UK conducted in 2004 show that, far outweighing other factors, teachers considered that greater relevance to real life was the most important change needed to improve the quality of children's science education and their interest in science. As the report (Wellcome Trust, 2005) noted, there are various ways of making science relevant but even when ideas are available many teachers were deterred from implementing them by lack of funding, time and classroom assistance – all also mentioned in the research.
>
> The content of the curriculum also plays a large part in each of these inhibiting factors. Time for setting a relevant scene for science work is limited by both the amount and type of content that teachers have to cover. For instance the requirement that 'pupils should be taught to make and use keys' (Key Stage 2, National Curriculum for England, 1999) could be met as part of investigation of creatures and plants found locally, but it is all too frequently taught directly for lack of time. This pressure caused teachers frustration expressed by one of those surveyed:
>
> > I want to teach through investigations – that is how I was taught in my teacher training but it's time ... we will set it aside and we will just talk about it or I will do it [as a demonstration] at the front – the time is just not available.
> >
> > (Wellcome Trust 2005: 90)

Relevance can be in the form of connections to other curriculum subjects as well as to real life. Cross-curricular topics help this relevance and had been encouraged in the 1960s and 1970s, only to be criticised in the 1980s (DES, 1989) for fragmentation of the subject and activities that did not justify the label of 'science activities'. However, the move to discrete science lessons then led to isolation of science and to the resounding call for relevance.

Moreover the detailed specification in the curricula of items 'to be taught' loses sight of the 'big ideas' that are the eventual aims of science education for all pupils. Progression in developing these ideas is not clear; each small idea becomes an aim in itself rather than building to a broader understanding of scientific aspects of the world around.

Science curricula in the UK after 2005

England

In 2005 it was clear that the entire science curriculum was in need of renewal. Attention was first given to the secondary school curriculum, key stages 3 and 4. When attention was turned to the primary curriculum, the government set up a review in 2008, led by Sir Jim Rose, to consider the 'input' side of the curriculum as a whole. The terms of reference of the review excluded assessment and testing, the 'output' side of the curriculum. It is important to note that this was not the

Box 2.3 The Cambridge Primary Review

The Review of Primary Education in England, led by Robin Alexander and launched in 2006, conducted a fundamental review of primary education. Known as the Cambridge Primary Review, funded by a private foundation and therefore independent of government, it considered, in addition to the curriculum and assessment, a wide range of matters relevant to children's primary education, including children's development and learning, the relationship between schools and other agencies, teachers and their training, the structure of primary education as a whole and its relationship to pre-school and secondary provision. In scope it paralleled the comprehensive review of primary education by the Plowden report (CACE, 1967).

The review identified 12 curriculum aims in three groups relating to: the individual; self, others and the wider world; and learning, knowing and doing. It 'proposed that the primary curriculum be re-conceived as a matrix of the 12 specified aims together with eight domains of knowledge, skill, dispositions and enquiry' (Alexander, 2010: 265), one of the eight domains being science and technology. In defining the content it proposed that 'each domain should have national and local components, with time available for the local component across all domains set at 30 per cent of the yearly total' (p. 262).

only review of the primary curriculum at that time. The Cambridge Review, with a much wider remit, outlined in Box 2.3, was also in progress.

In November 2009 the DCSF announced the new National Primary Curriculum, based on the Rose Review recommendations, organised around 'Understanding English, communication and languages'; 'Mathematical understanding'; 'Scientific and technological understanding'; 'Human, geographical and social understanding'; 'Understanding the arts'; and 'Understanding physical development'. The proposals (DCSF, 2009) set out what children should be taught in each of these areas at 'early', 'middle' and 'later' stages. In comparison with the curriculum being replaced, the proposed programmes of study were less prescription and more process-rich work. Implementation was planned for 2011 but the necessary legislation was not passed before the 2010 General Election and the newly elected government rejected the proposals.

The existing curriculum thus remained in place, while the new government initiated, in early 2011, a further review of both the primary and secondary curricula in England. The Secretary of State was concerned to learn from countries which performed particularly well in the international tests of the OECD PISA (see Box 1.2). To this end the Department for Education carried out an analysis of the curricula of high-performing jurisdictions. The Secretary of State also set up an Expert Panel to provide advice and called for evidence from a range of individuals and organisations. The reports of the information provided from these sources were published and a draft of revised programmes of study was subsequently published in June 2012. Following a period of consultation, a further draft of programmes of study for key stages 1–3 was published in February

Box 2.4 Features of the draft National Curriculum for science, KS1 and 2 (England)

The draft primary curriculum divides the six years of primary school into three parts, KS1, lower KS2 and upper KS2, each of two years. The document for science sets out the programme of study for each key stage in very general terms, followed by the programme to be taught in each year. It states, however, that schools are 'only required to teach the relevant programme of study by the end of the key stage'. Such close specification of 'what pupils should be taught' goes against the recommendation of the Expert Panel that the programme of study should enable a few powerful ideas to be studied in depth. It also invites criticism that some content is introduced too early and some too late. Each programme of study includes 'working scientifically', but with the instruction that 'working scientifically must *always* be taught through and clearly related to substantive subject content in the programme of study'. There are non-statutory notes and guidance that give detailed examples of how 'working scientifically' might be 'embedded within the content of biology, chemistry and physics'.

The draft curriculum does not specify attainment targets except to state that 'By the end of each key stage, pupils are expected to have the knowledge, skills and understanding of the matters taught in the relevant Programme of Study.'

2013 for a two-month consultation. The final document, indicating what is to be implemented in 2014, was due to be published in autumn 2013.

Between the two draft versions there were changes in the requirements of where specific topics were to be taught but the structure, as outlined in Box 2.4, remained the same.

Wales

Soon after responsibility for education was devolved from Westminster to the Welsh Assembly Government (now the Welsh Government), reviews of the content of the National Curriculum and its associated assessment arrangements were initiated. A new curriculum, developed by the Department for Children, Education and Lifelong Learning (DCELLS) and covering the age range 3 to 18, was introduced in 2008. The primary years were divided into the Foundation Phase, which covers the pre-school years plus key stage 1 (children aged 3 to 7) and key stage 2 (for children aged 8 to 11). This arrangement took advantage of the earlier introduction of a Foundation Stage Curriculum and met some concern that formal subject studies were begun too early in some countries of the UK.

A non-statutory skills framework was developed across the full age range 3 to 18, giving guidance about continuity and progression in developing thinking, communication, ICT and number skills. The revised assessment arrangements include optional skills assessment materials for use, initially, in Year 5. The special attention to Year 5 aims to enable teachers to identify and support progression in these skills a year before pupils leave the primary schools.

In the Foundation Phase the skills are developed across seven statutory Areas of Learning, one of which is 'Knowledge and Understanding of the World' where the opportunities indicated include those relating to science concepts. For example, under 'Myself and other living things' are included the opportunities to

- learn the names and uses of the main external parts of the human body and plants;
- observe differences between animals and plants, different animals and different plants in order to group them.

'Myself and non-living things' includes opportunities to

- experiment with different everyday objects and use their senses to sort them into groups according to simple features;
- develop an awareness of, and be able to distinguish between, made and natural materials (DCELLS, 2008).

At Key Stage 2 the curriculum for science is set out as a separate section. It explicitly states that learners should be given the opportunity to build on the skills, knowledge and understanding acquired during the Foundation Phase and should be taught to relate their learning in science to everyday life, including current issues. The science skills at Key Stage 2 are identified under three headings: communication, inquiry and planning. As in the Foundation Phase, these skills are to be developed through a defined range of subject matter. At Key Stage 2 this is identified under 'Interdependence of organisms', 'The sustainable Earth', and 'How things work'. Box 2.5 indicates the range for 'How things work'. The Programme of Study statements are expressed as statements of 'what is to be provided as opportunities to study', in some contrast to what 'pupils should be taught' in the earlier National Curriculum for England and Wales.

Northern Ireland

Primary education in Northern Ireland has three phases:

1. Foundation (Years 1 and 2, aged 5–6)
2. Key stage 1 (years 3 and 4, aged 7–8)
3. Key stage 2 (years 5, 6, and 7, aged 9–12)

The Northern Ireland Curriculum for the primary school is set out in the same way for each of these three phases; statements describe a progression through the seven primary years. It was phased in from 2007, when it became statutory for Years 1 and 5. In each phase there are six areas of learning (plus Religious Education as required by the Northern Ireland Department of Education):

1. Language and literacy
2. Mathematics and numeracy

Box 2.5 Welsh National curriculum for science: Key Stage 2 'How things work'

Pupils should use and develop their skills, knowledge and understanding by investigating the science behind everyday things, e.g. toys, musical instruments and electrical devices, the way they are constructed and work.

They should be given opportunities to study:

1. The uses of electricity and its control in simple circuits

2. Forces of different kinds, e.g. gravity magnetic and friction, including air resistance

3. The ways in which forces can affect movement and how forces can be compare

4. How different sounds are produced and the way that sound travels

5. How light travels and how this can be used (DCELLS, 2008).

Level descriptions for use in statutory assessment and reporting by teachers (national testing was ended in 2004) were revised to reflect the changes in the programme of study and to clarify the path of progress between levels. The eight-level (plus exceptional performance) description of progress and attainment is retained. Attainment Targets at each level, expressed in narrative form, describe progression in skills and how knowledge is obtained through working scientifically. In addition a 'science levels poster', spelling out progression across the levels in more detail, is provided to help teachers' planning, not for assessing pupils' progress.

3. The arts

4. The world around us

5. Personal development and mutual understanding

6. Physical development and movement

Specified outcomes include cross-curricular skills (communication, using mathematics and ICT) and thinking skills and capabilities (managing information, being creative, thinking, problem-solving and decision-making, working with others and self-management). Science, history, geography and technology contribute to learning in 'The world around us'. The statutory requirements are that pupils should have opportunities to develop knowledge, understanding and skills in relation to subject matter set out under four themes: 'Interdependence', 'Place', 'Movement and energy' and 'Change over time'. For example, for 'Change over time', the statutory requirements are that pupils should be enabled to explore:

■ ways in which change occurs in the natural world;

■ how people and places have changed over time;

■ positive change and how we have a responsibility to make an active contribution (CCEA, 2007: 86).

Box 2.6 Northern Ireland Curriculum Key stage 1: science and technology suggestions for 'The world around us'

Interdependence

- How we grow, move and use our senses, including similarities and differences between ourselves and other children
- The variety of living things in the world and how we can take care of them
- Some living things that are now extinct

Place

- The range of materials used in my area
- Sound in the local environment
- How animals use colour to adapt to the natural environment
- Animals that hibernate and the materials they use

Movement and energy

- The use of electricity as an energy source and the importance of using it safely
- Animals that migrate
- The importance of light in our everyday lives
- Different sources of light, such as traffic lights, candles or stars
- Devices that push, pull and make things move
- Design and make simple models

Change over time

- The effect of heating and cooling some everyday substances
- Changes in the local natural environment, including how they can affect living things

(CCEA, 2007: 87).

Thus science is not identified as a separate subject and its content is only minimally specified. However, there are suggestions for the contributions of science, history and so on, to these themes. Box 2.6 gives these suggestions for science and technology at Key Stage 1.

The curriculum document provides suggestions for teaching approaches and for building each phase on earlier experiences. A spiral curriculum is recommended and the nature of progression through stages 1 and 2 is made explicit in a series of statements such as: (to progress) 'from recognising a fair test to designing and carrying out fair tests', 'from using everyday language to increasingly precise use of subject specific vocabulary, notation and symbols'.

Scotland

In Scotland the curriculum revision is set within a wider programme entitled 'Curriculum for Excellence', which was established in 2004 following a national debate about education. While guidance on the curriculum content is central, the programme has implications for teachers and other staff, curriculum organisation and the qualifications system. An extended period of review, research, preparation of draft proposals, consultation, redrafting and planning by schools finally achieved the implementation of the new curriculum in 2011. As in the case of the *5 to 14 Curriculum Guidelines* introduced in the early 1990s, the curriculum is advisory and non-statutory. Eight 'curriculum areas' are identified in the curriculum:

1. Expressive arts
2. Health and wellbeing
3. Languages
4. Mathematics
5. Religious and moral education
6. Sciences
7. Social studies
8. Technologies

In each of these areas the curriculum is set out as statements of 'experiences and outcomes' from ages 3 to 15. The pre-school years (aged 3 and 4) and the primary school years are divided into three stages:

1. Early (pre-school and P1 – ages 3 to 6)
2. First (P2 to P4 – ages 7 to 9)
3. Second (P5 to P7 – ages 10 to 12).

The curriculum guidance for science expresses 'experience and outcomes' in statements combining learning processes and skills with knowledge and understanding. These statements are grouped under four main areas (plus Topical science), each subdivided as follows:

1. *Planet Earth* (Biodiversity and interdependence; Energy sources and sustainability; Processes of the planet; Space)
2. *Forces, electricity and waves* (Forces; Electricity; Vibrations and waves)
3. *Biological systems* (Body systems and cells; Inheritance)
4. *Materials* (Properties and used of substances; Earth's materials; Chemical changes)
5. Topical science

Progression within each of these areas is identified by the statements of experiences and outcomes across the primary stages and into the secondary years, although there is not an entry for each sub-area at every one of the levels. The 'topical science' area is for consideration of matters relating, for example, to ethics, how the media report science and aspects in the news at various times. There are frequent cross-links to other areas of the curriculum, particularly to social science and Health and Wellbeing studies.

Box 2.7 gives examples of these statements for the Early, First and Second levels in relation to the area 'Energy sources and sustainability', a sub-area of 'Planet Earth'.

Box 2.7 Examples of draft experiences and outcomes for science in Scotland's Curriculum for Excellence

Planet Earth: Energy sources and sustainability

Early stage (pre-school and P1)
I have experienced, used and described a wide range of toys and common appliances. I can say 'what makes it go' and say what they do when they work.

First (P2 to P4)
I am aware of different types of energy around me and can show their importance to everyday life and my survival.

Second (P5 to P7)
By considering examples where energy is conserved, I can identify the energy source, how it is transferred and ways of reducing wasted energy.

Through exploring non-renewable energy sources, I can describe how they are used in Scotland today and express an informed view on the implications for their future use.

Comment: diverse approaches, similar aims

Perhaps the main message from this brief look at the new curricula developed in the four countries of the UK is that there are very many ways of setting out the intended learning experiences in science! In some ways there seem to be moves in opposite directions in the structure of the curriculum. For instance, while Scotland has removed science from the envelope of Environmental Studies, the new Northern Ireland curriculum has science as part of The World Around Us to which history, geography and technology also contribute. Some other differences are:

■ The place of science in the first two years of school: the Welsh National Curriculum defers more formal study of science to Key Stage 2 but there is a specific programme of study for Key Stage 1 in the draft English National Curriculum for science.

■ The skills that are identified: the new national curricula for Wales and Northern Ireland specify cross-curricular skills but do not identify specifically scientific skills such as are identified in the draft National Curriculum for

England under 'working scientifically'. Although the draft declares that the content should be studied by working scientifically, it is only in the Scottish Curriculum for Excellence that science skills and content are combined in the specification of experiences and outcomes.

■ The detail of the description of progression across (key) stages: programmes of study are set out as requirements for key stages of two years in the draft National Curriculum for England, as well as being offered as guidance for each year. In Wales Key Stage 2 is undivided, extending across four years, whilst in Northern Ireland Foundation and KS1 are two years, with KS2 spreading across three years. In the Curriculum for Excellence, progression is set out across equal three-year stages.

However, despite appearances of form, there is much in common in the aims of the revisions in the different countries; just different ways of achieving these aims. In particular there is a general intention to:

■ provide for greater relevance to real life and other learning;

■ make a place for current issues of concern, such as sustainability;

■ reduce content to allow greater attention to skills and processes;

■ give teachers more freedom by less prescription;

■ identify progress in skills and ideas;

■ improve continuity from pre-school to school and from primary to secondary.

Of course there are possible dangers in some changes. For instance, less prescription could be taken as a signal to spend less time on science. Relevance could mean cross-curricular topics that risk returning to a superficial treatment of science. Avoiding such pitfalls depends on teachers seizing the opportunities offered by revised curricula to enable their pupils to develop scientific understanding and skills. As yet, the progression towards big ideas is not explicit in the UK national curriculum: perhaps that is for the next round of revision.

Summary

This chapter has described how the goals of learning science at the primary school level are expressed in the curriculum requirements at the national level in the countries of the UK. Considerable changes in how science is included in relation to other subjects and in the detail of specification have taken place since the late 1980s when national curricula were introduced. Whilst curriculum statements were quite similar across the UK until about 2005, since then there has been considerable divergence in the requirements or guidelines in England, Northern Ireland, Scotland and Wales. However, while differing in structure and detail, these four countries have produced curricula which share the aim of making science more relevant to children's everyday lives and reducing prescription of content to allow more emphasis on the development of skills and working scientifically.

Further reading

Harlen, W. (2008) *Science as a Key Component of the Primary Curriculum: A Rationale with Policy Implications,* London: Wellcome Trust.

Harlen, W. and Jarvis, T. (2011) What happens in other countries? in W. Harlen (ed.) *ASE Guide to Primary Science Education,* new edition, Hatfield: ASE, 195–203.

Johnson, A. (2013) Is science lost in 'The World Around Us?', *Primary Science*, 126: 8–10.

3

Primary school science in action

Introduction

Having looked at the compelling reasons for teaching science in the primary school in Chapter 1, and at the bare bones of curriculum requirements in the countries of the UK in Chapter 2, here we begin to put some flesh on the bones through some examples of classroom actions. There are multiple steps between the intentions of a programme of study and the experiences of children that will enable them to develop the ideas and skills intended. These examples show what some of the end products – the learning activities and interactions – look like. There are five short case studies between them spanning the primary school years, each beginning with some background information before describing one or more lessons on a topic. The rest of the book is about the steps that have to be taken – in planning, preparing, resourcing, evaluating and assessing – in order to provide for such opportunities for learning in science.

Key features of primary science practice

Although not to be taken as exemplary practice, these examples show some of the different ways of implementing the important features of effective science education practices in primary schools. At the end of the chapter we discuss some of the key features common to all the cases, despite their obvious differences. However, it is perhaps useful to be alerted to some of these important features at this point.

First is engagement. It is clearly important for children to be engaged in the topic, to be motivated to learn. Ideally this would come about because they are working to answer questions they have raised and to which they want to know the answer. In such ideal circumstances the natural curiosity about the world around that drives all scientific endeavours would focus their attention. But in a full class it is unrealistic for children to be pursuing their individual interests and making their own ways towards understanding. In practice, the teacher introduces topics that enable the development of certain ideas and skills through questions or problems to be solved. Generally this is based on knowledge of the children, their experience, stage of development and what is likely to intrigue them. The skilled teacher presents the selected topic in a way that captures the children's curiosity so that they engage with the questions or problems as their own. In the following examples, the teachers find different ways of setting the scene for scientific investigations to take place.

A second key feature concerns the provision of 'things' for the children to talk about, manipulate and use in answering their questions. Providing real objects can be quite a challenge in some topics where first-hand interaction is out of the question, for example, in the study of the solar system, phases of the Moon and the cause of day and night. The example of work on these topics (p. 46) shows how objects and actions can be used to enable active learning even in such unpromising contexts.

A third aspect is to tap into the knowledge the children already have about the topic, so that they can use relevant existing ideas and develop them into more powerful ideas. Accessing these ideas means that children have to communicate them in one way or another, through talk, writing, drawing or action. Among these, talk is the most immediate which can be used at any time and in a variety of contexts, thus constituting a fourth key feature.

Fifth is involving children in using inquiry skills, that is, in generating, gathering and interpreting evidence in developing their understanding of events and phenomena. The importance of these skills in cognitive development is discussed later, in Chapter 6, but here we see what it means for children to be using them in some quite different situations. Even at this early stage it is important for children not just to use, but to be aware of using, these skills of scientific inquiry as a foundation for understanding the nature of scientific activity.

Finally, what stands out in these examples is the extent of careful planning but also teachers' willingness to adapt their plans in response to feedback from observing and interacting with the children. The activities clearly would not take place without detailed planning but teachers do not adhere rigidly to their plans when things do not work out as intended.

Case studies

Kathy's 5/6 year olds and the dog's ball

Background
Kathy was starting a new topic with her class of 5 and 6 year olds. The class had previously undertaken a topic focusing on materials, looking at the best materials for mopping up a spillage on the kitchen floor. This had been introduced through a DVD about a cartoon dog, 'Discovery Dog', projected onto the interactive white board (IWB). As a way of recording their project, they had produced a big, illustrated book. Reviewing this book enabled them to revisit some of the things they had done and talked about, such as predicting, fair testing and safety, reminding them of the language they had used as well as recalling what fun it was.

The activities

The new project began with a short animation in which a naughty puppy had managed to burst the dog's favourite ball, had chewed another to a pulp and had lost another over the garden fence. The children saw the different events depicted on the IWB and read the words, as well as hearing them. The teacher was able to pause as they went along the four pages of pictures and text, to ask questions and respond to comments by the children. She let the children chip in with memories of balls that had popped after being bitten by a dog ('it was round and then it looked like a dish'), or what they knew of puppies and how they behave ('my Gran's got a dog and it chews the chairs').

The teacher focused the class on the problem of how they might find a good bouncy ball for the dog. *If you went to a shop to buy a ball you wouldn't just pick one without trying it would you?*

Pick a really bouncy one out and then e-mail him to tell him.

Get him another football.

The children began to suggest particular balls and those used when in play or sport. But before going further Kathy asked them to 'have a think', then to talk in pairs for a couple of minutes (talking pairs was a common element of their lessons), to consider how they might help the dog find a really good bouncy ball. Bringing the children back together, Kathy asked them for their ideas.

We could get a lot of balls and have a vote on them.

We could find which balls bounce and which don't, because Discovery Dog likes bouncy ones.

Yes we could have a vote on it.

We could get some balls and bounce them. But not in the classroom.

A brief discussion followed about the potential problems of bouncing balls all over the classroom. The teacher then showed the class the large box full of different balls that she had collected. How would they find which was the bounciest? The children began to settle on the idea of selecting out the relatively more bouncy balls and then focusing on these for further testing.

It was then playtime, after which they reconvened in the school hall. With the children sat on the floor with the box of balls in the middle, Kathy reminded them of the problem and they recalled some of their discussion from before playtime. She then passed some of the children a ball and encouraged them to describe it. The balls were passed around during the discussion and all the children had chance to look at the balls and describe them.

The initial discussion was wide-ranging, with children pointing to and describing balls. Kathy praised children for observing well and using good describing words.

That looks like a dog's ball, that small pinky one.

This one is all rough and dull looking.

Oh look this one is a mini rugby ball.

Kathy asked for more explanation –

It's not a round

It's an oval shape.

What makes them all balls?

They are all round.

But the rugby ball isn't.

When it bounces it goes the other way.

Some might be bigger.

Some might be smaller.

Some might be rough.

Different colours and shapes.

That one looks like the Earth [a map printed on the ball].

Bumpy.

Patterns.

Do you think patterns on the ball would make a difference?

No, it bounces the same.

That one looks like a dog's ball. It is a dog's ball.

Some are not sports balls, and some you kick and some you bat.

That's different to all the others because it's got holes in it.

Some are hard.

There's a criminal [i.e. chemical] inside that one; it lights up.

This has air inside it.

How do we know?

It can pop and go flat.

That's a sponge all through.

The teacher then brought the children back to the issue of 'bounciness'. *How are we going to find out, with all these different balls, which are the bounciest?*

Get a ball each and bounce it.

Good idea. How many bounces? The class settled on ten bounces from around waist height. The children were then asked to choose a ball they think might be a good bouncer. There were enough to go around. They spread out around the hall as they selected their ball, continuing to discuss and describe their selections.

The green one.

Why do you think that one?

Because I think it will go high.

The orange one, it's squashy.

The red one. It looks like it's bouncy. The rubber might make it bouncy.

The dog ball … it looks bouncy and dead hard.

That one, because I have used it before and it's bouncy.

Once balls had been selected one of the children asked to change hers. *Why do you want to change?*

It's too squashy to bounce much.

Anyone else want to change? There was further discussion as the children moved around.

I chose this particular one because it's very tight full of air.

Because bigger balls bounce highest.

Oh, so who chose a small ball?

To avoid the chaos of having too many balls being bounced at the same time, they agreed to having four children at a time bounce their balls ten times and the others to vote on the 'best'. The children were, in this way, encouraged to focus on observing the balls bounce. The process was very swiftly carried out and the class identified the best ball in each of the groups.

How could we find out which of these balls is the best bouncer?

We could have a vote again?

We could measure it.

How could we measure it?

We could stick the balls together …

You could catch it and measure it with a ruler how high it is.

We could put post-it notes on the board to see how high it is.

We could use blocks to see how high.

We could drop it down from a table and see if it goes back up to the table.

We could try which bounces quickest.

Trying this last idea allowed the children some further play and exploration, but was rejected as a good way to test the balls, because different children bounced them in different ways, and some children failed to catch them every time. So it really was not a fair test.

At this point the lesson was due to end. The teacher suggested that they take the selected balls back to the classroom and put them in the basket ready for the next day, when they would try some of their ideas for finding the best bouncer. A child pointed to one of the selected balls, and said

> That ball doesn't bounce good in the wet.

I'll make a note of that idea; we could test that out too.

Throughout the lesson the teacher took photographs of the children working – sitting discussing the balls, all bouncing balls, bouncing in fours and voting. This then provided the basis of the record of the investigation which would be used to create the big book. It meant that the children were not being distracted by having to write anything, which takes a long time for these young children. The big book and the selected balls provided the record of this lesson.

Chris's class investigating ice

Background

Chris's class of 6 and 7 year olds were working on a broad topic of changing materials. The children had made a collage using natural materials, they had baked cakes and made animals out of clay, they had developed appropriate language to describe materials and had experience of making predictions. They were now moving on to look at ice. Chris wanted the children to explore ice, describe it and, by thinking about how to slow down melting, to consider fair testing.

The activities

In the morning the children were told that there was something different about their classroom. A notice on the door read 'Penguins in Year 2, take care!' The children were encouraged to creep into the classroom, which was in semi darkness and rather cool. They found some footprints on the floor, a large 'iceberg' in the middle of the room, and two penguins sitting on it. The iceberg was constructed from the polystyrene packing materials around a new television, and some tinsel to make it glisten. Ice cubes were found in crevasses in the iceberg, and around it, along with some small pebbles. The children's imagination was fired and they were full of questions about icebergs, ice and the penguins. It transpired that the two penguins (puppets), Flapjack and Waddle, spent much of their time in the freezer department of the local supermarket but had been banned for leaving footprints in the ice cream. They had arrived with plenty of ice borrowed from the supermarket.

The children were given ice cubes on small dishes to explore and asked to look after them for the morning. The literacy lesson that morning involved the children in describing their ice, finding lots of 'icy' words and, after much discussion, writing some sentences about 'what I know about ice'.

The afternoon began with Chris calling the register, including Flapjack and Waddle, and some discussions with the two puppets. Chris asked where penguins come from and what sort of temperatures they are used to. The children knew they came from the Antarctica and that this was a very cold place where it was difficult to keep warm. They talked about how people generally preferred warmer climates. The teacher showed the children a big book about penguins. They discussed how flocks of penguins keep warm, huddling together and taking turns to be in the centre of the group. Chris emphasised the fact that this meant that all the penguins had an equal chance of keeping warm, that they made it fair.

Chris reviewed with the children what they know about ice, using their sheets from the literacy session. 'Ice melts in the sun', 'There are cold icebergs', 'Ice can build you a house', 'Ice is frozen water', 'Ice is "see-through"', 'Ice can be dangerous'. One child then told how he had swallowed an ice cube once. In discussion it was established that his warm body had melted the cube, although it had felt very cold and hard going down. Chris asked the children to describe their ice cubes. *Who rubbed it on their forehead?* Many hands went up. *How did it feel?*

Cold and wet.

What happened to your ice cube?

It gone watery.

Spread over the dish.

Runny.

Melted.

The penguins confided that, having borrowed the ice from the supermarket, they were keen to find the best place to store their ice so that it would not melt too quickly. Chris brought some more ice from the store cupboard. She had kept it in a freezer bag wrapped in layers of paper. Chris pointed out that the ice that was in the 'iceberg' crevasses had not melted away. She wondered why this was.

Maybe the penguins cuddled it under their legs.

But wouldn't that make it warmer?

There was not just one block, but a lot of blocks together.

The class found this idea extremely difficult and Chris realised that, apart from this one child they were not yet ready to consider it. She said that they would come back to this 'brilliant' idea later.

The children decided to put ice cubes in different places in the classroom and see how long they took to melt. Flapjack then selected an ice cube from the tray to test, and Waddle selected a large cube made in an ice cream tub. The children could immediately see that this was not fair. They discussed how to make their test fair.

Back at their tables, each group was given four ice cubes on small dishes and asked to think about where they might put them. The teacher gave them a simple worksheet for planning and recording, as in Figure 3.1.

The children began to discuss where they would place their ice cubes. Some children asked to put their ice cubes in the freezer, some wanted to put them in the school office (as it always seems cold in there). This caused a good deal of discussion about which was the coldest place, but for their investigation they had to stay in the classroom.

Where it was	Prediction	Result
1.	I think	
2.	I think	
3.	I think	
4.	I think	
I think the ice changed because		

Figure 3.1 What happens to ice?

Many found the worksheet a challenge. However, they were seen to be moving around the room, some held out their hands to test the temperature of different locations. Chris circulated among the groups, asking them to explain why they had chosen particular places. She was keen to find out their ideas about why the ice melts. 'Why do you think that might be a good place to keep the ice?' One thing that emerged was that a number of children seemed to believe that sunlight was a factor and that putting ice in the dark (as in the store cupboard or in the cardboard (Peter's) house) would slow down melting. However, when one child suggested wrapping the cube in plastic the other children rejected the idea 'because that would make it warmer'.

The children went out for break and on returning looked at their ice cubes. Chris asked them to think about which was the best place to keep the ice cubes for longest.

At the end of the afternoon the children sat on the floor to discuss their findings with Chris, Flapjack and Waddle. It was agreed that the coolest place in the classroom was on the windowsill. The children thought that the cold wind coming in kept the cubes frozen for longer. Yet the cubes in the Iceberg were still there. Paula, having thought about the problem, suggested that 'The polystyrene might have kept it cooler than the cups did'. Again other children struggled, finding this emerging idea of insulation a challenge.

The final part of the lesson considered the problem of how to get ice back for Flapjack and Waddle to take back to the supermarket. The children were asked to think about this overnight as a follow-up lesson would look at making ice from water.

In reviewing her lesson Chris felt that the children had enjoyed the lesson and that they had been able to explore ice and become aware that ice melts at different rates in places of different temperatures. During the practical activity she had focused her observations on a small number of children whom she felt might have difficulty in setting up an investigation. As she discussed the work with the children she found that they had not really grasped the purpose of the activity. They were struggling with the notion of fair testing and had difficulty understanding what was meant by a prediction. Many of the children had trouble completing the worksheet. Although individual questioning revealed that they were able to make and support their predictions, their difficulties were in articulating this in writing. She felt that some children were still at the stage of exploring and describing materials, while others were at a point where they understood the idea of a fair test, could make predictions and could describe and compare the properties of materials. However most were not able to record their ideas clearly in the table provided. She decided that, in the next lesson, she would focus more on fair testing and on prediction and perhaps find less demanding ways to record findings. (See page 304 for Chris' lesson plan.)

Explaining day and night

Background

This account is based on a case study by Fitzgerald (2012) using a range of research techniques to record the lessons of two primary teachers in Western Australia who were selected as being 'effective primary science teachers'. One of the teachers, Lisa, used a unit on astronomy from the Australian primary science programme 'Primary Connections' with a class of 8 and 9 year olds. Although an experienced teacher with a science degree, she used the unit because, she explained, instead of focusing on preparing the content of the lessons she could focus her attention on modifying aspects of the unit to suit her pupils' learning needs and interests. The programme promotes an inquiry-based approach through a five-phase lesson structure called 5Es: Engage, Explore, Explain, Elaborate and Evaluate.

The activities

As a stimulus to engaging the children's interest at the start of the unit the teacher showed two YouTube clips: one a series of satellite images of the Earth and the other a series of time-lapse photographs of changes in a city over 24 hours. She said: 'I wanted to start them thinking about what causes day and night, and I wanted them to start to make connections about things that they see in their own life and own experience.' After the children had watched the clips Lisa asked them to express their feelings as well as their observations. She responded to each contribution in a positive way. Then, as a whole class, they brainstormed the differences between day and night and what they knew or thought about what caused the daily changes. She used a TWLH (what you think you know (T), what you want to know (W), what you have learnt (L), how you know what you have learnt (H)) chart, completing only the T and W sections in the first lesson. What some children thought they knew about the Sun, Earth and Moon was revealed in this discussion:

Teacher	What are some of the things that we think we know already about the Sun, Earth and Moon? Ben, start us off.
Ben	When the Moon is a crescent, it's in the shade
Teacher	In the shade? Can you explain that just a little more, Ben?
Ben	It's in the shade of the Earth and when the Sun comes around the Earth is blocking the Moon, so it only gets a little bit of Sun and you can see a shadow
Teacher	OK. Thank you for clarifying that for me, Ben. Great. Simon, what else do we think we know?
Simon	That the Sun and Moon travel from one side of the world to the other each time.
Teacher	OK Interesting. Leah?
Leah	The Sun shines at day and goes away at night
Teacher	Thank you very much for that, Leah. Andrea?
Andrea	One side of the Earth has the Sun and the other side of the Earth has the Moon.

Teacher	Great. Rachel, last one.
Rachel	When the Sun goes away, it's the Sun having a rest.
Teacher	OK

When asked what they would like to know, their questions included: 'How does the Sun disappear at night?' 'What is the Moon made of?' 'How does the Earth spin if there is no wind or air?'

In the second lesson children worked in groups brainstorming words which they thought were connected to the Sun, Earth and Moon. These were shared with the whole class as a way of continuing the thinking in the first lesson. In an attempt to gather each child's ideas about the topic Lisa gave them a worksheet but realised that this was not the best way of eliciting their ideas. She found the children confused by the ideas about the Earth's movement around the Sun and the Moon's movement around the Earth. Consequently for the next three lessons the children worked with concrete objects as she scaffolded their understanding of the relative sizes and the movements of the Sun, Earth and Moon. Lisa showed them three spherical objects – a peppercorn, a marble and a basketball – and they discussed how these could be used to represent the Moon, Earth and Sun. In order to help understanding of how the very large Sun could appear to be about the same size as the much smaller Moon, they took some balls of very different sizes outside the classroom where they could look at how they appeared when held a long way away. Through these activities they realised that a very large object held a long way away could appear to be the same size as a small object that was much nearer. Then the children made their own scale models of the Sun, Earth and Moon, requiring them to think again about the relative sizes.

In order to show that the rotation of the Earth would result in the Sun appearing to move, the children explored the position of the Sun through shadow activities out in the playground. The shadows of sticks were marked at regular times, giving plenty of opportunity for making and testing predictions about the length and position of the shadow at different times. Using a model Lisa showed how the Earth spinning caused day and night. In groups the children then worked out a role-play to show their understanding of day and night. Each group practised their role-play in which they used themselves as objects to explain how day and night occur and then performed it to the whole class.

The responses of the children when asked about their experiences showed that they appreciated that the concrete experiences through models, animation and role-play helped their learning. For example, one explained how she felt the role-play helped by: 'actually showing us how the Sun just stays still while the Earth spins around and the Moon spins around the Earth' (Fitzgerald, 2012: 62). At the same time, the children's activities provided Lisa with feedback on the children's ideas. For example, she noted that some of the children's performances indicated an alternative idea in which the Moon had a role in causing day and night. This misunderstanding proved to be very persistent, and was still evident in some of the children's explanations of day and night at the end of the unit.

In her original plan the teacher intended to cover a good deal more ground relating to the relative positions and movement of the Sun, Earth and Moon but she found the ideas in the unit were quite challenging for her 8 and 9 year olds. So she reduced the range of the ideas to be covered at this stage and focused on how day and night can be explained without reference to the Moon.

Graham's class investigating soil

Background

Graham was introducing science activities within an overall topic about growing food to his class of 9 and 10 year olds. He planned that the children should discuss and investigate the differences between types of soil. He had in mind that the children should undertake some investigations of sandy, loamy and clay soil, so he provided samples of each of these, to which some of the children contributed samples that they brought from gardens at home. He wanted the investigations to advance the children' ideas, but felt it was important to start from their initial ideas and questions. It would have been easy to ask the children to find out, for example, 'Which soil holds most water?' 'Does water drain more quickly through some soils than through others?' etc., and to start the children's investigations from these questions. These are perfectly good questions for children to investigate and likely to be among those the children ended up investigating, but he wanted to hold back his questions to find out what the children would ask and what ideas they had.

The activities

The first part of the work was an exploratory phase of looking at the different soils. In groups, the children were given samples of the three main types, some hand-lenses, sieves, disposable gloves and some very open instructions:

- Separate each of the soils into the different parts that it contains.
- Find out what is contained in all the soils.
- Find out what is different in each soil.
- Think about how these differences might affect how well plants grow in the soils.

This task required children to use their ideas about different materials in making their observations. It encouraged them to look closely at the soil and to think about the differences they found. During this activity the teacher visited each group to listen in to what the children were saying about the types of soil. Many of their statements at this stage contained hypotheses and predictions. The children were quick to say which they thought would be best for plants to grow in (the darkest coloured one) and to identify the ability to hold water as a property that was needed.

There was then a whole-class discussion, pooling findings and ideas from different groups. Graham said that they would test their ideas about which was best for growing plants when they had found out more about the soils and the differences that might make one better than another. What would the plants need to grow? Water was the most popular answer. Some mentioned 'fertiliser' and there was a discussion of what this meant in terms of the soils they had looked at. It was eventually identified with the bits of leaves and decayed plant material they had found, particularly in the loam. Graham introduced the word 'humus' to describe this part of the soil.

No one mentioned the presence of air in the soil until the teacher asked them to think about the difference between soil that was compressed and the same soil in a loose heap. He challenged them to think about whether there was the same amount of air between the particles in each soil and whether this was likely to make a difference to how well plants would grow in it.

The discussion identified four main differences to be investigated: the differences in the amount of water held in the soil; how quickly water drained through each one; the amount of humus in each; and the amount of air. Each of the six groups in which the children were working chose one of these and set about planning how they would go about their investigation. Although having different foci, the investigations of all the groups were relevant to developing understanding of the nature and properties of soil so that, when they did the trial of which enabled plants to grow best, they might be able to explain and not just observe the result.

The investigations provided opportunities to help the children develop their inquiry skills, in order to carry out systematic and 'fair' tests through which they would arrive at findings useful in developing their ideas. He asked them first to plan what they would do and identify what they would need in terms of equipment. He probed their thinking about what variables to control and what to observe or measure by asking questions such as 'How will you be sure that the difference is only caused by the type of soil? How will you be able to show the difference?' He had ideas, gathered from various sources, about useful approaches but kept these 'up his sleeve' to be introduced only if the children did not produce ideas of their own. Graham encouraged the children to make notes of what they found as they went along and then use these to prepare a report from each group to the whole class. He told them that they should report what they did and what they found, but also say whether it was what they had expected and to try to explain the differences they found.

At the end of the practical work and after a period for bringing their ideas together in their groups, each group in turn presented a report, while other children were given opportunity to question. Graham refrained from making comments at this stage and asked questions only for clarification. When all the reports had been given he listed the findings for each soil and asked the children to decide which might be best for growing some seedlings. The choice was not as obvious as some children had initially thought, so they were very keen to try this next investigation and find out what really would happen.

Graham then turned to the samples of soil that the children had brought from home. In order to compare them with the three soils they had investigated he suggested mixing some of each with enough water to loosen the parts from each other and allow the constituents to separate as they settled to the bottom. They then used these observations on what they had found out about soil to predict which might by 'good growing' soils. These samples were then included in the seedling trials.

Before going on to set up the next investigations, Graham asked the children to reflect on which parts of the work just completed they had enjoyed most, which would they do differently if they could start again and what they now felt they could do better than before.

Science week for Year 6

Background

With the help of a colleague from the regional Science Learning Centre, some additional equipment borrowed from the local high school and college and contributions from the local police, teachers in one large primary school in England planned a science week for their Year 6 (10–11 years olds). The idea was to devise a cross-curricular theme with a science focus after pupils had completed their national tests. The teachers wanted the children to experience science as it is applied in the real world and to raise the profile of investigative work, which they recognised had been neglected in the preparation for the tests. They agreed that they wanted greater emphasis on group work and discussion than on writing.

Working with an adviser from the Science Learning Centre three class teachers planned the week together. They decided on a forensic science topic as likely to fire the pupils' imaginations and provide the potential to use many aspects of science as well as other subjects. The idea was to set up a 'crime' in school. The crime agreed was the theft of the two annual 'rounders trophies', for which children were to compete and were to them valued objects. The trophies were kept in a shed in the school grounds. They planned that the possible culprits could be one of the lunchtime supervisors, the head teacher, the school caretaker or one of the class teachers. Although the three teachers were involved in the lengthy planning, all the members of the school staff, including the non-teaching staff, were in the picture. The planning also involved the local police and the Scene of Crime Officer (SOCO) agreed to participate.

In planning the week the science coordinator was very keen to ensure that the science was not lost in the role-play, or other activities. She felt that the science had to be rigorous. However, the opportunities through the week for work on citizenship, drama, PSHE (personal, social and health education) and literacy skills were also clearly present.

The particular areas of science identified were:

■ Materials and their properties – identifying fibres, chromatography
■ Characteristics of living things – fingerprints, DNA
■ Scientific inquiry – evidence, observation, hypothesising, recording.

The activities

On the Monday morning the pupils arrived to find a police car in the school yard, and a shed cordoned off with yellow striped tape. The Year 6 classes were gathered in a hall to be informed about the crime. The SOCO spoke to the children and told them that he would need their help. He asked for ideas about evidence to look for and immediately received suggestions for fingerprints, hair, footprints. He emphasised the importance of not touching anything until photographs and notes had been taken. Then, in turn, groups dressed in white overalls and hoods, and given cameras, went with the SOCO to explore the scene of the crime.

The shed had a broken window and some 'blood' on the floor. A crow bar had been used to prise open the lock. A ginger beer can and a section of a shopping list lay on the floor. Also found were footprints in the mud outside and some pieces of fabric. The pupils noticed that the footprints leading away from the shed suddenly stopped. They hypothesised that the criminal had removed his or her shoes at this point.

They took photographs with a digital camera and collected evidence to take back into the classroom. There they worked together in groups to consider the evidence, with photographs from the scene printed out. They discussed and developed a list of suspects on the basis of the evidence they had about staff who had access to the shed, or who had some motive. They devised interview questions and went to interview each of the suspects, recording their responses to share with others. One group observed the lunchtime supervisor had a tear in her blouse, this provided a reason to compare fibres from the fabric found at the scene of the crime. They used a digital microscope borrowed from the secondary school to look at the fibres found at the scene and to compare them with those of the lunchtime supervisor's blouse.

The police fingerprint expert came to the school to show the pupils how to take fingerprints from the ginger beer can. The pupils then collected sample fingerprints from all the suspects and compared them with the ones from the can using magnifying hand lenses. Moulds of prints, photographs and measurements were taken and the footprints were identified as those of the classroom teacher (who kept his bike in the shed). Meanwhile the head teacher was eliminated 'because his foot is in a plaster cast'.

The pupils wanted to analyse the handwriting on the shopping list found in the shed. They did this in two ways. First they asked each suspect to write something on similar paper. Then they collected the suspects' pens in order to analyse the ink and compare it with that on the list, using chromatography. The teachers showed them how to do this, practising on coloured candy-coated chocolate beans (smarties). They saw how the colours separated as the dye spread across the damp filter paper. They then used these skills to test small fragments of the shopping list found at the scene of the crime, comparing it with the pens used by the different suspects. In doing this, and using the handwriting analysis, they were able to identify the handwriting as that of the school secretary.

For the analysis of the 'blood' the children were told about DNA and about Professor Howard Jeffries who had developed a test for DNA. The equipment was borrowed from, and the requisite chemicals donated by, the local college so that the pupils could carry out their own DNA testing. This was done with the help of the adviser from the Science Learning Centre (who also runs sessions for teachers on how to do DNA testing). The process was described as 'basically chromatography by putting 200 volts through DNA to split it up'.

When all the evidence was put together the conclusion reached was that the class teacher was the culprit.

Although the main aim was not to emphasise conventional recording and writing, the pupils were keen to write articles for the school magazine. There were also many discussions about matters beyond the science of solving the crime, such as about safety, the role of the police, the nature of evidence. The pupils had really enjoyed the week and the teachers felt they had learned a great deal in a really engaging way. The three teachers directly involved in the planning agreed that, although it had been very challenging, they would want to run a similar week the next year.

One teacher was worried about the ethics of being dishonest with the pupils by telling them that this was a real crime. Another argued that children had soon 'cottoned on' that it was not real but realised that joining in seriously enabled them to have fun and do lots of new things. Essentially the children were encouraged to join in the pretence and enjoy themselves.

The key features in the case studies

At the start of this chapter we identified six key features of classroom practice that appear to be significant in helping children to learn science:

- Engaging children in answering questions
- Providing materials for investigations
- Linking to children's existing ideas and skills
- Children talking and reporting
- Children using science inquiry skills
- Teachers planning and using feedback

The form that each of these features takes varies across the five examples, which span the age range from 5 to 11 years. The variation is partly a reflection of the different topics but mainly because of the changes in children during the years of primary education. For example, the meaning of 'relevance' differs considerably. Relevance is important at all stages, so that pupils see a point in what they are asked to do. However, in the later primary years what is seen as relevant is closer to real life rather than the imaginative stories that often inspire the activities of the earlier years, as in Kathy's and Chris's classes. Indeed, in some primary schools older pupils take an active part in making real decisions about, for instance, reducing the energy use in the school, through projects which include monitoring energy consumption and temperature to avoid waste through overheating.

We now look briefly at how these features of practice are present but take different forms in the examples.

Engaging children in answering questions

All of the teachers went to considerable lengths to plan and provide some initial stimulus to grab the children's attention and set a question for them to answer in a real, or simulated, context. Kathy told her 5/6 year olds a story about a puppy, using cartoons presented on the interactive white board. Chris set up a simulated 'iceberg' in the classroom which her 6/7 year olds were willing to accept as real enough. For the older pupils, in Year 6, a more convincing simulation was appropriate in the form of a 'crime scene'. For the 8 and 9 year olds, engagement in thinking about day and night might have been more challenging, but showing the changes across a city over 24 hours, using time-lapse photography, was a novel way of looking at something familiar which triggered curiosity about the cause of the changes.

Providing materials for investigations

Children of primary school age learn best when they can observe and investigate objects, materials and events at first-hand. In the early years they have limited ability to deal with abstract ideas and need to do and see things for themselves. Teachers have to provide materials and objects for the children to manipulate and also for them to use in their investigations. In Kathy's and Chris's classes they dealt with familiar things – balls and ice – extending their ideas about them through investigation. Equivalent manipulation of objects was not possible in the case of the Sun, Earth and Moon, of course, but Lisa provided concrete experience in several ways: from the images in the time-lapse sequence, the models of the Earth, Moon and Sun, and using themselves to act out their relative movements. This enabled some of the children to have the experience of the 'actual' objects, but for others having to use a ball, or person, to represent the real things was a difficult step to take. Graham's class certainly investigated the real things and perhaps because soil might have seemed too familiar to excite interest, he gave them time to explore and to look closely at the different samples. Investigating the crime scene gave the Year 6 pupils a variety of first-hand experience, from using chromatography to using a digital microscope.

Linking to children's existing ideas and skills

In the first four examples the teachers made particular efforts to find out the ideas the children already had about the objects and materials to be investigated:

- Kathy discussed what the children knew about balls before she showed them the collection of different ones. When they were handling the balls they continued, through their comments which she freely encouraged, to indicate what they expected balls to be like.

- Chris explored the children's ideas about ice melting, before they set about the activity of keeping it from melting.

- After the children had watched the 'day and night' images, Lisa explored the ideas the children had about the differences and cause of changes every 24 hours. She also tried using a worksheet to gather the children's ideas about the movements in the solar system but this was not found to be helpful as the children did not have sufficient grasp of the relative positions to make sense of the questions.

- In Graham's class the children's ideas about the factors that made one soil better than another for growing plants were the starting point. Noting that they did not mention air, he extended their first ideas so that a more complete set of variables, including air, were investigated. Developing a better understanding of the nature of soils and their role in plant growth was an important goal for Graham to be built up over several lessons, of which this was just the start.

Children talking and reporting

There was a good deal of talk, question and answers and reporting in different ways in all the classes and it played an important part in giving the teachers access to the pupils' ideas. Of particular value in the development of their ideas, however, is the informal talk among groups of children where they exchange ideas and realise that there are different views from their own. Finding out what others think is a key factor in developing more widely shared ideas. Douglas Barnes (1976) calls this 'co-constructing' ideas; helping each other to make sense of things. In simple terms it means 'putting our heads together', which we know so often leads to a better understanding than anyone working things out alone. Kathy's very young children needed the structure of the whole-class context in order to be encouraged to talk and to listen to each other's comments. Chris's pupils sat in groups to talk about their task but each one decided where to put his or her ice cube individually, not as a shared decision. Like Kathy, both Chris and Lisa made a point of discussing and using relevant words. The work of different groups was drawn together in different ways – by performance in Lisa's class, or reporting in other cases. In Graham's class, where groups tried different things, the reporting was of particular value since combination of their results was important in achieving an overall class result.

Children using science inquiry skills

The idea of 'fairness' in comparing objects or materials is a useful introduction to 'being scientific' for young children, even if it is only one form of scientific inquiry. Kathy and Chris guided their pupils into setting up 'which is best?' type investigations with familiar objects. For Chris's class the development of these skills was only at the starting point and it was clear that in several cases the children needed more opportunities to develop them. Chris built into her planning the penguins' unfair suggestion to start the children thinking about fair testing. Kathy and Chris avoided telling the children what to do ('put one ice cube here and another here' or 'hold the balls at the same height and see which bounces higher when they are dropped'), but instead gave the children the opportunity to decide what to do. This not only gave them some ownership of their investigations, but provided the opportunity for them to begin to use and develop skills such as planning a fair test, making a prediction and communicating a result.

In Lisa's class opportunities to use inquiry skills were provided by the concrete activities with the balls and shadow sticks. The children made predictions about how far away the ball representing the Sun would need to be to appear the same size as the much smaller ball representing the Moon. They also identified and used patterns in the positions of the shadows of their stick at various times.

The 'crime' activities in the Year 6 science week were particularly rich in potential for developing systematic and careful collection of data, for recognising the importance of recording and understanding how to use data in arriving at conclusions. However, it does not require an elaborate set up (fun though it was) to develop these skills and understanding of scientific investigation. Graham asked his pupils to plan their investigation and expected them to keep notes to help them in reporting. He also encouraged their reflection on how they could have improved their investigations, thus focusing their attention on the process and not just the outcome of their investigations.

Teachers planning and using feedback

In all cases the amount of careful planning is an impressive aspect of the work. However, apart from the Year 6 science week (which was exceptional and probably motivated by the filming of the week for Teachers' TV), this was not laid on for a special occasion. One might well ask: why did the teachers go to all this trouble rather than using alternative approaches which would have involved less preparation? The answer surely lies in the teachers' conceptions of how children best learn. We discuss this in Part 2 of this book. But it is also the case that the lessons described were at the start of a topic and the work would continue over some time. Kathy built in the opportunity to revisit parts of the children's work by taking photographs and creating a 'big book' for discussion later. This would enable the children to continue to learn from these activities. For Chris's class, too, there was a great deal of further discussion and investigation if the full value of the activities was to be exploited. So by no means every lesson would require the amount of preparation clearly necessary for the lessons we have glimpsed here. In fact the effort would be largely wasted if the investigations were not followed by time for reflection and consolidation of the learning they provided.

In all cases the topics fitted into the long-term plans of each school's programme, devised to ensure progression in development of conceptual understanding and skills and meet the national curriculum requirements. In his medium-term planning, Graham worked out how the work on soil fitted into the current term's work and built on what the children had done previously about what was needed for plant growth and how it would lead on to ideas about the formation of soil and the need to preserve its fertility in order to grow food. In his short-term planning, he worked out what both he and the children would do, considered some of the questions he would pose and prepared himself with information about the ideas children might have and with suggestions for activities from sources such as the *Rocks, Soil and Weather* Teachers' Guide of Nuffield Primary Science. Similarly Lisa used an existing well-developed published curriculum unit so that planning did not need to be started from scratch.

A further feature of the teachers' planning was their willingness to adapt and change their plans according to the feedback they gathered from the pupils' reactions. Chris noted that her young children found the idea of insulation difficult and decided not to follow up on this line of reasoning about what would keep the ice from melting. Also Chris, like Lisa, found that using worksheets was not helpful in exploring children's ideas and helping their planning. Lisa also responded to her pupils' difficulties with the effects of movements of the Sun, Earth and Moon by reducing her goals to focus on the one area, of day and night. In using feedback to adjust their teaching these teachers were incorporating an important aspect of formative assessment into their pedagogy.

Summary

This chapter comprises accounts of activities in five different classes, between them covering the ages 5 to 11 years. Each account provides some background information and one or more lessons on a topic. All the examples describe real events in real classes and are not intended as models, although they reflect several features of effective practice in science education for young children. They also indicate how classroom procedures and expectations change as children progress through the primary years. Some significant features have been discussed under the headings of

- Engaging children in answering questions

- Providing materials for investigations

- Linking to children's existing ideas and skills

- Children talking and reporting

- Children using science inquiry skills

- Teachers planning and using feedback

These points are discussed in later chapters of the book.

Further reading

Primary Science Review, 92 (March/April 2006) includes a number of articles on using stories, poems and puppets to engage children in science, including:

'Involving young children through stories as starting points' by Jill Cavendish, Bev Stopps and Charly Ryan.

'Puppets bringing stories to life in science' by Brenda Keogh, Stuart Naylor, Brigid Downing, Jane Maloney and Shirley Simon.

'Goldilocks and the three variables' by Graham Lowe

Primary Science Review, 90 (Nov./Dec. 2005) includes the following articles on the theme of forensic science:

'The baker did it!' by Ian Richardson (on how forensic science activities can engage children in developing their inquiry skills)

'Murder' by Ivor Hickey, Colette Murphy, Jim Beggs and Karen Carlisle (describing how children can carry out DNA finger printing)

'Fibres, blood and broken glass' (Bob Tomlinson talking to Alan Peacock about the work of Scene of Crime Investigators)

CHAPTER

4

Experiences that promote learning in science

Introduction

This chapter attempts to identify some important characteristics of classroom experiences that promote learning in general and in science in particular. The evidence used comes from classroom events, such as described in the case studies in Chapter 3, from systematic research and also from what is known from neuroscience about changes in the brain that accompany learning. The last of these reflects the argument that, even though we identify learning with change in observable behaviour – in what pupils show they know and can do – learning must have something to do with what happens inside the brain. So we begin by looking at what is needed to help learning from a different perspective than the classroom – what is known about the changes inside our heads when learning takes place.

After this brief foray into events at the micro-level, we return to the large-scale level of behaviour that we can more easily observe. Drawing on information at these two levels, we identify the characteristics of experience that are most likely to be effective in promoting learning in science. Finally, we illustrate how these can be used as criteria in evaluating activities and in deciding how to adapt or elaborate activities to increase their value for learning.

What do we learn about learning from neuroscience?

There has been a considerable expansion in our knowledge of the functioning of the brain, made possible largely because of the development of non-intrusive techniques for finding out about links between external behaviour and internal brain activity. One result of this has been the more than ten-fold increase since the early 1980s in publications linking neuroscience and education (Reid and Anderson, 2012). The advances in technology for detecting brain activity mean that it is no longer necessary to depend on investigations with non-human animals or humans with brain disorders. Studies show that learning changes the brain both in structure and size and so it is worth exploring, with appropriate caution, what neuroscience can say about learning.

Trying to relate the ideas and behaviours of a person to the function of cells in the brain is one of the great challenges facing neuroscience. This is partly because understanding of the brain is still at an early stage, but also because there are estimated to be 15 to 32 billion cells in the brain (OECD, 2007: 36–7) and a large number of these will be involved in even the simplest actions, such as decoding a word. It makes sense that there should be some relationship between what happens inside the brain and response to the world around, but a great deal has yet to be worked out about the nature of the connections. Meanwhile, what can we learn about learning from what is already known about the brain?

The brain

Our brains are composed of neurons, cells which are made up of a main part, called the cell body, with dendrites and an axon attached. Dendrites are thread-like, branching structures which grow out of the cell body, whilst the axon is in most cases a single fibre, thinner than a dendrite thread and much longer than the cell body. An axon running down the spinal cord (which is an extension of the brain) can be up to a metre long.

The activity of the brain depends on communication between neurons. There are other nerve cells in the brain, called glial cells, but these do not transmit messages. The communication is through electric signals which are the result of movement of ions (atoms that have a positive or negative charge), within and surrounding the neuron. Without going into detail of how charges move into and out of a neuron, it is enough for our purposes to know that these electric signals are transmitted by one neuron to another by axons and received from another neuron by dendrites. There is a small gap (synapse) between the terminal of an axon of the cell sending a message and the dendrite of a receiving neuron. If several signals are received in a cell body this can 'excite' the cell body and send a signal across the gap to another neuron. To communicate with the target cell, the axon has to release chemical signals across the gap. Communication between neurons is increased by an insulating layer of myelin which forms a fatty sheath around the axon.(see Figure 4.1).

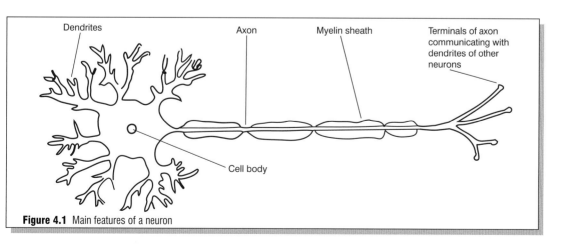

Figure 4.1 Main features of a neuron

Box 4.1 Growth of the brain

Much of the spectacular increase in brain size after birth is actually attributable to the development of these processes acting as lines of communication between neurons, rather than simply to the addition of more neurons.

(Greenfield, 1997: 141)

Each neuron can communicate with a large number of others, forming networks. It is these networks of communications that enable the brain to carry out its functions. At birth, the human brain has most of the neurons it will ever have; the brain development from there onwards comprises growth of communication among the neurons (Box 4.1).

At the same time, lines of communication between neurons that are no longer used are 'pruned'. Thus there is enormous potential for different connections to be made in response to changing environmental stimuli. The relationship between the internal changes in the brain and the external environment, which is under the influence of education, is of particular interest in improving the effectiveness of learning and teaching.

Memory

Memory is described by Greenfield (1997) as 'the cornerstone of the mind', for it is the basis of our adaptation to experience, which of course means learning. The difference between short-term and long-term memory is well known, but this is not the only difference within the overall concept of memory. Short-term memory, also known as working memory, used in the recall of series or numbers such as a telephone number or a series of actions, requires constant repetition. Otherwise the memory will fail in about 30 minutes, or sooner if there is distraction by other things happening. But when something is rehearsed and remembered for more than this time the memory will probably last for a few days (Greenfield, 1997: 159) and then may be held in long-term memory.

There are several types of long-term memory, for each of which there is a different type of short-term memory. Information such as a telephone number, which has to be consciously recalled, is described as explicit long-term memory. Another type is described as implicit, because it is more automatic, like riding a bicycle. Evidence from the study of people who have lost some of their memory from brain damage shows that these two types of memory are not processed in the same part of the brain. Not only are different parts involved in processing implicit and explicit memory, but these processing locations are also different from where memories are stored. Experimental studies have shown that there is no one location in the brain where long-term memories are held. Rather they appear to be distributed through the outer layer of the brain (the cortex).

By using various non-intrusive techniques for identifying which areas of the brain are being activated during learning, it is possible to show how dependence on short-term memory changes with practice and gives rise to activity in the longer-term memory parts of the brain. Such investigations have explored the conditions that favour memorisation. They confirm, for example, that writing down a problem and some representation of how it was solved, improves the ability to solve problems. 'In such situations, it can be particularly helpful for pupils to show their working, since, apart from many other advantages, external representations can help offload some of these heavy demands upon working memory' (Howard-Jones *et al.*, 2007: 17).

Critical periods for learning

Can neuroscience tell us about the best time for certain experiences? The question of whether there are certain critical times for learning particular things is not as certain as it was once thought to be. For one thing, it depends on what is being learned. The main distinction is between those functions which are developed naturally in a normal environment – relating to the operation of the senses and to movement, for instance – and those which depend on particular experiences such as provided in education. Whilst there is some evidence of critical periods during the early years for the development of the function of those parts of the brain dealing with the senses (see Box 4.2), this is less so for learning that is dependent on specific inputs. Although it is easier to learn certain things earlier in life than later, this is because greater changes occur in the brain in childhood. But changes continue to some extent throughout life.

There are periods when the brain seems to be developing particularly significantly. The first three years are one of these, relating particularly to language development. Another is adolescence, when the main changes are in the increase in the myelin insulating the axons and in 'pruning' of synapses. Until these changes have taken place, adolescents do not show the same abilities as adults in respect of processes such as 'directing attention, planning future tasks, inhibiting in appropriate behaviour, multitasking, and a variety of socially-oriented tasks' (Howard-Jones *et al.*, 2007: 9).

The brain continues to change and develop beyond adolescence and is well-designed for lifelong learning and adaptation to new situations and experiences. These changes show in structure and size of the brain, as illustrated in Box 4.3.

Box 4.2 Critical times in early development of the senses

Greenfield (1997) recounts the story of a boy who, as a baby, had one eye bandaged for two weeks to help treat an infection. Later he was found to be blind in this eye even though the eye itself was completely normal. The explanation was that this happened at a critical time for the establishment of connections between eye and brain. The brain, not receiving signals from the eye treated it as if it were not there and the neurons were not connected to this eye, but instead had been taken over by the other eye. Had the bandaging taken place later, after the normal connections had been established, it would not have had the same impact on the brain. In general, during the time when most connections are being made, up to the age of 16, a neuron that is insufficiently stimulated to make contact with other neurons will die.

> **Box 4.3** Physical change associated with learning
>
> In a study of juggling, the brain areas activated at the beginning of a three-month training period increased in size by the end of it. After three months of rest, these areas had shrunk back and were closer to their original size. This graphic example of 'if you don't use it, you lose it' demonstrates the potential importance of education in mediating brain development throughout our lives.
>
> (Howard-Jones *et al.*, 2007: 21)

Emotions

The chemicals in our bodies that relate to emotions have a modifying effect on the working of the networks of neural connections (Zull, 2004). The main ones relevant to learning are adrenalin, which affects the heart rate in preparation for unusual action (fighting or fleeing), and dopamine, which is related to feeling pleasure and satisfaction. The close relationship of feeling and thinking shows in the pleasure we feel from solving a difficult problem and in frustration from not being able to understand something. The pleasure is not only a reward for completing a task successfully but is a motivation for tackling further tasks. We all know how the response of other people to our suggestions or ideas can affect our feelings about ourselves and our willingness to offer further ideas. Recognising this relationship means taking the emotions into account in helping learners to use and change their brains. Some implications are identified in Box 4.4; others are discussed in Chapter 13.

> **Box 4.4** The importance of feeling good about learning
>
> As part of the teacher's art we must find ways to make learning intrinsically rewarding. Learning should feel good, and the student should become aware of those feelings. To achieve this goal, we need to make two things happen. First, classes and assignments should lead to some progress for students, some sense of mastery and success. Second, students should work on topics and activities that naturally appeal to them.
>
> (Zull, 2004: 70)

Imitation

Claxton (2007) reports that cognitive neuroscientists now believe that our brains have evolved to make us disposed to learn by imitation. So-called 'mirror neurons' in the cortex automatically prime us to mimic what we see others doing around us, and that disposition towards imitation is one of the main ways in which cultural habits of thinking and learning transmit themselves from generation to generation (Hurley and Chater, 2005).

Just as children moderate their emotional responsiveness by watching how those around them react, so they pick up from others learning dispositions such as 'persisting in the face of difficulty', 'relishing a challenge', 'pausing to reflect' and 'honest self appraisal' (or, of course, their reverse). As Vygotsky (1978) suggested, habits of mind are contagious. So we might surmise that the effective learner is (selectively) open to this contagion.

Some cautions

Considerable words of caution are needed before we make claims that link the insights from neuroscience about what is going on inside the brain to the external environment. The desire to explain behaviours in terms of brain functioning is responsible for some over-interpretation of neuroscience findings, often as a result of assuming that what is true for people with brain injury or illness is true for the non-clinical population (Reid and Anderson, 2012). In particular, Reid and Anderson (2012) have identified a number of 'neuromyths' in education for which they say there is no evidence. For example:

- Evidence does not support the idea that large parts of the brain are underused, thus providing potential for training for better functioning. Whilst learning leads to more connections being made between neurons, this is not the same as awakening large parts of the brain that are not being used.

- There is little evidence to support the notion that the left and right hand sides of the brain work in different ways and that some people are left-brained and others right-brained. In normal brains, most functions require brain activity in both hemispheres (Goswami, 2012).

- Nor is there support for different 'learning styles' (Goswami and Bryant, 2007). An activity such as talking requires several different areas of the brain to be working. However, the remarkable ability of parts of the brain to take over functions from other parts that are damaged shows that areas can become active in quite different processes (see Box 4.5).

Implications for learning in general

Many of the programmes and activities that are claimed to be brain-enhancing follow principles that have been found to be effective in classrooms. As Reid and Anderson (2012: 185) point out, these principles

> have led to a range of teaching techniques that have a strong common-sense appeal, such as introducing movement in the classroom, encouraging self-regulation, scaffolding for transfer of information into long-term memory and using mnemonic devices. However, often these methods defy a connection with the neuroscientific evidence base broadly invoked to support them.

With these cautions in mind, probably the best we can say is that evidence supports, but does not prove, the value of

Box 4.5 The boy with half a brain

The story of Nico, as told by Battro (2000), is about a boy who developed severe epilepsy after his first year. The seizures became so bad that at the age of three years seven months, half his brain (the right hand side) was completely removed. This not only cured the epilepsy but he very soon became able to operate at a normal level for his age in language, mathematics, arts and music, which are often thought of as being under the dominance of different halves of the brain. Indeed his only limitation was in writing things down and in drawing. However, given access to a computer, he made good drawings and his writing was normal when using a word processor. Thus it was only in the physical aspects of performing these tasks where he was deficient; the cognitive aspects were not deficient. The importance of the computer should not be underestimated, since it helped him to compensate for a deficiency (he had a disabled left hand) that could have impeded learning in several areas. Battro describes the computer as an 'intellectual prosthesis'. As might be expected, such was the interest in Nico that his development across a range of abilities was tested frequently and it was found to be completely normal. Of course it is not yet known how he will develop in later life, but his story so far is a remarkable testimony to how half a brain can take over the functions of a whole brain, at least in a young child.

- practice – repeating an action increases the growth and strength of links between neurons;
- motivation – through the experience of success in meeting a challenge;
- externalising thinking – in the way mentioned earlier, by making some concrete representation, by writing, drawing, talking or using a computer, so that not everything has to be held in memory;
- engaging several parts of the brain, particularly those concerned with the senses, with action, reflection and abstracting meaning;
- linking to existing knowledge – there is an area of the brain activated when we try to make something meaningful by relating it to what we already know. Once meaning is created through these associations the new information becomes more memorable.

There are also some more general conditions for learning that are supported and others that are not supported by evidence relating to the brain. Among those that are known to help learning are:

- having breakfast (studies show that missing breakfast interferes with learning and that a cereal-rich breakfast improves memory);
- having enough sleep;
- avoiding caffeine (in cola drinks, for instance);
- avoiding dehydration (although there is no evidence for the value of drinking large amounts of water when not dehydrated).

Research studies supporting these points can be found in the OECD publication (2007) listed at the end of this chapter.

Implications for learning science

All that we have said so far applies to all learning and so to learning in science. Is there anything more that is specific to science? From brain investigations perhaps the most relevant is that 'a concept in science may depend on neurons being simultaneously active in visual, spatial, memory, deductive and kinaesthetic regions, in both brain hemispheres' (Goswami and Bryant, 2007). This indicates the need for a wide variety of different kinds of experience: being able to touch and manipulate objects; using language; linking to previous experience; reasoning; reflection.

Beyond this we must move from the microscopic level of brain cells to the level of macroscopic observable behaviour of an individual. At this level the brain is treated as a 'black box' and the evidence of effectiveness comes from how the child responds to the environment and shows learning through change in behaviour.

Bringing together what we know about learning in general and what we know about learning in science from experience (such as the examples in Chapter 3) and research, leads to the following as important characteristics of learning experiences. They should

1. be interesting, relevant and appealing to the children;

2. build on their previous experience and promote progress;

3. involve use of the senses, action, reflection and making meaning;

4. encourage talk, dialogue and the representation and communication of ideas and events in various forms;

5. help to develop scientific concepts, inquiry skills and attitudes of and towards science;

6. provide opportunities for working cooperatively and sharing ideas with others.

We now look at these in a little more detail and show how they can be used as criteria to evaluate activities and adapt ideas from curriculum materials.

Interesting and relevant

This must be considered in relation to all the children, both boys and girls, and those of different social and ethnic backgrounds, so that activities are accessible to all. Interest is not always spontaneous and can be encouraged by, for instance, displaying materials in the class prior to a new topic, with questions to stimulate curiosity, or in other ways such as in the case studies in Chapter 3, namely: clips from videos, CDs, simulations of real events, using materials brought in by the children, role-play and stories. It is useful to recall, however, that what 'relevance' means changes as children get older and what engages and interests them also changes. Toys and make-believe stories are less likely to be regarded as relevant by an 11 year old than by a 5 year old.

Lack of perceived relevance is likely to be an important reason why attitudes to science become less positive in the later primary years (Murphy and Beggs, 2003). So it is important to address this aspect of classroom activities, but doing so is not always easy. Real-life events are often complex and involve several ideas, so there is a dilemma as to whether they should be 'tidied up' to demonstrate certain relationships or principles. In doing this, the essential links to real life – the 'relevance' – can be lost. Some degree of extraction from real events is generally necessary, but it should always be possible to see a link between what is learned and real events.

Linked to previous experience and to progress

For activities to be meaningful and engaging, they should help children to understand and find out more about the things that they have encountered directly or indirectly and to develop further the ideas and skills they have previously used. It should be possible for children to make a link between new experience and previous experience. At the same time they need challenges to move forward, so, in the enduring words of the Plowden Report, over forty years ago:

> The teacher's task is to provide an environment and opportunities which are sufficiently challenging for children and yet not so difficult as to be outside their reach. There has to be the right mixture of the familiar and the novel.
>
> (CACE, 1967: para. 533)

As we have seen, there is evidence from studies of the brain that supports the importance of making links and requiring learners to make conscious efforts to make sense of new experience in terms of what they already know. We will see, in Chapter 6, how this process involves inquiry skills in generating 'bigger' ideas from 'smaller' ones. There is also evidence to support the importance of experiencing success for motivating learning. But children need to experience successively more complex ideas and sophisticated ways of thinking to support their learning in order to experience satisfaction. Thus a sense of progression is needed.

When they enter school children will start from the ideas they bring with them and during their time in the primary years will develop ideas and skills that are a foundation for secondary school science. It is easier to see progression over this large span of years (for instance in the national curricula or guidelines discussed in Chapter 2) than it is from month to month or even from year to year. Nevertheless it must be there and be built into the school's overall plan for science (see Chapter 20). One of the criticisms of primary school practice before the advent of the national curricula in the countries of the UK was that children often repeated activities from year to year. With the reduction in the detail of the curricula and the number of topics studied, it is important that this situation does not recur. This means teachers being clear about the aims of activities and how they fit into the overall progression from age 5 to 12.

First-hand action using the senses

We have seen that activity in all parts of the brain is important for learning and science has the special value of enabling direct interaction with materials in which sight, sound, smell, touch and, when safe, taste, can be involved. Encouraging these interactions is therefore extremely important for learning science. Through first-hand manipulation, children learn that in this way they can find answers to some of their questions, just as do scientists (see Box 4.6). As children get older they become more able to manipulate some things in their heads and to learn from secondary sources, such as books, films, CDs, television and computer programs, but the link to reality is essential for understanding (see Chapter 8).

Box 4.6 Active learning

Science education begins for children when they realize that they can find things out for themselves by their own actions: by sifting through a handful of sand, by blowing bubbles, by putting salt in water, by comparing different materials, by regular observation of the moon and stars.

(Harlen, 2001b: 4)

Reflection and making meaning

Reflection, like practice, means going over actions, but in the mind, rather than physically. Revisiting something by visualising it – seeing it in the mind – is known to activate most of the brain areas associated with actually seeing it. It can help in relation to strengthening networks of neurons and memory. Thus time used in reviewing activities before going on to the next is time well spent on learning. Reflection about how things were done can improve skills. Reflection about what was found that was not known before can produce new meaning and develop ideas.

Talk, dialogue and representation in various forms

We will be considering the value to learning of various forms of verbal interactions in Chapter 7. Here all that needs to be emphasised is that we know that learning is encouraged by 'thinking aloud', when learners make clear for themselves and others how they are making sense of things and what they understand and do not understand. It is the main way for teachers to have access to children's thinking, particularly in the early years, when children are not skilled enough in writing and drawing to express their ideas.

Evidence from studies of memory indicates that holding ideas or facts in short-term memory long enough for them to be taken into long-term memory is helped by using some external prop. Representing their developing ideas in some way, perhaps through drawing, modelling, role-playing and actions that demonstrate relationships or changes in the world around, requires children to make some external representation of their knowledge. Finding a way of representing in actions an event such as water evaporating into the air and then condensing to form clouds and rain forces thinking about 'Is it like this … or that?' 'What comes first, the rain or the cloud?' So these opportunities are not just useful for adding fun to science but also help children to rehearse their ideas, to go over and refresh what they know. They help children to reflect on what they understand and whether it makes sense when put in a different form.

Development of scientific concepts, inquiry skills and attitudes

The potential for the development of science concepts depends to a greater extent on the content of the activities than in the case of the other characteristics of activities. Developing understanding of science concepts is a central purpose of science education, so the content of activities should involve relevant scientific ideas. Even when the main aim of an activity is the development of inquiry skills, it may scarcely be described as a 'science activity' unless the skills are used in relation to content that involves scientific ideas (see Chapter 12).

Inquiry skills are sometimes referred to as process skills, since they are involved in the processes of interacting with materials and in the 'processing' of information so gained, but inquiry (or enquiry) is the term now more widely used. They include physical skills of manipulation and mental skills that are central to reasoning and to the development of understanding. Developing inquiry skills means using them. So what is important is that children have opportunity, for example, to raise questions, to suggest ways of answering them, to make predictions, to propose explanations (hypotheses), to collect evidence and to interpret it in relation to the question being investigated (see Chapter 6).

In relation to attitudes, it is useful to distinguish between attitudes towards science and the attitudes that are part of engaging in scientific activity. We are concerned with the latter here, meaning willingness to act in certain ways that promote scientific understanding. These are attitudes such as open-mindedness, willingness to consider evidence, flexibility in taking new evidence into account (see Chapter 13). It is the decline in attitudes of the first kind, shown in children's liking for science or willingness to continue studying it, that has raised concern about the impact of science education in some countries. There is not much evidence about change in children's willingness to think scientifically, since this has not been assessed except insofar as it is involved in understanding the nature of science.

Working cooperatively and sharing ideas with others

The process of learning science involves the development and change in the ideas that individuals hold. The direction of change is from children's own ideas, which may be unscientific (as we will see in Chapter 5) towards ideas that are more widely shared because they explain a range of phenomena. Expressing ideas and listening to others is an important part of this process. But sharing and changing ideas can be risky and it is important for teachers to take steps to avoid a classroom atmosphere that would inhibit children airing and sharing ideas, perhaps by being too competitive or anxious to get 'the right answer'. So it is important, for example, for teachers to show genuine interest in what the children think, by phrasing questions carefully and allowing time for children to give considered answers (see Chapters 7 and 10 for more discussion).

Criteria for evaluating and adapting activities

The characteristics of activities that are learning opportunities listed earlier can be turned into criteria to evaluate already planned activities for their learning potential, to help in planning new activities and to adapt existing activities to enrich their learning potential. All this can be done whilst adhering to content requirements, for in most cases it is the way the children interact with the materials, with each other and with the teacher, not the content of the activity, which makes the difference between a richer and a poorer learning opportunity.

Evaluating activities

The criteria can be expressed as questions to apply to activities. Box 4.7 shows how they can be used in evaluating the lessons in one of the case studies, the activities that Graham carried out with soil.

Reviewing Graham's lesson using this framework also reveals certain aspects where opportunities for learning could have been increased. For instance, he might have been more explicit in encouraging children to exchange views and reasons for their views about the soil samples in small groups; he could also have discussed with the children what to include in their reports. Of course, these things may well have been done, but just not recorded in the case study. Thus this kind of analysis is useful at the stage of planning activities as well as for teachers' reflection on their lessons.

Adapting or elaborating activities

When there are many ideas for activities available in curriculum materials it is not necessary for teachers to start from scratch, but it is often possible, and indeed necessary, to adapt activities to ensure that they provide rich learning experiences for children. Take the example of the activity presented to children on the work-card in Box 4.8. There are some obvious reasons why this is limited as a learning

Box 4.7 Evaluating Graham's lessons about soil

Were the activities interesting and relevant to the children?
Interest was created by the prospect of growing seedlings and using soil samples from their own gardens. Since the work was within an overall topic of food, the prospect of growing something that they could eat would have increased the relevance. The activities allowed for a range of different kinds of interaction with the materials which would cater for different needs. Children with learning difficulties may have only gone so far as to feel, smell and look at the soils to appreciate their differences.

Did they build on previous experience and promote progress?
The children had previously planted seeds and had experience of seeing them grow into seedlings. So they were aware that there were roots in the soil which were important in determining the health of the plant. The children's idea of soil as a single, and not very interesting, substance was developed into one that recognised different types and constituents. Further development into understanding of how soil is formed might follow from these observations of what it contained. Their inquiry skills and attitudes were also advanced through conducting careful comparisons and seeking explanations, not just describing them.

Were the children able to use a range of senses and learn actively?
The children used sight, smell and touch in the free exploration of the soils, when they handled the soils and looked carefully using magnifying lenses, and in the controlled investigation of specific questions. The opportunities of this activity were well exploited; other senses might be more appropriately used in other activities. The children were active mentally and physically in planning and then carrying out their tests.

Did the children reflect and make meaning from their activities?
Graham set aside time at the end of the investigations for the children to reflect on what they had found and how they had found it.

Did the children talk and represent their ideas in other ways?
The initial group work in the exploratory phase involved talk in small groups and the whole-class discussion gave opportunities for more formal reporting from each group and structured exchanges. We do not know whether the children made drawings of the differences they found in soils during their group investigations. In some investigations drawing would help to focus observation, requiring children to move between the representation and the real things, refining their identification of differences.

Could they develop scientific ideas, use inquiry skills and demonstrate scientific attitudes?
Ideas about important differences between soils were developed; for example, their ideas advanced from the initial one that dark soils were more fertile. There were many opportunities to use and develop observational, planning, interpretation and communication skills. They were encouraged to compare their expectations with their findings and to reflect on how to improve their investigations. The careful collection of evidence and use of it to decide the best soil encouraged willingness to change their ideas on the basis of evidence.

Could they work cooperatively and share ideas with each other?
The reporting to and questioning by each other suggests an atmosphere in which ideas are shared.

Box 4.8 Parachute workcard

- Cut 4 pieces of string 14 inches long

- Cut a 14-inch square from sturdy plastic

- Securely tape or tie a string to each corner of the plastic

- Tie the free ends of the 4 strings together in a knot. Be sure the strings are all the same length

- tie a single string about 6 inches long to the knot

- Add a weight, such as a washer, to the free end of the string

- Pull the parachute up in the centre. Squeeze the plastic to make it as flat as possible

- Fold the parachute twice

- Wrap the string loosely around the plastic

- Throw the parachute up into the air

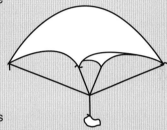

Results The parachute opens and slowly carries the weight to the ground.

Why? The weight falls first, unwinding the string because the parachute, being larger, is held back by the air. The air fills the plastic, slowing down the rate of descent. If the weight falls quickly a smaller object needs to be used.

experience although it is certainly an activity most children would enjoy. There are some positive points which are worth considering before looking at how it can be adapted.

It is capable of relating to children's interests across a broad spectrum, with no obvious gender or cultural bias. Thus it meets the first criterion. It uses simple and safe materials, which are familiar and cheap and it would be an easy activity for teachers to manage. It also meets the criterion of children using their senses directly and being active. However, they have no invitation to be reflective, or to develop their own ideas about what happens. The children manipulate materials, but only according to instructions. This can be a good start when particular techniques have to be learned, but they would learn more about what is going on by interacting with the materials more independently.

Using the criteria relating to the characteristics of learning experiences reveals several ways in which the activity could contribute more to pupils' learning.

Building on children's experience and promoting progress
Children's experiences of air resistance are many and not restricted to parachutes. Children could relate it to more everyday events, such as riding a bicycle in a strong wind and the 'helicopter' wings of sycamore seeds seen

drifting gently down to the ground. They should be encouraged to think about air resistance in relation to horizontal movement, in yachts and sailing ships, as well as in slowing aircraft to land on short runways and aircraft carriers. They can be challenged to think about the kind of materials and construction needed in each case.

Work-cards can have a useful role as part of a topic in which there is a progression in ideas, but for this they need to provide incentives for children to question and find ways of answering their own questions. In this case the instructions could provide an initial experience and to encourage children to raise questions which this material could so easily be used to answer: what happens if there is no weight on the sting? More weight? A bigger/smaller canopy? A different shape? Alternatively the activity might begin with the experience of throwing several parachutes, of different sizes and even shapes, and noticing how they fall. This would provide the context for expressing their initial ideas about what is happening and opportunity for comparing them with evidence.

Encouraging talk and representation of events
When children have to follow instructions, their talk is focused on the details of what they have to do rather than on the purpose of doing it or what they are learning from it. 'Where do you tie the strings?' 'Don't put the weight there, it has to go here.' 'You need to throw it like this.' This might be necessary at the start but after the initial experience, there is room for much more educationally useful talk focused on 'why' rather than 'what'. The later directions could ask the children to explain what is happening, to discuss in groups how to make the parachute fall more/less quickly, to agree on how to test their ideas and then to do it. Other questions would no doubt arise, about the effect of the suspended load, which could be discussed in groups or with the whole class.

This is a good example of an activity where children could be asked to make an annotated drawing of what they think is happening and why changing certain things changes the way the parachute falls. Children could be encouraged to work in groups to add labels and arrows to show their ideas about the forces acting.

Developing ideas and inquiry skills
A main point of the activity is to enable children to recognise the role of air in slowing down the fall of the parachute. With this in mind it would be useful for children to observe how quickly the parachute falls when it is not allowed to open. Exploration of larger and smaller parachutes might further children's ideas about the effect of the air. The question of why the parachute falls at all could also be discussed, leading to recognition of the main forces acting on the parachute when it is falling. Giving the 'answer' to why the parachute moves slowly is not allowing the children to use and explore their own ideas. Rarely does the explanation of an event by others lead to understanding; the children have to work it out for themselves.

The provision of precise instructions removes the opportunity for children to investigate and think out for themselves how to make a parachute. Opportunities for children to develop their inquiry skills are further limited by the lack of any investigation once the parachute is constructed. There are many variables which affect the fall of the parachute, such as shape, area, length of strings, which children could explore in a controlled way as they test out various ideas and try to find answers to questions they raise for themselves. More investigations planned by the children would give the chance of them to review their work critically and to improve their future inquiries.

Working cooperatively and sharing ideas
Even within the context of a worksheet, there could be instructions for pooling ideas within a group, planning how to find 'what happens if...' and preparing a group report to others when they meet together as a class to listen to reports of each other's progress and share ideas. Different groups might investigate different variables and so ideas about explanations could be tested in different ways – does the explanation for the effect of changing the size of the canopy also explain what happens when the shape is changed? Or when there is a hole in the canopy?

Creating richer opportunities for learning

There are three main consequences of modifying activities in these kinds of ways:

- First it will depend more on the teacher than on the content of the activity. In the case of the work-card, although careful wording can go a long way in encouraging children to use their own ideas and think things out for themselves, there is less room for the children to make their own links and pursue their own questions.

- Second, it will undoubtedly take up more time. This has to be weighed against the much greater learning which takes place. Even if the same time as required for a modified parachute activity were to be used for several activities of the original kind, there would still be no opportunity for developing real understanding. Fewer activities, with more opportunity for different kinds of learning, for discussion, for reflection and for developing skills, will be a greater contribution to learning with understanding.

- Third, it requires a different kind of lesson planning. Planning to allow children to use and develop their own ideas requires more, not less, planning than preparing prescribed activities. It means thinking about the teacher's and the children's role in the activities. This is taken up in Chapter 20.

Summary

This chapter has considered the characteristics of classroom activities that optimise opportunities for learning science. The characteristics were drawn from what is known about learning in general from studies of the brain and from examples of effective classroom practice and research. The characteristics identified related to the potential of activities:

- to be interesting and relevant to children;

- to build on their previous experience and promote progression in learning;

- to require use of the senses and physical and mental activity;

- to encourage reflection and the extraction of meaning;

- to involve talk and representation of experience in different forms;

- to foster the development of science concepts, inquiry skills, scientific attitudes and cooperative working.

Using an example from Chapter 3 we have illustrated how the criteria can be used in evaluating and in planning and adapting activities to increase the opportunities for developing scientific understanding, skills and attitudes. We have also noted that such changes have implications for the role of the teacher and for the time spent on different parts of activities to allow children to develop their understanding. Spending time on fewer well planned activities that provide a range of learning opportunities can be more productive than a larger number with restricted opportunities for learning.

Further Reading

Dela Sala, S. and Anderson, M. (eds) (2012) *Neuroscience in Education: The Good the Bad, and the Ugly*, Oxford: Oxford University Press.

Greenfield, S. (1997) *The Human Brain: A Guided Tour,* London: Phoenix.

Hall, J. (2005) *Neuroscience and Education: What Can Brain Science Contribute to Teaching and Learning?* Spotlight 92, Glasgow: SCRE Centre, University of Glasgow.

Murphy, C. and Beggs, J. (2003) Children's perceptions of school science, *School Science Review,* 84(308): 109–16.

OECD (2007) *Understanding the Brain: The Birth of a Learning Science,* Paris: OECD.

Wellcome Trust (2013) *Inside the Brain, Big Picture,* 17 (spring 2013): http://www.wellcome.ac.uk/Education-resources/Education-and-learning/Big-Picture/All-issues/Inside-the-brain/index.htm.

How children learn

5

Children's own ideas

Introduction

The next four chapters are about children's learning, mostly concerned with how we can best provide for it in school. However, it is important to recognise that children are learning without formal intervention, beginning at birth and continuing throughout life. This chapter therefore looks at some of the ideas that children have worked out for themselves and at reasons for taking them into account in developing children's scientific understanding. A great deal has been uncovered about the ideas that children form and bring to school and the fact that these ideas exist is no longer a surprise. Indeed, some of the ideas described in this chapter are well known. This does not, however, diminish their importance as starting points. The arguments for this remain as firm as ever. We therefore begin this chapter with a brief review of these reasons and then look at some examples of children's ideas. The chapter concludes with a list of characteristics of children's ideas which give clues to helping children to develop more scientific ideas. We return to these later, in Chapter 11.

Reasons for taking children's ideas seriously

The studies of Piaget in the first part of the twentieth century revealed that not only were young children eager to interact with the things in their environment, but as a result they developed ideas about the world around. Researchers who replicated these studies in various parts of the world have found remarkably similar ideas arising in quite different contexts. It was soon realised that the existence of these ideas, which were often in conflict with the scientific understanding of events and relationships, had an impact on children's learning in science. Systematic research into children's ideas in science began in the late 1970s with work mainly at the secondary level. The main work of this kind at the primary level began with ground-breaking studies in New Zealand in the 1980s (Osborne and Freyberg, 1985) and the SPACE (Science Processes and Concepts Exploration) project in the UK (1987–92). The SPACE project studied children's ideas across the full range of the curriculum for children aged 5 to 11 years, resulting in 10 research reports (see Further Reading).

There are several reasons why we should start, in developing children's scientific ideas, from their initial ideas, rather than just 'telling them the correct ideas'. There are theoretical reasons, related to how children learn, which will be explored in Chapter 6. There are also practical reasons: it just does not work. If we simply ignore children's ideas or insist on them 'learning' the correct idea when they still have their own ideas, they will possibly memorise the correct one, but without really believing it, and will hold on to their own ideas to make sense of real phenomena around them.

But the strongest reason of all comes from looking at what the children's ideas are. This reveals that the ideas are the product of thinking about experience (necessarily limited experience) and are not childish fantasy. The ideas they form depend both on the extent of experience and on the processes of thinking about it. So it is important to consider not only what the ideas are but how the children arrived at them. It may be just insufficient evidence (for instance, assuming that 'all wood floats' because they have never seen wood that does not float), or there may be faulty reasoning through not using the evidence that is available to them (assuming that things that sink are heavier than things that float).

The children have reasons for what they think and unless they are helped to have even better reasons for thinking differently and more scientifically, they will retain their own ideas. So this is why we now look at some examples of children's ideas, mostly from the Science Processes and Concepts Exploration (SPACE) research.

Some examples of children's ideas

The Earth in Space

The case study of Lisa's lesson in Chapter 3, reported by Fitzgerald (2012), contained many examples of children's ideas about the reasons for day and night on Earth and the appearance of the Moon. Given the complexity of the relations among the objects in the solar system it is not surprising that children's ideas are different from the scientific view. But it is also clear that children think about their experience of these events which are part of our daily lives and have developed some ideas about what might explain them. For example, the ideas that the crescent Moon is in the shadow of the Earth was expressed by Ben (p. 46). This idea is by no means unique to Ben, for the same explanation was reported by the SPACE project research (Nuffield Primary Science, 1995a: 93), where Niall wrote about his drawings of the different phases the Moon: 'This is a drawing of the Moon as it moves. It is different because as the world moves it casts a sadow (sic) over it in different places.'

This view accepts that the whole Moon is still there when only part can be seen and is an advance on the idea often expressed by younger children who consider that the Moon itself changes shape. There are also some who believe that there is more than one Moon (Nuffield Primary Science, 1995b: 26).

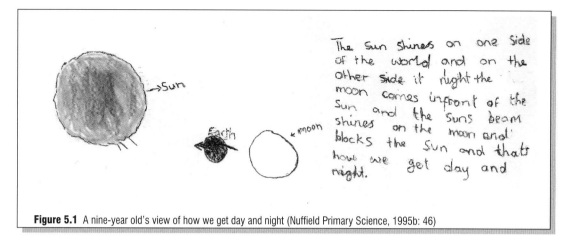

Figure 5.1 A nine-year old's view of how we get day and night (Nuffield Primary Science, 1995b: 46)

In Lisa's class there were many children who held to the view that the Moon has a role in causing day and night on Earth. Again, different researchers have reported very similar ideas, as in Figure 5.1. Clearly the children have not been taught this and it is interesting that, at opposite parts of the globe, they have arrived at similar ideas at to explain their observations.

What's inside an egg

Research in the SPACE project studied the ideas of children about what was happening inside hens' eggs that were being incubated in the classroom. The most popular idea was that there was a miniature but mainly complete animal inside the egg, feeding on what was there. This is evident in the drawings made by the children when asked to depict what they thought was inside an egg while it was incubating.

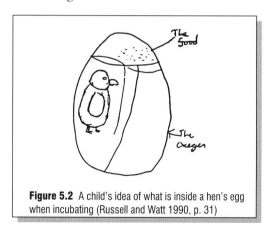

Figure 5.2 A child's idea of what is inside a hen's egg when incubating (Russell and Watt 1990, p. 31)

An alternative was that the complete animal was inside simply waiting to hatch. This is perhaps not surprising, given that children may have seen nature TV programmes showing birds hatching from eggs.

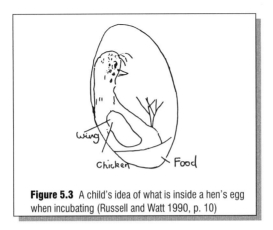

Figure 5.3 A child's idea of what is inside a hen's egg when incubating (Russell and Watt 1990, p. 10)

There was also the view that the body parts were complete but needed to come together.

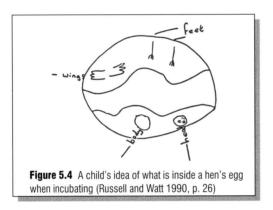

Figure 5.4 A child's idea of what is inside a hen's egg when incubating (Russell and Watt 1990, p. 26)

The more scientific view that transformation was going on inside the egg was evident in some children's ideas. It was also clear that the children used knowledge derived from experience of reproduction of pets and observations of human babies when trying to understand what was going on inside the eggs.

Growth in plants

When asked 'What do you think plants need to help them grow?' infant (5 to 7 year old) children generally mentioned one external factor. For example, Figure 5.5 suggests that light is necessary.

Other young children mentioned soil or water or sun, but rarely all three. Characteristically the younger children made no attempt to explain why these conditions were needed or by what mechanism they worked. Junior children, however, made efforts to give explanations, as in Figure 5.6.

Figure 5.5 A young child's idea of what plants need to help them grow (unpublished SPACE Research)

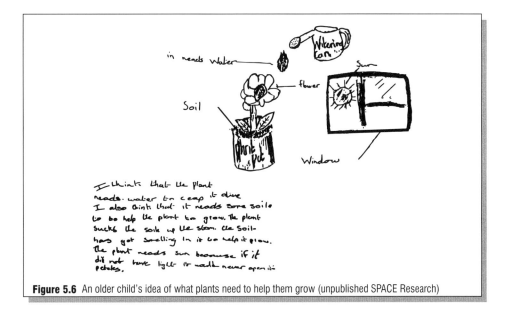

Figure 5.6 An older child's idea of what plants need to help them grow (unpublished SPACE Research)

How sounds are made and heard

Children's ideas about sound were explored after they had opportunity to make sound with a variety of instruments. The instance in Figure 5.7 suggests no mechanism for sound being produced by a drum or for it being heard; it is as if being 'very loud' and 'listening hard' are properties which require no explanation.

The simplest mechanism suggested is that the impact of hitting produces 'sound'. In contrast, Figure 5.8 explains the sound in terms of vibration. But notice that the vibration comes out of the drum through 'the hole'. A very common understanding of children was that sound travelled through air, or at least through holes in solid objects and not through the solid itself.

The notion of 'vibration' was associated with sound in ambiguous ways, sometimes sound being the same as vibration and sometimes having some cause and effect relationship to it. Figure 5.9 illustrates this struggle to connect the two.

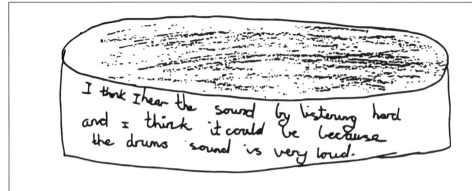

Figure 5.7 A young child's idea about how a drum makes sound and how the sound is heard (Watt and Russell 1990, p. 36)

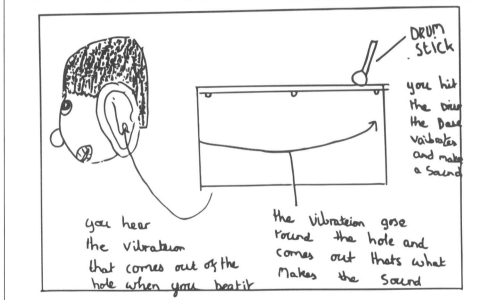

Figure 5.8 An older child's idea about how a drum makes sound and how the sound is heard (Unpublished SPACE research)

How we see

It is very common for children (and indeed some adults) to regard the eye as an active agent in seeing, rather than being a receiver of light from a source or reflecting surface. This view corresponds with the feeling of moving the eye to look from one place to another and with the words we use such as 'casting a glance' or 'looking hard'. Figure 5.10 was a 10 year old's drawing of how someone would see the bottle standing on the table when the light was turned on. When asked why the person would not be able to see the bottle in the dark, if the eye was sending something to the bottle, the child explained that the eye doesn't

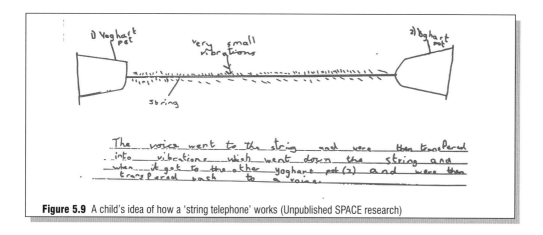

Figure 5.9 A child's idea of how a 'string telephone' works (Unpublished SPACE research)

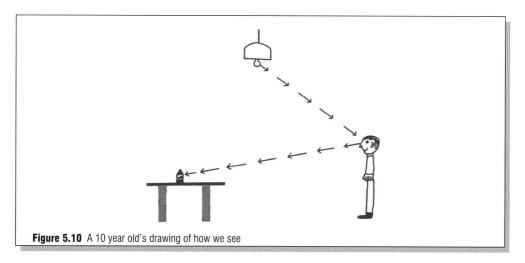

Figure 5.10 A 10 year old's drawing of how we see

work without the light. The light acts like a switch, turning the eye on. With this explanation the child was able to hold onto the idea of the eye sending out a beam to what was being seen – but only when 'turned on'!

Forces

Children's ideas about how things are made to move and what makes them stop were explored in various contexts, including the 'cotton reel tank' which is propelled by the energy put into twisting a rubber band. Again the younger children found no need to explain more than 'it works because you're turning it round' and 'it stops because it wants to'. Another 6 year old could see that the pencil (used to twist the rubber band) was important but the idea of why went no further than its presence:

> When we wind it up it goes because of the pencil. When the pencil goes to the tip it stops.

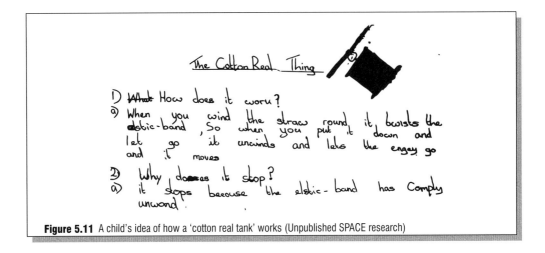

Figure 5.11 A child's idea of how a 'cotton real tank' works (Unpublished SPACE research)

Energy was mentioned in the ideas of older children (Figure 5.11) but the meaning the word was given is not entirely consistent.

Ideas about solids, liquids and gases

The idea that air is all around, including inside 'empty' containers, was expressed in some way by most junior age children but by a much smaller proportion of 5 to 7 year olds. This statement by an 8 year old shows a child who has not yet acquired an idea of air as a substance, although its presence is accepted:

> You can't see the air, but sometimes you think there is nothing in there 'cos you can't see anything, but it isn't a matter of seeing, it's a matter of knowing.

Even young children have relatively little difficulty in identifying something hard, such as steel, as solid, and something watery as a liquid. A 5 year old, after activities with liquids, managed to give a general definition:

> Liquids are all kinds of things that don't stay where you put them. They just run. If you put them on the table it runs along the table.

But where does talcum powder fit? One explanation was:

> It's something like a kind of liquid, but it isn't a liquid, its talcum powder. It goes fast like vinegar and it's not a solid because you can put your finger through it. It's a bit solid, but not like a liquid. A liquid feels wet and this doesn't.

> (Quoted in Russell *et al.*, 1991)

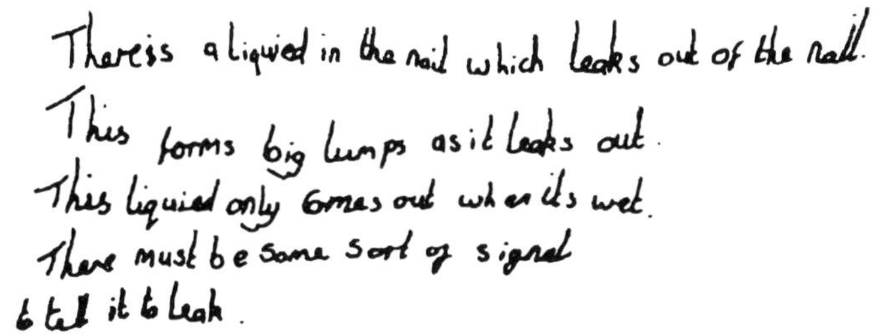

There is a liquied in the nail which leaks out of the nall.
This forms big lumps as it leaks out.
This liquied only comes out when its wet.
There must be some sort of signal
to tel it to leak.

Figure 5.12 An 8 year old's idea about rust

Ideas about change in materials

In relation to changes in materials, too, there is a stage in which there seems to be no need for explanation. Children use their experience of finding rust under bubbles of paint on metal gates or bicycle frames to conclude that rust is already there under the surface of metal, hence there is no need to explain what causes it to form. For example, an 8 year old wrote the explanation in Figure 5.12. There are other examples of children's ideas in Chapter 16, Figures 16.1 and 16.4.

Characteristics of children's ideas

It is not difficult to see that there is some reasoning, albeit limited, behind these ideas and that they may well make sense to the children themselves. In many cases it is easy to see why children might come to hold these ideas. They reflect what the children have experienced and clearly indicate effort to make sense of their experience. Would anyone know what is inside an incubating egg unless they had seen it? But clearly this doesn't stop children thinking about it and forming their own ideas.

It is precisely because of this that we must take these ideas seriously. If we just ignore them, the children may well hold onto them, since non-scientific explanations often seem more rational to children than the scientific ones. For instance, it makes more sense to conclude that puddles dry up because water seeps away through the ground, than that water particles fly off the surface into the air.

Drawings are particularly useful in conveying children's ideas since they try to represent what they know, or think they know. Often their drawings do not reflect real things but the ideas children have of these things. For example, young children's drawings of vehicles with wheels often show all the wheels on one side although these are not in fact all visible at once, or animals with four legs equally spaced along the body (Figure 5.13). They know cars have four wheels and dogs four legs and represent this idea rather than what a car or dog looks like. Such drawings indicate a correct idea of the parts but not how they relate to each other.

Even with the article in front of them young children will draw something that is more like a symbol than a representation of the object. For instance trees are frequently drawn as in Figure 5.14.

Figure 5.13 A 6 year old's drawing of herself with her dog

Figure 5.14 A 5 year old's tree

When some children were asked to draw some leaves they included a stem that was not actually there (Harlen, 2001a). Similar findings were reported by Tunnicliffe and Litson (2002) in a study of children's drawings of apples. They found that children added a stalk and leaves that were not present on the apple they were asked to draw, but were typical of drawings of apples found in books. It seems that children have developed a mental model of common objects such as a tree or a car which over-rides observation of the real things. There are implications here for both art and science, where children are often asked to draw what they have seen.

Although we have given only a few examples, there are many similar ideas that have been revealed by research and enable us to identify some characteristics. It is helpful to bring these general features together since they point to what teachers may be able to do to help children develop more scientific ideas. Box 5.1 brings together some characteristics illustrated by the examples.

We return to these characteristics in Chapter 11, for they give important clues as to how to help children develop more scientific ideas. When we do so we need to start from their ideas and help them, through scientific reasoning and use of inquiry skills, to change them or replace them with ideas which fit the evidence better than their own.

Box 5.1 Some general characteristics of children's ideas

- Generally, children's ideas *are* based on experience but this experience is necessarily limited and therefore the evidence is partial. So children may well consider rust to be within metals, as illustrated in Figure 5.12, if they have only noticed it when it appears under paint or flaking chromium plating.

- They may hold on to earlier ideas even though contrary evidence is available because they have no access to an alternative view that makes sense to them. In such cases they may adjust their idea to fit new evidence rather than give it up, as in the idea that 'light turns the eye on' (page 83).

- Children pay attention to what they perceive through their senses rather than the logic which may suggest a different interpretation. So if the Sun appears to move around and follow them, then they think it *does* move in this way. Since we see the Moon rather than the Sun at night, then the Moon must be blocking the light from the Sun (Figure 5.1).

- Younger children particularly focus on one feature as cause for a particular effect rather than the possibility of several factors. For example, children of 6 or 7 might mention water or light or soil as needed by plants to grow, but not all of these (Figure 5.6).

- Although it may satisfy them, the reasoning children use may not stand comparison with scientific reasoning. For example, if they were to make genuine predictions based on their ideas, these ideas would be disproved. But instead they may 'predict' what they know to fit their idea.

- They often hold different ideas about the same phenomenon when it is encountered in different contexts. For example, while they may realise that exposure to air helps washing to dry outside, they often consider that puddles on the road dry up only because the water leaks through the ground.

- Children may use words without a grasp of their meaning. We have seen this in relation to 'vibration' (Figures 5.7 and 5.8) but many more examples could be cited, common ones being 'floating', 'evaporation', dissolving and reflection.

- Their representations of common objects often reflect a mental image, influenced by illustrations in books, rather than the details of real objects that are there to observe (Figures 5.13 and 5.14).

Summary

This chapter has provided some examples of the ideas that children form about the world around through their own thinking. Although often differing from the scientific view these ideas clearly arise from experience and thinking, both necessarily limited.

The examples of children's ideas show that they are the product of reasoning, and so make sense to the children. It follows that these ideas have to be taken seriously and addressed in helping children to come to hold more scientific ideas. Some general features have been drawn from the examples. Taking note of these characteristics can help to indicate how more scientific ideas can be developed. This approach is taken further in Chapter 11.

Further reading

Harlen, W. (2007a) The SPACE legacy, *Primary Science Review*, 97: 13–15.

Harlen, W. (2001) *Primary Science: Taking the Plunge,* 2nd edn, Portsmouth, NH: Heinemann.

Resources online

SPACE Research Reports available on the National STEM Centre website: http://www.nationalstemcentre.org.uk/elibrary/collection/982/space-research-reports

Light http://www.nationalstemcentre.org.uk/elibrary/resource/4548/space-project-research-report-light

Electricity http://www.nationalstemcentre.org.uk/elibrary/resource/4547/space-project-research-report-electricity

Evaporation and condensation http://www.nationalstemcentre.org.uk/elibrary/resource/4549/space-project-research-report-evaporation-and-condensation

Forces http://www.nationalstemcentre.org.uk/elibrary/resource/4543/space-project-research-report-forces

Growth http://www.nationalstemcentre.org.uk/elibrary/resource/4540/space-project-research-report-growth

Materials http://www.nationalstemcentre.org.uk/elibrary/resource/4541/space-project-research-report-materials

Processes of Life http://www.nationalstemcentre.org.uk/elibrary/resource/4539/space-project-research-report-processes-of-life

Rocks, Soil and Weather http://www.nationalstemcentre.org.uk/elibrary/resource/4542/space-project-research-report-rocks-soil-and-weather

Sound http://www.nationalstemcentre.org.uk/elibrary/resource/4544/space-project-research-report-sound

Earth in Space http://www.nationalstemcentre.org.uk/elibrary/resource/4546/space-project-research-report-the-earth-in-space

6

Learning through inquiry

Introduction

This chapter considers how children's ideas are developed through scientific inquiry and the factors and conditions that are important in developing children's understanding in science. In the first part examples from Chapter 3 are used to suggest a framework, or model, of how different parts of classroom activities come together to help children develop their understanding through inquiry. In the context of cross-curricular topics it is particularly important that the potential for developing scientific understanding is recognized and exploited. The model is based on the observation that learners bring ideas from earlier experiences to try to make sense of new experiences or answer new questions. Some of these will be the naïve or non-scientific ideas exemplified in Chapter 5. The model identifies the role of inquiry skills in helping children to develop more scientific ideas and to move from small ideas towards 'bigger' ideas. We also discuss how inquiry in science differs from inquiry in other subjects and the form it takes, depending on the type of question that sparks inquiry.

Learning in the case studies

Kathy's lesson

Kathy's lesson (pp. 38–42) starts with a question, stimulated by a story and made real by a collection of different balls. The initial question 'which ball is best for a dog?' is turned through discussion into an investigable question: 'which is the bounciest ball?' (We discuss the nature and importance of investigable questions later, p. 93, and also in Chapter 12.) The children make lots of suggestions based on their previous experience of balls ('The red one. It looks like it's bouncy') and they suggest explanations ('The rubber might make it bouncy'). Their various predictions as to which might be the best ball are then challenged by the teacher's question: 'How do you know?' The teacher asks for the children's ideas on how to collect data that can provide evidence of 'bounciness'. Through discussion of many different suggestions they agree the procedure, which is in two parts.

In the first part they carry out an investigation in four groups and as a result find four balls which they judge to be the bounciest. The second part – not described in the case study – comprised a further round of planning and data gathering with these four balls. Then the final result was compared with their predictions. The record of the whole inquiry enabled the children to look back and reflect on what they had done and learned, not just about balls but how to answer a question through scientific investigation.

So we can identify several stages in the inquiry:

■ the initial question and discussion that refines the question;

■ the exploration and observation of the materials;

■ hypotheses and predictions about which would be good bouncers;

■ planning how to test the predictions (to see which is the best bouncer);

■ collecting data (two parts);

■ putting different results together;

■ interpreting the result (deciding the bounciest);

■ recording and reflecting.

These stages involve actions which help the children to learn how to investigate. In the context of the subject of this chapter it is also important to ask: what science ideas did this activity help to develop? These young children brought to the activity ideas about particular balls in their experience. They certainly extended their knowledge of different balls, but they also learned more about the materials of which balls are made. Through the activity there was therefore opportunity to develop understanding of the range of materials used in everyday objects. They also add to their understanding of how questions can be answered through investigation.

Graham's lesson

Looking back at the description of Graham's lessons on soil (p. 48) we can identify stages similar to those in Kathy's lesson. In Figure 6.1 the stages in the children's activities and thinking are set out diagrammatically

The children were given a new experience in the form of the soils to observe and a question about how the differences between the soils might affect how well plants would grow in them. In exploring and making a prediction about which soil would be best they used their existing ideas, which led them to suggest dark, damp soils. Further discussion and prompting by the teacher led to the identification of four properties that might be relevant. Thus four investigable questions were identified (Which soil holds most water? Which lets water through most easily? Which has most air? Which contains most humus?). Different groups investigated these questions, each planning an investigation to test their predictions about a particular property.

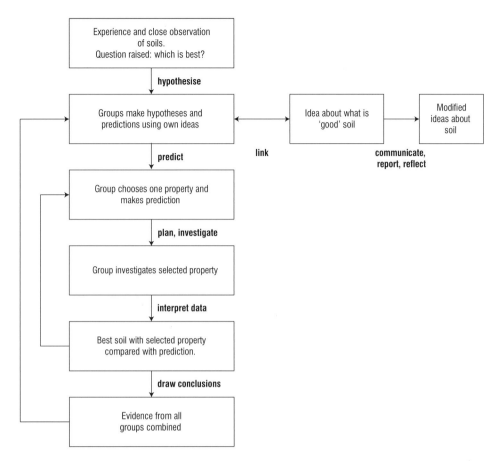

Figure 6.1 Inquiry in Graham's lesson

The data collected by each group were interpreted to answer that group's particular question and then the results from various groups were combined and interpreted. Although the different properties were investigated in parallel the outcome was the same as if the investigations had been carried out in succession. When all the results were combined, they found that what they predicted initially was not supported by the evidence. As a result, their idea about soil was modified: dark soil is not necessarily the most fertile according to the combination of properties they had investigated. They had learned not only that their initial ideas were limited but they had reasons for changing them and reached a better understanding of the properties of soil.

In their subsequent work with the soils, they would go through the cycle of thinking again – this time with a more informed idea as a basis for predictions. Throughout the whole sequence of activities, and particularly at the end, there were opportunities to communicate, report and reflect on what they were doing so that they would become aware of the processes indicted by the arrows in Figure 6.1.

Science in the 'crime' investigation

It is particularly important to be able to identify the science learning in considering cross-curricular topics such as the Year 6 science week (pp. 50–52). By definition, not all activities in a cross-curricular theme are focused on learning in science, but it is important to ensure that opportunities for developing understanding in science are not missed. In this example, the overall question of who committed the crime was broken down into a number of questions for investigation. It is in answering the investigable questions that the opportunities for learning in science are to be found.

The science week was full of activities with the potential for developing science concepts. However, it would have been easy for the search for the 'culprit' to have overshadowed the science learning. For instance, there were predictions as to who might have had opportunity or motivation to commit the crime but the predictions that led to developing scientific ideas were different ones, related to the various investigations. As in the parallel tests of soils in Graham's classroom, there were several pieces of information to bring together from separate investigations. In the chromatography the prediction was that it would be possible to match colours in the ink on the shopping list with the ink in the pens of the suspects. Testing this and finding it was possible strengthened their understanding of the properties of these materials. Similarly their predictions about finger-print patterns were tested and the results increased their ideas about human characteristics as well as helping them to solve the crime.

Lisa's class

In Lisa's class the new experience was presented in the form of images of a city by day and night. This engaged the children in thinking about the cause of day and night, revealing various hypotheses. Some of their ideas involved the Moon but most explained the changes by the movement of the Sun round the Earth. Lisa introduced a model of the Sun, Earth and Moon to enable the children to explore the effect of various movements suggested by the children and also the idea that she introduced of the Earth spinning rather than the Sun moving. The children had opportunity to plan how to investigate these possibilities using the model and gather evidence from trying them out. Interpreting their observations in relation to alternative explanations helped them to modify their ideas about day and night.

A model of inquiry-based learning in science

We could identify sequences of thinking and actions similar to those set out in Figure 6.1 for Graham's class in all the activities described in the examples in Chapter 3 and in other classrooms where children are actively investigating and using evidence to extend their understanding. This suggests a general framework, as in Figure 6.2.

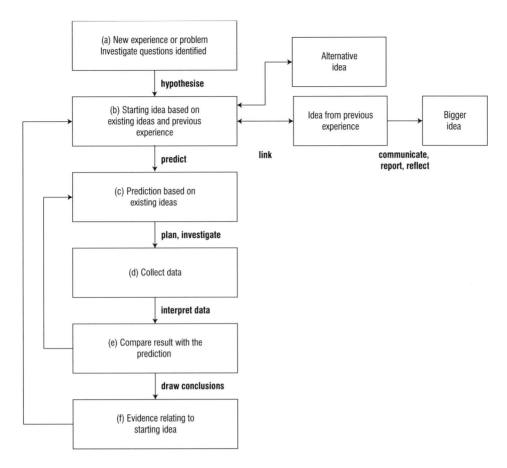

Figure 6.2 A model of learning through inquiry

The process begins when a learner tries to make sense of some phenomenon or to solve a problem. In such situations we all start from the ideas we already have, creating a hypothesis that the explanation is found in these ideas. Scientists and others working scientifically then proceed to see how useful these starting ideas are by making a prediction based on the hypothesis, because only if ideas have predictive power are they valid.

Starting with an experience to be explained, or a question that has been raised, the first two stages, (a) and (b) relate to making a link with previous experience. The link may be made because of some physical property or event or something else that calls it to mind, such as a word or situation. Pooling different ideas in a group discussion is particularly useful here; it means that the experience used is greater than that of any one individual. Creativity and imagination also have a part. Indeed, in the case of the scientist faced with an unexpected phenomenon, it is the ability to try ideas outside the immediately obvious that may be the start of a 'breakthrough'. If the initial question needs to be refined, it is at this stage that it is turned into one or more investigable questions.

The stages (c), (d) and (e) are concerned with working scientifically to test the starting idea by making a prediction and gathering data to see if what is predicted actually happens, showing that the idea 'works'. More than one prediction and test is desirable, through the sequence (c) to (e), in order to see if the suggested explanation is useful, hence the loop back from (e) to (c).

From these results a tentative conclusion (f) can be drawn about the initial idea (b). If the evidence shows that the idea gave a good explanation then it is not only confirmed, but becomes a little more powerful – 'bigger' – because it explains something more. Thus 'small' ideas, so described because they relate to particular individual situations, gradually become bigger because they relate to several situations and eventually become generalised to a set of conceptually related properties or phenomena. If the evidence does not support the explanation given by the starting idea, then an alternative idea has to be tried. But knowledge that the initial idea is not the answer is also useful. It is just as important to know what doesn't work as what does work.

Figure 6.2 models the process of building understanding through collecting data as evidence to test possible explanations in a scientific manner, which is described as scientific inquiry.

Introducing alternative ideas

Inquiry starts from the existing ideas that children have and use to explain the event or attempt to answer the problem, consistent with a constructivist view of learning. For various reasons these ideas may not provide a useful answer or explanation and an alternative idea has to be sought. Take the following example.

In the course of inquiry into heat conduction of different materials, children in a middle school class placed their hands in turn on three surfaces in the classroom – one metal, one wooden and one of polystyrene foam. The subsequent events unfolded as follows.

- The metal felt considerably colder than the other two surfaces (a), which raised the question: why?

- The children immediately said that the metal felt cold because it was at a lower temperature (b), because that was usually the case when something felt cold, as when touching an object just taken out of the fridge or touching things out of doors on a cold day (link to previous experience).

- The investigable question was then identified as 'does the metal feel colder because its temperature is lower?'

- Their teacher asked them what they would expect to find if they measured the temperature of the surfaces and they predicted that the metal would be lowest, the wood next and the foam about the same as their hands (c).

- Using a temperature sensor connected to a computer to collect data (d) they tested their prediction and found almost no difference among the three surfaces.

- They were so surprised by this that they wanted to repeat it and to try it in different places (e) to (c). In particular they wanted to take the surfaces out of the classroom to where it was colder. The result was the same, no difference in measured temperature, although the metal still felt much cooler than the other surfaces.

- It was clear that their idea that the metal was at a different temperature from the other was not explaining what they found (f). An alternative was needed.

- The teacher helped them to link to a different experience by asking them to think of things that had made their hands cold. Among the suggestions was snow-balling. With a little scaffolding (see p. 169) the teacher helped them to realise that what caused their hands to feel cold was loss of heat (alternative idea)

- Could this account for the hand on the metal getting cold? (Back to (b).) If so, then the hand would really be colder after touching the metal than after touching the other surfaces (c).

- A fair test of this was devised by the children (d).

- This idea seemed to be confirmed (e) to (f).

To see whether they could apply this idea, the teacher challenged them to predict what would happen if the surfaces were all warmer than their hands rather than colder. For safety's sake their predictions were not tested, but various experiences were collected that helped to provide supporting evidence – the handles of cooking pans being wooden or plastic rather than metal, the kinds of gloves that keep our hands warm and so on.

What if there is no accessible alternative idea?

Alternative ideas are not always as easily found or accepted as happened in this example. Children may ignore contradictory evidence in interpreting findings and hold on to their initial ideas even though these do not fit the evidence. The example in Box 6.1 illustrates a common way in which children deal with the situation in which they may not have the experience from which they could draw alternative ideas or they resist ones that are suggested. One approach is that, instead of trying an alternative, they modify the idea they do have in order to accommodate conflicting evidence. It seems characteristic of human beings to try to explain things and if ideas that really fit are not available then less satisfactory ideas will be used. It is more comfortable to modify an idea than to abandon it, especially if it is your only way of making any sense of an observation.

In such circumstances teachers have to decide what alternative ideas are within the reach of the children and support them in trying out ideas that can explain the phenomenon. This is described as scaffolding and we say more about it what it means, with examples, in Chapter 11.

> **Box 6.1** Children holding on to ideas because there is no alternative accessible to them
>
> Faced with the evidence that smooth varnished cubes of wood stick to each other when wet, several groups of 11 year olds concluded that the blocks became magnetic when wet (Harlen, 2006b: 20). The resemblance of a block sticking to the underside of another, without anything to hold them together to a magnet picking up another magnet or a piece of iron was clearly very strong. An equally good alternative explanation was not available to them and so they held onto their view of magnetism, modifying it to accommodate the observation that the blocks only stuck together when wet by concluding that 'they're only magnetic when they're wet'. Had they had experience, say, of 'suction cups' being held to a surface when air is forced out from under the cup, they might have used a different linking idea – that air pressure can 'stick' things together.

Scientific and non-scientific ideas

Another problem in introducing alternative ideas arises when children's ideas are non-scientific. So we need to consider when an idea is scientific and when it is not. According to modern philosophers of science (e.g. Popper, 1968) an idea is scientific 'when it can be disproved'. This is a simple but profound statement that, in straightforward language, means that

- if there is no possibility of evidence being used to contradict an idea or theory, then it is not scientific;
- but if the theory or idea can be used to make a prediction that can be checked against evidence, which could either agree or disagree with it, then it is scientific.

Thus the test for whether an idea or theory is or is not scientific is not whether the evidence does or does not confirm it, but whether it is possible to find evidence to disprove it. Often, in science, technological development enables evidence to be found that disproves a theory for which there had previously only been confirmatory evidence. This is how Newton's theories were overtaken by those of Einstein, but this did not mean that his ideas were unscientific. The very fact that they could be disproved by evidence meant that they were scientific. This is because, even if the evidence agrees with the prediction, that does not prove the theory to be 'correct', for there is always the possibility of finding further evidence that might not agree with the prediction. This is explained by Stephen Hawking in Box 6.2.

Are children's ideas scientific?

This may seem a long way from the primary classroom, but it explains why we want children to express their ideas and question in terms that are testable. The ideas children create can be scientific if they are testable and falsifiable and the fact that they are often disproved by the evidence makes them no less scientific.

Box 6.2 Science as falsifiable

Any physical theory is always provisional, in the sense that it is only a hypothesis: you can never prove it. No matter how many times the results of experiments agree with some theory, you can never be sure that the next time the result will not contradict the theory. On the other hand, you can disprove theory by finding even a single observation that disagreed with the predictions of the theory.

(Hawking, 1988: 10)

Learning science and doing science proceed in the same way. Indeed, we find many parallels between the development of ideas by the scientific community and the development of children's ideas. For example, both are influenced, and to some extent formed, by the reactions and alternative views of peers. The ideas of both are provisional at any time and may have to be changed to be consistent with new experience or evidence not previously available.

Children also have non-scientific ideas, because they cannot be tested, as in the examples in Box 6.3.

Box 6.3 Children with untestable ideas

Luis had an idea about what made snow melt, which was that it was caused by the presence of air; he did not consider heat. He wanted to preserve some snow and said that it would not melt if it were put in a jar with a lid on to keep out air. His first attempt led to the snow melting when the jar was brought into a warm room. He said that there was still some air there and that if the jar were to be packed with snow it would not melt. But however much snow was put into the jar he still said that there was room for air. He had, therefore, turned his claim into one which was irrefutable, since on his assertion it would never be possible to have only snow in his jar.

Emma was convinced that something that did not float would do so if the water was deeper. To try to test this, more water was added. But it was never enough and all the time she maintained her claim that it would float in very, very deep water. Again, the idea had become untestable.

The role of inquiry skills

Using the model of learning through inquiry to reflect on learning enables us to identify the role that inquiry skills play in developing scientific ideas. The outcome of children's investigations will depend on whether the inquiry skills, such as those labelling the arrows in Figure 6.2, are carried out 'in a scientific manner'. For young children, particularly, this is not always the case.

Suppose that the tests that the children in Graham's class carried out were not 'fair', because the soils were not compared equally. Or suppose that the children testing the surfaces did not use the temperature probe correctly and came up with findings that supported their sensations. In such cases the results of their investigations would not lead to change in ideas. We can see that development of the children's idea is dependent on the extent to which inquiry skills have really been used.

If the observing, predicting, testing, etc. is rigorous and systematic, in the way associated with scientific investigation, then ideas which do not fit the evidence will be rejected and those which do fit will be accepted and strengthened. But it may not be the case that the testing has this quality. The skills of young children – and those of some adults – may not have developed to the appropriate degree.

Thus the extent to which ideas become 'bigger' or more powerful (by explaining more phenomena) depends both on the way ideas from previous experience are linked to new experience and on how the testing of possible explanatory ideas is carried out, that is, on the use of the inquiry skills. So inquiry skills involved at all stages have a crucial part to play in the development of ideas. This is one important reason for giving attention to helping children to develop their inquiry skills and to become more conscious of using them with appropriate rigour. The other reason, of course, is that by reflecting on their learning they develop skills needed for making sense of new experiences in the future and for learning throughout life.

Identifying inquiry skills

There is no definitive list of inquiry skills. Each science curriculum spells them out in different words and detail. A useful list of what children may be doing when undertaking inquiry, adapted from a report by an international group including scientists and science educators (IAP, 2006) is given in Box 6.4.

It is not expected, and indeed rarely feasible, for children to undertake all the activities in Box 6.4 in any one inquiry. There are different types of inquiry (see below) which require greater emphasis on some skills than on others. However, there are four main groups of skills which ought to be represented in any activity that is described as 'science inquiry':

- raising questions, predicting and planning investigations (concerned with setting up investigations)
- gathering evidence by observing and using information sources (concerned with collecting data)
- analysing, interpreting and explaining (concerned with drawing conclusions)
- communicating, arguing, reflecting and evaluating (concerned with reporting, reflecting and applying).

In Chapter 12 we discuss the nature of progression and how to help development in these groups of skills.

Box 6.4 Science inquiry in action

Children will be

- gathering data by observing and manipulating real objects where possible or using other sources;

- pursuing questions which they have identified as their own even if introduced by the teacher;

- taking part in planning investigations with appropriate controls to answer specific questions;

- using and developing skills of gathering data directly by observation or measurement and by using secondary sources;

- using and developing skills of organising and interpreting data, reasoning, proposing explanations, making predictions based on what they think or find out;

- working collaboratively with others, communicating their own ideas and considering others' ideas;

- expressing themselves using appropriate scientific terms and representations in writing and talk;

- engaging in lively public discussions in defence of their work and explanations;

- applying their learning in real-life contexts;

- reflecting self-critically about the processes and outcomes of their inquiries.

Learning through inquiry in other subjects

Inquiry is a term used both within education and in daily life to refer to seeking explanations or information by asking questions. Within education, some inquiry skills can be applied in several subject domains, such as history, geography, the arts, as well as science, mathematics, technology and engineering, when questions are raised, evidence is gathered and possible explanations are considered. In each area different kinds of knowledge and understanding emerge. What distinguishes scientific inquiry is that it leads to knowledge and understanding of the natural and made world through direct interaction with the world and through the generation and collection of data for use as evidence in supporting explanations of phenomena and events as represented in Figure 6.2. This is expressed in a formal definition of inquiry-based science education (IBSE), as in Box 6.5.

There are similarities and differences between inquiry in science education and in other subjects, such as history, geography and mathematics. The similarities include:

- starting with a question or a problem;

- making some connection with questions or problems of a similar kind which have been previously encountered and solved;

> **Box 6.5** Definition of inquiry-based science education
>
> IBSE means students progressively developing key scientific ideas through learning how to investigate and build their knowledge and understanding of the world around. They use skills employed by scientists such as raising questions, collecting data, reasoning and reviewing evidence in the light of what is already known, drawing conclusions and discussing results. This learning process is all supported by an inquiry-based pedagogy, where pedagogy is taken to mean not only the act of teaching but also its underpinning justifications.
>
> (IAP, 2012)

- seeking solutions through observation, exploration, and through actual or virtual experiments;
- using some agreed strategies and techniques for accessing, analysing, interpreting and using evidence.

Differences arise from the subject matter and so will vary. For instance in the case of mathematics there are differences in:

- The kind of questions or problem that are the subject of inquiry. In mathematics these do not need to relate to real life, as they do in science.
- How problems are expressed. An important part of the process of inquiry in mathematics is transforming a problem into a form that can be solved using mathematics.
- The processes of investigation and experimentation. In mathematics these are not limited to observation of or manipulation of the real world.
- The basis for accepting solutions to problems. Whereas in science ideas are accepted – and only provisionally – if predictions based on them are found to be consistent with new evidence, in mathematics inquiry the validity of solutions is demonstrated through logical arguments. This means that when a solution to a mathematical problem has been proved to be true there can be no further evidence to invalidate it. This is quite contrary to scientific explanations, theories and models which are those that fit the facts known at a particular time and are regarded as provisional and can never be proved (as expressed in Box 6.3).

Inquiry is not the only approach used in mathematics, history, geography, etc. of course. Nor it is the only approach in science, for there are aspects of learning science, such as knowledge of scientific vocabulary, conventions and use of equipment, best learned through direct instruction. Thus not all science teaching will be concerned with the specific outcomes of learning through inquiry. However, knowledge of facts and procedures are means to the end of developing understanding through inquiry, which should remain the main focus of science education.

Different kinds of inquiry in science

The description of inquiry in Figure 6.2, whilst showing how ideas develop through collecting and using evidence, oversimplifies the process of inquiry. It is a rather more varied, non-linear sequence of events which takes place in different ways according the kind of question being addressed. Not all the inquiry activities listed in Box 6.4. will be required in every inquiry, but experience across a range of different kinds of inquiry will provide opportunity to use and develop the key inquiry skills.

There are different ways of describing types of inquiry. Turner *et al.* (2011) have produced a guide for teachers describing five types of inquiry, with many examples of each. Some of these overlap with the following five types based on the kind of question leading to the inquiry.

'Which … is best?'

This question leads to the type of inquiry which is most familiar to many primary teachers. These inquiries involve the manipulation and controls of variables to make tests 'fair'. The first step is for children to engage with the question, which, although being raised by the teacher, has to be presented in a way that engages the children. The way in which Kathy presented the question about the dog's ball and Chris set up the inquiry of how to keep an ice cube from melting provide good examples. By starting with a real question pupils gain ownership of the problem and a formulaic approach, perhaps with a work-card offering a 'recipe' for finding the answer, can be avoided. The inquiry then involves a good deal of thinking about how to compare the objects or conditions in a 'fair' way so that the only differences are known and are not caused by variations in other conditions or in the way they were tested. It is a good introduction to the concept of variables – things which change or can be changed.

'Is there a pattern in … ?'

These questions arise when there is a possible relationship between variables associated with the behaviour of a thing or substance. Examples are: the note produced by blowing across the top of a bottle with different amounts of water in it; the length of a shadow cast by the sun and the time of day; the number of turns given to a wind-up toy and how far it will go. These inquiries involve the same skills as 'which is best' inquiries since the effect of changes in one variable have to be tested fairly, with other variables or conditions kept the same. However, there is additional emphasis here on the interpretation of findings. They also provide valuable opportunities for developing the skills of presenting data in the form of graphs, tables or charts.

In some cases the relationship leads to an explanation of one variable in terms of another. For instance, after finding that the tighter a string the higher the note produced by plucking it, it is reasonable to conclude that tightening is the cause of higher notes. But there is need for caution here. In other cases there may be another factor causing one thing to vary with another. For example, the fact that trees of the same kind with more growth rings tend to be taller does not mean that one causes the other; there is another factor that links the two. So these inquiries can provide experiences that help children to distinguish between an association between things and a cause and effect relationship.

'What happens when … ?'

These questions lead to inquiries into what happens, either as a natural process unfolds or when some action is taken. Examples are seeing eggs hatch, raising butterflies or silk worms, observing the expansion of water on freezing, seeing what things dissolve in water. Usually these concern the behaviour of particular living things or substances, not comparison between things. For example, the use of technology, such as the bird box camera in Box 6.6, provides opportunities for children to understand the needs and processes of living things.

The fact that the whole school and wider community were fascinated by the nesting birds demonstrates clearly that information seeking is relevant at all ages, building up a stock of personal experiences that are needed to make sense of later experiences. In this case information seeking was an end in itself, but in other situations it might be a forerunner for hypothesis-generating inquiries.

'I wonder why … ?'

The first step in answering these questions is to consider possible reasons why and then to test them out. 'I wonder why footsteps echo in some places on the path?' 'I wonder why the mirror in the bathroom steams up when I have a shower?' 'I wonder why there are plants growing in the pavement under the street lamps?' Children will have some ideas about what causes these things and should be encouraged to think of possible explanations (hypotheses) based on what they know. It may be possible to test out possible explanations by investigating the

---

Box 6.6 A bird box in the classroom

Despite their rural location the 5–7-year-old children in Sally Buckle's class were unfamiliar with the diversity of life around them. Raising their awareness, sensitivity and care for living things was a key aim. With the help of a grant a solution was found by setting up a bird box in the school grounds with a micro camera placed in it, linked to a monitor in the classroom, showing the blue tits who set up home in the box in real time. The monitor was constantly switched on and became like another window in the classroom. Children were able to record the nest building, egg laying and hatching, and feeding the fledglings. Although the death of the adult male meant that most of the fledglings did not survive, the whole community were by that time enthralled by the experience.

(Based on Barker and Buckle, 2002: 8–10)

phenomenon directly or by using a model, as Lisa's children did in answering 'why do we have day and night?' But in some cases finding answers will involve using secondary sources – searching the internet or reference books – which may stimulate further investigation at the same time as making them aware that they can collect data in different ways.

'How can we ... ?'

These questions may lead to inquiries where the end product may be an artefact or a construction that meets particular requirements – a model bridge that will support a certain load, for example. These are problems of a technological nature, though involving many scientific inquiry skills and ideas. It is not necessary to make a clean distinction in children's activities between science and technology, but it is important for the teacher to be aware of the difference and of the particular learning that can be developed through these activities. In making decisions about organising the practical work it is important to keep in mind the features that enhance the value of first-hand experience: the physical interaction with materials, the discussion and social interaction.

Summary

This chapter has provided a model of learning through inquiry through analysis of the examples in Chapter 3. The model has been used to

- show how children, starting from their existing ideas, can develop more scientific and powerful ideas about the world around through collecting, interpreting and using data;

- highlight the central role that inquiry skills have in developing children's scientific ideas;

- indicate how alternative ideas can be introduced when children's own ideas do not explain experiences adequately.

We have briefly mentioned the characteristics of scientific, as compared with non-scientific, ideas. We have also considered the use of inquiry in other subjects, and the similarities and differences between inquiry in science and mathematics. Finally we have noted that there are various types of inquiry in science and the form an inquiry takes will depend on the type of question being asked.

Further reading

Turner, J., Keogh, B., Naylor, S. and Lawrence, L. (eds) (2011) *It's Not Fair – or is it?* Hatfield: ASE and Sandbach: Millgate House Education.

Learning through talking

Introduction

This chapter presents evidence and arguments for the value of children's talk in developing their understanding in science, as well as in communicating ideas and information to others. It begins by considering talk described as 'dialogic talk', where thinking is made explicit and different views can be combined in coming to a shared understanding of observations or findings. We consider the meaning in theory and in practice of 'dialogic teaching', in which the teacher encourages children to express their reflective thinking. The concept of argumentation and the extent to which primary pupils can engage in it is also considered.

More formal spoken language also has a role in reporting, where there is need for a classroom climate in which children listen and respond positively to each other and make an effort to communicate effectively. The organisation of group and class discussions is considered and in the final section questions relating to the introduction and use of scientific words are addressed.

The importance of talk

Douglas Barnes was one of the first educators to focus on the importance of talk in the classroom and to distinguish between speech as communication and speech as reflection. Throughout this book there are many references to the value of children discussing with each other, exchanging ideas and developing their own views through trying to express them and to explain them to others. This involves both communication and reflection. The reflective part is sorting out their own ideas, indeed 'thinking aloud'. The communication is sharing with others and involves listening as well as presenting in a way which is coherent and understandable by others. Barnes claims that both are needed and that it does not serve learning to focus only on the more formal communication since 'if a teacher is too concerned for neat, well-shaped utterances from pupils this may discourage the thinking aloud' (Barnes, 1976: 28). More recently Robin Alexander has taken further the discussion of oracy in the classroom, presenting it, as in Box 7.1, as essential to learning.

In his publication *Towards Dialogic Teaching* Alexander (2008) brings together evidence from international studies and from projects such as the ORACLE

Box 7.1 Talk as the foundation of learning

Talk has always been one of the essential tools of teaching, and the best teachers use it with precision and flair. But talk is much more than an aid to effective teaching. Children, we now know, need to talk, and to experience a rich diet of spoken language, in order to think and to learn. Reading, writing and number may be the acknowledged curriculum 'basics', but talk is arguably the true foundation of learning.

(Alexander, 2008: 9)

---

project (Galton *et al.*, 1980) which involved intense observation of primary classroom interactions, to show 'the relative scarcity in English classroom of talk which really challenges children to think for themselves' (Alexander, 2008: 14). Research conducted after the introduction of the National Curriculum and assessment (for instance, Galton *et al.,* 1999) showed that little had changed in 20 years. Yet the theoretical arguments and research evidence continue to build up a firm case for the importance of children thinking for themselves and for the key role of talk in enabling them to do so.

It is clear from this that we are concerned with a particular kind of talk; not the chatter of the playground, but talk in which children are engaged in thinking and initiating as well as responding. The context for this is the interaction with the teacher and with other pupils that Alexander describes as 'dialogic' teaching.

Dialogue or dialogic talk?

Dialogue is defined as a conversation between people but in the context of classroom interchange it has a rather more precise meaning. To signal this, the term 'dialogic talk' has been adopted to describe the kind of interchange where there is an aim of exploring in depth a situation, problem or possible answer. Box 7.2 gives an example of dialogic talk among two girls and their teacher.

The teacher does little here except to encourage the girls in their struggle to work out their answer and to explain their reasoning. Just the occasional 'Why do you think that?', the acknowledgement 'I see', and reinforcement 'A little raw', encourages their exploratory talk. We can see from this interchange about the eggs how the girls use evidence to check their ideas. This comes through most clearly in Allyson's 'if we work on the principle that', where she relates what she predicts on the basis of her judgement to the observation of how quickly the egg floats up in the salty water, but it also occurs throughout. It is worth noting in passing that the origin of her idea is previous knowledge about how to distinguish 'good' from 'bad' eggs.

Contrast the dialogic talk in Box 7.2 with that in Box 7.3, where June and David are working on the same problem. In the absence of the teacher, at this particular time, they seem to regard the task as one where giving an answer is more important than having a reason for the answer. June, particularly, seems keen to move to early closure.

Box 7.2 Dialogic talk with the teacher present

Deidre and Allyson were investigating the way in which three whole hens' eggs, labelled A, B and C behaved in tap water and in salty water. They knew that one was hard-boiled, one soft-boiled and one raw. They had to find out which was which.

This is how the eggs landed up just after being placed in the salty water. The transcript begins with the teacher approaching them after they had been working alone for some time.

Deidre:	... hard-boiled.
Allyson:	I know
Teacher:	(coming up to them) Can you tell me how you're getting on?
Deidre:	I think that C is raw.
Allyson:	We both think that C is raw.
Teacher:	Do you?
Deidre:	B is ...
Teacher :	(to Allyson) Why do you think that?
Allyson:	Because when you put eggs in water bad ones rise to the top.
Deidre:	(at the same time) Because it ... we put them all in ...
Teacher:	Bad?
Allyson:	Yes, I think so – or it is the good ones? ... well, I don't know.
Teacher:	Yes?
Allyson:	... they rose to the top, so ...
	(Deidre is putting the eggs into the salty water)
Deidre:	... that's the bottom (pointing to C)
Allyson:	... if it's raw it should stay at the bottom.
Teacher:	I see.
Deidre:	So that's what we think, C is raw and B is medium and A is hard-boiled.
	(Allyson starts speaking before she finishes)
Allyson:	... and I think that B is hard-boiled and she thinks that B is medium.
Teacher:	Ah, I see. (To Deidre) Can you explain, then, why you think that?
Deidre:	If we put ... er ... take C out (takes C out, puts it on the table, then lifts A and B out) and put these in, one after the other. Put A in – no B first. That's what ... Allyson thinks is hard-boiled, I think it's medium. If you put that in ... (she puts B into the salty water)
Allyson:	... 'cos it comes up quicker.
Deidre:	It comes up quick. And if you put that in. ..
	(She puts A into the salty water. It goes to the bottom and rises very slowly.)
Allyson:	And that one comes up slower.
Deidre:	So, I think that one (pointing to A) is hard-boiled because it's ... well ...
Allyson:	I don't. I think if we work on the principle of that one (pointing to B). Then that one comes up quicker because it's, you know, not really boiled. It's like a bit raw.
Teacher:	A little bit raw.

Allyson:	So, therefore, it'll come up quicker.
Deidre:	Yes, but it's not bad.
Teacher:	What'll it be like inside?
Allyson:	Runny
Teacher :	It'll be runny still, I see.

Having agreed that C is the raw egg, Deidre and Allyson disagree about the identity of the other two eggs. Allyson has a reason for considering B is hard-boiled on the basis that 'bad ones rise to the top', so she considers that B behaves as if it had had something done to it. But she does not articulate the consequences of this until Deidre attempts to give her reason. Then it is as if Deidre's reason, which she interrupts, sparks off her own thinking.

Box 7.3 Group discussion without the teacher

David:	Look at that one, this one, look, June.
June:	That one's the one that's not boiled.
David:	How do you know?
June:	Oh, I'm not stupid
David:	Shall I put them in there, or in there? (*On the table or in the container where they were first*)
June:	Put them in there.
	(*David puts the one he took out in the container and June brings out the other two eggs*)
June:	There's B ... (*as she passes them to David who places them carefully*). Now put them in the salty water.
	(*David picks up A and puts it in the jar of salty water*)
David:	A floats. A.
June:	B (*She puts B in. It sinks*) sinks.
David:	C.
	(*He puts it in the salty water. It goes to the bottom and slowly begins to rise again.*)
June:	Sinks.
David:	Yea, look ... no, it doesn't.
June:	No ... that one (*she points to C. Pauses, uncertain for a moment*) No, how are we going to tell ...
David:	That one's ...
June:	Hard-boiled. The one at the bottom's hard-boiled. Put C hard-boiled. (*She instructs David to write. But it isn't C which is at the bottom.*)

Even here, though, there are signs that they are close to becoming more involved. David's 'How do you know?' could have sparked June into explaining her ideas, had she been less defensive. Later on, when an egg which she declares 'sinks' begins to rise up again there is potential for questioning, but it goes no further. How could this potential have been exploited; how, more generally, can we encourage interchanges which involve reflective thinking? Clearly the teacher's role is important, even though it seems very low-key in Box 7.2.

Dialogic teaching: the teacher's role

The importance of the teachers' role in setting the context for the exchanges that lead to learning is emphasised by Barnes:

> The quality of the discussion – and therefore the quality of the learning – is not determined solely by the ability of the pupils. The nature of the task, their familiarity with the subject matter, their confidence in themselves, their sense of what is expected of them, all these affect the quality of the discussion, and these are all open to influence by the teacher.
>
> (Barnes, 1976: 71)

In their discussion of different kinds of communication in the classroom Asoko and Scott (2006: 160) quote this exchange between teacher and some 8/9 year olds. The children are looking at a shadow of a piece of paper in the shape of a face. The paper has holes cut in it for the eyes and mouth.

Teacher:	So what are the mouth and eyes?
Amy:	Holes
Teacher:	Yes, and what goes through the holes?
Amy:	Light
Teacher:	The light. So what's making the shape of the face?
Perdip:	The paper's blocking the light
Teacher:	The paper's blocking the light, isn't it, to make the face. So it's a shadow. So what does that tell you about light? How does it travel?
Fiona:	At light speed
Teacher:	Yes, I know it travels at light speed but does it travel in wavy lines?
Perdip:	No. straight.

This illustrates a common pattern in classroom discourse in which

- the teacher asks a question (what are the mouth and eyes?)
- the student responds (holes)
- the teacher makes an evaluative comment (yes …),

then

- asks another question (what goes through the holes?)

and the pattern of 'question-response-evaluation' is repeated. This discourse involves plenty of interaction between teacher and children but in it the authority of the teacher is unmistakable. The teacher is seeking particular answers and there is little encouragement to reflect and make their own sense of what they are looking at.

Contrast this with the role of the teacher in Box 7.2 where the teacher encourages deeper thinking, use of evidence and clarity of meaning, and shares in the exchanges rather than dominating them. The approach of Deidre and Allyson's teacher gives several clues to positive encouragement of reflective thinking:

- joining in as part of the group, without dominating the discussion;
- listening to the children's answers and encouraging them to go on ('I see', 'Yes?');
- asking the children to explain their thinking;
- probing to clarify meaning ('what'll it be like inside?').

Not all aspects of the teacher's role can be illustrated in one short interchange and indeed much of it is in setting a context and a classroom climate which encourages exploratory thinking and talk. Important in this respect are:

- expecting children to explain things, which involves valuing their ideas even if these are unformed and highly conjectural;
- avoiding giving an impression that only the 'right' answer is acceptable and that children should be making a guess at it;
- judging the time to intervene and the time when it is better to leave a children-only discussion to proceed.

The presence of the teacher changes a discussion quite dramatically, for it is difficult for him or her not to be seen as an authority (see also Chapter 16, p. 241). Left alone, children are thrown on to their own thinking and use of evidence. But, as we see with June and David, the absence of a teacher does not always lead to a productive interchange and it is not difficult to imagine how a question from a teacher could have supported the move towards inquiry which David seemed to be making. The teacher needs to monitor group discussions, listening in without intervening, before deciding whether 'thinking aloud' is going on usefully or whether it needs to be encouraged.

Whole-class dialogic teaching

Although it is easier to illustrate the teacher's role in establishing dialogic talk in the context of small group work, the features listed above apply equally to whole-class discussions. The key feature of such whole-class activity is to engage in 'joint inquiry' in which pupils bring their different ideas to the shared learning task (Barnes and Todd, 1995). The collection of findings from the different groups by Graham in his class (p. 48) is an example of such a context. Although we don't have details of the oral exchanges, it seems that he asked questions for clarification and may have asked groups to explain how they came to their conclusions, as well as giving the pupils the chance to query and challenge so that they understood what each group had done and found. Bringing the findings together was an opportunity for all to be involved in the thinking that led to the eventual decision about the different soils.

A whole-class discussion is the obvious context for this kind of discussion. It can also be the context for rather different exchanges, where teachers are more authoritative and controlling not just of the interactions but of the content of the talk as well. In such cases, instead of sharing in the creation of understanding, children become recipients of someone else's understanding. Alexander (2008) makes a point of clearly distinguishing between the whole-class context and the kind of interactions and thinking that takes place within it. It is important that good examples of whole-class dialogic teaching are not interpreted as reasons for wholesale use of whole-class teaching where most children are passive receivers.

Encouraging argumentation

We should not be put off by technical terms, nor use them unnecessarily, but it is often useful to use a special word to make an important distinction. Using 'dialogic talk' rather than 'discussion' is one example; 'argumentation' is another. It means arguing about evidence, particularly when that evidence can be interpreted in different ways. To call it plain 'argument' suggests that it is little different from the exchange of opinion that characterises everyday disputes (who should be first, for instance). To call it 'discussion' – although it is one type of discussion – leaves out its particular function in developing reasoning about whether evidence supports one or another conclusion or hypothesis.

Young children find it difficult to entertain different interpretations of evidence, but they make a start when helped to identify alternative reasons for observations. For example, Chris's class (p. 42) mentioned different reasons for some ice cubes melting more quickly than others and Lisa's class gave a range of causes of day and night. Older primary children can begin to argue more thoughtfully about the interpretation of evidence as, for example, when Deidre and Allyson contested their views on which eggs had been boiled.

Speech as communication

This is the more formal side of using talk, where shared conventions and expectations have to be observed if others are to be able to make sense of what is said. It is part of socialisation to be able to describe in a way comprehensible to others what has been done or thought about and to be able to listen to others, attending not only to the words but to the implicit messages conveyed by tone of voice and manner. Giving attention in this way is not an automatic response of children, as teachers know all too well; it is a behaviour that has to be taught. Box 7.4 sets out some ways of providing the classroom climate

Box 7.4 Creating an atmosphere for productive oral reporting

- Providing guidelines for preparing presentations and a structure for ensuring that each report can be heard and given attention

- Giving an example in the teacher's own response, of showing interest, asking questions for clarification, making positive comments, etc.

- Making use of children's ideas in comments, thus encouraging children to do the same ('That's an interesting idea you have about ...' 'Tell us how you think it explains ...').

- Encouraging children to respond to each other and not just to make statements of their own ideas.

- Listening attentively and expecting the children to do so.

- Setting up expectations that children will put effort into their presentations to each other and try to make them interesting, and giving time for and help in preparation with this in mind.

in which children have opportunity for reporting orally to others in a setting where they know that others will be listening and where they have to convey their information clearly.

These things have to become part of the general way of working, since expectations that children will respond to what their classmates say are set by the pattern of previous lessons as well as by the response on a particular occasion. Then the telling and listening can have a role in the development of children's ideas as well as in their communication skills. It means that they go back over their activities and make sense of them for themselves so that they can make sense of them for others.

Organising class and group discussions

In setting up discussion the (perhaps obvious) point is to ensure the attention of all involved. For a whole-class discussion the location of the children is significant in avoiding distractions. Occasionally it may be necessary to hold a brief discussion during the course of practical activities, for the purpose of bringing together observations which have been made, reporting progress or sharing information which will help everyone (including instructions about safety if unexpected hazards have arisen). On these occasions it may be advisable to move the children away from the materials they are working on in order to ensure their attention. The discussion will only last a few minutes and it will be no hardship for the children if they are cramped in a small space for this time. It is intended to help them with their work when they return to it; otherwise interruption should be avoided until the time for warning of the impending end of the group work session.

Apart from these infrequent interruptions, whole-class discussion will be at the beginning and end of the group work, with group discussion in between.

Whole-class discussion at the start of a lesson

The initial discussion is the key to setting up group work which is sufficiently clear and motivating to ensure that children begin work promptly and with enthusiasm. Some motivating starting activities are discussed in Chapter 11. Whether the purpose is for children to continue work already begun or to start on fresh activity, the essential function of the initial discussion is to ensure that children know the purpose of their work (see Chapter 18) and what role is expected of them.

Group discussion during the lesson

Group discussions are important parts of practical work; children should be encouraged to talk freely among themselves. The teacher will visit each group for various purposes – to monitor progress, to encourage exchange of views, to offer suggestions, to assess. It may only be necessary to ensure that the talk is productive (as in Box 7.2) but other groups may need more input. Since it is almost impossible for teachers to 'hover' without their presence affecting the children, it is best to make clear what is intended. 'I'm not going to interrupt; just carry on' or 'Tell me what you've been doing up to now'. During a teacher-led group discussion, the teacher should show an example of how to listen and make sure that everyone has a chance to speak. When the teacher withdraws from the group the children can be left with the expectation that they should continue to discuss, 'You already have some good ideas, now see if you can put together some more suggestions.'

The noise, which discussion inevitably generates, is part of the working atmosphere. If the noise level becomes unacceptable it should be possible to spot the reason:

- too much excitement about certain activities?
- children waiting for equipment and not 'on task'?
- 'messing about'?

Once diagnosed, appropriate action can be taken – for example, by diluting the excitement by staggering work on certain activities, organising equipment for easier access, checking the match between the demand of an activity and the children's readiness to respond.

Whole-class discussion at the end of the lesson

Holding a whole-class discussion at the end of a practical session, whether or not the work is completed, should be the normal practice. The reasons for this strong recommendation have been well articulated by Barnes in Box 7.5.

It is important to warn the children in good time for them to bring their activity to a stage where equipment can be put away and to allow five or ten minutes for reviewing and reporting ongoing work. At the end of the activities on a particular

Box 7.5 The value of discussing activities that have been completed.

Learning of this kind (from experience of manipulating objects, visits or group discussions) may never progress beyond manual skills accompanied by slippery intuitions, unless the learners themselves have an opportunity to go back over such experiences and represent them to themselves. There seems every reason for group practical work in science, for example, normally to be followed by discussion of the implications of what has been done and observed, since without this what has been half understood may soon slip away.

(Barnes, 1976: 30–1)

topic a longer time for whole-class discussion should be organised and children given time beforehand to prepare to report, perhaps with a demonstration, to others.

Introducing scientific words

The importance of introducing children to scientific vocabulary is made clear in both new and 'old' curriculum requirements and guidelines. For example, the 2014 National Curriculum (DfE, 2013) states that, at key stage 1, pupils should be taught to 'use simple scientific language to talk about what they have found and communicate their ideas to a range of audiences in a variety of ways'. At key stage 2, the requirement is to 'use some scientific language' in years 3 and 4, and to 'read, spell and pronounce scientific vocabulary correctly' in years 5 and 6. The ability of children to 'express themselves using appropriate scientific terms and representations in writing and talk' was also included in the skills to be developed through inquiry (Box 6.4).

Teachers have to decide the answers to the difficult questions of when and how new words should be introduced. Should they use the correct word from the moment of children being involved in an activity in which they might use it and insist on them using the word? Or should they allow children to 'pick up' words as they go along? We know that children pick up and use scientific words quite readily; they often enjoy collecting them and trying them out as if they were new possessions. At first one of these words may have rather a 'loose fit' to the idea which it is intended to convey. Does it matter if children use scientific words without knowing their full meaning?

Before trying to answer some of these questions, it is useful to reflect on the notion of the 'full meaning' of scientific words.

Different levels of meaning

Most scientific words (such as evaporation, dissolving, power, reflection) label concepts which can be understood at varying levels of complexity. A scientist understands energy in a far broader and more abstract way than the 'person in the street'. Even an apparently simple idea of 'melting' is one which can be grasped in different degrees of complexity: a change which happens to certain substances when they are heated or an increase in energy of molecules to a point which overcomes the binding forces between them. This means that the word melting may evoke quite a different set of ideas and events for one person than for another. Now, to use the word 'melting' in a restricted sense is not 'wrong' and we do not insist that it is only used when its full meaning is implied. Indeed the restricted meaning is an essential step to greater elaboration of the concept. We should, perhaps, accept children's 'loose' use of words as a starting point to development of a more refined and scientific understanding of the word.

For example, take the child's writing in Figure 5.9 (p. 83) where, in describing how the sound is transmitted in a yoghurt pot string telephone, he explains how vibrations go down the string. The word 'vibration' is certainly used in a manner here which suggests that the child understands sound as vibration, until we notice that he writes that the voice is 'transferred into vibrations' at one end and 'transferred back to a voice' at the other. It seems that the sound we hear is not understood as vibration, but only its transmission along the string. It may be that ideas both of sound and of vibration have to be extended, so that vibration is something which can take place in air and occur wherever sound occurs, which will take time and wider experience, but he has made a start. And he is not wrong in using 'vibration' in the way he has done.

When to introduce new words

Teachers seem to be caught between, on the one hand, giving new words too soon (and so encouraging a verbal facility which conceals misunderstanding) and, on the other, withholding a means of adding precision to thinking and communication (and perhaps letting children continue to make use of words which are less than helpful).

The value of introducing the correct word at a particular time will depend on whether

- the child has had experience of the event or phenomenon which it covers;
- the word is needed at that time;
- the word is going to help the child to link related things to each other (since words often give clues to these links).

In other words, *if a word will fill a gap, a clear need to describe something which has been experienced and is real to the children, then the time is right to introduce it*. With young children one of the conditions for the 'right time' is the physical presence or signs of the phenomenon to which the word refers. Only then can we hope to fit the word to an idea, even loosely.

How to introduce new words

The above argument suggests that, until the moment for introducing the word is right, the teacher should use the language adopted by the children in discussing their experiences. Then, once the word is introduced the teacher should take care to use it correctly. For example, if children have been exploring vibrations in a string, drum skin, a tissue paper against a comb, and wanting to talk about what is happening to all these things, it may well be useful to say 'what all these are doing is called "vibrating"'. Before this the children and teacher may have called it by descriptive names: trembling, jumping, moving, going up and down, etc. A useful way of ensuring that the new word and the children's words are connected to the same thing, suggested by Feasey (1999), is to use them together ('the thing that's trembling or vibrating') until the new becomes as familiar as the old.

Much more experience of a concept has to follow so that the word becomes attached to the characteristic or property rather than to the particular things present when it was first encountered. But there is no short cut through verbal definitions in abstract terms.

Words describing inquiry skills

It is not only 'concept' words that children need to learn to use correctly. Edmonds (2002: 5) makes the point, in the context of teaching children for whom English is an alternative language, that: 'Children are unsure what is required of them when they are asked to predict, hypothesise or interpret.' This applies to all children, however, as do the suggestions in Box 7.6, for alternatives to giving verbal definitions of processes.

Box 7.6 Suggestions for conveying the meaning of processes

Some of the most effective strategies appear to be:

- Teacher modelling the procedures with a group or the whole class; demonstrating the whole procedures of planning parts or the whole of an investigation

- Providing examples of the kind of procedures the teacher has asked for

- Identifying and sharing clear criteria for what the procedure would look like if completed successfully

- Looking through pieces of other children's work where they have carried out the procedure or skill and making a running commentary on what the child has done

- Detailed feedback and discussion on the child's work.

(Edmonds, 2002: 5)

Summary

This chapter has considered various aspects of oral communication in the classroom. The main points have been:

- Children's talk can take an important role in the development of their understanding when it takes the form of 'dialogic talk', which is characterised by 'thinking aloud' about a situation or problem.

- The teacher's role in discourse intended to help children's learning is one of taking part as an equal member of the group, encouraging explanations and helping to clarify meanings.

- Primary children can be encouraged to consider alternative explanations and to use evidence to argue the pros and cons.

- More formal talk for reporting requires a classroom climate in which children listen and respond positively to each other and make an effort to communicate effectively.

- Whole-class discussion is needed at the start of a lesson to motivate engagement and at the end to reflect on what has been learned and discuss its implications.

- Scientific words for processes as well as concepts are best introduced when the children have experienced the event or phenomenon that they represent.

Further reading

Alexander, R. (2008) *Towards Dialogic Teaching,* York: Dialogos.

Asoko, H. and Scott, P. (2006) Talk in science classrooms, in W. Harlen (ed.) *ASE Guide to Primary Science Education,* Hatfield: ASE, 158–66.

Dawes, L. (2004) Talk and reasoning in classroom science, *International Journal of Science Education,* 26(6): 677–95.

Eccles, D. and Taylor, S. (2011) Promoting understanding through dialogue, in W. Harlen (ed.) *ASE Guide to Primary Science Education,* new edn, Hatfield: ASE, 77–84.

8

Learning through ICT

Introduction

In this chapter we focus on the ways in which information and communication technology (ICT) can support and enhance children's learning in science. In particular we consider the role of digital technologies in learning: from the most obvious use of computers in supporting written communication to the less common use of digital multimedia to enhance observation and visualisation; from the solo use of mobile technologies to access information to the collaborative group work afforded by social networking. All of these technologies are now readily available to so many of our youngest children in their lives outside school that the challenge of harnessing them in the cause of science learning is not one educators can choose to avoid. What is essential, however, is that how we use ICT must be firmly linked to discussions in other chapters about the importance of learning and understanding constructed through children discussing ideas, thinking, exploring and developing the skills and attitudes of science.

We begin by noting how children interact with technology and the value of building on this facility in the classroom. The main section provides examples of how ICT can support different aspects of inquiry in science, from enhancing observation, to collecting evidence, to testing ideas with models and simulations.

Digital natives and digital literacy

Although we cannot assume that all children have equal access to digital technologies outside school, they have been born into a digital world where the mobile phone is ubiquitous and where instant communication is the norm. Children – and their younger teachers at least – are digital natives (Frand, 2000) and, indeed, in the developed world high proportions of senior citizens might be described as digital immigrants making use of the internet, satellite navigation systems, Skype and Facebook. Large amounts of money are spent in many countries in introducing ICT to schools (see e.g. Hall and Higgins, 2007) and a report of an evaluation of ICT in schools in England (Ofsted, 2011b) found that ICT teaching was good or outstanding in two-thirds of primary schools. It would seem that the significant levels of investment have, to a large extent, paid off. Both children and their teachers are more confident and proficient than

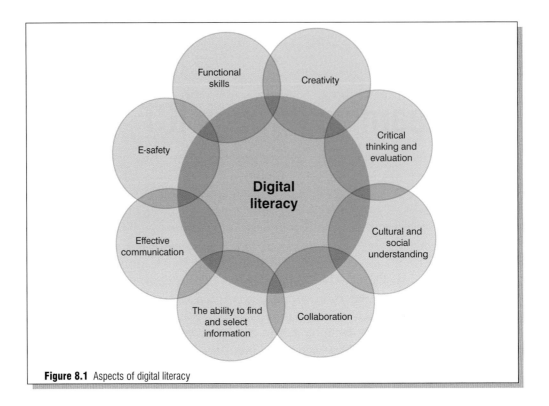

Figure 8.1 Aspects of digital literacy

ever before. Schools are making efforts to use ICT to enhance learning across the curriculum. The focus then has turned from the introduction and use of ICT in conventional teaching towards more thinking about the ways in which technology is used safely to genuinely enhance learning.

Given the ubiquity of technology and the ease of access to it, we cannot shield children from it, as perhaps we thought we might when social media first came on the scene. Parents and teachers need to teach them to use it safely to their advantage as learners. Young people should acquire the skills and attitudes, as well as the knowledge of the tools available, to be able to access, select and manipulate data in all its various forms, to synthesise the information gained and so construct new knowledge. They need to be able to create ways to explore and to communicate their knowledge and ideas in real-life situations both individually and collaboratively (Ng, 2010). This facility has been described as 'digital literacy', represented diagrammatically by Futurelab (2010) (see Figure 8.1).

The digitally literate classroom

The range and variety of ways in which ICT can be used is daunting and there is a tendency for teachers to stick with a narrow range of easily available tools that the children know well. Expanding this range of tools will achieve more than novelty since it has been demonstrated that the ICT rich and digitally literate classroom does lead to greater learning:

Project learning, group work, field trips, creative expression and many other teaching strategies that foster inquiry learning are given new impetus, vitality and effectiveness through the integration of digital media in the process. In this regard, we observed a variety of digital tools in use in primary classrooms – digital cameras, video cameras, audio recording devices; animation, picture story and text captioning software were especially popular. We recommend that schools consider the pedagogic potential of a broad range of digital technologies alongside the more frequent emphasis on the need for more and better computers and network access.

(CRILT, 2009: 10)

Over recent years the importance of learning to use ICT has been the focus of attention, but the 2013 National Curriculum for England also includes understanding computers as a separate subject in primary and secondary schools. It is important to emphasise that we are concerned here *only* with the use of computers as aids to communication and with other communication technologies which can be used in learning.

The case for the digitally literate science classroom

Reimann and Goodyear (2004) looked at ICT and science and concluded that ICT can help with

1. increasing motivation
2. providing highly interactive experience and rich feedback to engage with learning
3. providing tools that demonstrate what has been learned
4. providing for communication and collaboration
5. facilitating data collection and presentation
6. connecting science to students' real-life experiences
7. increasing students' self-management of their own learning and
8. catering for differences in learning.

They cited Webb (2005), arguing that in science education the benefits go beyond the list above in that they promote cognitive development. The point here is that, by using digital tools effectively, children are able to concentrate fully on what is to be learned. When we first learn to drive a car it seems impossible to concentrate on using the clutch and changing gears whilst also navigating traffic safely. But once gear change becomes automatic then the higher order challenge of driving safely can be dealt with. Similarly, where children experience a new tool (such as a data-logger, or tablet), they need time to become proficient but, once they are, they are free to use it in higher order thinking. This has been described as reducing the cognitive load. Tamim *et al.* (2011) found that students in classrooms where ICT was used regularly were likely to perform 12 percentage points higher in their studies overall than those in more traditional classrooms.

The digitally literate science classroom: examples

Having looked at some evidence for using ICT in the classroom, this section gives two examples of ways in which ICT can help to enhance, and provide access to, good science learning experiences for children.

The birds topic
A teacher of 9 year olds in an urban school used ideas by Byrne and Sharp (2002) for a topic that would involve the use of databases. The annual National Bird Survey of the RSPB (Royal Society for the Protection of Birds) provided the starting point. A member of the local RSPB came to the school to talk to a class about the Big Garden Watch project and about birds in their locality. The children decided to set up a bird watch project of their own to run throughout the spring term.

Groups of children took on different tasks:

- One group found images of birds on the internet and explored the different identification keys available to find one they could easily work with and then created a display for the wall next to the window looking out onto the bird table.

- One group experimented making bird seed cakes and deciding where best to place bird feeders.

- Another group explored the best bird tables to use and sourced an inexpensive one.

The children's teacher found out about a project in another authority that involved movement-activated webcams being placed in each of a number of school bird boxes over the spring and summer. The children had monitored the website looking into the nests.

Once the bird table and feeders had been set up, the children organised a rota to observe the birds on the table at different times in the day (including during breakfast club and after school club) over a two-week period. Groups used the digital camera to film birds on the table and took photographs. A database of birds and times of visiting was built up and explored to find out which birds visited at different times of the day. The children were able to create and interrogate the database and use it to make comparisons with the national data produced as a result of the RSPB project. They designed a web page for their school website, which included profiles of the most regular visitors and of the most rare. They were able to insert a video clip into their web page and an animation based on photographs taken at different times of the day.

A group of children wrote a report on the nest box experiment in the local authority newsletter and another group negotiated with the head teacher for the school to get involved in the following year's RSPB garden and school bird watch survey.

Since the publication of Byrne and Sharp's article, more opportunities have been developed for children to be involved in similar inquiries and communication. There has been an expansion in the number of individuals and

RSPB Love Nature

Thanks to St Mary's Church of England Primary, Folkestone, for these pictures. Great shot of the rabbit tracks!

Like · Comment · Follow post · 23 January at 11:02

37 people like this.

Steve Black brilliant well done st marys
23 January at 11:09 · Like · 1

Figure 8.2 Children's photographs placed on Facebook by their teacher

schools posting on the RSPB Facebook page, offering photographs and giving and receiving comments about their work.

In this example it is clear that the starting point for the topic was not using ICT but involving the children in an extended project that would continue to hold their interest, so that the children themselves would raise and find ways to solve questions of importance to them. They used their senses and enhanced this with photography and videos; and they took part in drawing and close observation, extensive dialogue and collaborative work. There is no doubt that they were enhancing their inquiry skills. The work gave them the skills and knowledge to be able to use the larger data sets available through the RSPB, which in turn reinforced the relevance of their topic and so promoted learning further. More recently the children in St Mary's school (see Box 8.2), undertaking a similar project, were able to disseminate their findings – and so take part in a wider dialogue giving them a sense of contributing to the growth of knowledge about birds nationally – when their teacher put photographs they had taken onto Facebook (note that Facebook does not allow children under 13 to join).

Mobile learning

In a much more explicit attempt to explore the use of ICT, in this case mobile learning, in teaching science, Loi and colleagues (2011) developed a project using smart phones and a managed learning environment (MLE) as a new way to support children learning about bodily systems.

The topic began with a game in class to help the children to identify what they already know about the body systems and for the teacher to identify gaps in their understanding. Using their smart phones, and linked to the project on the MLE, the children then reflected on their learning and completed a section recording 'what I Know', 'what I Want to know' and 'what I have Learned' (KWL) (see Chapter 16). Each child was then given an experiment to undertake at home related to a bodily system. These included, for example, what happens to the heart beat after exercise? One of the systems for study was the digestive system where children explored what happens to an apple when chewed in the mouth. The children video-recorded their experiments for discussion in pairs and as a class. The children went on to record their learning and, through software on their smart phones, to create sketchy animations of the digestive system. These were peer assessed and improved before sending to the teacher, who again made suggestions in class for improvements. Finally, the children were asked to interview their parents to find out what they knew about the digestive system, to identify gaps and then to teach them something they did not know. These interactions were recorded for discussion with a partner back in class.

The children very much enjoyed their project and when tested performed better than comparable classes taught in the more traditional ways. The researchers observed that the pupils developed an increased level of self-discipline in the class, for example, organising a rota for charging the phones. There was a lot of social interaction, with children sharing YouTube videos they had found and answers from web searches. The children were much more willing to ask questions of each other and the teacher and they asked fewer questions about lesson instructions and more about the subject matter. This last point is important because it underlines the shift in the quality of student learning that this type of approach can lead to.

The classroom example described here reflects the aims of the Wolverhampton based Learning2go project (http://www.learning2go.org) which has been working to embed mobile learning in the city since 2003. The initiative, coordinated by the e-Services team of Wolverhampton City Council, shows how successfully mobile learning can be used to give children access to 'anywhere, anytime' learning. Learning2Go is developing new ways of delivering exciting and motivating learning both in and beyond school.

The functions of ICT and the role of the learner

As the nature and variety of ICT and associated software increases, it becomes more and more difficult to categorise its different tools; often one tool has several different functions. As we have argued above, ICT offers affordances for learning, that is, it helps children to access learning opportunities more readily. It does this in many ways by enabling them to:

- observe phenomena that they would find difficult to do otherwise (e.g. digital microscopes);
- record data more readily (e.g. data-loggers or using time-lapse photography);
- gain access to information quickly and easily (e.g. using web searches, or a Skype meeting with a scientist);
- go beyond what can be accessible in the primary classroom (e.g. see the Earth from a satellite);
- explore and consolidate ideas (using games and simulations);
- present information in detail to support analysis (simple databases); and
- present ideas in ways that engage others and so stimulate discussion and engagement in the topic (e.g. by putting information on a social network site or a VLE, or video conferencing with pupils in another school).

The examples in the next section illustrate some of these categories and the motivation for learning that ICT creates.

Enhancing observation

Developing the skills of observation is a crucial element of inquiry. Using their senses, paying close attention and using tools, such as hand lenses to see more clearly, or thermometers to gauge temperature changes, support the development of observation skills. ICT provides opportunities from simple magnification, as in the use of digital microscopes or, as described in Box 8.1, the use of a visualiser. This has the added advantage of supporting discussion and collaboration. Data-loggers, as described in Box 8.2, allow the observation of fine differences that would be otherwise difficult to detect and record. Data-loggers have the added advantage of recording the data digitally.

Facilitating the recording of information

In the birds topic described earlier, the children began the project by using digital cameras to record the birds visiting the feeders. This was much easier than trying to draw the birds or learning all the names of the different birds before beginning. Their enthusiasm and a clear record of the birds helped the children subsequently to use bird books to find out about the birds and learn their names. Digital cameras and video are now common tools in the recording of information. Data-loggers again are invaluable in helping to record data in ways which are clear to the children.

The use of data-loggers and movie creators was explored in the DREAMS (Digitally Researched Engaging and Motivating Science) project (2009). This project, funded by the Primary Science Teaching Trust and based in Northern

---

Box 8.1 Observing fruits and seeds

The teachers and children in a Hertfordshire Infants school became very excited by the arrival of a visualiser. This looks like, and can be used as, a digital projector, displaying extremely clear two- and three-dimensional images on a screen. It is possible to zoom in and out and to freeze and split the screen to allow comparisons to be made. Children can share the experience of close observation of objects that they might otherwise use a hand lens or a digital microscope for. The children of Cunningham Hill Infants School were studying fruit in their art project, but the detail they were able to capture, as shown in their drawings in Figure 8.3 provides an ideal opportunity to learn about seeds and reproduction in plants.

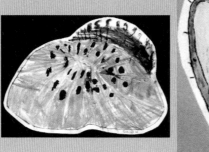 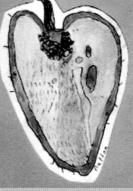

Figure 8.3 Children's drawings of a closely observed kiwi fruit and a pepper

---

Box 8.2 Data-logging

Ofsted (2011a) reported on the work of a class who were studying a topic on the Second World War. Their task was to find out, with the help of light sensitive data-loggers, which material would be the best for blackout curtains. The teacher demonstrated the use of the data-loggers and gave the children plenty of practice recording the light levels in the room. Once the children had learned how to annotate the graphs they produced, they were ready to address the question of blackout curtains. The children looked at the materials and made their predictions and tested a range of different options before agreeing on which combination of fabrics was the best.

Ireland, developed the use of digital resources within primary science. Digital resources such as computer microscopes, movie-creators and data-loggers were used to extend the means by which children capture and communicate information about the world around them. Data collected using a range of research methods showed that the use of the digital resources (data-loggers, computer microscopes and video cameras)

> brought about a statistically significant increase in pupils' enjoyment of science and enhanced their engagement and motivation. The resources also

increased pupils' perceptions of the 'usefulness' of science and made it less difficult and more relevant to their everyday lives. In providing alternative ways to capture data and present results, the resources allowed for greater creativity in terms of the scope and nature of the inquiry activities and the methods used to report on them.

(McCullagh, 2009: 4)

Gaining access to information

A Teachers' TV video recording of a lesson to illustrate the use of formative assessment (http://vimeo.com/5184675) showed a class of 10 and 11 year olds revising their understanding of light. The teacher gave them the intended learning outcomes and asked them in pairs to demonstrate their understanding. They designed and carried out their own investigations, for example, looking at the formation of shadows and the transparency of materials. The children were also free to leave the classroom to visit the school library and, more often, to search online for explanations and to check their own definitions. One girl, searching for information about light, read out to her partner 'we see a light source when the light from the source enters our eyes. But beware you should never look directly at the sun because the amount of light travelling from the sun will damage your eyes very quickly.'

Access beyond the classroom

A major advantage offered by the internet is the access it can give to information that is beyond the classroom. Lisa, described in Chapter 3, used YouTube videos to show a series of satellite images of the Earth and a time-lapse photographs of a city over 24 hours. These were used to stimulate interest in a way that static images in books could not have achieved. The internet provides many other opportunities to move beyond the confines of the classroom with video clips and virtual tours of places of interest, or to connect with other schools, scientists and other experts through email, video conferencing or internet video phone connections.

Explore and consolidate ideas

Revisiting ideas learned previously, either for reinforcement or as revision is important in building understanding. It is important to ensure that it is motivating for the pupils rather than a drudge. This can be done in many ways. For example

- Reviewing records kept over the course of a project. In Kathy's class in Chapter 3 this was done by creating a Big Book. Alternatively this could be done using a website, or in the form of a podcast, enabling groups or the class to go back and review what they did and what information they used, giving purpose and meaning to revision.

- The opportunity to play games and undertake quizzes is also a fun way to consolidate learning, using websites such as BBC Bitesize or Askabout Ireland (see web references).

- Simulation and modelling software, and spreadsheets and databases, enable pupils to test out ideas.

Test out ideas using simulations

With the introduction of digital cameras that are easy for children to use in schools time-lapse photography has now become accessible to them. They can also make their own simulations and animations, as in Box 8.3. Once children see how simulations are made they are better able to understand those they see on screen. In some cases simulations are the only way to provide opportunity for children to test their ideas – for instance in understanding how movement of the Earth and Moon in relation to the Sun lead to day and night and seasonal changes, or how blood flows around the body. In using ICT in this way pupils are testing out ideas. This can be done in groups who can then discuss these ideas and build on them (this also helps in the process of making sense of the information). The teacher has an important role to play in mediating what children are learning, because, as Sutherland *et al.* (2004) observed, with simulations often the knowledge the pupils construct as a result can be quite different from that intended by the teacher.

Box 8.3 Animating the growth of a bean

A Year 2/3 class were looking at life cycles. In pairs they grew beans, keeping a diary of the changes they observed. The children then made a story board of the different stages of the life cycle. The class teacher, Wendy, then arranged the children into groups to focus on: (i) seed germination; (ii) seed growth; (iii) seedlings; (iv) flowering; and (v) forming seeds. Each group then made a play dough model of the bean at their allotted stage and took a series of photographs manipulating the model each time to show the small changes they had observed. Wendy was then able to download all the photographs into an animation package (slowmation) which the children then recorded a narrative over the animation.

(Hoban and Nielsen, 2010)

Present information to support analysis

Young people were often heard complaining about having to 'write up' their science work in ways that took the shine off the excitement of learning. ICT provides opportunities for the learning to continue beyond the initial activity and into the presentation and reporting. A pupil from the DREAMS Project mentioned above is quoted as saying:

We had learned all the facts about smoking, but when we then made our advertisements about the dangers of smoking we were learning it again and hearing what other groups were saying as we could watch their video.

(McCullagh, 2009: 39)

Collaborate with others/engage in dialogue

One of the problems with early use of ICT was that children spent time on their own interacting with a computer screen. With the development of mobile technologies and new soft and hardware the possibilities for collaborative learning have mushroomed. The visualiser described in the example on p. 124 allows groups to see and explore objects together supporting dialogue and enhancing learning. In Boxes 8.4 and 8.5, the interactive whiteboard is used to support dialogue. In Box 8.4 this is not for whole class teaching but for use by a small group, so encouraging productive talk. In Box 8.5 the whole class is involved.

Box 8.4 Use of IWB to promote group collaboration

In a study of the use of interactive white boards in supporting learning Kershner *et al.* (2010) closely observed groups of children as they worked together to observe and explore animal teeth. The children were seen using exploratory talk, which Barnes (2008) has argued is the most productive for learning (see Chapter 7).

> The children monitor and evaluate their progress and each other's work, as when Natalie receives Adam's drawing efforts as: 'That looks like an elephant's foot!' and Adam then comments on Noah's later effort as 'I'm not meant to be rude, but they look a bit like a necklace.' They regularly erase unwanted work and begin to comment more explicitly on the design aspects, talking about 'putting lines on …' and using their own teeth as a model. The children eventually reach the tiger. They quickly decide that tigers' teeth are 'sharp' and 'big' and then continue.
>
> (Kershner *et al.*, 2010: 376)

They were able to collaborate more effectively with a large image of an animal and its teeth, while other groups jostled around smaller printed pictures. They could draw and write and easily erase until they had negotiated an outcome they were all happy with.

Box 8.5 Whole-class involvement through use of an IWB

Greg's class of 4 year olds were looking at everyday objects, thinking about the properties of the materials from which they were made. Greg typed their descriptions onto a computer. The children then took photographs of the objects which were uploaded and displayed on the interactive whiteboard. In discussion the children were able to connect the text to the objects. Then, using their 'magic fingers', children were able to move the objects around the board to sort them into groups. The lesson helped children to make the connection between objects they had seen and handled and the images on the screen, and promoted a great deal of purposeful discussion.

Present conclusions in engaging ways

One of the most obvious uses of ICT is in the communication of findings to others. Children can create engaging PowerPoint presentations, colourful posters, podcasts, or web pages with embedded video clips to present to audiences of other classes or parents and families. This can be much more motivating for the class than the traditional report and as such extends the learning. Thinking hard about what the information means and how to present it is a powerful way to extend learning.

> Using the video was far better and made you try harder as you knew it was important. Because it was going to be on the video we wanted to get it right. You had to make sure you said the right thing and you had to know what you were talking about.
>
> (DREAMS project, McCullogh, 2009: 39)

Practice and reinforcement

We know that children from a very young age enjoy playing games on computers. Although some might not provide a wealth of learning, engaging in games does mean that the children become adept at finding their way around the technology. There are lots of games and quizzes available free on the internet that are specifically designed to support or, more often, to reinforce learning (e.g. the BBC learning zone – see websites). It is worth selecting games that relate closely to the topic children are tackling in class. This might seem an obvious point but, in the same way that teachers observe that books that have never left the library shelf are suddenly in demand, so children's enthusiasm for a game will be heightened if they are currently immersed in learning the concepts it covers.

Box 8.6 A novel way of deepening understanding

Ofsted (2011b) reported on a Year 4 class where children drew on their learning about habitats to create a podcast where a 'reporter' interviewed an 'animal'. The children planned the reporter's questions and considered the animal's replies, and added sound effects by layering and modifying sounds they recorded. The children developed their scientific understanding of habitats, learned new skills in using technology and did it all with great enthusiasm.

Summary

In this chapter we have discussed how the use of ICT can enhance children's learning in science. ICT is not a substitute for first-hand experience or for the discussion and interaction that are key features of good primary science, but it can, when well planned and understood, provide valuable opportunities to support, extend and represent learning in a way that is motivating for children and their teachers.

We have noted and illustrated through practical examples the value of ICT in supporting

- observation of phenomena that they would find difficult to do otherwise
- recording and displaying data
- gaining access to information quickly and easily
- going beyond what can be accessed in the primary classroom
- exploring and consolidating ideas (using games and simulations)
- organising data to support analysis
- presenting ideas in ways that engage others and stimulate discussion.

Recent years have seen a leap in the practice of using ICT effectively so that it supports all aspects of effective learning in science.

Further reading

Crompton, Z and Davies, E. (2012) Making movies, *Primary Science,* 123: 8–9.
Nicholson, D. (2011) Using a visualiser in primary science, *Primary Science*, 118: 23–9.
Qualter, A. (2011) Using ICT in teaching and learning science in W. Harlen (ed.) *ASE Guide to Primary Science Education,* new edn, Hatfield: ASE, 61–9.

Websites
Askabout Ireland http://www.askaboutireland.ie/learning-zone/primary-students
BBC Bitesize http://www.bbc.co.uk/bitesize/ks2/science
BBC Learning Zone http://www.bbc.co.uk/learningzone
The DREAMS project: http://www.stran.ac.uk/informationabout/research/dreamsproject
Hertfordshire Development Centre http://www.thegrid.org.uk/learning/ict/technologies/index.html
RSPB birdwatch http://www.rspb.org.uk/birdwatch
RSPB schoolswatch http://www.rspb.org.uk/schoolswatch
The South East Grid for Learning http://birdbox.segfl.org.uk

The teacher's role

Providing for learning outside the classroom

Introduction

Learning takes place in a wide range of environments at different times and in various social contexts. It is common to distinguish between formal and informal contexts for learning; formal ones being schools and colleges and informal ones being outside such institutions. Informal learning takes place in a wide range of situations, from family discussions to field visits organised by schools. Our focus here is on those activities which are organised by the school and are intended to contribute to curriculum learning just as much as what happens in the classroom. Whether within or outside the classroom there is an active role for the teacher – in interaction with learners and in ensuring active engagement with the learning environment. We look at various aspects of this role in this part of the book: questioning in Chapter 10; supporting the development of children's conceptual understanding, skills and attitudes in Chapters 11, 12 and 13; and using ICT in Chapter 14.

In this chapter we consider the benefits of learning outside the classroom and its particular value for primary science. We provide examples of different types of experiences and locations and make some suggestions about how to plan for and make the most use of these precious events.

Why learning outside the classroom?

The need to extend learning experiences

After the introduction of the national curriculum and assessment in England the amount of 'fieldwork' being experienced by secondary school pupils plummeted because teachers did not see how it related to the curriculum, could not link it directly to assessment and worried about finding the time in a crowded curriculum (Fisher, 2001). Similarly, in primary schools the time taken to visit a museum or local supermarket became more difficult to justify when so much content needed to be 'covered' in the prescribed curriculum. In addition to these curriculum constraints the issues of health and safety became such that, in some cases, teachers shied away from taking the risks associated with journeys out of school. In general, young people are more protected and less active than they were in the past .The increase in the costs of school visits, especially transport costs, added to the problem. Few would argue that this was a loss to the general education of young people. Indeed the House of Commons Education and Skills Select Committee, reporting in 2007, underlined the significant benefits of learning outside the classroom.

Since that time several factors have come together to bring learning outside the classroom to the fore. Helped by the reduction in prescription in successive revisions of national curricula and guidelines, teachers have more confidence in using the outside environment to meet their requirements. In addition there have been increasing concerns about a lack of exercise by young people, and poor diet leading to health problems. Understanding more about food production as well as developing an appreciation of the outdoors is seen as a way to counteract this. Further, there are worries that a lack of understanding of the natural world may leave future citizens unable to take informed decisions about the impact on the environment of human activities. In primary school science in particular, the opportunities offered for relevant, exciting and memorable experiences with resources, environments and experts not normally found in the classroom means that learning outside of the classroom is essential.

Outside activities also helps children to experience and enjoy a wider range of activities. In our increasingly controlled and technologically rich world, many children have come to expect to be entertained in their leisure hours rather than to make their own entertainment. Whilst a previous generation played out of doors when not at school, many of today's young people are holed up indoors, sitting staring at large or small screens. This contrasts with the image described by Peacock (2006a) of an idyllic childhood in the Lake District where he roamed far and wide, fishing in streams and climbing trees. We may not all have had such freedom or such opportunities to discover the natural world by ourselves, and simple nostalgia for our own childhoods may not be sufficient reason to go to the trouble of trying to recreate these experiences. However, there is growing unease at the lack of freedom for children to learn through play and exploration, which in turn means that they are not learning how to take risks and make decisions for themselves.

In 2006 the government published the *Learning Outside the Classroom Manifesto* (now archived but still available at the URL at the end of this chapter) which linked learning out of doors to key learning objectives, for example:

> Learning outside the classroom is not an end in itself, rather, we see it as a vehicle to develop the capacity to learn. It provides a framework for learning that uses surroundings and communities outside the classroom. This enables young people to construct their own learning and live successfully in the world that surrounds them. There is strong evidence that good quality learning outside the classroom adds much value to classroom learning. It can lead to a deeper understanding of the concepts that span traditional subject boundaries and which are frequently difficult to teach effectively using classroom methods alone.
>
> (DfES, 2006: 3)

Box 9.1 The benefits of learning outside the classroom

- Improve academic achievement
- Provide a bridge to higher order learning
- Develop skills and independence in a widening range of environments
- Make learning more engaging and relevant to young people
- Develop active citizens and stewards of the environment
- Nurture creativity
- Provide opportunities for informal learning through play
- Reduce behaviour problems
- Improve attendance
- Stimulate, inspire and improve motivation
- Develop the ability to deal with uncertainty
- Provide challenge and opportunity to take acceptable levels of risk
- Improve young people's attitude to learning

(DfES, 2006: 4)

The contribution to learning in general

Arguments for teachers spending the, not inconsiderable, time and effort involved to provide opportunities for learning outside the classroom include the mounting evidence that such experiences have a significant impact on children's learning, their motivation to learn, their social skills and general attitude to school. It provides access to resources that would otherwise be unavailable, including the physical environment, and specialist or expensive equipment from which to learn, and also to the intellectual resources of the specialists who offer support for learning in certain sites, such as countryside rangers, museum curators, farmers, employees in factories and other industrial settings.

There is a broad consensus that taking children out to experience the environment and to work in exciting and different settings has a significant impact on the quality of their learning and on the relationship between teacher and pupils. Pupils learn about society and how to work together, they develop an understanding of the relationship between nature and society. Dillon *et al.* (2005: 22) describe the cognitive, affective, interpersonal/social and physical/behavioural impact of learning outdoors. Similarly *Learning Outside the Classroom Manifesto* listed the advantages as in Box 9.1.

The particular contribution to learning in science

In relation to science, in addition to the development of positive attitudes to learning science, working out of the classroom provides the opportunity to develop and apply scientific skills and understanding in the real world. Interactive and informal learning environments have an important role in demystifying science, for parents and the general public as well as for children.

Specific benefits for science include, for example, the development of an understanding of the relationship between the food we eat and farming. Dillon *et al.* (2005) point out that, although farming takes up a significant proportion of the countryside and is a huge industry, in the UK as in much of the developed world, the farming and food have become disconnected for many people. If young people are to contribute to debates about sustainability, a reconnection needs to be made. Similarly in terms of the environment, the issues are complex, but having the chance to explore the natural world and to see the interrelationship between people and their environment gives young people a foundation on which to build their views of the world and their own relationship to it and to make informed decisions about such matters as the need to recycle materials.

The quotations in Box 9.2 bring together some of the important aspects of learning outdoors. In the first case the girl experienced something brand new and learned not to be afraid of the animals she found, her interest was aroused and she really enjoyed the experience. In other cases, where children might have been expected to know a lot about the environment (Ambleside being in the heart of the Lake District National Park), having a project to work on focused their energies and helped them to value their own beautiful surroundings. Without this they might not have appreciated the need or the means to preserve it. In the final quote the ranger makes a link between memory and long-term learning similar to that described in Chapter 4 where we discussed neuroscience and Susan Greenfield's description of memory as the 'cornerstone of the mind' and the basis of our ability to adapt to our environment, that is, to learn. In this case, as in the other two, children were also motivated to revisit these sites and to continue to use and learn from them.

Box 9.2 Some views on the benefits of getting out of the classroom

An 8 year old from inner London on her first experience of pond dipping: 'there were lots of different animals, lots of legs and all slimy. It took away my fear.'

(Getting Out of the Classroom: A Day with the RSPB, Teachers' TV)

A 14 year old girl living in a rural area (Ambleside), after working in her local environment: 'We used to take it all for granted – you know, the hills and the trees ... now, we take it for granted that we don't pick wild flowers, things that are illegal and anti-social, like litter and campfires.'

(Peacock 2006b: 15)

A ranger discussing the value of school visits: 'Children's memories and learning from the visit were closely related. Strong themes are positive personal and social gains of direct and novel outdoor experiences in big landscapes, appreciation of methods of enquiry into the natural world (scientific and artistic) and interest in revisiting the National Park.'

(Dillon *et al.*, 2005: 23)

Extending the range of resources for learning

A valuable benefit of using out of school locations for learning is that they provide access to resources – physical, human and intellectual– which are not available to the teacher in the classroom.

Physical resources

Most of the physical resources for learning science in the primary school can be simple, familiar everyday objects, and may be easily accessible (see Chapter 22). However, there are times when so much more could be learned with access to appropriate equipment or environments. Box 9.3 describes the visit of a class to the beach with David, a ranger. Clearly the beach in itself is a valuable resource, but also the classroom provided by the local oil company and the photographs developed with the support of that company meant that key images could be presented and discussed in relation to the topics under study. The opportunities provided by museums and hands-on science centres are considerable, such as the example given later in Box 9.6 of a model of NASA mission control and the chance to 'fly' in a space ship. No less significant are the opportunities offered by the local supermarket to help children understand how groceries are organised, how bread is made, how food is stored and kept fresh: all valuable additions to the curriculum.

Box 9.3 Learning on a North Wales beach

This visit of Year 1 and 2 children from a small former mining community in north Wales was to a beach where the area of the dunes is designated as a site of special scientific interest. A large oil company, with a gas processing plant near the beach, funds some conservation work as well as school visits. The company provides a classroom, and supports its staff and rangers in working with schools in the area on a number of projects. In this case the focus was on the environment and conservation. The school had arranged transport for the day, the help of four adults and all the necessary negotiations with parents about packed lunches, etc.

While it rained in the morning the children worked in the classroom in five groups, each with a teacher or helper. The sessions were led by David, the ranger, who showed photographs of the area including the lighthouse, dunes and other things they were likely to see on the beach. He included some less pleasant images – litter, dog mess, graffiti on a 'you are here' map and warning signs – which were discussed in the context of helping children to realise that 'we really have got to look after our beach' and what to do if they find things damaged.

In the afternoon, as the children walked towards the sea break of dunes with the project leader, he reminded them that the dunes were there to hold back the stormy seas and keep the land safe. As they walked through the dunes the leader stepped off the duck board walkway and focused the children on the marram grass.

David: Look at this grass, can you see it? Feel it.
Pupil: It's dry and hard.

continued ...

Box 9.3 continued

David:	Yes. Even though it's been raining and raining all morning. Why do you think that is?
Pupil:	The sand is dry.
David:	(*picking up some sand and running it through his fingers*): It might have rained a lot but the rain has just run through it. So how does the grass survive?
Pupil:	It doesn't need a drink.
David:	It does, it needs water badly and so has to grow very long roots.

He asked a child to walk about 3 metres away from him in order to show how long the roots are. He explained that the long roots mean the grass can get water, and that the roots criss-cross each other to make nets that hold the sand together.

After a good hour of searching the beach, helped by the earlier discussion of what might be found, the children then walked back through the dunes a different way so that they could climb quite high and look back at the lighthouse. They could see where foxes had been and where rabbit holes were on the far side, and again discussed the fragility of the dunes.

Human resources

No teacher can hope to be an expert in all areas. Learning from experts is a valuable extension of the resources that can be harnessed to support the curriculum. This might mean making use of an amateur photography club to produce photographs of a local site for a visit, or the expertise of parents, carers and others in the community. One school developed a thriving gardening club under the guidance of the school caretaker and a parent who was also a professional gardener. The garden is used by all children throughout the school as part of their curriculum (Davids, 2008). Museums, galleries, gardens, farms and other places of work also provide access to a great deal of expertise. A number of businesses have also opened their doors to educational visits, often providing educators based in specially designed centres to support learning (see Box 9.5).

Intellectual resources

Museums and galleries, and especially hands-on centres, have worked extremely hard over recent years to develop materials to support pupil learning and to explore ways of presenting exhibits that support learning. These locations are now much more child and teacher friendly, providing hands-on experiences, specially designed exhibits and specially trained educators. Most centres have developed materials that can be sent out to schools to help prepare for a visit and that suggest follow-up work. For instance, in Scotland, the four Science Centres, the Royal Botanic Gardens, National Museums of Scotland, the two national parks, Scottish Natural Heritage, Historic Scotland, the Royal Zoological Society and local botanic gardens all offer educational programmes matched to the Curriculum for Excellence guidelines in various areas of the curriculum. In addition, there is a wealth of material online that can be used to support visits, or used in other work, through websites such as the 24 Hour Museum (www. culture24.org.uk). It remains the role of the teacher to make the best use of these resources, as we discuss later in this chapter.

Locations for learning outside the classroom

There are many ways to categorise locations for learning. We divide them here into natural locations, museums and wildlife centres, places of work and a few 'others'.

Natural locations

This includes parks, seashores, woods, meadows and school grounds. In some there may not be a formal structure for visitors and so the teacher's knowledge of the area is important. The school grounds and immediate surrounding area is probably the most inexpensive and under-used outdoor opportunity. One great advantage of making more use of the local environment is that repeat visits can be made. Fradley (2006: 15) wanted to include the outside environment more and in particular to take the children out for a weekly walk. Making sure that her pupils were adequately clothed and shod was a challenge. She sent a letter home to parents as in Figure 9.1.

Dear Parents

Welly Walks from Elm Class

This year I would like to use the outside environment more within my teaching; the children are really interested in the world around us. This week we went for a short walk and had a great time talking about bees and collecting nectar, the lifecycle of a caterpillar and seed dispersal linked to sunflowers. When we returned to the classroom the children wrote beautifully about aspects of the walk they enjoyed and did colour mixing to paint sunflowers in the style of Van Gogh as well as pastel pictures. Real experiences such as these are very valuable.

I would like the children to bring in wellies and a very waterproof coat every Friday in order for us to go out for short walks. Sometimes we will go around the village to link in with our geography topic; at other times we will be collecting thoughts, ideas and possibly creatures to fit in with our other subjects. It will be great to find out more about the rain. All the children will obviously need to be adequately protected from the weather so if you have any spare wellies or waterproofs I would like to have some for the classroom

Figure 9.1 Preparing for working out of doors

The option of walking around the local area is necessarily dependent on parental permission, and the environment. A busy city location might be inappropriate, but getting out into the grounds to experience rainfall or to measure wind speed with paper windmills is possible for most schools. Many teachers recognise that the pedagogic skills needed for a successful trip are not quite the same as those needed in the classroom (Kiseil, 2007). This can lead to a lack of confidence, especially on the part of inexperienced teachers. Accompanying more experienced staff on visits is a good way to learn, as is making use of organisations that provide expert trained staff. Forest schools, for example, in which educational experiences are led by trained specialist staff using the outdoor environment of the forest as a classroom, are becoming widespread in England and Wales. An evaluation of two forest school projects by the New Economics Foundation highlighted how they can increase young people's self-confidence and self-esteem (O'Brien and Murray, 2007). They provide opportunities for learning, particularly for those who do not do as well in the school classroom.

Welly Walks, forest schools and others focus on general learning, although they include many opportunities for science learning, as Jane Adams describes when writing about her school's involvement with the National Trust Guardianship Scheme which enables links with NT wardens (Adams, 2006: 7). Other activities can have science as the main focus of work and make use of the school grounds or nearly park.

In some schools joining in national events such as the Great Bug Hunt supported by the Association for Science Education (see *Primary Science,* June 2012) or the RSPB's Big Garden Birdwatch can spark long-term interest and use of the school environment. For example, Ripple Primary School created an outdoor classroom and nature garden designed to enable children to watch birds, grow vegetables, pond-dip, raise butterflies, etc. The Year 6 teacher, James Davis, reported that the children were showing such an interest in the wildlife starting to visit the area that he decided to enter his class into the 'Great Bug Hunt'. As winners they were able to afford, among other developments, a flat screen TV linked to a camera in a bird box. They also set up a school blog in which the children were able to put suggestions or simply share an experience that they had had whilst in the area. The teacher wrote with enthusiasm about this project:

> The most satisfying aspect of this project is that there is a real sense of ownership from the children. This is their area and they look after it in all seasons! The most important aspect through is that this resource has shown many children that learning can be fun. I would recommend that all schools have an outdoor classroom and nature garden and that you get involved in the Great Bug Hunt to get you started.
>
> (Davis, 2012)

Working outside the classroom as described in Box 9.3 provides children with the opportunity to use and develop their skills of observation and prediction in this case on the beach. Carefully organised beach scavenger hunts offer so much that is exciting and interesting, providing children with a sound basis for further class work on identification of items found, using online research and other sources. Other opportunities can come from links with university departments who are keen to develop links with schools. Owen *et al.* (2008) describe how a school gained through children working with professional scientists to do environmental research on their local river, something that might otherwise have been beyond the ability of the school staff to offer.

Places of work

Children's learning is enhanced where they see its relevance to their lives and to the world beyond school. The *Every Child Matters* agenda (DfES, 2004) refers to economic wellbeing, within which an understanding of the world of work is considered important. Visits to places of work can promote an understanding of how science contributes to our lives, and how useful an understanding of science is to future employment. Local supermarkets, fire stations, green grocers and garden centres can provide valuable locations for visits.

Farms, as mentioned earlier, provide opportunities for many links between science and everyday life; they are also places of work. There are some concerns about health and safety of children during visits on account of contact with animals and machinery. But Bill Graham, of Farming and Countryside Education (FACE), points out how simple measures can be taken by teachers and farmers to guard against any potential hazards. FACE helps farmers to prepare for educational visits and so farms are in turn able to help schools in planning visits. As well as experiences ranging from animal breeding to the conditions needed for plants to grow, farms are great places to demonstrate how science and technology are being applied in the workplace. They are also places where some key issues relating to the impact of human activity on the environment have to be faced, as pointed out by Graham in Box 9.4, quoted from an article which provides information about a very useful set of websites relating to farm visits.

Box 9.4 Learning from farm visits

Farmers use a large array of high-tech equipment, including global positioning systems (GPS), similar to those found in cars, with which pupils may be familiar. Many of their activities contribute to sustainability, including growing plants that are used for fuels and in manufactured products. For example, *Miscanthus* (elephant grass) is grown as a biofuel and for its fibres in boards, willow is burnt for electricity generation and corn starch is used for biodegradable plastic manufacture. Farmers also maintain and encourage wildlife by leaving the edges of their field with longer grass to encourage a range of insects and wild flowering plants, and replanting hedgerows as protection and food for small mammals and birds. There are choices to be made about using genetically modified plants and animals, methods of controlling disease and whether to use fertilisers or not. These are issues that affect all our lives, the directions of society and, indeed, the future of the planet.

(Graham, 2012: 17)

Building up a long-standing relationship with a local farm or local company can provide continuity for pupils and additional advantages as pupils become familiar with the site and make links with the work that some of their parents do. In the case of a local power company, as described in Box 9.5, the school gains considerably from the continued connection.

Box 9.5 Getting to know local industry

A class of 7 year olds visited a local gas-powered electricity-generating power station. The company has a staff-training centre that is also used to host school visits. The company funds a significant number of class visits for local schools each year as part of its community responsibility. The children from this local school will visit the station at least twice during their primary school career. On each visit, where possible, a member of staff who is also a parent of a child in the school is released to join the group. This helps to make the link with employment and also adds to the expertise available to the children on their visit. Older children have a chance to look around the power station while, for health and safety reasons younger ones remain in the classroom at the site.

After safety talks, including dressing up in reflective clothing and hard hats, the children worked in small groups with helpers provided by the company to study electricity. They made circuits, tried out switches, looked at a prototype electric car and then worked with a small model electric car studying conductors and insulators. Each group tried each activity; one involved generators.

Generators

A group of five children were shown pictures in the power station exhibition of the large gas-powered electricity generators in the main power station. They also looked at scale models of wind turbines and water driven turbines. The parent who worked in the station was able to explain that some energy is needed to turn a generator in order to produce electricity. In this station the energy comes from gas.

Each pupil was then handed a small, hand-held generator, wires and a bulb in a holder. They were asked to connect up the generator and turn the handle. This caused much excitement. One pupil commented: 'The faster you go the brighter the bulb'. The teacher used this to ask pupils to try for themselves. 'Go slower. What happens to the bulb? Go faster. What happens to the bulb?'

The teacher then gave each child a cell to connect up instead of the bulb. This caused the generator handle to turn, much to the delight of the pupils. The teacher did not go into detail but simply explained that the electricity was causing the handle to turn, so energy was coming from the 'battery' to the generator, instead of the other way round.

Science museums or centres, zoos and wildlife centres

Unlike classroom learning where there tends to be a linear sequence of activities and ideas, one building on the other, each relying on what has previously been learned, museums, galleries and hands-on centres tend to provide non-linear units of activity. These may be around a theme, such as 'Light and Colour' or 'Lavatories through the Ages', but visitors can experience exhibits in more or less any order, remaining at each for as long as they wish. Thus the museum relies on curiosity and intrinsic motivation on the part of the general visitor. For school visits this can mean that the amount learned is fairly limited. In a study of pupils visiting fairly formal museums, Bamberger and Tal (2007) concluded that learning in museums is optimised when pupils have a guided choice as to the areas that they are encouraged to explore. This gives the opportunity to make links with their classroom learning and enables the best use to be made of the expertise and knowledge of the museum staff.

Tunnicliffe (2001) found that groups visiting museums with adults asked significantly more questions and made more statements of knowledge than groups without adults. The importance of adults, of prior preparatory learning and of information available to pupils at their level was suggested by Bowker (2004) who, when researching visitors to the Eden project, found that children change their views of plants even in a single day visit (from boring to interesting), but that, unless interesting plants and information are pointed out to them, they don't always notice things for themselves. In a further study of the learning achieved in an Eden workshop focused on teaching children about the use of tropical plants for survival, Bowker and Jasper (2007) found that although pupils' understanding did increase significantly, they did not make the link between what they had learned and the way indigenous peoples might use these plants. Such connections need to be made explicit by those leading the workshops. All this suggests that, for maximum benefit to be obtained by pupils, careful planning is crucial, with teachers, helpers and museum educators sharing an understanding in how best to support the visit.

Box 9.6 Out of this world

In visits to the National Space Centre (http://www.spacecentre.co.uk/home/) teachers were keen to ensure that pupils learned about the relationship between the Earth, Moon and Sun in order to meet the requirements in the English national curriculum. Children visited the main exhibitions looking at models of the solar system and many other exhibits, touring in groups accompanied by a parent or school helper.

The Space Centre included a section called the Challenger Centre which consisted of a NASA-like 'Mission Control' with a bank of computers sending electronic messages to the 'Space Craft' (entered through an air locked door). Flight Directors, from the museum, ran a role play in which pupils were allocated roles, with half in mission control and half in the spacecraft. The challenge was to find and send a probe to a comet. The Flight Directors asked questions to bring out children's knowledge and understanding before starting. Half way through the visit the pupils had the opportunity to change over so that all had a chance to experience mission control and space flight and to take on roles such as the life support team who conducted water supply tests.

(Jarvis and Pell, 2005)

Jarvis and Pell (2005) investigated any influence on children's attitudes to science of a visit to the UK National Space Centre (Box 9.6). They found that in the main exhibits, where helpers had a knowledge of or interest in science or were experienced teachers or helpers, the children were more focused and engaged more with the exhibits. However, a number of the groups were fairly directionless. Questionnaires before and sometime after the visits showed that these experiences had not contributed to increased interest in science in general or space in particular. However the feedback from the Space Challenger experience was more positive.

The space-craft was amazing. I've never had an experience like this before. It felt real.

It's really exciting science … You felt important because you had your own little job.

Other locations

Almost any location can provide learning opportunities. Visits to castles with a focus on history can also contribute to the science curriculum: pushes and pulls, levers and pulleys are fascinating when linked to the mechanisms for a portcullis, or how a magellan operates. Visits to a concert hall can provide just the background for work on sound and music, and regular trips to the swimming pool offer obvious opportunities to study floating and sinking. All visits, whether out into the school grounds or week-long school trips abroad, require careful planning. We now consider some key points that have emerged from research in terms of planning to ensure learning.

Preparing for a visit

Research suggests that the most effective visits, wherever they might be, are those where the aims and objectives are clear and planning is carefully designed to achieve these objectives. Where possible all those involved in the visit should contribute to and be aware of the aims of the wider project that includes work prior to the visit and follow-up work. DeWitt and Osborne (2007) developed guidelines as a result of extensive research where they focused particularly on developing interaction and dialogue as the means to engender learning (see Box 9.7).

The Primary Science Teaching Trust (PSTT) website provides a professional development unit on planning for visits to hands on science centres. Advice is given under five headings: 'Why visit?'; 'Arranging the trip'; 'In the classroom'; 'On the day'; 'Link'. The information and ideas apply equally to many other visits (http://www.pstt.org.uk/resources/continuing-professional-development/enrich-science-learning.aspx).

Box 9.7 Guidelines for planning visits (adapted from DeWitt and Osborne (2007))

Select a good venue

The best organised locations produce resources that are attuned to the needs of the teacher and pupils, that fit with the curriculum as planned by the teacher. This means that museums, hands-on centres etc. that are willing to meet with teachers beforehand and adapt their materials to suit are likely to be more effective. In turn, then, visits where teachers have taken up the offer of a pre-visit and shared planning are likely to be the most successful both in terms of pupil and adult enjoyment and in terms of learning achieved.

Provide a clear structure

A clear structure and purpose for the planned activities for the visits, linked to pre-visit activities (including the opportunity to practise any skills they might need on the visit) and post-visit follow-up lessons enhances pupil learning. Pupils should know what to expect before they arrive and have a clear idea about what they need to focus on during their visit. Ideally they will have planned strategies for recording experiences, observations and information to take away with them.

Encouraging joint productive activity

During a visit it is helpful to have pupils working in pairs or small groups with an objective, such as a display, or some other need to report back on what has been learned. This gives a focus for and encourages dialogue with each other and with the group helper. A degree of choice in selecting displays or activities enables them to select things of greatest interest to the group and which have personal relevance to them.

Support dialogue, literacy and/or research skills

Visits where pupils are encouraged to discuss ideas and to think of follow-up research and ways to report back on their finding encourages productive dialogue during the visit and sustains interest and learning beyond it. Use can be made here of online materials provided by the centre visited or other similar places. Jarvis and Pell (2005) also suggest that sending letters home to parents telling them what is planned or what was learned can encourage discussion at home, so extending the learning further. They also recommend that teachers should review and recall learning and experiences from visits later in the year and when working on related science topics.

Making the most of a visit

One of the major factors limiting the number of experiences schools can offer outside the classroom is the cost. This was cited as the third most important factor in limiting teachers' choice in the Wellcome Trust science survey of primary teachers (Wellcome Trust, 2005). Other issues include concerns about health and safety, worries about the time taken by visits and the effect this might have on coverage of the curriculum and finally concerns that inexperienced teachers and others have about coping in very different teaching situations.

Here are some suggestion for addressing these concerns, emerging from the examples given earlier and similar experience of working out of the classroom.

Developing confidence

- Teachers who are inexperienced at managing trips should always get advice and guidance from more experienced staff, and wherever possible, should have the opportunity to accompany others as a helper in order to develop some of the skills necessary. Putting two or more classes together can help.

- Science Learning Centres provide courses on managing out of school activities and there are also the freely downloadable CPD units provided by the PSTT (see websites).

Justifying the time and keeping down the costs

- It is worth thinking about the immense value that school visits can bring to pupil learning. Once this is factored in then the funds become less difficult to prioritise.

- Transport costs can be reduced by planning trips for several classes on the same day, making use of the same bus. In some areas clusters of schools combine trips and share costs.

- The idea of Welly Walks is inexpensive and the children gain a great deal from this approach. Making use of free sites close to school, such as supermarkets, green grocers and other businesses can keep the costs to a minimum.

- There are many businesses willing to fund and otherwise support schools. Making links in this way can bring a range of benefits, particularly where longer-term relationships are established.

Health and safety concerns

- The key to safe learning outside the classroom is careful planning and taking good advice.

- As already emphasised, pre-visits are important in planning the learning. These same visits help to ensure that a risk analysis is thorough. There is a wealth of guidance including 'Health and Safety of Pupils on Educational Visits' published by the DfE and available free or to download.

- Local authorities often have an outdoor education officer, and advice on their websites, and schools should have their own policies in place.

- Most museums, hands-on science centres, national parks and other places that host school visits regularly will publish their own risk assessment which can help guide teachers in their planning.

- All those involved in a trip, or undertaking any activities outside the classroom, should be aware of the risks and the procedures to deal with any problems. This includes all helpers. For example, in the visit to the power station, the staff at the station separately from the children briefed all the helpers. This was followed up with a briefing for the children.

Summary

This chapter has considered the value to learning in general and science in particular that comes from working out of the classroom. The main points have been:

- Learning outside the classroom has significant benefits for pupil learning in terms of social, personal and academic development as individuals and as citizens.

- These values are increasingly recognised by policy-makers who actively encourage more learning outside the classroom

- As prescribed curriculum requirements are being relaxed, teachers have more freedom to provide a richer and more varied learning experience within and outside the classroom.

- Visits extend the range of human and material resources available for learning not otherwise accessible to teachers and pupils.

- Well planned visits, especially those that fit into the year planning provide the motivation for pupils to continue their learning back in school.

- There are many different types of locations available for visits, not all requiring expense.

- Careful preparation with pre-visits to plan good curriculum coverage and a rigorous risk assessment ensures a productive and enjoyable visit.

Further Reading

Adams, J. (2006) Starting out in your own backyard, *Primary Science Review*, 91: 7–10.

Davids, S. (2008) Growing faster than their sunflowers, *Primary Science*, 101: 5–8.

Dixon-Watmough, R. and Rapley, M. (2012) The Great Bug Hunt is back! *Primary Science*, 123: 24–6.

Fradley, C. (2006) Welly Walks for science learning, *Primary Science Review*, 91: 14–16.

Graham, B. (2012) Visit a farm? Surely not! *Primary Science*, 122: 15–17.

Websites

The PSTT website has a section on planning for visits to hands-on science centres
http://www.pstt.org.uk/resources/continuing-professional-development/enrich-science-learning.aspx

Department for Education (2006) *Learning Outside the Classroom Manifesto*. Available for download from https://www.education.gov.uk/publications/standard/publicationdetail/page1/DFES-04232-2006

10

Teachers' and children's questions

Introduction

Teachers' questioning practice is one of the most important factors in determining children's opportunities for developing their understanding and their inquiry skills. Three aspects of this practice are discussed in this chapter. First we look at the kinds of questions that teachers can ask to encourage children's active inquiry, and at the importance of giving sufficient time for children to answer questions. The second part deals with encouraging children to ask questions. However, when children ask questions, they have to be answered, or at least addressed in some way. This is often a worry to teachers who feel that their knowledge of science is not adequate. So in the third part we look at ways of dealing with the different kinds of questions that children ask.

Teachers' questions

Questioning is frequently mentioned in discussing the teacher's role and is perhaps the main means of finding out their ideas and of encouraging children's thinking and use of inquiry skills. In the detailed study of primary classroom interactions conducted by Galton *et al.* (1980) in the ORACLE study of 1976, questions formed 12 per cent of all the teacher behaviours observed. When the study, involving children in England at Key Stage 2 (8–11 year-olds), was repeated 20 years later, the proportion overall was 16.2 per cent. But there were significant changes in the types of questions asked. The proportion of all questions that were 'closed' increased in that time from 18.3 per cent to 34.6 per cent, which Galton *et al.* (1999) suggested was due to the larger incidence of whole-class teaching. The researchers' summary of the findings in 1998 is given in Box 10.1.

The findings reported in Box 10.1 echo other research analysing classroom discourse such as that by Alexander (1995). Occasional questioning of what the children know is expected, but it seems that far too many questions are of this type. The change that is needed is not in the number of questions asked but in their form and content. This is particularly important in a constructivist approach to learning science, where questions have an important role in finding out children's ideas and encouraging their active learning through inquiry.

Box 10.1 Questions asked by teachers

In summary, teaching in today's primary schools at Key Stage 2 is very much a matter of teachers talking and children listening. Of this talk by far the largest amount consists of teachers making statements. When questions are asked of children, these questions require them either to recall facts or to solve a problem for which their teachers expect a correct answer. Open or speculative or challenging questions, where children are required to offer more than one answer are still comparatively rare. Even in science, where the highest percentage of open question was recorded, teachers were three times more likely to require a single correct answer than they were to invite speculation.

(Galton *et al.*, 1999: 33)

Box 10.2 Open and closed questions

Open questions give access to children's views about things, their feelings and their ideas, and promote enquiry by the children. Closed questions, while still inviting thought about the learning task, require the child to respond to ideas or comments of the teacher. For example, these open questions:

   What do you notice about these crystals?

   What has happened to your bean since you planted it?

are more likely to lead to answers useful to both teacher and children than their closed versions:

   Are all the crystals the same size?

   How much has your bean grown since you planted it?

Closed questions suggest that there is a right answer and children may not attempt an answer if they are afraid of being wrong.

The form of questions

In relation to form, the important distinctions are between open and closed questions (Box 10.2) and between person-centred and subject-centred questions (Box 10.3).

When the purpose of the question is to explore children's reasons and ideas behind them, or to encourage their inquiry-based thinking, person-centred questions are clearly essential. At other times, too, they are a more effective, and a more friendly, way of involving children in discussions which help them in making sense of their work. However, a study by Smith *et al.* (2006) of the impact of the National Literacy and Numeracy Strategies in England showed that a very small proportion of questions asked were open and that pupils responses were very short – limited to three words or fewer for most of the time. The researchers concluded that:

Far from encouraging and extending pupil contributions to promote high levels of interaction and cognitive engagements, most of the questions asked were of a low cognitive level designed to funnel pupils' response towards a required answer.

(Smith *et al.*, 2006: 408)

Box 10.3 Person-centred and subject-centred questions

A *subject-centred* question asks directly about the subject matter; a *person-centred* question asks for the child's ideas about the subject matter. Subject-centred questions are such as:

Why do heavy lorries take longer to stop than lighter ones?

Why did your plant grow more quickly in the cupboard?

cannot be answered unless you know, or at least think you know, the reasons. By contrast the person-centred versions:

Why do you think heavy lorries take longer to stop than lighter ones?

Why do you think your plant grew more quickly when it was in the cupboard?

can be attempted by anyone who has been thinking about these and has some ideas about them, whether or not correct.

The prevalence of closed and subject-centred questions is not confined to England. Research in the US – where person-centred questions are described as 'authentic' and subject-centred as 'test' questions (Nystrand et al., 1997) – found the latter to be overwhelmingly predominant. 'Authentic' questions are identified as 'dialogic' (see Chapter 7) because they signal to pupils that the teacher is interested in what they think 'and not just whether they can report what someone else thinks or has said' (quoted in Alexander, 2008: 15).

The content of questions

Elstgeest (2001) distinguished between 'productive' and 'unproductive' teachers' questions. The latter are questions that ask directly for facts or reasons where there is clearly a right answer. The former are far more useful in helping children's investigation and thinking. There are different kinds of productive question, set out in Box 10.4, which serve different purposes in encouraging inquiry.

Questions for different purposes

It is evident from what has just been said that questions should be framed so that their form matches their purpose. Here are some examples of questions for different purposes.

Box 10.4 Elstgeest's types of productive questions

- *Attention-focusing questions* have the purpose of drawing children's attention to features which might otherwise be missed. 'Have you noticed ... ?' 'What do you think of that?' These questions are ones which children often supply for themselves and the teacher may have to raise them only if observation is superficial and attention fleeting.

- *Comparison questions* – 'In what ways are these leaves different?' 'What is the same about these two pieces of rock?' – draw attention to patterns and lay the foundation for using keys and categorising objects and events.

- *Measuring and counting questions* – 'How much?' 'How long?' – are particular kinds of comparison questions which take observation into the quantitative.

- *Action questions* – 'What happens if you shine light from a torch onto a worm?' 'What happens when you put an ice cube into warm water?' 'What happens if ... ' are the kinds of question which lead to investigations.

- *Problem-posing questions* give children a challenge and leave them to work out how to meet it. Questions such as 'Can you find a way to make your string telephone sound clearer?' 'How can you make a coloured shadow?' require children to have experience or knowledge which they can apply in tackling them. Without such knowledge the question may not even make sense to the children.

Questions for finding out children's ideas

The following questions were among those designed to be used by teachers to find out children's ideas in the SPACE project. They are the kinds of questions that led to the children's work presented in Chapter 5. These particular questions were used when children had been involved in handling, observing and drawing sprouting and non-sprouting potatoes (Russell and Watt, 1990: A-10):

What do you think is coming out of the potato?

What do you think is happening inside the potato?

Why do you think this is happening to the potato?

Do you think the potato plant will go on growing?

Can you think of anything else that this happens to?

They can readily be seen to be open, person-centred questions. They encouraged children to express their thoughts before starting investigations, giving teachers information about the kinds of ideas the children were bringing to their activities. We say more about these questions and their value in the context of assessment for learning in Chapter 16.

Questions for developing ideas

According to the kinds of ideas the children start from, activities to develop them may take various forms, as discussed in Chapter 11. Questions can be used to initiate children's investigation of their ideas. For example, questions of the kind:

What evidence would you need to show that your idea works?

What would show that … was better than …?

What could you do to make it even better?

require children to think through the implications of an idea and extend its application.

When the development of children's ideas seems to require further experience and comparisons between things, then attention-focusing, measuring and counting and comparison questions are the most useful. For applying ideas, the problem-posing questions are appropriate. For discussing the meaning of words, it is best to ask for examples rather than abstract definitions, through questions such as: 'Show me what you do to "dissolve" the butter', 'How will you know if the sugar has dissolved?' and other ways of introducing scientific words discussed in Chapter 7.

Questions for encouraging inquiry skills

Questions can be framed so that children have to use inquiry skills to answer them, giving the teacher the opportunity to find out how far the skills have been developed. Examples of questions relating to some inquiry skills, set in the context of children investigating a collection of different seeds, are given in Box 10.5.

Giving time for answering

Allied to the careful selection and framing of questions to promote thinking and action is the need to allow time for children to answer and to listen to their answers. Questions that ask children to think require time to answer. Teachers often expect an answer too quickly and in doing so deter children from thinking. Research shows that extending the time that a teacher waits for children to answer increases markedly the quality of the answers (Budd-Rowe, 1974). This is a case where patience is rewarded and time saved overall by spending a little more in allowing children to think about their answers before turning to someone else, or rephrasing the question. The time given for answering has become known as 'wait time' or alternatively 'thinking time' (see Box 10.6).

Later research with teachers found that increasing wait time for answering, without feeling the need to 'fill the silence' has led to

more students being involved in question-and-answer discussions and to an increase in the length of their replies. One particular way to increase participation is to ask students to brainstorm ideas, perhaps in pairs, for two or three minutes before the teacher asks for contributions. This allows the students to voice their ideas, hear other ideas and articulate a considered answer rather than jumping in to utter the first thing that comes into their head in the hope that it is what the teacher is seeking.

(Black *et al.*, 2003: 35)

Box 10.5 Questions encouraging particular inquiry skills

Observing

- What do you notice that is the same about these seeds?
- What differences do you notice between seeds of the same kind?
- How could you tell the difference between them with your eyes closed?
- What difference do you see when you look at them using the lens?

Predicting

- What do you think the seeds will grow into?
- What do you think would make them grow faster?
- What do you think will happen if they have water without soil?
- What do you think will happen if we give them more (or less) water/light/warmth?

Planning

- What will you need to do to find out ... (if the seeds need soil to grow)?
- How will you make it fair (to be sure that it is the soil and not something else which is making the seeds grow)?
- What equipment will you need?
- What will you look for to find out the result?

Interpreting

- Did you find any connection between ... (how fast the plant grew and the amount of water/light/warmth it had)?
- Is there any connection between the size of the seed planted and the size of the plant?
- What made a difference to how fast the seeds began to grow?

Responding to children's answers

As Alexander points out:

There's little point in framing a well-conceived question and giving children ample 'wait time' to answer it, if we fail to engage with the answer they give and hence with the understanding or misunderstanding which that answer reveals.

(Alexander, 2008: 25)

Box 10.6 'Wait time'

In 1974 Mary Budd-Rowe published significant research on teachers' questions in elementary science classes in the USA. She reported that teachers waited on average less than one second after asking a question before intervening again if no answer was forthcoming. Teachers tended to rephrase the question or ask a different one that the children could answer more quickly – invariably making the question more closed and fact-related. Research in the UK confirmed that this situation was far from being confined to American classrooms.

Budd-Rowe found that when teachers were advised to increase the 'wait time' after asking questions requiring explanations, the children's answers were longer and more confident. Also:

- the failure to answer decreased

- children challenged, added to or modified each other's answers

- children offered more alternative explanations.

Several different ways of responding to children's answers are described by Mercer (2000). Common ones used in the primary classroom are illustrated in the exchange in Box 10.7, reported by Fitzgerald (2012).

The teacher conducts the question and answer session by calling on each pupil to answer her, allowing, in this exchange, no pupil–pupil interaction. Her response to children's answers is to accept them with an approving comment ('fantastic', 'great', 'that's interesting'), even when the response needs to be clarified (in what way does Naomi think a shadow is like a reflection?). Such automatic praise for giving an answer, no matter what, can easily deter careful thinking and lower expectations. Similarly, repeating a child's answer ('They're grey' and 'Bit like a reflection') is not particularly useful unless it leads to clarification. Although,

---

Box 10.7 Responding to children's answers

Teacher : Tell me what you know about shadows. Anything that you know about shadows at all. Ruby?

Ruby: You can never catch your shadow.

Teacher: Oh, that's interesting. We're going to test that in a minute, Ruby. Keisha?

Keisha: They're grey.

Teachers : They're grey? OK. So you're talking about colour. Fantastic, Keisha. Naomi?

Naomi: They're like a reflection.

Teacher: Bit like a reflection. Oh, Naomi is trying to use from science words. Great. Rachel?

Rachel: It changes shape and size when the Sun moves.

Teacher: Oh, fantastic. Thank you, Rachel. Yolanda?

Yolanda : The Sun has to be shining so that you can see it.

Teacher: Very good …

(Fitzgerald, 2012: 77–8)

---

in this example, the teacher was gaining useful information about the children's ideas, she was missing the opportunity to advance their thinking.

Children's questions

Asking questions is an important means for both adults and children to try to understand the things around them. When engrossed in the study of something new we use our existing knowledge to make sense of it and try out the ideas we already have to see if they fit. When we find a gap between what we already know and making sense of something new, one way of trying to bridge it is to ask questions. We might do this immediately by asking a question if there is an authority present, as might happen at an exhibition, on a guided tour, or in a class or lecture. At other times the question may remain unspoken but guides us to a source of information which is then more efficiently used because we know what ideas or information we are looking for.

But we all, adults and children alike, ask a number of different kinds of question as well as those seeking information or ideas. Some questions are rhetorical and some just show interest; neither of these expects an answer. Some questions are asked to establish a relationship with someone, or to gain a response; some to attract attention; some even to irritate or harass (as in Parliaments).

Children's questions that arise from curiosity and the desire to understand have a key part to play in learning science. However, it is important not to discourage any questions by implying that only some are worth answering. At the same time, while we recognise the value to children of encouraging the expression of their questions, including the vague and unspoken ones, it is helpful to their learning if they begin to recognise the kinds of questions which can be addressed through scientific inquiry.

Children who realise that they can find out answers to 'what, how and why' questions by their own interaction with things around have made the best start they can in scientific development. They realise that the answer to 'Why do daisies spread out their leaves?' 'Why do paper tissues have three thin layers rather than one thick one?' 'What happens when you turn a mirror upside-down?' are to be found directly from observations and actions on the daisies, the tissues, the mirror.

Encouraging children's questions

The importance of children's questions means that the classroom should foster the curiosity from which they arise. Here are some ways of doing this:

- Provide plenty of interesting materials for children to explore.
- Make provision for children to bring into the classroom material and objects they find interesting, since what intrigues them is likely to be shared by other children.
- Set up a 'question corner' or a 'question of the week' activity where there are materials to stimulate inquiry that might be incorporated into class work.

Box 10.8 A stimulating display of familiar things

A display of different tools, nuts and bolts and screws was set up with a 'question box' enabling children to post their questions on small pieces of paper. The apparently gender-biased subject matter in fact produced no bias in the interest and questions the display stimulated. When the box was opened and each question considered, girls were as ready as boys to come up with reasons for different sizes and shapes of heads of screws, why screws had threads but nails did not or whether the length of the handle of a screw driver made any difference. They followed up some suggestions through practical investigations and others were left pinned to the display board awaiting information from an 'expert'. The work added considerably to their experience of materials and their properties as well as showing that questions were valued.

- While introducing new or unusual things to stimulate curiosity, provide familiar materials as well (see Box 10.8).
- Encourage children to question as well as to report what they have done and say what they don't understand.
- More generally, and importantly, regularly extend the invitation 'what question would you like to ask about ...' either orally or in writing on work-cards or worksheets.
- And, resist the temptation, as a teacher, to do all the question raising

Handling children's questions

Despite the value to children's learning of encouraging their questions, many teachers are worried about answering children's questions and, perhaps unconsciously, adopt classroom strategies that reduce opportunities for children to ask questions. So if questioning is to be encouraged, being able to handle the questions that children raise has high priority.

Fortunately handling questions is a skill which can readily be developed. It requires thought about the kind of question being asked, about the likely motive for asking it and knowledge of how to turn a question into one which can be a useful starting point for investigation. The word 'handle', rather than 'answer', is used deliberately here. One of the first things to realise – perhaps with some relief – is that at times it is better not to answer children's questions directly (even if the teacher does know the answer). But it depends on the question which is asked and so we look now at what is appropriate for different types of question.

Responding to different types of question

Most questions that children ask fall into five groups:

- Comments that are expressed as questions but which require a response that is not an answer.

- Philosophical questions that have no answer that scientific inquiry can provide.
- Requests for simple facts such as names or definitions.
- Requests for explanations that would be too complex for children to understand.
- Requests for explanations that children could find through inquiry.

Here are some suggestions of how to handle these different types. But the first step is to identify the type of question and, if this is not clear, ask the children to clarify or rephrase what they want to know.

Comments expressed as questions

These are questions which children ask when they are intrigued or excited. The questions don't really need to be answered but there has to be some response which acknowledges the stimulus which gave rise to the question. For example, here is how an infants' teacher handled a question from a 6 year old when she and a group of children were examining a bird's nest:

Child: How do they weave it?
Teacher: They're very clever ...
Child: Birds are very clever with their beaks
Child: Nobody would ever think they were because they're so small
Teacher: Yes, it's wonderful isn't it? If we turn this right round and let you have a look at this side ...

The child's question was used to maintain the close observation of the nest and a sense of wonder. The teacher might have replied 'Look carefully and see if you can tell how it is done?' but perhaps she judged that this was too early a stage in the exploration for focusing on one aspect, but her response leaves open the possibility of returning to the subject in this vein if the children's interest is still there. Another way of putting this is that she judged the question to be a way of expressing wonder rather than a genuine query. In effect, the child might just as easily have said 'Look at how it's woven!'

Philosophical questions

This is another category of questions to which the response has to be of the 'yes, isn't it interesting/intriguing' kind, sharing the wondering behind the question. 'Why do we have birds and all different things like that?' is such a question. Taken at face value the only answer is to say that there is no answer. However, we should not read too much into the exact words children use. They often phrase questions as 'why' questions, making them sound philosophical, when the answer they are wanting is much more related to 'what makes it happen' rather than 'why does it happen'. When children's questions seem philosophical the initial step is to ask them to explain their question. It may well then turn into a question in a different category, but if not it should be treated as an interesting question but one to which no one can give a definite answer.

Requests for simple facts

These are questions which satisfy the urge to name, to know, to identify. These are questions to which there are simple factual answers which may help the children to give a context to their experience and their ideas, as for example, in Box 10.9, about the bird's eggs. The teacher may know the answers and if so there is no point in withholding them.

Requests for names of things fall into this category, as do definitions which arise in questions such as 'Is coal a kind of rock?' While names can be supplied if they are known, undue attention should not be given to them. Often children simply want to know that things do have a name and, knowing this, they are satisfied. If work requires something to be named and no one knows the proper name at that moment then children can be invited to make up a name to use. 'Shiny cracked rock', 'long thin stem with umbrella', 'speedy short brown creature' will actually be more useful in talking about things observed in the field than their scientific or common names. Later the 'real' names can be gradually substituted.

Some requests for simple facts cannot be answered. Young children often have a view of their teacher as knowing everything and it is necessary to help them to realise that this is not the case. When the children asked 'Where are the birds now, the ones who built the nest?' they were expecting a simple question to have a simple answer. In this case the teacher judged that the kind of answer they wanted was 'They've probably made their home in another shed, but I really don't know

---

Box 10.9 Questions about nests and eggs

The children looking at the bird's nest asked 'Where did it come from?' 'What kind of stuff is this that it's made of?' 'How long do the eggs take to hatch?' In this case the teacher knew where the nest had come from and helped the children identify the 'stuff' as hair. But for the length of hatching she did not have the knowledge and the conversation ran on as follows:

Teacher:	Well, you've asked me a question that I can't answer – how many days it would take – but there's a way that you could find out, do you know how?
Child:	Watch it...
Child:	A bird watcher...
Child:	A book.
Teacher:	Yes, this is something you can look up in a book and when you've found out...
Child:	*(who had rushed to pick up the book by the display of the nest)* ... I've got one here, somewhere.
Child :	... here, here's a page about them.
Teacher :	There we are ...

The children were engrossed in the stages of development of a chick inside an egg for some time. The question was answered and more was learned besides. Had the book not been so readily available the teacher could have suggested that either she or the children could look for the information and report back on another day.

---

for sure' rather than an account of all the possibilities, including migration and whether or not birds tend to stay in the same neighbourhood. A straight 'I don't know' answer helps children to realise the kinds of questions that cannot have answers as well as that their teacher is a human and not a superhuman being.

Questions requiring complex answers

Apart from the brief requests for facts, most questions children ask can be answered at a variety of levels of complexity. Take 'Why is the sky blue?' for example. There are many levels of 'explanation' from those based on the scattering of light of different wavelengths to those relating to the absence of clouds. Questions such as 'Why is soil brown?' 'Why do some birds build nests in trees and others on the ground?' 'How do aeroplanes stay up in the air?' fall into this category.

They seem the most difficult for teachers to answer. The difficulty lies in the fact that many teachers do not know the answers and those who do will realise that children could not understand the answers. There is no need to be concerned, whichever group you fall into, because the worst thing to do in either case is to attempt to answer these questions!

It is sometimes more difficult for the teacher who does know the scientific explanation to resist the temptation to give it than to persuade the teacher who does not know not to feel guilty about not being able to answer. Giving complex answers to children who cannot understand them is underlining for them that science is a subject of facts to memorise that you don't expect to understand. If their questions are repeatedly met by answers which they do not understand the children will cease to ask questions. This would be damaging, for these questions particularly drive their learning.

So what can be done instead of answering them? A good answer is given by Sheila Jelly in Box 10.10. Turning questions in this way enables teachers to treat difficult questions seriously but without providing answers beyond children's understanding. It also indicates to children that they can go a long way to finding answers through their own investigation, thus underlining the implicit messages about the nature of scientific activity and their ability to answer questions by inquiry.

Questions which can lead to investigation by children

Teachers looking for opportunities for children to explore and investigate will find these are the easiest questions to deal with. The main problems are: resisting the urge to give the answer because it may seem so evident (to the teacher but not the child); and storing such questions when they pop up at an inconvenient time.

Questions which can be profitably investigated by children will come up at various times, often times which are inconvenient for embarking on investigations. Although they can't be taken up at that moment the question should be discussed enough to turn them into investigations and then, depending on the age of the children, picked up some time later. Some kind of note has to be made and this can usefully be kept publicly as a list of 'things to investigate' on the classroom wall, or just kept privately by the teacher. For younger children

> **Box 10.10** 'Turning' complex questions to find related investigable ones
>
> The teaching skill involved is the ability to 'turn' the questions. Consider, for example, a situation in which children are exploring the properties of fabrics. They have dropped water on different types and become fascinated by the fact that water stays 'like a little ball' on felt. They tilt the felt, rolling the ball around, and someone asks 'Why is it like a ball?' How might the question be turned by applying the 'doing more to understand' approach? We need to analyse the situation quickly and use what I call a 'variables scan'. The explanation must relate to something 'going on' between the water and the felt surface so causing the ball. That being so, ideas for children's activities will come if we consider ways in which the situation could be varied to better understand the making of the ball. We could explore surfaces, keeping the drop the same, and explore drops, keeping the surface the same. These thoughts can prompt others that bring ideas nearer to what children might do.
>
> (Jelly, 2001: 44, 45)

the time delay in taking up the investigations has to be kept short – a matter of days – but the investigations are also likely to be short and so can be fitted into a programme more easily. Older children can retain interest over a longer period – a week or two – during which the required time and materials can be built into the planned programme.

The five categories of questions and ways of handling them are summarised in Figure 10.1.

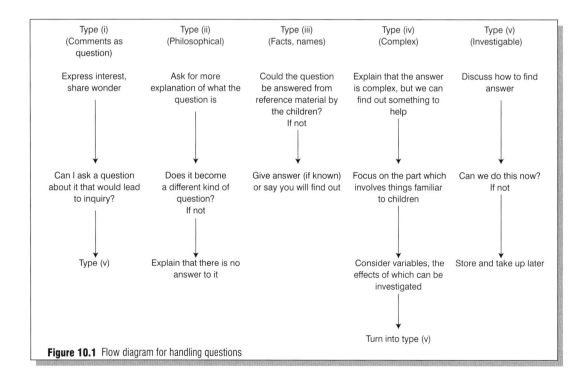

Figure 10.1 Flow diagram for handling questions

Summary

This chapter has concerned issues relating to questions: questions asked by teachers, ways of encouraging children's questions and ways of handling the questions that children ask. The main points have been:

- Research in England shows that teachers ask many more 'closed' than open questions and the difference has increased coinciding with an increase in the amount of whole-class teaching from 1976 to 1996.

- The form and content of questions should match their purpose and the kind of response that the teacher is seeking from the child (attention, action, problem-solving, etc.).

- When teachers ask questions that require thoughtful answers, children need time to think about their answers.

- Teachers should avoid responding to children's answers by uncritical praise or repetition in a formulaic way which fails to advance or clarify their ideas.

- Children's questions are valuable for a number of reasons: they show the gaps that the children feel they need to fill in their understanding; they can provide the basis for children's investigations; and they give children the opportunity to realise that they can find things out for themselves and satisfy their curiosity.

- Teachers can encourage children to raise questions by providing interesting and thought-provoking materials in the classroom, mechanisms for inviting questions, such as a question box, and an atmosphere that welcomes and encourages questioning.

- Children will ask all kinds of questions and not just those which can lead to investigations. In order not to deter questioning, teachers need to be able to handle these different kinds. The first step in doing this is to recognise the type of question so that the appropriate response can be given.

Further reading

Elstgeest, J. (2001) The right question at the right time, in W. Harlen (ed.) *Primary Science: Taking the Plunge,* 2nd edn, Portsmouth, NH: Heinemann.

Galton, M., Hargreaves, L., Comber, C., Wall, D., and Pell, T. (1999) Changes in patterns of teacher interaction in the primary classroom: 1976–96, *British Educational Research Journal*, 25(1): 23–37.

Goldsworthy, A. (2011) Effective questions, in W. Harlen (ed.) *ASE Guide to Primary Science Education,* new edn, Hatfield: ASE, 69–76.

Jelly, S.J. (2001) Helping children raise questions – and answering them, in W. Harlen *Primary Science: Taking the Plunge,* 2nd edn, Portsmouth, NH: Heinemann, 36–47.

11

Helping development of scientific understanding

Introduction

This chapter is concerned with the action that teachers can take to help children's progress in developing scientific ideas. It is now well established that by the time they come to the classroom children have already formed ideas about the things they have encountered and it is important to take these as the starting point. Some key characteristics of these ideas were identified in Chapter 5. Here we revisit them and suggest strategies teachers can use for helping children to develop more scientific ideas, that is, ideas supported by evidence and widely shared in the scientific community. Since the process of forming 'bigger' and more scientific ideas, as discussed in Chapter 6, depends on the use of inquiry skills, the development of these skills is a key factor in developing understanding and will be considered in Chapter 12.

Starting from children's ideas

Progression in scientific ideas

Whilst it is clear that we need to take children's ideas seriously and use them as the start for developing more scientific ideas, we need also to be clear about where we are going. Although various curricula and programmes indicate the content that children should encounter at different stages, it is sometimes difficult to see how these combine into a coherent progression in ideas. So before looking at specific actions that can be taken, it is helpful to have an overview of the general direction of change. What is it that we call 'progression' in ideas? In what ways are 'big' ideas different from 'small' ones? Thus we begin with the overall patterns that describe progress from limited 'small' and sometimes unscientific ideas towards 'bigger' ideas that help understanding of the world around us.

From 'small' to 'bigger' ideas
A major aim of science education is to help children develop 'big' ideas. A 'big' idea in science is one that applies to a range of related objects or phenomena, whilst what we might call 'small' ideas apply to particular observations or

experiences. 'Worms can live in soil because they can slither through small spaces and can eat things that are in the soil' is an idea that applies to worms only. It is transformed to a bigger idea when it is linked to other ideas, such as 'fish can live in water because they can breathe through their gills and find food there', to form an idea that can apply to all animals. Eventually this idea may be linked to ideas about the habitats of plants, to become an even bigger idea about living things in general, that organisms have evolved over very long periods of time to function in certain conditions.

From descriptive to explanatory ideas
Children's early experiences build up their knowledge of what is there, what is happening in the world around them, as opposed to explaining why. Through identifying and naming common animals and plants they learn that there are different kinds of living things that are found in different places. Later, their ideas provide explanation. For example, that because living things need energy from food as well as air, water and certain temperature conditions, they are found in places that provide the particular conditions each requires. This aspect of progress is seen in the development of models that explain what is found in the surrounding world.

From personal to shared ideas
It is characteristic of young children to look at things from one point of view – their own – and this is reflected in their ideas. These are based on their personal experience and their interpretation of it. As children become older and willing to share how they see and how they explain things, their ideas are influenced by those of others, including their teacher, other adults and other children. Thus ideas are constructed on the basis of social and educational interactions as well as their own thinking.

Through becoming aware of others' ideas and sharing their own, children negotiate meaning for their experiences and for the words that are used to communicate them (such as 'habitat'). In this way children derive assurance that their understanding is shared by others. It is central to learning in science that children have access to the views of others and to the scientific view, but at the same time retain ownership of their own developing understanding.

From concrete to abstract ideas
This dimension of progression follows from the 'growth' of ideas resulting from using an idea derived from previous experience to try to explain a new experience, as suggested in the model of learning introduced in Chapter 6 and represented in Figure 6.2 (p. 93). The more related phenomena and events an idea can explain the bigger it becomes. As an idea grows it is expressed in more abstract terms – as when ideas related to pushes, pulls and twists are encompassed in ideas about 'force'.

Developing understanding

These overall dimensions of progress are the kind of changes that it is helpful to have in mind and to encourage in children whatever the content of their activities. However, there is an important consequence of looking at the development of ideas as a progression. It implies that what it means to 'understand' something will change in the course of children's learning. Explanations and even descriptions of events and phenomena will be given in different ways at different points in learning.

Understanding is not, then, something that a learner either has or has not. Its meaning constantly changes. At certain points all of us may have had the experience of thinking that we understand something, then something comes along to challenge this and we have to develop a new understanding. So it is with children, they understand to the extent that the ideas they have fit their experience and help them to explain things around them. But when their experience is extended, as it will be through experiences in daily life as well as through planned encounters at school, understanding may require change in their ideas of how things work or what they are. So we should try to ensure that their ideas keep pace with the change in experience.

Developing ideas to keep pace with expanding experience does not make earlier ideas 'wrong'. But it is important to distinguish between ideas that are limited and incomplete, but nevertheless productive in providing a basis for further learning, and those that are inaccurate and unproductive because they inhibit progress. It is useful to have these points in mind as we now look at ways of encouraging development of ideas.

Strategies for developing children's ideas

In Chapter 5 we looked at some examples from research into children's ideas. Although these ideas are different from the scientific ways of thinking about the phenomena involved, it is not difficult to see why children come to hold them. They result from children trying to make sense of events and phenomena using their own limited experience and thinking. We also referred to research that indicates that these ideas should not be ignored. Ideas that children have worked out for themselves make sense to them and will not be replaced by simply giving them the scientific view. A child has to realise that the scientific ideas are more useful than his or her own for helping understanding of what is going on.

Some general characteristics of children's ideas were set out in Box 5.1 (p. 87). We now take up the matter of how to help children to use more scientific ideas in the way they understand the world around – 'more scientific' meaning ideas that fit a wider range of experiences. Each of the characteristics of children's ideas, briefly identified in the left-hand column of Box 11.1, indicates some action that could help children to change their thinking. In the right-hand column are some suggestions for action.

Not surprisingly, given the interdependence of ideas and inquiry skills, some of the strategies involve development of inquiry skills, linking to Chapter 12.

Box 11.1 Strategies matched to the characteristics of children's own ideas

Characteristic	Strategies for development
Ideas are based on (inevitably) limited experience.	Give experience selected to show that things can behave contrary to the child's idea, e.g. that heavy things can float, seeds can germinate without soil.
Children may hold on to their ideas despite contrary evidence if they have no access to an alternative view that makes sense to them.	Scaffold the introduction of alternative ideas. Ask children to consider evidence in relation to other ideas than their own – from information sources or other children. Encourage application of new ideas.
Children base their ideas on the appearance of change rather than on the whole process.	Encourage attention to what happens during a change and not just at the start and end, e.g. to observe closely whether anything has been added or taken away when a quantity appears to change.
Younger children, particularly, focus on one feature as an explanation.	Encourage observation of other factors that might also explain why something happens, e.g. that plants need light (and sometimes heat) as well as water.
Their reasoning may not be scientific.	Help them to develop the inquiry skills to find and use relevant evidence (see Chapter 12).
Their ideas are tied to particular instances and not connected to other contexts where they could apply.	Refer to other contexts in which the same idea is applicable, e.g. is there something vibrating in a wind instrument that produces sound just as the vibration of a drum skin?
They may use words without a grasp of their meaning.	Find out what they mean by a word through asking for examples; give examples and non-examples of what words mean and introduce scientific words along with children's own expressions (see Chapter 7).
Their representations reflect a generalised idea of an object rather than observed details.	Help children to identify differences between, for instance, different kinds of trees, flowers, boats, or other vehicles.

Some are actions that can be taken in the course of children's work without introducing new experiences (for instance, the discussion of the words the children are using). Others require more planning to provide new experiences as the subject for children's inquiry.

1. Extending children's experience

Extending the range of types of material, living things, and events in children's experience is a central purpose of primary science activities. Sometimes this new experience is enough in itself to challenge existing ideas and prompts children to be more cautious in their generalisations. It can change generalisations to more guarded statements:

- almost all wood floats (not ebony or lignum vitae);
- most conifers are evergreen (but not all);
- sound travels through the air (and through solids and liquids as well).

These are not only matters of definition but also matters of explanation, when used, for example, to 'explain' that something floats because it is made of wood.

Often children's ideas indicate the experience that is lacking. For example, the quite common idea that rust forms inside metals and leaks out on to the surface (see Figure 5.12, p. 85) can be challenged by cutting through a rusty nail. It is more difficult to provide more relevant experience of things that cannot be directly seen by the children; the insides of living things and of themselves, for instance. This is where visits outside the classroom, particularly to science centres and interactive displays in museums, can play a really special part in children's learning.

Interactive museums or science centres often have curriculum-related exhibits that are designed to take into account children's ideas and find intriguing ways of challenging and advancing them. For example, in a science centre for 3–12 year olds, the staff designed an exhibit about the human skeleton which takes into account research about young children's ideas of the bones in their body. This shows that children may view their body as a 'bag of bones' or as having strings of many small bones which could not provide support (see Figure 11.1). The interactive exhibit that was produced enabled a child to sit on and pedal a stationary bicycle which was next to a large sheet of glass that acted as a mirror. When the child begins to pedal and looks at the image of his or her legs in the glass, a skeleton is superimposed on this image, showing the moving bones in the legs. This experience was found to have a much greater impact on children's ideas about bones in the body than classroom lessons about the human skeleton (Guichard, 1995).

Information from other sources can also be found from the websites that museums and various industries and organisations set up to help education, and from CD-ROMs. The children's ideas about what is inside the egg (p. 80) will no doubt be changed by access to photographs of the development of egg embryos and discussion of other evidence of the changes in form and in size that take place in the reproduction of all living things, to be found in books or CD-ROMs. More and more industries and commercial organisations have education sections which give children learning opportunities that cannot be provided in the classroom, as in case studies in Chapter 3. Ideas about the origins and processing of food can be developed by visits to a farm or dairy or a supermarket (see Chapter 9).

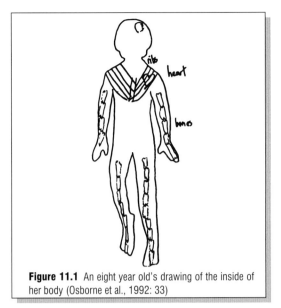

Figure 11.1 An eight year old's drawing of the inside of her body (Osborne et al., 1992: 33)

Experiences of these kinds become the 'new experience' leading to the development of ideas, as represented in Figure 6.2 (p. 93). As children use their initial ideas in investigating them they find these ideas inconsistent with the evidence from the new experience. They need to be able to consider different ideas, leading us to the next strategy in Box 11.1.

2. Introducing new ideas

While we can often see how to challenge children's unscientific ideas, it is not always clear how they find more scientific ones to replace them. There is an important role for the teacher here; one which has, perhaps, been underplayed in discussing constructivist approaches to learning (which sometimes gives the impression that children will arrive at new ideas through thinking about new experience for themselves). It is also a subtle role, since we must avoid giving the 'right' answer that children have to accept whether or not it makes sense to them. We have to ensure that the new ideas are taken into the children's own thinking. In order to do this, children need

- access to ideas different from their own;
- support in trying out the new ideas in relation to their existing experience;
- opportunities to apply them to new experiences.

Here are some suggestions for how these can be provided.

Access to different ideas
New ideas need not necessarily be introduced by the teacher. They can also come from books, the internet, CD-ROMs, videos and from people who visit

the classroom or places that are visited by the children. Other children are often a source of different ideas and these may include ideas that are closer to the scientific view than the ideas of a particular child. Whatever the source, children are likely to need encouragement and support while trying out new ideas.

Analogies and models may provide the new idea that children need in order to understand something. The difference between a model and an analogy is discussed by Maloney and Curtis (2012) who define an analogy as a 'word model', and use the word 'model' for a physical representation. However, the two terms are often used interchangeably. Analogies can provide a link between one situation (A, which a child wants to understand) and another (B, more familiar) which is thought to illustrate the idea or process in action in A. For instance, it is common to illustrate the water cycle (A) using a boiling kettle and condensing the water vapour on a cold surface (B). The problem for the children is making the link between the pieces of equipment in A and B. As a consequence, the kettle often ends up in a child's representation of how rain is formed from clouds in the sky!

Often the models which adults think up to represent difficult concepts, such as water flow in pipes as an analogy of flow of electricity in a circuit, can cause more problems in understanding the analogous situation in the first place. A small-scale research (Jabin and Smith, 1994), which involved trying different analogies for electric circuits, seemed to show that it was the effort made to create a link with something already familiar to the children which had an effect rather than the nature of any particular analogy. Asoko and DeBoo (2001), presenting a collection of analogies used in primary science, warn that analogies can introduce irrelevant or misleading features and may be as difficult to understand as the phenomenon they are supposed to explain.

Support in trying new ideas
This is where 'scaffolding' new ideas comes in (see Box 11.2).

Scaffolding is particularly important in relation to ideas which cannot be tested out in practice. It is difficult, for example, for children to understand that, if a moving object stops, there must be a force acting to stop it. Many children accept or offer the reason as being 'friction' but don't go as far as realising that without friction the object would not stop moving. Scaffolding is necessary here, just as it is in relation to ideas about the Earth in space, the causes of day and night, the seasons, and phases of the Moon (see Lisa's scaffolding of these ideas in Chapter 3). These are cases where the teacher may have to lead children to take a few steps without realising why until they can look back. For example, children are unlikely to decide on their own to make a model of the Sun, Moon and Earth to explain why we see the moon in different phases. So the teacher takes the initiative and sets up the situation that enables the children to 'see' a spherical object looking like a half-moon and then they can make the connection.

Opportunities to try out new ideas in different situations
Given that the new idea is a scientific one, it should help children make sense of further experience. Helping children to do this will secure the new idea in their

---

Box 11. 2 Scaffolding children's ideas and skills

Scaffolding means supporting children in considering an idea or a way of testing an idea that they have not proposed themselves but are capable of making 'their own'. The judgement of when this is likely to be possible has to be made by the teacher, taking into account the existing ideas or skills of the children and how far they are from taking the next step. It often means the teacher making links for the children between experiences and understanding they already have but have not linked up for themselves.

In theoretical terms, it means finding what Vygotsky (1978) introduced as the 'zone of potential development'. This is the point just beyond existing ideas, where the learner is likely to be able to use new ideas with help. What the teacher does in scaffolding is to suggest the new idea and provide support for the children while they use it and, finding it helps to make sense, begin to incorporate it into their thinking. The teacher might ask children to 'Try this idea' or 'Try looking at it this way' or 'Suppose ...' An example might be 'Suppose the water that disappears from the puddle goes into the air?' or 'Suppose the Sun is not moving but the Earth is turning round ...' Each of the 'supposed' ideas can be used to make a prediction that can be tested and as a result children can see that they do help to explain experience.

Scaffolding can be used to develop skills, too. It is indeed familiar in teaching new skills such as using a microscope or a calculator. In these cases the learner needs first to be told what to do, may need a reminder later and eventually uses the skill confidently.

It is important to underline that scaffolding ideas is not the same as telling children the 'right answer'. It is essentially enabling children to take a further step in progress that is within their reach. It depends on teachers having a good knowledge of their children's ideas and skills and using this in deciding the next steps and helping children to advance their thinking.

thinking as well as expanding their understanding of things around them. It also gives the teacher the opportunity to see how secure the new idea really is. It may be necessary to stop and return to familiar ground if the signs are that the new idea is still a little wobbly. However, if new ideas can be successfully applied, this brings a feeling of enjoyment and satisfaction in learning. For example:

- Can eclipses be explained in terms of the movement of the Moon round the Earth and the Earth round the Sun?

- Can the ideas about reducing friction be used to explain why ice skates have knife-edged blades?

3. Developing reasoning about changes in appearance

Some of the well-known, and often replicated, results of Piaget's investigations with children showed that young children may judge by appearance rather than reasoning about when a quantity of a material has changed. A child might claim that, for example, there is more in a lump of clay after it has been squashed out than when it is in a ball. Learning that things are not always what they seem to be is important in science. Reasoning often has to overcome appearance, as for instance when salt or sugar dissolves in water and appear to have vanished. The action that the teacher can take is to draw attention to the whole process of change, to reverse it where possible (as with the clay) and provide some evidence that will overcome the visual sensation of change.

4. Encouraging attention to more than one factor

Another feature of young children's thinking, related to the one just discussed, is that it is unidimensional. One view of things, or one factor, is considered when there are others that need to be considered to explain particular phenomena. This shows, for instance, in children saying that plants need water or light to grow, but not both and rarely adding air or heat. There are very many ideas in science that involve a combination of factors (such as the meaning of something being 'alive') so it is important to encourage children to think in terms of all possible factors and not just the first that comes to mind. Having children brainstorm in groups about, for example, what we need to maintain good health, will not only gather more ideas but help them to realise that a combination of factors is involved.

5. Developing children's inquiry skills

The model of developing understanding through inquiry, in Figure 6.2 (p. 93), shows that inquiry skills have a determining role in what ideas emerge from the process. Unless these skills are carried out in a scientific manner the resulting ideas may be unscientific in the sense of not reflecting the evidence. Ways of helping children develop skills of finding and using relevant evidence are discussed in Chapter 12.

6. Creating links between events with a common explanation

Children develop ideas about events in terms of the particular features of those events. These are 'small' ideas, fitted to each particular instance and not joined up even though there is a shared explanation. For example, children commonly explain the disappearance of water from puddles only in terms of draining away through the ground, while they may explain the drying of damp clothes on a washing line in terms of some action of the air. The children could be helped to link these two: could the air have something to do with the puddle drying up, too? Some investigations, testing this idea in relation to puddles, could make this a useful idea in both situations. Further examples of water disappearing could then be drawn into the range of things explained in this way. The idea has then become one that applies more widely, that is, it has become a bigger one.

In other cases the small ideas are ones that refer to different aspects of a phenomenon, and need to be brought together. For instance understanding why thing don't fall off the side of the Earth means bringing together the ideas that:

- things fall downwards;
- the Earth is spherical;
- 'down' means towards the centre of the Earth.

Another example is putting together ideas about light and how we see to understand the formation of images in mirrors or lenses. This depends on understanding that:

- we see an object when light from it enters our eyes;
- putting a mirror or lens between the object and our eyes changes the path of the light;
- we interpret the path of the light as a straight line from the object to the eye.

If all these ideas are understood it may be possible to bring them together to realise that the eye does not 'see' the change in direction that the mirror or lens has caused and so interprets it as if it came in a straight line, so the object is interpreted as in a different place than it really is.

7. Discussing the meaning of words

Suggestions of ways of introducing scientific vocabulary to children and finding out the meaning they attach to words can be found in Chapter 7 (pp. 113–115).

8. Discussing children's drawings

It is significant that we learn a great deal about children's ideas from how they represent objects and events in their drawing. It is no accident that much of the evidence of children's ideas collected in the SPACE project and the examples in Chapter 5 take the form of drawings. Part of children's development in representation is drawing something that is more like a generic symbol for an object than an attempt to produce a picture of a particular object. Drawing a lollipop tree (Figure 5.14) is an example, but it may also indicate the conception of a tree as a trunk with leaves. To develop the concept of a tree as something more than this requires more experience and discussion of real objects and the help of a teacher in developing the skills needed to represent observed details (Morgan, n.d.). Computer programs that enable children to draw (and change their drawings more easily than on paper) can also help (Williamson, 2006).

Selecting strategies for helping progression in ideas

It is not until teachers take steps to find out children's ideas (in ways discussed in Chapter 16) that they can decide what is the appropriate action to take. The appropriate action can be decided by diagnosing the shortcomings of the children's ideas and selecting from the kinds of strategies that we have discussed. This requires, of course that we pay attention to children's ideas and take them seriously.

Summary

This chapter has described some general trends in the development of children's ideas about the world around them. The notion of progression has been described in terms of moving from 'small' to 'big' ideas, from description to explanation, from personal ideas to shared ideas and from concrete to abstract. It has noted that the meaning of 'understanding' something changes as ideas progress.

Some strategies for helping children's progression in scientific ideas have been suggested, matched to the particular characteristics of the ideas that children initially hold. The main points have been:

- It is important to start from the ideas that children have in trying to help their progress towards more scientific ones.

- A range of different strategies can be used to help development, the selection depending on the nature of the ideas that children hold.

- There are many sources of alternative ideas for children to test, including other children as well as information sources.

- When alternative ideas are introduced, the teacher should scaffold their use and give opportunity for application in a variety of contexts.

Further reading

Asoko, H. and DeBoo, M. (2001) *Analogies and Illustrations: Representing Ideas in Primary Science,* Hatfield: ASE.

Russell, T. (2011) Progression in learning science, in W. Harlen, (ed.) *ASE Guide to Primary Science Education,* new edn, Hatfield: ASE, 17–24.

12

Helping development of inquiry skills

Introduction

In Chapter 6 we showed that inquiry skills have a central role in the development of scientific understanding. We noted that, if these skills are not well developed, relevant evidence may not be gathered, or some evidence may be disregarded. As a result, preconceptions may be confirmed when they should be challenged. So the question of how to help development of skills, which we take up in this chapter, is an important one. As in the discussion on development of scientific ideas, we first consider the overall development of inquiry skills and suggest three dimensions of progress that apply across the skills. Then we consider the action that teachers can take to help the development in the four groups of skills identified in Chapter 6. These are skills concerned with: setting up investigations; collecting data; drawing conclusions; and reporting, reflecting and applying. Finally we note the contribution of scientific inquiry to the development of cross-curricular skills needed for thinking and continued learning throughout life.

Inquiry skills and the development of understanding

In the case studies in Chapter 3 the teachers collected materials (ice, balls, soil samples, models) or took children to an environment (or created it in school) for children to explore and observe. Their observations were focused by a question – often starting with a 'which is best' question or a 'what is going on here' question and leading to a 'how do we find out' question. The children's ideas based on earlier experience led them to suggest answers and their teachers encouraged them to gather more information which enabled the children to test their ideas. This was followed by interpreting their results, drawing conclusions and by communicating and reflecting on what they found. The understanding emerging from the inquiry, as noted in Chapter 6, depends on what and how information is gathered and used, in other words on the skills of observation, hypothesising, questioning, predicting, planning, interpreting, drawing conclusions, communicating and reflecting.

Progression in inquiry skills

If we want to help development in inquiry skills we need some idea of what changes signify progress from early to more advanced skills. One of the differences between experts and novices in any field is that experts are able to function at a more general level than novices. One of the aims of education has been expressed as releasing thought from particular contexts (Hodson, 1998).Children at the primary level are functioning as novices, who learn particular skills in particular contexts and generally are not able to transfer skills from one subject area to another – which can happen even within the different biological and physical areas of science, much to the frustration of secondary science teachers. This is why we have identified, as one dimension of progression in inquiry skills, the ability to use them effectively in unfamiliar as well as in familiar contexts. This is one of the three main dimensions of progress across all the skills suggested in Box 12.1.

With these overall changes in mind, we now consider what teachers can do to help develop the four groups of skills proposed in Chapter 6.

- raising questions, predicting and planning investigations (concerned with setting up inquiries)
- gathering evidence by observing and using information sources (concerned with collecting data)
- analysing, interpreting and explaining (concerned with drawing conclusions)
- communicating, arguing and evaluating (concerned with reporting, reflecting and applying).

For each group of skills some action that teachers can take and the types of questions that it is useful to ask are given in Boxes 12.2, 12.3, 12.4 and 12.5.

Strategies for development of inquiry skills

Helping development of questioning, predicting and planning skills

Box 12.2 sets out some key ways of helping children to develop these skills. The importance of children asking questions, and the kinds of response to different kinds of questions has been discussed in Chapter 7. Here we are concerned with encouraging the kinds of questions that lead to inquiries that children can undertake.

Identifying investigable questions
We have mentioned on several occasions the significance in science of being able to put questions in an investigable form. One of the actions that teachers can take is to make time to discuss with children explicitly what this means and how to do it, using some examples. The AKSIS project (Goldsworthy *et al.,* 2000) produced lists of questions for discussion with children in structured

---

Box 12.1 Dimensions of progression in inquiry skills

From simple to more elaborated skills

This is the most obvious dimension, comprising the development of ability to perform more aspects of a skill. A parallel in another field is the development from just being able to move round an ice-rink on skates to being able to jump, twist and dance and still land on your feet. Both might be called 'ice skating' but one is much simpler and less elaborated than the other. In the case of science inquiry skills it is the difference between observing main features and observing details, between predicting what might happen in vague terms and being more specific, between concluding that a change in one variable does affect another and identifying the direction and nature of the relationship.

From effective use in familiar situations to effective use in unfamiliar situations

All inquiry skills have to be used in relation to some content and it is not difficult to appreciate that what the content is will influence the way children engage with it. Some children who may be able to make a reasonable prediction or plan an inquiry about, say, how far paper darts will fly, may be less likely to do these things effectively in relation to the effect of resistance in an electric circuit. The reason is that some scientific knowledge is always involved in using inquiry skills because the skills have to be used on some science content; there has to be something to observe, to investigate, to make predictions about. Whether or not knowledge of this content is the main obstacle in a particular case depends on familiarity with it. A consequence of this is that the extent to which young children can conduct scientific inquiries can only be assessed when they are engaged in inquiries about things familiar to them or ones they have thoroughly explored.

From unconscious to conscious action

Unconscious action here is means doing something without recognising just what one is doing. For example, noticing something without making a conscious effort to observe it, or finding an answer to a question by inquiry without recognising the kind of question that is being answered in this way. The kind of thinking that is at the conscious end of this dimension is meta-cognition, being aware of one's thinking and reasoning processes. It is often considered that primary children are not able to stand back from their inquiries or problems and reflect on how they tackled them and so opportunities to do this are not offered. Involving children in such thinking (as in the AKSIS and CASE projects mentioned later) has, however, provided some more positive evidence. Giving children more opportunity of this kind may well advance the development of their inquiry skills and thus their ability to make sense of the world around.

---

activities designed to make children aware of the need to clarify questions. The idea is to help children realise that questions such as: 'Does toothpaste make a difference to your teeth?' 'Is margarine better for you than butter?' can only be answered when the meaning of 'making a difference' and 'better for you' have been clarified. There has to be some indication of the kind of evidence that could be collected to answer the question (even if, in these cases, the children might not be able to collect it themselves). One of the AKSIS activities is to ask

---

Box 12.2 Developing skills of questioning, predicting and planning

Action that teachers can take

- Stimulate curiosity through classroom displays, posters, and inviting questions through a question board or box.

- Help children to refine their questions and put them into investigable form.

- Ask children to use their suggested explanations for something to make predictions: 'what do you think will happen if your idea is correct?'

- Provide opportunities for planning by starting from a question to be answered by inquiry without giving instructions.

- Scaffold planning a fair test using a planning board (see Figure 12.1)

- Talk through an inquiry that has been completed to identify how it could have been better planned.

Teachers' questions

- 'what would you like to know about …?'

- 'what do you think will happen if your idea is correct?'

- 'what do you think will happen if … or when …?'

- 'what do you think will make this go …?'

- 'what will you need to do to find out …'

- 'how will you be make it "fair"?'

---

children to decide whether in certain questions it is clear what would have to be changed and what measured to answer the question. The children can then be asked to reflect on their own questions and reword them to make clear how they could be investigated.

Using ideas to make predictions
Children's predictions are often implicit and helping to make them explicit and conscious enables them to see the connection between an idea and the prediction from it that is tested. For example, children may explain the moisture on the outside of a can of drink, just taken out of the fridge as having come from the drink inside the can. Asking 'what do you think will happen if you put an empty can in the fridge and then take it out?' will make them use this idea to predict something that can be tested. If children are helped to make predictions in simple cases and to think about the way in which they do this, the process will become more conscious and more easily applied in other contexts.

Opportunity to plan how to answer a question by inquiry
Too often children's thinking about what is required in planning an inquiry is by-passed because they are given written instructions to follow, as in the

parachute activity in Box 4.8 (p. 71). It also happens when their teachers guide their activities too strongly, as in the following classroom observation of a teacher introducing an activity to find out if ice melts more quickly in air or in water at room temperature:

> You'll need to use the same sized ice cubes. Make sure you have everything ready before you take the ice cubes out of the tray. Put one cube in the water and one close to it in the air. Then start the clock ...

Here the children will have no problem in doing what is required, but they may have little idea of why they are doing it. If they did, they might challenge the need for a clock in this activity!

In the early years, children's experience should include simple problems to which they can easily respond 'How will you do this?' For example, 'How can you find out if the light from the torch will shine through this fabric, this piece of plastic, this jar of water, this coat sleeve?' Often young children will respond by showing rather than describing what to do. With greater experience and ability to 'think through actions' before doing them they can be encouraged to think ahead more and more, which is one of the values of planning.

Supporting (scaffolding) planning

If children are to develop the ability to plan there must be opportunities for them to start from a question and work out how to answer it, or to make a prediction and to think out and carry out their own procedures for testing it. To take these steps by themselves is asking a great deal of young children and of older ones unused to devising inquiries. They will need help, which subsequently can gradually be withdrawn.

Planning a fair test can scaffolded (see Box 11.2) by using a planning board. The original planning board was developed in 1972 as part of a Science 5/13 unit on Working with Wood. Several variants on it have been devised since, but the main features remain much as in the original description shown in Figure 12.1.

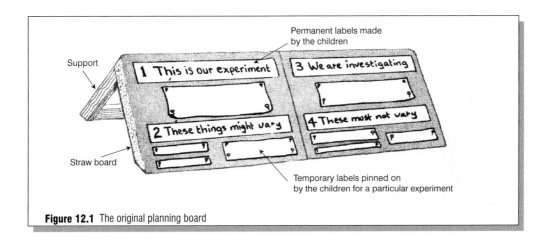

Figure 12.1 The original planning board

Reviewing a complete inquiry

For older children, help in planning can begin, paradoxically, from reviewing an inquiry which has been completed (whether or not the children planned it themselves), helping them to go through what was done and identifying the structure of the activity through questions such as:

- what were they trying to find out?
- what things did they compare (identifying the independent variable)?
- how did they make sure that it was fair (identifying the variables which should be kept the same)?
- how did they find the result (identifying the dependent variable)?

Planning continues throughout an inquiry and indeed the initial plan may change as the work progresses and unforeseen practical obstacles emerge. However, it is important for children to recognise when they make a change to their plans and to review the whole plan when a change is made. Writing plans down is a useful activity because it requires forward thinking, actions carried out in the mind.

Helping development of gathering evidence by observing and using information sources

Box 12.3 summarises some actions that teachers can take and the kinds of questions they can ask to encourage these skills. In the case of observing, the first essential is something to observe. As children will spend most time in the classroom it is important for this to be rich in opportunities for observation – displays of objects related to a theme, posters, photographs, living things, etc. – with sources of further information nearby.

Providing time is significant in encouraging observation, perhaps more than for other inquiry skills. Children need time to go back to things they may have observed only superficially or when a question has occurred to them about something they want to check. A display enables children to use odd moments as well as science activity time for observing and so increases an important commodity in the development of this skill.

Not all observations are made in the classroom, of course, and careful preparation for expeditions outside is important if things are not to be missed. There is less opportunity to revisit objects and so it is essential for the teacher to explore in advance the place to be visited, keeping the capabilities and knowledge of the children in mind (see also Chapter 9).

Invitations to observe

Some children need encouragement to observe and to do this carefully, with attention to detail. Question cards placed by displayed objects: 'Try to make this bottle make a high and a low sound', placed next to a bottle three-quarters full of water, encourages interaction. 'How many different kinds of grass are there here?', placed next to a bunch of dried grasses, encourages careful observation.

Box 12.3 Developing skills of gathering evidence by observing and using information sources

Action that teachers can take

- Provide informal opportunities for using the senses for gathering information by
    - regular display of objects and phenomena for children to explore, with relevant information books or CD-ROMs accessible nearby;
    - a collection of objects relating to a new topic two or three weeks ahead of starting it to create interest;
    - time for observing.
- Encourage observation through 'invitations to observe' – cards placed next to objects or equipment displayed, encouraging observation and attention to detail.
- Teach the correct use of instruments that
    - extend the senses, including time-lapse photography and the digital microscope;
    - can measure change or differences, such as sensors and probes (see Chapter 21).
- Teach the techniques for using information sources such as reference books and the internet/intranet.
- Set up situations where observations are shared.
- Organise visits to observe events and objects outside the classroom (see Chapter 9).

Teachers' questions

- 'What do you notice that is the same about these ...?'
- 'What differences do you notice between the ... of the same kind?'
- 'What differences do you see when you look through the lens?'
- 'How much longer, heavier, ... is this than ...?'
- 'What did you notice about the places where you found the most ...?'
- 'What more can you find out about ... from the books and the internet?

Or, next to a 'cartesian diver', made from a dropper floating in water inside a large plastic bottle, a card asking 'what happens when you squeeze the sides of the bottle?' In this case there are several things to observe including how the level of the water inside the dropper's tube rises when the bottle is squeezed, which helps to explain why the dropper sinks. So the card could ask 'What do you notice that could explain what happens?'

Using aids to observation and data collection
Observing is the basis of all means of collecting data in a practical situation. Where attention to detail or to small differences is necessary it will be appropriate

to extend senses by using an instrument such as a hand lens or stethoscope and to use measuring instruments to quantify observations. Observation aids, such as the use of a hand lens, can be taught through a card with a drawing placed next to some lenses and selected objects in the classroom display. Older children with the required manipulative skill can learn to use a microscope through similar informal opportunities. Other techniques, such as the use of sensors involving computers, need more formal instruction.

Data can also be obtained from secondary sources, of course, from books, displays, film, television, computer-based sources, and children will need to know how to use these sources properly.

Reporting and discussing observations
Sharing observations helps children to become aware of what can be found by careful observation and so more conscious of this skill. Making a point of spending a few minutes, as a whole class, discussing what has been noticed about things on display, for example, may draw the attention of some children to things they have missed. Asking questions about details during this discussion will help children to pay attention to them in further observation.

Helping development of analysing, interpreting and explaining

Analysing and interpreting results means going further than collecting individual observations and recording them. It means trying to find patterns that relate various pieces of information to each other and to the ideas being tested. As with other inquiry skills, children need the opportunity and encouragement to do these things if they are to develop these abilities. Some of ways teachers can help are summarised in Box 12.4.

Linking results to the question under investigation
This is a vital aspect of interpretation which can made all the difference in ensuring that inquiry leads to the development of understanding. The main thrust is to ensure that children use the results of their inquiries to advance their ideas. Asking 'How does this compare with what you expected/predicted?' brings the children back to the reason for their enquiry and to thinking about the ideas they were testing.

As an example, consider children measuring the length of the shadow of a stick at different times of the day. They must go beyond just collecting the measurements if the activity is to have value for developing ideas. Important outcomes from this activity include:

■ identifying a pattern in the decreasing and then increasing length of the shadow;

■ realising the possibility of using this pattern to make predictions about the length at times when the shadow was not measured, or the time of day from the measurement of the shadow;

Box 12.4 Developing skills of analysing, interpreting and explaining

Actions that teachers can take

- Plan the topic or lesson to make sure that the thinking does not stop when data have been collected or observations made and recorded.
- Provide time and opportunities for children to identify simple patterns or relationships which bring their results together.
- Ensure that results are used to decide whether a prediction was confirmed or whether a question was answered.
- Talk about what has been learned about the phenomenon investigated, not just the observed effects.
- Encourage identification of overall statements (conclusions) that bring all observations together.

Teachers' questions

- 'How did what you found compare with what you expected?'
- 'Did you find any connection between … and …?'
- 'What did you find makes a difference to how fast … how far … how many …?'
- 'What do you think is the reason for …?'

- developing ideas about how shadows are formed;
- developing ideas about the movement of the Earth in relation to the Sun.

All depend on *using* the results the children obtain, so the development of the skills required is important. The central part of the teacher's role is to ensure that results are used and children don't rush from one activity to another without talking about and thinking through what their results mean.

Identifying patterns in results or observations
Sometimes children implicitly use patterns in their findings without recognising that they in fact do so. Teachers can help to foster greater consciousness of the process by discussing simple patterns, such as the relationship between the position of the Sun and the length of the shadow (or the equivalent in a classroom simulation using a torch and a stick). The starting point must be the various ways in which children express their conclusions. For instance there are several ways of describing the relationship between the length of the shadow and the position of the Sun:

the shadow is shortest when the Sun is highest

the shortest one is when the Sun is high and the longest when it is low

its length depends on where the Sun is

the higher the Sun the shorter the shadow

All of these show thinking about the set of information relating to the position of the sun, or other source of light, and the length of the shadow, but the first three are incomplete expressions of it. The last one refers to all the data in one statement and says not just that there is a relationship, but what this is. Discussion will help children to realise this but it is quite an advanced skills and should not be short-circuited by teaching a formula for 'the great/small -er X, the short/long -er Y'.

Helping development of skills of communicating, arguing and evaluating

Communication by children plays an important part in their learning. Some actions that teachers can take to encourage communication and reflection are summarised in Box 12.5. In Chapter 7 we noted how thinking and speaking are connected; how we 'talk ourselves into our own understanding'. So regular class discussion of what children have found in group activities is important for development of understanding and for recognising how the skills of collecting and interpreting information were used in arriving at this understanding. Such exchanges are particularly useful if they are conducted so that children question each other, ask for explanations as well as descriptions and suggest improvements in what was done.

Using a notebook
The same arguments apply to writing as to talking, but children need more help to develop the skills of using personal writing to support their thinking. Providing children with a personal notebook is a start. However, they also need to recognise its function not just as an aid to memory, but also as a means of organising their thinking, through writing rough notes and recording observations.

It is important for personal notebooks to be seen as informal, a place where words do not have to be marshalled into sentences. This can liberate children from seeing writing as a chore – one that deters some from activities, even ones they enjoy, 'because we will have to write about it afterwards'. Just as informal talk helps reflection so does informal writing. Teachers can help this benefit by suggesting making notes – 'you might want to think about this and write down some ideas in your notebook before starting' – and by showing an example of using a notebook themselves. Children should begin using notebooks as soon as writing becomes fluent. It is probably best to introduce them to the whole class, encouraging those less able to write to draw and use what words they can.

Time for discussing what and how to report
Children will need to draw upon their notes in preparing for reporting on what they have done when the class gets together at the end of an activity or topic. This is an opportunity for them to realise the value of making notes. It is also the occasion for thinking about what is needed for formal reporting. Different occasions may require different forms of report. Not every activity needs to be written up formally and displayed. (We saw that Kathy was content to have the selected balls as the record of the children's activity: p. 42.) But the

Box 12.5 Developing skills of communicating, arguing, reflecting and evaluating

Actions that teachers can take

- Provide opportunities for oral reporting and time for preparing so that procedures and ideas are shared.

- Provide children with a personal notebook for recording and reflection.

- Discuss with children how they might use their notebook and set aside time for them to use it.

- Provide ideas about how to record certain kinds of information, using tables, drawings with labels and symbols.

- Discuss ways of communicating particular information to particular audiences.

- Discuss criteria for evaluating reports and provide time for peer and self-assessment (see Chapter 18).

- Give time to review activities and reflect on, for instance, whether questions could have been better expressed, other variables controlled, measurements repeated, etc.

Teacher's questions

- 'How are you going to keep a record of what you do and find?'

- 'What kind of chart/graph/drawing do you think is the best way to show the results?'

- 'How can you explain to the others what you did and what happened?'

- 'How can you show that (what evidence do you have that) your conclusion is right?'

- 'What other conclusions can you draw from your results?'

- 'If you did this again, is there anything that you would change?'

occasional preparation of a report that could be displayed to other classes, parents or at a science fair is an opportunity for children to think about the audience when deciding what words, diagrams or other illustrations to use for effective communication.

Arguing: providing evidence to support claims

In this context arguing does not mean the contesting of views and opinions that we associate with everyday arguments. Rather it is the process of supporting claims and conclusions with evidence. For that reason the word 'argumentation' has been coined. Sometimes children assert what they would like to happen rather than what does happen, particularly if the latter challenges their preconceived ideas or beliefs. They need to realise and ensure that what they report and claim in science is based on evidence. The actions the teacher can take, suggested by Osborne *et al.* (2004), include modelling behaviour of expecting children to give a justification for their views, encouraging children to challenge each other ('how do you know that?') and to expect counter-arguments.

Some general strategies for developing inquiry skills

When we look across the action suggested for helping development of these groups of skills we find some common themes. Frequent mention has been made of certain points which appear to be key strategies that can be applied to all inquiry skills. These are:

- Providing opportunity to use inquiry skills in the exploration of materials and phenomena at first-hand.

- Asking questions that require the use of the skills (and allowing time for thinking and answering).

- Providing opportunity for discussion in small groups and as a whole class.

- Encouraging critical review of how activities have been carried out.

- Providing access to the techniques needed for advancing skills.

- Involving children in communicating in various forms and reflecting on their thinking.

Developing cross-curricular skills

In addition to the skills that are specifically used in developing scientific understanding through inquiry, there are skills to which inquiry-based work in science and other areas of the curriculum contribute.

Learning how to learn

Inquiry in all subjects has a particular role in helping children to develop the skills needed to continue learning outside and beyond formal education. These skills are described by James *et al.* (2007) as skills of 'learning to learn' rather than 'learning skills'. The main reason is that the latter phrase suggests that there is something to be learned in the same way as 'language skills' or 'learning to play a musical instrument'. Rather, what is to be learned is the practice, or a set of practices, that lead to learning. These skills are not about learning particular subject matter but about the process of learning itself. The aim of developing learning how to learn skills is that someone with these skills will in theory be able to go about learning without help. That is, they become autonomous learners. Autonomy is seen as a key aim in education, often used interchangeably with phrases such as 'independent learning', 'taking responsibility for one's own learning', 'self-determination' and 'self-regulation' (Boud, 1988, quoted in James *et al.*, 2007).

The importance of learning how to learn follows from the widely recognised expansion of knowledge and the accelerating change in daily life, largely resulting from scientific and technological advances. (Just consider the impact of the mobile phone and the i-pad and the complex electronics of the modern car.) Future citizens need to be able to adapt to the many changes that will be a constant feature of their lives. The consequences for education are described by the OECD as in Box 12.6.

Box 12.6 Impact of constant change

Students cannot learn in school everything they will need to know in adult life. What they must acquire is the prerequisites for successful learning in future life. ... Students must become able to organise and regulate their own learning, to learn independently and in groups, and to overcome difficulties in the learning process. This requires them to be aware of their own thinking processes and learning strategies and methods.

(OECD, 1999: 9)

In the process of learning how to learn children become able to use strategies for learning new things, not just at school but in other contexts, and develop the attitudes that motive continued learning. Goals relating to reflection and learning autonomy may be regarded as more relevant at later stages of school than in the primary years. But, like many goals which seem too complex for young children, there are essential foundations to be laid in the primary school. The first step in reflecting on learning is to become aware of what one is actually learning. We can help this process through ensuring that children know what they are learning and why. Then by reflecting on what has been learned, and how, children gradually start to take more conscious control of their learning, and become able to pursue learning independently.

Some strategies for doing this are similar to those of using assessment for learning; for instance, the communication of goals to children, the type of feedback given by the teacher and the encouragement of self-assessment. We return to these in Chapter 18.

Thinking skills

Thinking skills are widely taken to be those concerned with identifying patterns, finding order and relationships that help in making sense of things around us. The idea that thinking skills can be enhanced by special teaching was tested and confirmed by the Cognitive Acceleration in Science (CASE) project developed over many years by Adey and Shayer (1994). Their work was initially with secondary school pupils but programmes for children aged 5–7, 7–8 and 8–9 years were later produced.

The materials for the youngest children provide activities in which children work in groups with specially designed materials which involve them in sorting and sequencing, classifying in different ways and considering situations from different points of view. Group working is a key part of the programmes and teachers have a key role in stimulating children to help each other. Research during the trials of the materials showed that they 'work best when children work in groups with a range of abilities and differences. It is advised that teachers choose groups of mixed gender, ethnicity, language, ability and personality' (Robertson, 2004: 6).

For older children various key features of dealing with a problem form the core of the experiences for each situation. As an example, Serret (2004) described how the topic of making sandwiches can be exploited to develop thinking. The children start by discussing their favourite sandwiches and the different ingredients that can go into a sandwich (different types of bread, fillings and dressings, such as mayonnaise). This ensures familiarity with the content. Then they are challenged to work out how many different sandwiches can be made with a given range of ingredients. The next stage is for the teacher to ask them how they came to their answer, what they discussed and how they tackled the task. This leads to questions about what they had to think about and what was important in solving the problem. Finally they are asked to link what they have learned to other areas, such as how they could use the same methods to solve other problems and whether a sandwich could be part of a healthy diet.

Experiences of this kind encourage both teacher and pupils to change their ideas about what it is to be a good learner, that is, not someone who knows all the right answers and doesn't need or have help from or give help to others but someone who works things out carefully together with others. They also challenge established notions about intelligence and the extent to which it can be changed and developed by practice.

Activating Children's Thinking Skills (ACTS) (McGuinness, 2000) is an example of a cross-curricular approach to developing thinking processes and strategies. The ACTS project originated in Northern Ireland, from where it spread throughout the UK and beyond. It was developed in collaboration with teachers of 8 to 12 year olds but has been adapted for older pupils. Essentially it identifies

Box 12.7 Some types of thinking in the ACTS framework

- Sequencing, ordering information
- Sorting, classifying, grouping
- Analysing part/whole relationships, compare/contrast
- Making predictions, hypothesising
- Drawing conclusions, giving reasons for conclusions
- Distinguishing fact from opinion
- Determining bias, checking the reliability of evidence
- Relating causes and effects, designing a fair test
- Generating new ideas, brainstorming
- Problem-solving, thinking up different solutions
- Testing solutions
- Planning
- Making decisions, weighing up pros and cons.

(McGuinness, 2000: 7)

a framework of thinking skills such as in Box 12.7. These are used in analysing the curriculum to target contexts where there is potential for developing some of the kind of thinking in the framework. For instance, sequencing can occur in history (sequencing events and changes in a period being studied, constructing a time line) as well as in science (sequencing the stages of development in the life cycle of a frog or butterfly).

Summary

In this chapter we have suggested three main directions of change that indicate development of inquiry skills:

- from simple to more elaborate skills;

- from effective use in familiar situations to effective use in unfamiliar situations;

- from unconscious to conscious action.

In more detail we have proposed what teachers can do to help progress in specific skills, considered in four groups concerned with: setting up investigations, collecting data, drawing conclusions and reporting, reflecting and applying. Actions the teacher can take and questions to ask have been proposed for these groups and general strategies that apply to helping all inquiry skills have been brought together. These apply also to other skills briefly discussed – learning how to learn and thinking skills – which can be developed across the curriculum as well as in science education.

Further reading

Osborne, J., Erduran, S. and Simon, S. (2004) Enhancing the quality of argumentation in school science, *Journal of Research in Science Teaching*, 41(10): 994–1020.

James, M. *et al.* (2007) *Improving Learning How to Learn*, London: Routledge, ch. 6.

Harlen, W. (2001b) *Primary Science: Taking the Plunge*, 2nd edn, Portsmouth, NH: Heinemann, chs 6, 7 and 8.

Website

http://www.education.gov.uk/schools/toolsandinitiatives/tripsresearchdigests/a0013261/themes-thinking-skills

Provides links to a number of articles about cognitive acceleration and thinking skills.

13

Teaching for enjoyment, motivation and scientific attitudes

Introduction

We are concerned in this chapter with the classroom conditions which have direct impact on children's response to their activities and thus on their learning outcomes. These are not features of the learning environment that are easily measured and consequently attract less attention than they merit, yet they are critical to the achievement of some of the more important of aims of education. A good deal depends, not on the materials and physical resources, but on teachers' actions, language and behaviour.

In the first part of the chapter we discuss the features of a classroom that support learning for all pupils through taking account of their emotional response to particular tasks. This includes recognising the importance of how children see themselves as learners. In the second part we consider ways of motivating engagement and persistence in learning and how to encourage intrinsic, as opposed to extrinsic, motivation. The third section, on attitudes, begins by considering attitudes to learning in general and the teacher's role in developing positive attitudes. Finally we propose ways of helping children's development of attitudes specifically relevant to learning science.

What schools teach: the whole curriculum

Children learn in school far more than the official curriculum and even more than the wider curriculum that is implicit in aims such as learning how to learn, developing scientific literacy, thinking skills and so on. Beyond this they are learning from what they observe and experience in the behaviour of those around them – the teachers, other pupils and the interactions among them. This learning has been described as the 'hidden curriculum'. Atkin and Black argue that:

> Of particular significance, students learn about the behaviour of adults in situations of responsibility. Does the teacher punish the entire class when

a child or a small group misbehave? The hidden curriculum includes serious attention to personal and social behaviour, such as taking turns and respecting the ideas of other students. It includes how fair teachers seem to be and whether they give even chances to all students. Do they humiliate those who misbehave? How do they handle situations in which a student accuses another of bullying, or copying, or lying? Does the teacher seem to have favourites?

(Atkin and Black, in press)

Everything that happens in the classroom takes place within the ethos or social climate created by the teacher. The teacher and other adults in the school clearly have important roles in helping children to develop values and respect for themselves and others as well as confidence in their ability to learn and willingness to engage in learning. Before a teacher can have any chance of gaining access to children's ideas and skills, it is necessary to establish a classroom climate in which children feel that is it 'safe' to express the ideas they have and in which these ideas are valued and taken seriously, not disregarded or ridiculed. The point is well made by Keogh and Naylor (2004):

As adults we realize how close the connection is between self-esteem and having our ideas accepted and valued. Children are no different. If we want children to 'think out loud', to be creative in their thinking and to argue about alternative possibilities, then we need to provide the kind of learning environment in which they feel comfortable to do that. They need to know that they can make mistakes or give wrong answers and still feel good about themselves.

(Keogh and Naylor, 2004: 18)

Such an atmosphere cannot be created overnight. It results from teachers showing by example how to respect others' ideas, how to be sensitive to others' feelings and to value effort and attitudes of perseverance, responsibility and openness (see Box 13.1). An environment that lays the foundation for continued learning should not only accept, but also motivate, change in ideas and ways of thinking. Above all, we need to create a desire to learn, to understand things around us and to make this enjoyable.

The importance of affect

How children feel about themselves and the ideas that they encounter in the classroom influences their learning. 'Feelings of wonder, delight, amusement, interest, influence, disinterest, boredom and disgust will clearly impact in different ways on the learning task – sometimes favourably, sometimes unfavourably' (Hodson, 1998: 54). Children's feelings about learning tasks are affected by many different factors including ones in their personal background which are beyond the influence of the school. But the school can have a role in relation to the impact of other factors, relating to their previous experience of

Box 13.1 Creating a classroom climate for learning

- Find out about individual children's interests, likes and dislikes, as well as their previous experience and home background.
- Respect differences in ideas, resisting making judgemental comments.
- Seek to understand how children come to form their ideas.
- Use language, particularly in relation to learning in science, that children understand.
- Check that children have understood the aims of learning tasks in the way intended.
- Provide an example of respecting children's feeling and expect them to do the same for each other.

similar tasks, the response of others to what they have done and how their ideas are received. For instance:

- Previous success in a task similar to the one to be undertaken is likely to encourage children to try hard; constant failure will most likely create reluctance.
- If others have responded well to a child's contribution, (s)he is more likely to join in with others and offer ideas than if these contributions have been ignored or the child made to feel 'silly'.
- The non-scientific ideas that children have created for themselves and which have worked in everyday contexts may be so firmly held that they become part of their sense of themselves, which is challenged when the ideas are challenged (Abelson, 1988).

So sensitivity to children's feelings is as important in interaction with and among children as it is for adults. It is shown primarily in taking interest in children's feelings about their learning. But this interest has to be sincere. Children are not taken in by the superficial attention of their teacher, for it will be betrayed by manner and tone of voice as well as by whether anything happens as a result. A genuine interest creates an atmosphere in which children's own ideas are encouraged and taken as a starting point; where effort is praised rather than only achievement; where value is attached to each child's endeavours. In this atmosphere, a child who does not achieve as well as others will not be ridiculed or feel inferior. Box 13.1 summarises some other actions that teachers can take to make children feel comfortable, in the emotional sense, in the classroom.

Children's self-image as learners
An important part of the emotional context of learning is how children see themselves as learners and how they attribute their success or failure. Those who attribute their successes to their ability and hard work recognise that their learning is within their own control. When they are challenged by difficulty they try hard and when they fail they consider that they could succeed if they try hard

enough. So for these children failure does not damage their self-esteem. The reverse is the case for those who attribute their success to circumstances outside themselves, to chance, to luck or to their teachers. For these learners, experience of failure leads to loss of confidence, for they do not feel they are in control of whether they succeed or fail. Such learners try to protect their self-esteem by avoiding the risk of failure through selecting tasks well within their grasp.

Self-image is particularly important since it influences whether children are deterred by challenging work. Dweck (2000) has researched extensively the impact on their performance in school of children's view of themselves as learners. She has found that, in the face of difficulty, some children regard failure as inevitable and not within their capacity to change ('I'm no good at these problems'; 'I have a poor memory'). Others react differently, recognising that they need to find ways of overcoming the difficulty ('I'll try a different way'; 'I don't understand this bit but I can do the rest and then it might make sense'). When children of the same ability are given work well within their grasp, the difference between these two ways of responding is not noticed, but as soon as there is a challenge, those who feel that they cannot overcome it by making an effort are at a disadvantage, which will continue as they move through the school and inevitably encounter more challenges.

So what can teachers and others do about making sure that some children do not write themselves off as unable to tackle difficulties? Dweck makes a strong case for using praise to promote effort ('effort praise') and not to promote children's views of themselves as being 'intelligent' or 'smart' ('person praise').

Effort praise is preferred to person praise for learners of all abilities. For the low-achieving children, effort praise helps them to recognise the importance of effort and focuses them on ways of overcoming problems. It is advisable not to try to encourage achievement by person praise when these children do succeed,

---

Box 13.2 Effort praise for high-achievers

Anyone who has been in the presence of children who are doing really well at something knows that there is an almost irresistible urge to tell them how good, talented or smart they are at what they are doing. We are at a loss for other ways to show our delight and admiration. Effort praise hardly seems like an adequate substitute.

But effort and strategy praise when given in the right way can be highly appreciative of a child's accomplishments. If a child paints a lovely picture we can ask about and admire how he or she selected the colours, formed the images, or created textures. If a child solves a series of difficult maths problem, we can ask with admiration what strategies she or he used and we can admire the concentration that went into it …

In many ways, this kind of 'process' discussion is more appreciative of what the child has done than person praise. Person praise essentially ignores the essence, the true merit, of what was accomplished, and appreciates the work only as a reflection of some ability.

(Dweck, 2000: 120–1)

in the attempt to boost faith in themselves, for that encourages labelling and removes attention from effort. For the high-achieving children it is perhaps more difficult to avoid person praise, particularly when work seems to have been done perfectly. However, as pointed out by Dweck in Box 13.2, there are other ways of showing appreciation which focus on the work and how it was done rather than on the person.

Motivation for learning

Creating a supportive atmosphere by caring for children's emotional response is basic to motivating learning. But there is more than this in motivation for learning – which we can describe as the willingness to make the effort that learning often requires. There has to be something in it for the learner, some reward that makes that effort worthwhile.

It is useful to distinguish between motivation to become engaged in an activity and then, once engaged, motivation to continue despite difficulties and determination to do as well as possible. Motivating to engage takes different forms for children at different stages. For 5 and 6 year olds stories and fictional situations, such as used by Kathy and Chris (Chapter 3), readily encourage active participation in the narrative and in the activities that the stories suggest. Older children are more likely to be motivated by situations that seem real to them, relating to things around them.

Undoubtedly the best way of motivating learning is for children to enjoy it. There are many creative ways of introducing activities that make learning fun as well as engaging hard thinking. For example, Keogh and Naylor (2011) suggest the following:

- Testing 'myths' such as that if you drop buttered toast it always lands butter-side down.
- Ideas developed from recent news items, found through Primary Update (see websites).
- Links to topics in other subject, such as food rationing and blackout in a topic on the Second World War (Bird and Saunders, 2007).
- Concept cartoons (see Chapter 16).
- Using puppets (Simon *et al.*, 2008) to introduce problems and raise questions.

Once engaged, willingness to persist in an activity and overcome problems is often motivated by the prospect of a reward. There is an important distinction to be made between different types of reward: rewards that are unrelated (extrinsic) to the activity and what can be learned through it and those that relate (or are intrinsic) to the activity and the learning. The idea of motivating learning through extrinsic rewards and punishments is the basis for the approach to learning known as 'behaviourism' (Skinner, 1974). The underlying theory is that behaviours that are regularly rewarded will be reinforced and those that are repeatedly punished will disappear. The assumption here is that learning is under some control that is external to the learner. By contrast, the view that learning depends on the active participation of the learner means that it is under internal control and the reward is in the satisfaction in what has been achieved.

Extrinsic and intrinsic motivation

Although some psychologists identify other forms of motivation (e.g. McMeniman (1989) adds 'achievement motivation'), it is generally agreed that the chief distinctions to be made are between intrinsic and extrinsic. Intrinsic motivation means that someone engages in an activity because of the satisfaction that is derived from doing it. When there is extrinsic motivation the satisfaction comes from a result that has little to do with the activity – a new bicycle for passing an examination or an ice cream for finishing the homework! Some characteristics of extrinsically and intrinsically motivated learners are given in Box 13.3. From this we can see that intrinsic motivation is clearly desirable, since it leads to self-motivated and sustained learning. It is particularly relevant to learning to make sense of things around and not being satisfied until they are understood.

Motivating learning by rewards and punishments, described as extrinsic motivation is widely criticised and indeed there is evidence from research studies (Kohn, 1993) to suggest that the use of rewards is associated with reduction in the quality of children's work. The reason for this is that going all out for the extrinsic reward can lead to short-cuts and less thoughtful work. If the reward is in the doing or the learning that results, on the other hand, and the motivation is intrinsic, then this reward will be achieved by more thoughtful and careful work. To anticipate the discussion of feedback in Chapter 17, intrinsic motivation is more likely to be

---

Box 13.3 Intrinsic and extrinsic motivation for learning

Learners who are intrinsically motivated:

■ find interest and satisfaction in what they learn and in the learning process;

■ are 'motivated from within' and do not need external incentives to engage with learning;

■ recognise their own role in the learning and take responsibility for it;

■ seek out information, identify their learning goals and persevere;

■ know that what they achieve depends on their effort.

Learners who are extrinsically motivated:

■ engage in learning mainly because of external incentives such as gold stars, high marks;

■ may cease to learn, or at least decrease effort, in the absence of these external factors, learn what is closely related to the behaviour that is rewarded;

■ put effort into learning the things not because they have value for developing understanding, but in order to gain praise, reward or privilege.

encouraged by comments on children's work identifying what is good about it and giving suggestions for improvement, rather than grades or marks.

Encouraging intrinsic motivation

We must recognise, of course, that in practice it is difficult to work on the principle that all children will find satisfaction in learning all the time. The occasional bribe or threat relating to privileges will do no harm, providing that the regular expectation is to find satisfaction and enjoyment in working to the best of their ability. Celebrating this is an important intrinsic reward. In what other ways, then, can intrinsic motivation be encouraged? Experience from a range of studies of learning across the curriculum suggests that there are things that a teacher can do and things to avoid in aiming to create the climate to foster intrinsic motivation.

Positive action includes:

- Providing some choice of activities. This does not mean a free choice to do anything but a choice from among carefully devised alternatives, all seen by the children as having some relevance to them. The act of choosing gives the children some ownership of the activity and transfers some responsibility to them to undertake it seriously and complete it to the best of their ability.

- Involving children in identifying some reasonable objectives for the activity and some ways of achieving these objectives.

- Helping them to assess their own progress, using approaches such as the ones suggested in Chapter 18.

- Setting up activities in a way that requires genuine collaboration in pairs or small groups, so that the effort of all those involved matters and all are obliged to pull their weight.

- Showing confidence that children will do well; having high expectations.

- Encouraging pride in having tried and made a good effort.

Such actions set up a 'virtuous' circle, where children try harder and as result succeed, which raises their self-esteem. By the same reasoning, it is important to avoid the vicious circle or self-fulfilling prophesy whereby children see themselves as failing even before they begin a task and therefore make little effort, leading to failure which confirms their judgement of themselves. Again, we can identify actions that should be avoided.

Things to avoid include:

- Labelling children either as groups or individuals. This can happen consciously, as when children are streamed or grouped by ability and are referred to by a label, or unconsciously. It is difficult to imagine that being labelled 'the B class', reinforced by the uniformly low level of work expected, does not transfer to the children's self-image. Children are acutely sensitive to being treated in different ways from others and are not deceived by being described as the 'green' group when this means that they are the 'slow' ones.

- Making comparisons between children. This encourages competition and detracts from each child working towards his or her own objectives.

- Praising children for being 'clever' rather than for the effort and skill required to succeed.

Attitudes and learning

General approaches to development of attitudes

Attitudes show not in what children can do or know but in their willingness to use their knowledge or skills where appropriate. They are outcomes of learning that result from a range of experiences across which there is some pattern. For instance, an attitude of willingness to take account of evidence does not result from a single activity or even several activities around a topic. Instead it may result from extended experience in which the value of using evidence has been clear or from the example over a period of time of someone who showed this attitude in their behaviour. In other words, attitudes are picked up from a range of experiences: they are 'caught rather than taught', particularly from influential adults. Thus showing an example of the behaviour in practice is a key action that teachers can take. Others are: providing opportunity for children to make the choices that enable them to develop attitudes; reinforcing positive attitudes; and discussing attitude-related behaviour. We now look at these in a little more detail.

Showing an example
Given that attitudes are 'caught', showing an example is probably the most important of the positive things that teachers can do. To make a point of revealing that his or her own ideas have changed, for instance, can have a significant impact on children's willingness to change their ideas. 'I used to think that trees died after dropping their leaves, until ...', 'I didn't realise that there were different kinds of woodlice', 'I thought that it was easier to float in deep water than in shallow water but the investigations showed that it didn't make any difference.' The old adage that 'actions speak louder than words' means that such comments will not be convincing by themselves. It is important for teacher to show attitudes in what they do, not just what they say, for example by:

- showing interest in new things (which the children may have brought into school) by giving them attention, if not immediately, then at some planned time later, and displaying them for others to see, if appropriate;

- helping to find out about new or unusual things by searching books, the internet or using other information sources with the children;

- being self-critical, admitting mistakes and taking steps to make amends.

In a classroom where useful ideas are pursued as they arise and activities extend beyond well-beaten tracks, there are bound to be opportunities for these teacher behaviours to be displayed. Situations in which the teacher just doesn't know, or which bring surprises or something completely new, should be looked upon, not as problems, but as opportunities for transmitting attitudes through example.

Providing opportunity

Since attitudes show in willingness to act in certain ways, there has to be opportunity for children to have the choice of doing so. If their actions are closely controlled by rules or highly structured lesson procedures, then there is little opportunity to develop and show certain attitudes (except perhaps willingness to conform). Providing new and unusual objects in the classroom gives children opportunity to show and satisfy – and so develop – curiosity. Discussing activities while they are in progress, or after they have been completed, gives encouragement to reflect critically, but unless such occasions are provided, the attitudes cannot be fostered.

Reinforcing positive attitudes

Children pick up attitudes not only from example but from how others respond to their behaviour. When children show indications of positive attitudes, it is important to reinforce these behaviours by approval of the *behaviour*. As we have already noted, there is an important distinction between praising the individual (person praise) and reinforcing the behaviour (effort praise). It's important not to adopt a behaviourist approach of giving general praise of the person as a reward for behaving in a certain way, since this can reinforce the behaviour without an understanding of why it is desirable. As in the case of feedback to children about their work, which we discuss in Chapter 17, feedback about attitude-related behaviour should avoid judgement of the person.

For example, if critical reflection leads to children realising that they did not make fair comparisons in their experiment, the teacher's reaction could be 'well you should have thought of that before' or, alternatively, 'you've learned something important about this kind of investigation'. The latter is clearly more likely to encourage reflection and the admission of fault on future occasions. Moreover, if this approval is consistent it eventually becomes part of the classroom climate and children will begin to reinforce the attitudes for themselves and for each other. Those who have not developed positive attitudes will be able to recognise what these are from the approval given to others.

Discussing attitude-related behaviour

Attitudes can only be said to exist when they appear as a regular part of behaviour. In this regard they are highly abstract and intangible. Identifying them involves a degree of abstract thinking which makes them difficult to discuss, particularly with young children. However, as children become more mature they are more able to reflect on their own behaviour and motivations. It then becomes possible to discuss examples of attitudes in action and to help them identify the way they affect behaviour explicitly. When some 10 year olds read in a book that snails eat strawberries, they tested this out and came to the conclusion that 'as far as our snails are concerned, the book is wrong'. Their teacher discussed with them how the author of the book might have come to a different conclusion from them and whether both the author and the children might gather more evidence before arriving at their conclusions. The children not only recognised that what was concluded depended on the attitudes to evidence but also that the conclusions were open to challenge from further evidence, thus developing their own 'respect for evidence'.

Helping the development of scientific attitudes

It is useful to make a distinction between two kinds of scientific attitudes:

- attitudes towards science as an enterprise;
- attitudes towards the objects and events which are studied in science and the use of evidence in making sense of them.

In relation to the first, to develop an informed attitude towards science it is necessary to have an idea of what 'science' is. Without this, attitudes will be formed on the basis of the many myths about science and about scientists which persist in popular belief and in the caricatures which are perpetuated in the media and in some literature. Typically these portray scientists as male, bespectacled, absent-minded and narrowly concerned with nothing but their work (see e.g. Jannikos, 1995; Johnston, 2005). Science as a subject may be portrayed as the villain, the origin of devastating weapons and technology which causes environmental damage, or as the wonder of the modern world in providing medical advances, expanding human horizons beyond the Earth and being responsible for the discoveries which led to computers and information technology.

At the primary level the concern is to give children experience of scientific activity as a basis for a thorough understanding, which will only come much later, of what science is and is not and of the responsibility we all share for applying it humanely. So the main concern here is with the second kind, that is, with attitudes which we might call the attitudes *of* science, those which support scientific activity and learning.

Although development of scientific attitudes is not explicitly identified as an aim in national curricula it is widely acknowledged as an important outcome of science education. Most curricula make some reference in non-statutory statements to helping children to develop care, responsibility, concern and respect for all living things and the environment and make reference to valuing others' opinions, being sensitive to others' feelings and fostering curiosity. Other attitudes are implied in curriculum requirements for children to identify and use scientific evidence in supporting ideas and arguments. These fall into the category of attitudes *of* science and would also support learning in several subject areas.

The generalised nature of attitudes is such that no clear line can be drawn between 'scientific' and other attitudes, thus what we have suggested as needed to foster positive attitudes in general are equally applicable to attitudes relevant to developing ideas through exploration of the surrounding world, such as willingness to consider evidence and to change ideas and developing sensitivity to living things and the environment. This leads to the suggestions for actions that teachers can take in Boxes 13.4 and 13.5.

Box 13.4 Developing willingness to consider evidence and change ideas

Actions that teachers can take

- Protect time for discussing and interpreting evidence, thus conveying how important this is.

- Pay attention to the evidence children gather and make sure that none is ignored, thus setting the expectation of taking note of evidence.

- Provide an example, by talking about how the teacher's own ideas have been changed by evidence.

- Acknowledge when evidence does require a change of ideas ('we need to think again about this').

- Reinforce the importance of not rushing to conclusions with inadequate evidence by approval when children suggest that more evidence is needed before they can come to a conclusion.

Box 13.5 Developing sensitivity to living things and the environment

Actions that teachers can take

- Provide an example of responsibility for living things by checking on the health of animals and plants in the classroom, even if children have been assigned to look after them.

- Give opportunities for children to care for living things, temporarily brought into in the classroom (but check on their welfare, as just suggested above).

- Discuss the care that should taken when exploring the natural environment, such as replacing stones to preserve habitats.

- Show approval of thoughtful behaviour to living things.

- Ensure that, where possible, animals taken from natural habitats into the classroom for study are replaced afterwards.

- Provide bins for recycling that are used by staff and children.

Summary

In this chapter we have considered the unplanned learning that takes place through the 'hidden curriculum' in schools and the emotional reactions that can affect children's learning. We noted how children vary in their response to challenges and how important it is to support effort in such circumstances by praising children for succeeding through trying hard rather than for their ability or for 'being clever'. We have also considered how teachers can help the development of motivation, for example, by giving children some choice and responsibility for their learning, leading to ownership, involving children in identifying and working towards clear goals and assessing their own progress, setting up situations for genuinely collaborative work, raising children's expectations of themselves and celebrating effort as well as achievement. Intrinsic motivation for learning science is encouraged when children enjoy exploring and find satisfaction in making sense of the world around them.

In relation to attitudes towards learning in general and to learning science in particular the main points have been:

- Attitudes are ways of describing a willingness or preference to behave in certain ways.

- Attitudes in general and scientific attitudes in particular can be encouraged by teachers providing examples through their own behaviour, ensuring opportunities for children to make decisions and form their own ideas, reinforcing relevant behaviours and discussing the value of behaviours that lead to self-motivated learning.

- Ways have been suggested in which teachers can foster in children willingness to consider evidence and to develop sensitivity towards living things and the environment.

Further reading

Keogh, B. and Naylor, S. (2006) Access and engagement for all, in W. Harlen (ed.) *ASE Guide to Primary Science Education,* Hatfield: ASE, 151–157.

Keogh, B. and Naylor, S. (2011) Creativity in teaching science, in W. Harlen (ed.) *ASE Guide to Primary Science Education*, new edn, Hatfield: ASE, 102–10.

McCrory, P. (2011) Developing interest in science through emotional engagement, in W. Harlen (ed.) *ASE Guide to Primary Science Education,* new edn, Hatfield: ASE, 94–102.

Websites

Primary upd8: www.primaryupd8.org.uk (on subscription for non-ASE members or included as part of ASE e-membership for primary schools).

14

Teachers using ICT in the classroom

Introduction

In Chapter 8 we argued that science learning for primary school children can be significantly enhanced by ICT as part of the learning experience, especially when it is set in the wider context of a digitally literate classroom. It follows that science teaching is enhanced when the teacher has a good level of digital literacy and the skills to use ICT well. This entails keeping up to date with the extremely rapidly changing landscape of computer and other information technologies and with the greatly expanded range of technological tools now available for classroom use. This chapter considers the range and uses of ICT tools, with particular attention to how the teacher uses them in advancing children's learning. The first section lists four aspects of the use of ICT which structure the rest of the chapter. Most attention is given to two of these: the range of available tools and their selection for different purposes. Later sections deal more briefly with ensuring children's familiarity with ICT tools, and the importance of CPD for teachers.

What working with ICT involves for the teacher

A study of American teachers' engagement with and use of ICT found it to be a myth that more experienced or older teachers are less likely to use technology in their teaching than early career younger teachers (Richard Riley College, 2010). Although younger people might use technology more in their everyday lives, we all still need to develop an understanding of appropriate resources for the classroom. The study also produced the following recommendations for teachers.

- Be as fearless as children are in trying new technologies.
- Seek out or create opportunities to collaborate and learn from peers.
- Evaluate continuing education opportunities.
- Communicate with parents.

Making provision for young people to develop their digital literacy is a matter for the school, led by the ICT coordinator; making best use of this provision is a matter for the class teacher. Rudd (2007) argues that ICT contributes to learning where the teacher employs sound pedagogy: this is most likely to be the case when ICT is more than a prop for traditional practices but becomes so integrated into the curriculum that it transforms the approach to teaching and the quality of learning. Starkey (2010) suggests that this involves:

1. Having good understanding of available tools and ICT accessible resources and a willingness to spend time exploring their potential.

2. The ability to select resources and methods appropriate to the needs of the individuals in the class.

3. Understanding the capacity of the class to engage in purposeful activity with ICT in science. This includes knowing when this is not the best option.

4. Using ICT to support CPD – enhancing knowledge and skills, communicating with others and reflecting on the impact of ICT on pupils' science learning.

We now consider some examples of what these mean in practice.

Understanding available tools and resources

The tools and resources for ICT change rapidly and new ones are being developed all the time. This makes it difficult in a book to provide a list of resources that will not go out of date; certainly specific branded products will be overtaken by other, more powerful tools. Table 14.1 describes generic tools that are available at the time of writing.

Using ICT tools to enhance learning

Selecting ICT resources

For any ICT tool to be used effectively to support learning the teacher needs to be actively involved in helping children to make sense of their learning. Winnie (2012) argues that, although classroom technologies are now common, they are often not used to enrich or stimulate higher order thinking and reasoning. What this suggests is that, in selecting ICT resources, lesson planning must focus on learning science and the teacher needs a good understanding of the subject and a clear idea as to the intended learning outcomes.

ICT resources can support the teacher, but it is intervention by the teacher that helps children to achieve higher levels of thinking and so greater learning. This was illustrated in a study of teachers' use of computer games in teaching. It was found that, although some familiarity with the game was necessary, it was the teacher's knowledge of the curriculum that was more important to them in selecting and using games that would further pupils' learning (Sandford et al., 2006). Furthermore, teachers who had a clear idea about the learning outcomes they wanted their pupils to achieve were likely to spend time offering support and 'scaffolding' the children's learning while they played.

Table 14.1 Uses and value of ICT tools

Tools	Uses	Value
Interactive whiteboard	The large, touch sensitive screen linked to a computer enables all the functions of the computer to be used in an interactive way by the class and teacher.	Can present engaging materials including sound, video and colourful images which can be manipulated easily by the user. Can support lively whole class discussion giving teachers insights into children's ideas. Care needs to be taken to avoid use as an entertainer.
Presentational software: eg graphics programmes; word processing; desk top publishing	To present findings in attractive ways and to edit and modify reports as required. Graphics software enables children to draw or create animations and to create professional looking reports.	Once children have mastered the technical challenges the very act of translating their new ideas and findings for presentation helps them to explore and refine those ideas, especially when collaborating and as a group. Teachers can use these products to identify and explore children's developing ideas. Care needs to be taken to avoid presentation taking precedence over substance.
Data loggers, digital microscopes, data bases and spreadsheets and graphing programmes for data collection and manipulation	Data loggers have sensors to measure light intensity, temperature, sound etc. These can be recorded by the user and input to a database or spreadsheet or captured directly by a computer so that graphs, charts etc can be drawn. Digital microscopes allow close observation and capture of images on computers.	In science, where hands on investigations are so important the use of effective measuring instruments is helpful. Data loggers are accurate and quick, they can be used in and outside the classroom. Children need time to practise use of equipment otherwise the challenge of the technology can detract from the science learning.
Multi-media tools: including digital cameras, video cameras and associated software such as film editing software	Digital cameras, video cameras and audio recording equipment are now light and easy to use and images readily uploaded onto computers to enable analysis and presentation of findings.	A great advantage of these tools is that they allow numerous and immediate records to be made such that the images or sounds are more than just a general record but can be valuable data for exploration and analysis. They can be used both by the teacher, and, often usefully the children themselves. Again, care needs to be taken to avoid presentation taking precedence over the opportunities for learning.

Mobile technologies. Mobile phones, tablets and mobile sensors.	The introduction of ever smaller and more powerful mobile technologies opens up possibilities of activities beyond the classroom. Pupils can use their phones to record events outside school, at home, on field trips etc. Tablet computers provide access to information for pupils immediately and the opportunity to record information instantly.	Moving away from the fixed computer frees up teachers and pupils and allows more personalised use of technology. Shifting ownership and control to the children is a powerful motivator and has the potential to significantly change the pedagogy. This equipment can be expensive and so may be in short supply, and the applications (apps) for tablets and mobiles can be expensive. There is also a problem with relying on children having mobile phones etc or running up bills without parental approval.
Internet	Even the youngest children can access the web to make use of a huge array of information, resources, images, media answers to questions is readily available in most homes and schools.	The Internet provides teachers with a wealth of resources and, when children are purposeful in their use of the internet and know how to search and use it, it opens up a world of possibilities for them. Care needs to be taken to avoid 'surfing' with little purpose, and the safe use of the Internet is crucial. Schools usually have safeguards in place (such as limiting access to safe search engines), but teachers need to be aware of the risks and how to deal with them
Virtual learning environments (VLE) (a 'collection of integrated tools enabling the management of online learning, providing a delivery mechanism, student tracking, assessment and access to resources' (JISC, 2004))	Some, often larger, primary schools and secondary schools have their own VLE (these can be free such as Moodle, or by subscription).	VLEs provide a structured environment that can be accessed from anywhere, including mobile devices. They also allow the safe (private) use of blogs, and discussion board, and other social networking additions, space for students and teachers to upload materials. However, even more than school web sites the VLE needs to be managed and maintained.
Social media	Social network sites designed to be appropriate and safe for 9-13 year olds (and some for younger children) can be used and managed by teachers, often at no cost. Teachers can also set up blogs that are restricted to a limited group.	Important to supervise and ensure appropriate use.

> **Box 14.1** Using a simulation game
>
> Sarra's class of 9 and 10 year olds were considering how sound is transmitted through different materials. They had carried out experiments with sound insulation earlier. In groups the children used a software simulation of an experiment testing the sound insulation qualities of different materials. In order to support the children the teacher provided directions which included asking them to observe closely and make notes, to write down their predictions and note outcomes. The instructions also asked the groups to discuss how the simulation showed that the tests were fair, what factors were being changed, kept the same and measured.
>
> (Wegerif and Dawes, 2004)

In the example given in Box 14.1 the class teacher was clear that she wanted the children to learn about the effect of different materials on sound transmission, and she also wanted the children to develop their understanding of fair testing. Having the children step back from the game and think about what was happening helped them to develop their understanding of both the properties of materials and experimental design. The teacher was also able to look at their notes and listen to their discussions to consider the children's developing understanding and address any misconceptions as they used the simulation.

The potential of the simulation game described in Box 14.1 to support learning might not have been realised without teacher intervention. To move children's thinking on to higher levels takes careful thought. The importance of planning and of selecting appropriate resources to help meet the learning goal while also motivating and enthusing the children cannot be overstated. Starkey developed a model to show how learning activities using digital resources can support higher level thinking and learning. Figure 14.1 is based on Starkey's model of 'levels of learning' and describes the ways in which teachers may raise the level of learning by pupils through well-planned interventions, given in between the levels.

In Table 14.2 these levels are set out against various uses of ICT. As an example of application in practice, consider the 'doing level' in terms of the activities of the class described in Chapter 8, example 1: the birds topic. The children accessed information about different garden birds (*Doing*). By looking at images of birds beaks and at the type of food they eat (as found in books and from their own observations) children could see the connection (*Thinking about connections*). Then, helped by the teacher's intervention, children began to draw conclusions that birds are adapted to a particular habitat (*Thinking about concepts and working towards bigger ideas*). They realise that their observations are limited and they could gain more by looking at birds in other habitats (*Critiquing and evaluating*). A further step that they might have taken would be to share their ideas on a social network site and to obtain responses of support or challenge from others (*Sharing knowledge*).

Another example mentioned in Chapter 8 involved the use of data-loggers to investigate the best materials to use for blackout curtains. This is an example of the levels of learning in relation to the 'presenting information' use of ICT.

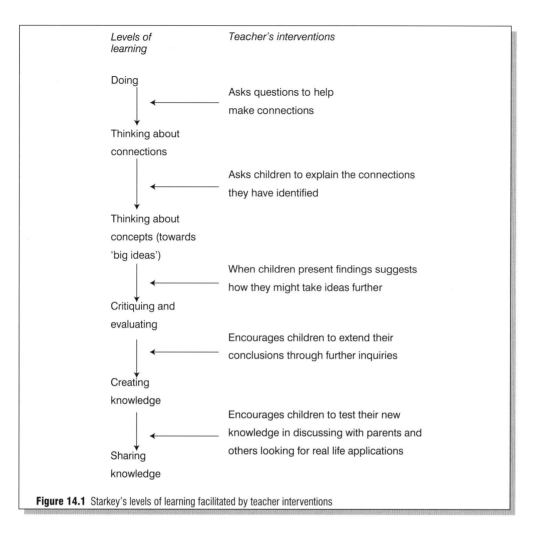

Figure 14.1 Starkey's levels of learning facilitated by teacher interventions

Little detail was given in Chapter 8, but we can envisage that the learning was developed along these lines:

- Children present findings as a chart of light levels based on data-logger readings, with magnified photographs of the various fabrics (*Doing*).

- Children present the connection between weave of fabric and ability to block light (*Thinking about connections*).

- Children draw conclusions that materials allow more or less light through depending on the degree of transparency/opacity (*Thinking about concepts and moving towards bigger ideas*).

- Children question whether it is the weave of the fabric or the nature of the material that is important (*Critiquing and evaluating*).

- Class argue that woven fabrics are not ideal as blackout but an opaque but flexible material as a window blind would be better (*Creating knowledge*).

Table 14.2 Starkey's model of levels of learning applied to uses of ICT

Levels of learning	Digital technology use				
	Accessing information	Presenting information	Processing information	Games or quizzes	Communicating
Doing	Pictures, graphs, data, film clips, audio clips, information	Using sound, pictures, words, video	Information processed or data/images manipulated in isolation	Play a game, take a quiz, enter a virtual world	Send, receive or read a communication
Thinking about connections	Connecting or comparing information from more than one source	Presented information has clear connections across formats or ideas	Connections made within or between processed information/data or images and relevant concepts	Links made between the game and own knowledge	Ideas shared and compared with other learners through a two way conversation
Thinking about concepts	Information explicitly develops conceptual understanding	Presentation has clear conceptual underpinning	Processed data or images has clear conceptual underpinning	Relevant concepts within the game/quiz identified and explained	Communication explicitly develops conceptual understanding
Critiquing and evaluating	Information and resources are critiqued and evaluated	Presentation methods and results are critiqued and evaluated	Process and product are critiqued and evaluated	The game is critiqued or evaluated within the conceptual context	Critique other people's work or ideas
Creating knowledge	New conceptual understanding building on or linking with accessed information	Critiqued and developed ideas, new knowledge presented	Ideas and new knowledge are developed	Original ideas are used to create a knowledge product in any medium	Through interaction and communication new knowledge is constructed
Sharing knowledge	The value of the product is determined by feedback (from beyond the classroom)				

■ The class teacher sets up a video conference meeting (using Skype) with a window blind manufacturer, allowing children to discuss their findings and in turn learn about other blackout materials (*Sharing knowledge*).

Other examples can be cited where there are different main uses of the ICT, but by careful intervention the activity is extended so that conceptual learning is developed. Without these interventions the activities can end with data being collected and graphed, but not used in developing understanding.

Use in assessment

In the same way that ICT can support teachers to support children's learning, it can also offer opportunities for teachers to find out children's ideas and use this information both formatively, in tailoring teaching to meet their needs, and summatively. If the lesson is well planned to ensure that the learning outcomes are achieved then teacher-based assessment can make use of the records made by their pupil (see Chapter 19). For example, where a class is encouraged to write a blog of their science work the teacher can use this for assessment purposes. Box 14.2 shows a section from a class science blog. In this case the teacher made the original post asking the class to explain what they understood by dissolving. She used this to gain insight into children's understanding and as the starting point for a class discussion as the topic got under way. At the end of the topic the teacher started another post asking the children to explain what they had learned. This approach is fun and allows the children to see each other's posts as well as the teacher, who is able to challenge some misunderstanding, such as the confusion between melting and dissolving.

Other approaches include the use of mind maps, which help children to articulate their ideas whilst helping teachers to assess understanding. The traditional, and often easiest, way is to use pencil and paper. However, there are apps available that are simple and easy to use and provide a functionality that paper and pencil cannot. There is often a cost involved in such apps (e.g. Popplet (see Further reading) could work out expensive unless used across the curriculum).

Using a different approach Mr Andrews (a regular blogger on primary teaching) describes his digitally literate classroom and how his class has been using a wide range of digital tools which they are encouraged to select according to their need (rather than teacher directed). In science topics are introduced to children as a series of learning objectives. The children work with a partner to plan how they will meet the learning objectives. On the blog Mr Andrews presents video clips created by the class to demonstrate their learning, although the class also use exercise books for reports, and other more traditional approaches. Figure 14.2 includes an adaptation of the blog post that showed Mr Andrew's class targets for a topic 'How we see things' and his explanation of the resources he makes available to the class. Here, the objectives are arranged as a progression, where the ideas are seen as working towards relevant curriculum requirements, with the outcomes at the top of the table corresponding to the Year 6 requirements of the new English National Curriculum.

Box 14.2 A science class blog

Mrs Clarke *Calling all Scientists- Can you help??*

Mrs Jones needs some help – she doesn't know a lot about the dissolving process and needs you to tell her what you already know about it.

Responses to *Calling all Scientists- Can you help??*

JohnT — Disolving is where a material goes rotten and dissolves until theres only a peice of material is left.I would say that when you leave something outside, the rain and the sun get to it, it starts to disolve.

JohnK — If I put a cup on the table and I put water in it and put a sweet like a refresher in it will dissolve.

Liam — When something dissolves, you can't see it.

Shelly — Dissolve means where it disapears onto something or into something.

India — I would say dissolving is where you put different things in with liquid to make it vanish e.g water and some tablets.

Laura — Disolving is were a liquid disappears onto a material, like wool or cotton, or it can disdapear in water and mix together.

Maria — Dissolving is if you put something into water it just dissolves or disappears.

Anwar — You put ice on a material and it will disappear, thats how it works.

Nico — Well dissolving is when something breaks apart like a paracetamol.

Jaycee — Dissolving is were a figure disappears.

Siobahn — It is when you leave an ice cube out and after a bit it will melt.

Mrs Clarke — Is that not called melting rather than dissolving Siobahn?

Hayleyw — Dissolving is when you put a tablet in a glass of water and it will dissipear in with the water and it will turn to liquid.

Connorp — What I know about dissolving is when carbon dioxide dissolves into water and reacts to form an acid. Carbon dioxide reacts to water to make carbonic acid. Thank you

Demi — Dissolve is where you put something in with something else e.g water (liquid) in with sugar.

Mrs Clarke — Have a look at this link and see if you were right? http://www.bbc.co.uk/bitesize/ks2/science/materials/changes_materials/read/4/

Understanding the capacity of the class to use ICT purposefully in science

In a number of the examples given in this and previous chapters, the selection of digital tools to support learning is determined by the value the resource can add to the learning experience. As Mr Andrews points out in his blog, the children in his class will not make use of digital resources if they are not helpful. In the examples given in Chapter 3 we discuss a topic where a class is looking at different soil types with a view to considering which will be the best for growing seeds. The most useful piece of equipment in the first lesson was the hand lens. Using a digital microscope might have helped, but having the whole class take

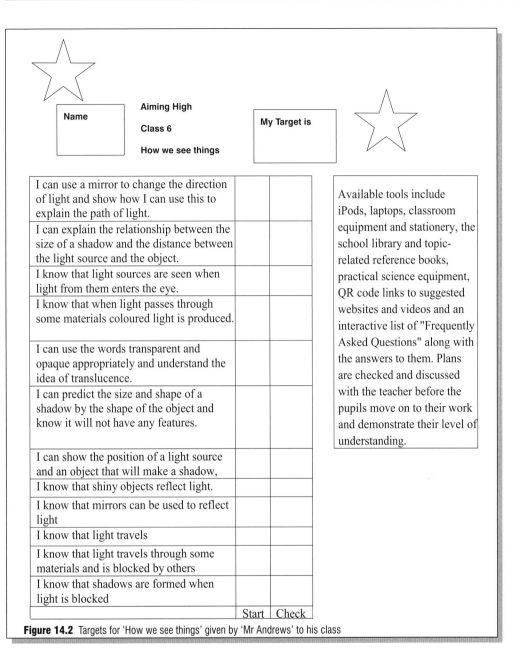

Figure 14.2 Targets for 'How we see things' given by 'Mr Andrews' to his class

turns would have been counterproductive, slowing down learning to no real advantage.

Where a resource would be helpful it is important to know the level of competence required of the children to use it. Children struggling with, or even so excited by the novelty of, some new piece of equipment can get in the way of learning. In a study of very young children's exposure to digital media Plowman *et al.* (2012) showed that, by the time the children in their case study entered school, nearly all had encountered digital media such as mobile phones, desktop and laptop computers and MP3 players. However, their competence and confidence varied greatly due to the kinds of technologies available in their homes and their opportunities to observe others and to participate in using them themselves.

It is useful to make an assessment of children's confidence in using digital tools. BECTA and ORC (2010) developed two useful self-assessment checklists (for lower and upper primary children). These ask children about their access and use of communications technology at home and their knowledge of how to: save a file to a computer; open a new document; find information online; download music, pictures or videos from the internet; send an email; use instant messaging software (e.g. MSN or Yahoo Messenger); add something to a wiki or blog; make a web page, wiki or blog; upload a video, picture or sound recording to the internet; send an attachment on an email; save a website as a favourite bookmark; create a podcast.

Whenever a teacher plans a topic using ICT tools it is important either to be sure that the children are confident with the equipment, or to give them the time to explore and practice in advance of their investigation.

Developing teachers' competence in using ICT

Activities described in all the foregoing sections underline the importance of the teacher's own digital literacy and the clear need to keep up to date. In a survey of teachers in England BECTA and ORC (2010) found that 75 per cent of primary teachers felt that they needed further development in using particular applications and devices. High proportions also agreed that they wanted further development in personalising learning, using assessment data and reporting online to parents as well as in using ICT for administration. These areas are all covered in online ICT CPD courses for teachers offered by the national professional association for ICT (NAACE). Many are free while some carry a fee (see website: ICTCPD4free). These are not science specific, but courses for primary teachers, such as those offered by National and Regional Science Learning Centres (see Chapter 25), often include an online element for participants and will reference the appropriate use of ICT.

One of the ways to keep on top of developments is to use the myriad of online resources available. Some require registration, such as the TES site, and others are, perhaps, biased to the particular interests of their funders, but they can provide lively discussion, tips and hints and examples of good practice. We have already mentioned a number of blogs by primary teachers and others interested in primary science. Useful and timely information and ideas can be gained and exchanged through Twitter, with feeds dedicated to science (from ASE) and primary science (Primary Science Geek). These change over time and so it is worth keeping an eye on what is available and signing up to those that are found helpful.

Summary

This chapter has been concerned with one of the most rapidly changing aspects of the primary classroom. The main points have been:

- the range and power of ICT tools available to children within and outside the classroom has mushroomed in recent years;

- as for any resources to support learning and teaching, the teacher's role is central if the resource is to advance children's learning;

- the effectiveness of computer technology in children's learning will therefore depend on the teacher's good planning and interventions designed to encourage children to make connections, to develop, evaluate and communicate ideas;

- selecting and using resources is dependent on the teacher having a clear idea of what it is the children will learn and the best way to go about creating opportunities that engage and motivate a class to collaborate and learn;

- although some children will be confident in the use of communications technology, this will not be the case for all, thus having an awareness of the level of understanding of individuals in the class is crucial, so that the demands of the equipment do not detract from the learning;

- teachers need to keep abreast of new developments and to find ways to maintain their own professional development in this area.

Further reading

Chippindall, J. (2012) Using free on-line survey software in your teaching, *Primary Science,* 121: 16–19.

Davies, D. (2010) Using new technologies creatively, in *Teaching Science Creatively,* London: Routledge, ch. 8.

Rees, C. (2013) Use of apps in science, *Primary Science* 127: 14–15.

Online resources (all of these can change or disappear)

Sites such as those of the Health and Safety Executive can give advice on internet and social networking safety www.hse.gov.uk/services/education/index.htm

The DigitalMe site provides in advice relating to use of social media: http://www.digitalme.co.uk/safe/

Some search engines such as MSN for kids are now limited to members, however, others, such as kidsclick and yahooligans, Google safe search and Ask Jeeves are readily available. These sites limit access to other sites to those that have been vetted.

Makewaves: this site is designed to be used by schools for social networking (e.g. blogs): https://www.makewav.es/about#

The popplet mind mapper is available as a free version and paid: https://itunes.apple.com/nz/app/popplet-lite/id364738549?mt=8

continued ...

CPD opportunities and advice for teachers

ICTCPD4Free is a website offering free and fee-paying ICT courses for teachers
http://www.ictcpd4free.co.uk/

TES has a very useful website with advice for teachers, helpful resources (although not all are free) and guides for making use of digital resources (e.g. how to set up a blog). Registration with the site is necessary. http://www.tes.co.uk/home. aspx

Twitter feeds

Primary Science Geek @priscigeeks

ASE Chat #asechat #teaching

Assessment for and of learning

15

Assessment purposes

Introduction

This first of five chapters on assessment clears some ground for later discussion of key aspects of assessment in the primary school. It deals with matters that are general to assessment in any subject area, leaving the discussion of matters specific to science for later chapters. We begin by defining assessment and related terms, distinguishing particularly between assessment and testing. The question of why we assess leads to identifying the purposes of assessment considered here as being for helping learning and for summarising learning. We then tackle questions of when and how to assess, involving decisions about what is relevant evidence, how to collect and interpret it and communicate the result. We discuss the meaning of reliability and validity in relation to assessment and how these two concepts interact. Finally we summarise the characteristics of formative and summative assessment.

Meaning and purposes of assessment

Meaning

Assessment in education is generally taken to be a process in which evidence is gathered about learners' achievements, interpreted and used for some purpose. It is in this sense that we use the term 'assessment' in this book, that is, as a process rather than a product. It is quite common, however, for the term to be used for the product (mark, grade, level, etc.) resulting from the process. So we may find this used in quoting various sources, but hopefully the context makes clear how the word is being used.

Related terms that are sometimes used interchangeably with assessment are 'evaluation' and 'appraisal'. An authoritative statement on the use of these words is given in an OECD report:

> The term 'assessment' is used to refer to judgements on individual student performance and achievement of learning goals. It covers classroom-based assessment as well as large-scale, external tests and examinations. The term 'appraisal' is used to refer to judgements on the performance of school-level

professionals, e.g. teachers and principals. Finally, the term 'evaluation' is used to refer to judgements on the effectiveness of schools, school systems and policies.

(Nusche *et al.*, 2012: 24)

It should be noted, though, that educational evaluation is the term used in some countries (particularly the USA) interchangeably with assessment to refer to the achievements of individuals. To make matters worse, some languages (such as Spanish) do not have separate words for assessment and evaluation, so again it is important to use the context to clarify the meaning of 'evaluation' and 'assessment' or to specify 'assessment of learning' where there is likely to be confusion.

There are many decisions involved in assessment concerning:

■ the range of evidence that is required to serve the purpose of the assessment;

■ how best to gather the evidence so that it is suited to the purpose;

■ how to interpret the evidence;

■ how to report and communicate the result to those who need to know what children are achieving.

Combining various ways in which evidence is collected and the various ways of interpreting and reporting it creates different methods of assessment. These range from standardised tests, where evidence is gathered when children are tackling carefully devised tasks under controlled conditions, to assessment carried out almost imperceptibly during normal interchange between teacher and children. The most appropriate form in a particular case should be decided by the purpose of the assessment.

Tests and other methods of assessment
While it is important to avoid jargon, is it necessary to be clear about meaning of various terms connected with assessment and to use them consistently. For instance the distinction between tests and assessment is central to current discussions about national testing and alternatives; to treat them as interchangeable would make nonsense of some important issues. Tests are one way of conducting assessment which is particularly suited to certain purposes. Tests are specially devised activities designed to assess knowledge and/or skills by giving precisely the same task to children who have to respond to it under similar conditions, which sometimes, but not always, involves time limits. Examinations are commonly combinations of tests or tests and other forms of assessment used for qualifications, entry into certain kinds of education or professions.

Tests are not necessarily externally devised; teachers prepare tests (e.g. of spelling, arithmetic) and some 'tests' can be embedded in classroom work and look very much like normal classroom work as far as the children are concerned. Also, regular classroom work can be assessed for reporting performance as well as for feedback to help learning. It is therefore more helpful to characterise assessment differences in terms of purposes rather in terms of methods.

Why do we assess?

There are two main reasons for assessing individual pupils in the primary school:

- to use the information to help learning;
- to find out and report on what has been learned at a particular time.

The first of these is described as formative assessment or assessment *for* learning (AfL). The second is described as summative assessment or assessment *of* learning. These are not different *kinds* of assessment but different purposes. Whether they serve their purpose depends on how the information is used. Formative assessment is, by definition, used to make decisions about how to advance learning while it is taking place. Summative assessment has several uses, including reporting to parents and other teachers, tracking progress and sometimes for grouping and selection. At the secondary level its uses include choosing courses of study, certification and selection for further or higher education. In principle, summative assessment should also help learning but in the longer term, through the decisions based on it, in a less direct way than in the case of formative assessment.

However, there are other ways in which information from assessment is used which have a considerable impact on teachers and schools and which cannot be ignored, although the main focus in this book is on assessment that helps learning and learning science in particular. The uses of results of assessment of individual pupils for evaluation of schools and the monitoring of national standards of achievement and for setting targets at school and national levels are highly controversial. The complex and sometimes technical arguments involved are discussed, for example, in Gardner (2012) and Harlen (2007). A brief overview of the impact of high stakes use of assessment results is given in Box 15.1.

When do we assess?

It may seem ominous to answer this question by saying 'all the time', or even 'at any time'. Such a reaction would indicate a view of assessment as something that causes anxiety – something we have to do but do not enjoy. Instead we should think of assessment as helping learning and therefore relevant at any point. Viewed in this way, it becomes part of the teaching. Take the case study of Chris's class, for instance (p. 42). At first reading it would be easy to assume that there was no assessment going on. There was no test at the end of the lesson, not even a quiz to find out what they had learned. But Chris 'circulated the groups asking them to explain why they had chosen particular places'. She could then understand their ideas and help them to try them out. She was able to respond within the lesson and ensured that the children knew the purpose of their activities.

Of course teachers have to plan and prepare lessons. However, not everything can be predetermined if challenges are to keep in step with children's development. There must always be room to adjust the pace – and even the direction – of the

---

Box 15.1 High stakes use of assessment results

The practice in England in 2013 is to use the percentages of pupils reaching level 2 at the end of KS1 and level 4 at the end of KS2 in mathematics and English in the evaluation of primary schools. (Until 2010, level 4 in science at the end of KS2 was also included.) The evidence used in deciding levels reached is obtained from national tests only. The consequences of pupils not achieving in the tests at the target levels can be severe, including the school being described as 'inadequate' in certain areas, being taken into different leadership or even closed. This is what is meant by the results having 'high stakes' attached. The publication of 'league tables' comparing schools with each other on the basis of results adds to the high stakes of the tests. To avoid the consequences of not meeting targets, inevitably teachers place emphasis on making sure that pupils' test results are maximised, with all that this implies for teaching to the test and giving practice tests (ARG, 2002). Since the range and number of items in the tests is limited to what can be included in short written tests, the effect is to narrow the curriculum and the teaching methods. Other well-documented consequences include teachers' focusing on children just below the target levels, spending a great deal of time in practising tests and reducing the use of assessment to help learning.

In other parts of the UK, in recognition of the problems just outlined, assessment arrangements have been changed to place greater emphasis in summative assessment on the use of teachers' judgements and avoid the creation of league tables.

---

lesson to respond to children's ideas and skills. We can see that Graham (p. 48) did this when eavesdropping on the groups exploring soils. He introduced the notion of humus and the need for air in the soil – ideas prepared but brought in by him only when they were not raised by the children. He also helped them to recognise what was needed in a group report on their work. Formative assessment means taking action as appropriate, but equally refraining from spending time on things the children already know or can do for themselves.

Processes of assessment

How do we assess?

We noted at the start of this chapter that assessment involves decisions about what evidence to gather, how to gather it, how to interpret it and how to report the resulting information. Note that 'evidence' becomes 'information' when it has been interpreted. A child's action or statement is evidence that could be interpreted in various ways and until interpreted it is only a fact. Once interpreted in terms of its significance for learning, the evidence has meaning and provides information about what the child can do or understands. (More correctly we should refer to 'data' rather than evidence, but this term is often taken to mean results of measurement that can be expressed in numbers; 'evidence' better expresses a range of different types of data.)

We deal here in brief outline with the 'what' and 'how' of collecting, interpreting and communicating evidence, taking up points about how they apply specifically to science education in later chapters.

Deciding what evidence to gather

Formative assessment is close to the learning, so the evidence required is everything that is relevant to learning at a particular time. The lesson goals, which will be communicated in some form to the children as discussed in Chapter 18, will be the main determinant of the evidence needed about cognitive development. Consequently, in line with her lesson goals, Chris was finding out what her 6 and 7 year olds knew about ice, what caused it to melt and what might prevent it from melting, and about their emerging ideas about a fair test. In the teacher's mind these lesson goals will be related to the broader concepts of change of state and development of inquiry and thinking skills identified as key concepts and processes in the curriculum. Information about the children's physical, emotional and motivational states will also be relevant for helping learning. Children who are upset, anxious or unwell are unlikely to make the effort that learning is likely to require.

A teacher may review children's work five or six times a year in order to monitor progress but make a formal summative report only once or twice a year. The information required for the latter will reflect evidence of learning from a series of lessons during the year, contributing to broader ideas, such as about 'the effects of heating and cooling on some everyday substances'.

Deciding how to collect evidence

The main methods for collecting evidence for assessment are

- observing children during regular work (this includes listening, questioning and discussing with them);
- studying the products of their regular work (including writing, drawings, artefacts and actions);
- observing children and/or studying the products of embedding special activities into the class work (such as concept-mapping, diagnostic tasks);
- giving tests (teacher-made or externally produced).

For formative assessment, regular work is a rich source of evidence about children's abilities and understanding which can be gathered through observation. But it is important to know what to look for in order to help progress. We give some ideas about this in Chapter 16.

Interpreting the evidence

Once evidence is gathered, it is interpreted in terms of what it means in relation to progress or achievement to date. This interpretation can be done in three main ways:

Box 15.2 The bases of judgements in assessment

Suppose that a teacher wants to assess a child's ability in knocking nails into wood. This can be described in different ways.

■ The teacher may have some expectation of the level of performance (knocking the nail in straight, using the hammer correctly, taking necessary safety precautions) and judge the child's performance in relation to these criteria. The judgement is made in terms of the extent to which the child's performance meets the criteria; that is, it is criterion-referenced.

■ Alternatively, the teacher may judge in terms of how the child performs at knocking in nails compared with other children of the same age and stage. If this is the case there will be a norm or average performance known for the age/stage group and any child can be described in relation to this as average, above average or below average, or more precisely identified if some quantitative measure has been obtained. (The result could be expressed as a 'knocking nails age' or a 'hammer manipulation' quotient!) The judgement arrived at in this way is called a norm-referenced assessment.

■ A third possibility is that the teacher compares the child's present performance with what the same child could do on a previous occasion – in which the case the assessment is child-referenced, or ipsative.

■ by reference to a description of what it means to be able to do something or to explain something that indicates ideas at a certain level (criterion-referenced);

■ by reference to what is usual for children of the same age and/or ability (norm-referenced);

■ by reference to what a child was previously able to do (child-referenced or ipsative).

Box 15.2 illustrates what these mean in terms of an example, which is not a serious suggestion but illustrates the principles.

How is the information communicated?
When the purpose of the assessment is formative, to help learning, then the information will be used by those involved in the learning – the teacher and the child – to decide about what are the next steps to take and how to take them. The way in which information is communicated from teacher to pupil is discussed in Chapter 17 and the role that pupils can take in Chapter 18.

If the purpose is summative (to summarise learning), then the judgement of what has been achieved will be used for reporting this to those who need this information. In addition to the child and his or her teacher, other teachers, including the head teacher, the parents and others with an interest in the progress of the children will want to know the results of the assessment. The information can be communicated in various ways, such as by scores from tests, grades, marks, levels and discursive accounts.

Tests scores give very little information about what children can and cannot do, being a summation over a diverse set of questions where the same total can be made up in different ways. A score also gives the impression of accuracy, which is far from being justified in consideration of the reliability and validity of tests (see later). Converting scores to levels or grades avoids this to a certain extent, but introduces other problems discussed later (Chapter 19).

In theory, reporting in terms of criteria which describe levels or grades can say something about what children have learned, but when a single overall grade or level has to combine many different domains it becomes almost meaningless. A profile giving information about different aspects is more meaningful. But expressing learning in terms of levels is only useful to those who know what they mean. For reporting to parents and students, the levels need to be explained or replaced by accounts of what the child can do (see Chapter 19).

How good is the assessment?

What we generally mean by 'good' assessment is practice that provides valid and reliable information through a process that is manageable and evidently useful. The validity and reliability of the results of assessment are key factors in deciding how effectively they serve the purpose of the assessment.

Validity
It is usual to define validity of an assessment in terms of how well what is assessed corresponds with the behaviour or learning outcomes that it is intended should be assessed. Determining the extent to which this is the case is complex and involves judgements of various kinds. The validity of an assessment depends, however, not only on its content but on how it is used. In the case of a test, for example, this may produce a valid result for some pupils, but not for others, perhaps for reasons of age, experience or reading ability. So validity is not a property of an assessment method or instrument regardless of the circumstances in which it is used.

Reliability
The reliability of an assessment refers to the extent to which the results can be said to be of acceptable consistency or accuracy for a particular use. It is often measured in terms of how likely it would be that the same result would be obtained if the assessment were to be repeated. Reliability depends on the procedure that is used. Thus tests comprising questions where children choose between fixed alternative answers (multiple-choice), that can be machine marked, are more reliable than ones that ask children to provide answers which then require some judgement in the marking. However, the latter may be a more valid test if the purpose is to find out what answers children can produce rather than choose. Here it becomes clear that attempts to make assessment results more reliable affect what is assessed – its validity. Indeed there is an inevitable interaction between the two, which is described in Box 15.3.

> **Box 15.3** The trade-off between reliability and validity
>
> These aspects of an assessment are not independent of one another, since if reliability is low this means that various unintended factors are influencing the result and therefore what is being assessed is uncertain. However, there is a limit to the extent that both reliability and validity can be high. To raise the reliability it is necessary to reduce the potential errors by using tasks and methods where outcomes can be consistently judged. This often means focusing on learning such as factual knowledge, where there is a clear right answer. But if the purpose is to assess skills and understanding, where we need children to generate rather than select answers, this would reduce the validity. On the other hand, to increase validity by including more open-ended tasks would reduce reliability because the marking would be less clear cut. Thus there is a trade-off between reliability and validity; increasing one decreases the other. There has to be a compromise and what this is depends on the purpose of the assessment.

For formative assessment validity is paramount; the assessment must provide information about all relevant goals and attributes related to learning. Reliability is less important because of the ongoing nature of the process. The information is used to inform teaching in the situations in which it is gathered. Thus there is always quick feedback for the teacher and any misjudged intervention can be corrected. Thus considerations of reliability do not need to impact on validity. This is not to say that teachers do not need to consider how they gather and interpret evidence, but they do not need to be concerned about accuracy in judging it in terms of grades or levels. Such accuracy is needed for summative teacher assessment, but formative assessment is concerned with the future, not with judgements about the past.

For summative assessment, however, reliability is important since its purpose is to provide information about where children have reached in their learning that parents and other teachers can depend upon. So attention has to be given to increasing reliability as far as possible without endangering validity.

Manageability
The resources required to provide an assessment ought to be commensurate with the value of the information to its users. The resources may be teachers' time, expertise and the cost both to the school and to external bodies involved in the assessment. In general there has to be a compromise, particularly where a high degree of accuracy is expected. There is a limit to the time and expertise that can be used in developing and operating, for example, a highly reliable external test or examination. Triple marking of all test papers would clearly bring greater confidence in the results; observers visiting all candidates would increase the range of outcomes that can be assessed externally; training all teachers to be expert assessors would have great advantages – but all of these are unrealistic in practice. Balancing costs and benefits raises issues of values as well as of technical possibilities.

The cost of formative assessment is negligible once it is incorporated into practice. The process of introducing it may well be considerable in terms of teachers' time for professional development. These costs, however, are integral to efforts to improve teaching and learning.

Summative assessment requires resources in terms of both teachers' and pupils' time. When tests developed by agencies outside the school or by commercial publishers are used, there is considerable financial cost and time taken in practising test-taking. Even if national tests and examinations are provided free to schools, the cost has to be borne by the system and can be surprisingly large, particularly when cost of development, postage and marking are added.

Characteristics of formative and summative assessment

We now bring together the points about assessment for the two main purposes that we are considering in this book – formative assessment (assessment for learning) and summative assessment (assessment of learning). In each case we consider what it is and why it is important.

Formative assessment

What it is

Formative assessment is assessment that helps learning. It does this through the process of 'seeking and interpreting evidence for use by learners and their teachers to decide where the learners are in their learning and where they need to go and how best to get there' (ARG, 2002). In other words it starts from what children already know and can do in relation to the goals of a particular area of learning and informs decisions about the steps needed to make progress.

Formative assessment can be represented as a cyclic process, as in Figure 15.1 where A, B and C represent activities through which pupils work towards the goals. If we break into the continuing cycle of events at activity A, evidence gathered in this activity is interpreted in terms of progress towards the goals of the work. Following the outer arrows round the cycle clockwise, this facilitates the identification of appropriate next steps and decisions about how to take them (leading to activity B). The cycle is repeated and the effects of decisions at one time are assessed at a later time as part of the ongoing process.

Describing the process in this way makes it appear far more formal and teacher-directed than is the case in reality. The actions indicated by the boxes in Figure 15.1 are not 'stages' in a lesson or necessarily conscious decisions made by the teacher. They represent a framework for thinking about what is involved in focusing on what and how children are learning and using this to help further learning. But of course it is the children who have to take the action; only they can do the learning. For this reason they are at the centre of the process and the two-headed arrows indicate their role as both providers of evidence and receivers of information. The developing theory of educational assessment, and various models within it, emphasises the important role that children have to play in their own assessment, as they come to understand the process, to learn to work

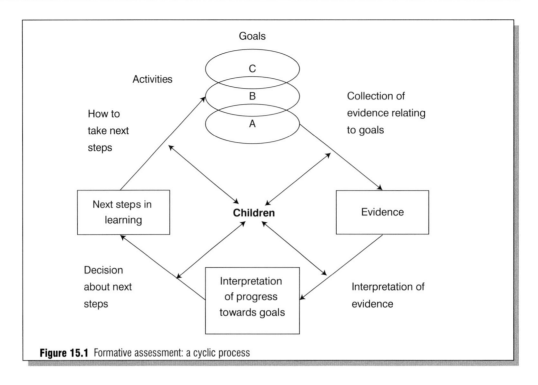

Figure 15.1 Formative assessment: a cyclic process

towards explicit standards and to modify what they do in relation to constructive task-related feedback from teachers (Gipps, 1994).

We look at various aspects of pupils' roles in self- and peer-assessment in Chapter 18.

Why it is important

The value of formative assessment is supported by both theories of learning and research into practice, as summarised in Box 15.4.

Formative assessment has to take account of all the aspects of children which affect their learning – not only the progress being made in knowledge and skills, but the effort put in and the other aspects of learning which are unspecified in the curriculum. It must be positive, indicating the next steps to take, not pointing out what is missing without identifying what to do about it. The teacher will have in mind the progression which is appropriate for the child, and this will be the basis of the action taken. Thus formative assessment is not a pure criterion-referenced assessment; it is more ipsative or child-referenced. The teacher will be looking across several instances in which a particular skill or idea is being used and will see variations and possibly patterns in behaviour. It is these variations (which would be seen as sources of 'error' if the purpose of the assessment were summative) that, in the formative context, provide diagnostic information.

So, to summarise, the characteristics of formative assessment are that it:

- takes place as an integral, not an occasional, part of teaching;
- relates to progression in learning;

Box 15.4 Empirical and theoretical support for formative assessment

The best known of several reviews of research studies on classroom assessment was carried out by Paul Black and Dylan Wiliam (1998a). They found a considerable positive impact of assessment on children's learning when certain conditions were in place. The main conditions were that the assessment:

■ involved sharing goals of learning with pupils,

■ helped pupils to know the standards to aim for,

■ provided feedback to help pupils know how to improve or move on,

■ involved pupils in the process of assessment and reflection of the information gained.

They also reported that 'improved formative assessment helps the (so-called) low attainers more than the rest, and so reduces the spread of attainment whilst also raising it overall' (Black and Wiliam, 1998b).

The theoretical reasons follow from the widely accepted theories of learning that emphasise the role of learners in constructing their own understanding. Formative assessment involves children in recognising where they are in progress towards goals and participating in decisions about their next steps in learning. The feedback provided through formative assessment has a role in regulating learning so that the pace of moving forward is adjusted to ensure the active participation of the learners. As in other regulated processes, feedback into the system is the important mechanism for ensuring effective operation. Just as feedback from a thermostat allows the temperature of a room to be maintained within a particular range, so feedback about learning helps to ensure that new experiences are neither too difficult nor too easy for learners (Harlen, 2006b).

■ depends on judgements which can be child-referenced or criterion-referenced;

■ provides feedback that leads to action supporting further learning;

■ uses methods which protect validity rather than reliability;

■ uses evidence from children's performance in a variety of contexts;

■ involves children in assessing their performance and deciding their next steps.

There is a good deal of common ground between formative assessment and learning through inquiry – both serve to develop learning with understanding and to enable students to take responsibility for identifying what they need to do to achieve the goals of their activities. It could almost be said that inquiry requires formative assessment. The additional features of formative assessment – the provision of formative feedback and the involvement of students in self- and peer-assessment – all support active engagement in learning and encourage students to take ownership of their learning and progress.

Summative assessment

What it is

Having described formative assessment as assessment that helps learning, there is a tendency to think of it as the 'good' face of assessment and to regard summative assessment as the 'bad' face. This is unfortunate because summative assessment has an important but different role in children's education. Its purpose is to give a summary of achievement at various times, as required. It may, and often does, have some impact on learning and the outcome may be used in teaching, but that is not its main rationale. We return to the relationship with formative assessment later, but for the moment represent the process as one of providing information purely for reporting achievement, as in Figure 15.2. Evidence used for this purpose may be gathered over time from regular activities or from special tasks or tests (see Chapter 19).

The interpretation is in terms of goals achieved over a period of time, not the lesson goals that are used in interpreting evidence for formative assessment. This marking or scoring can be carried out by the teacher or by an external agency, as in the case of some national tests and examinations. Only in the most informal classroom tests do students usually have a role in this process. Students are all judged by the same criteria, or mark schemes (rubrics), whereas, as noted earlier, in formative assessment criteria may be ipsative, or pupil-referenced, in order to help pupils recognise their progress from different starting points.

The interpretation necessarily reduces the richness of the actual performance to a score, category or mark that represents it; thus a great deal of information is lost. Depending on the use to be made of the result, the process of interpretation will include some procedure for increasing reliability. Where results are used to compare students, particularly where high stakes selection or grading is involved, steps are taken to check marking and moderate judgements by teachers or examiners.

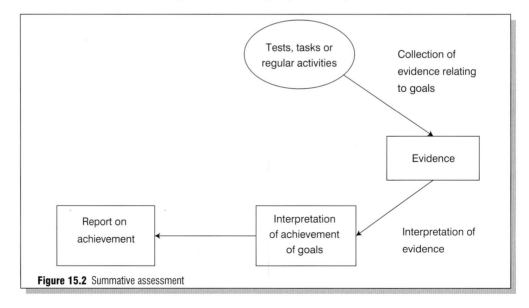

Figure 15.2 Summative assessment

Why it is important

Summative assessment is important for a number of reasons. Teachers need to keep records summarising children's performance at key points, such as the end of topics or terms, and to use these records in their planning. Children also need to keep track of their progress. Parents and children's next teachers at points of transition from class to class or school to school need records of what has been achieved. School principals and managers need to have records so that they can review progress of individual and groups of children as they pass through the school for use in school self-evaluation and curriculum planning. All these reasons mean that summative assessment is necessary and cannot be avoided. By contrast, formative assessment could be considered, in a sense, to be voluntary, in that teachers choose to use it.

Since the purpose is to report achievement to parents, other teachers, children, school governors, etc. then reliability of the information is important and the criteria have to be used uniformly. Thus, if the summary is based on a review of evidence gathered during teaching, some form of moderation, or procedure for quality assurance, is required. So the characteristics of summative assessment are that it:

- takes place at certain intervals when achievement has to be reported;
- relates to progression in learning against public criteria;
- enables results for different children to be combined for various purposes because they are based on the same criteria;
- requires methods which are as reliable as possible without endangering validity;
- involves some quality assurance procedures;
- should be based on evidence relating to the full range of learning goals.

The relationship between formative and summative assessment

The list of characteristics of formative and summative assessment show the differences between these two purposes; differences which should be kept very clearly in mind, especially when both are carried out by teachers. It is too often assumed that all assessment by teachers is formative or that assessment carried out frequently in any way is formative. Unless the assessment is used to help the ongoing learning, this is not the case. Where this happens the true value of formative assessment will not be realised.

Nevertheless, these are good reasons for expecting that all assessment should ultimately help learning (Harlen, 2010b). The uses of summative assessment suggested above indicate that, whilst summative assessment is not intended to have direct impact on learning as it takes place, as does formative assessment, it nevertheless can be used to help learning in a less direct way by informing decisions about appropriate future educational provision. There is also the opportunity to use evidence that is gathered to help learning, in order to build a picture that summarises learning at a particular time. This depends on the teacher having responsibility for summative assessment and on making a clear distinction between evidence and its interpretation. The process is discussed further, with examples, in Chapter 19.

Summary

This chapter has defined assessment as the process of deciding, collecting and interpreting evidence about children's learning and skills and using the information for some purpose. It has considered the why, when and how of assessment and the characteristics of assessment for formative and summative purposes. The main points have been:

- How assessment is best carried out depends on its purpose.

- The purposes considered in this book are assessment for a formative purpose (assessment *for* learning) and assessment for a summative purpose (assessment *of* learning).

- Testing is not to be equated with assessment; it is one way of conducting assessment.

- Evidence of children's achievements can be interpreted by comparing it with norms, criteria of performance or the child's previous achievement.

- Depending on the purpose of the assessment, different emphasis is laid on reliability (accuracy of the assessment result) and validity (what inferences can be drawn about children's achievements from the results).

- The characteristics of formative and summative assessment differ in how evidence is interpreted and in the use of information, more than in the methods used for collecting evidence.

Further reading

Harlen, W. (2005) Teachers' summative practices and assessment for learning – tensions and synergies, *Curriculum Journal*, 16(2): 207–23.

Harlen, W. (2010) What is quality teacher assessment? in J. Gardner, W. Harlen, L. Hayward, G. Stobart and M. Montgomery, *Developing Teacher Assessment*, Maidenhead: Open University Press.

Harrison, C. and Howard, S. (2010) Issues in primary assessment 1: assessment purposes, *Primary Science*, 115: 5–7.

Wiliam, D. (2008) Quality in assessment, in S. Swaffield (ed.) *Unlocking Assessment*, London: David Fulton, ch. 8.

16

Gathering evidence to help learning

Introduction

As we noted at the end of the last chapter, formative assessment is a continuing cyclic process which informs ongoing teaching and helps learners' active engagement in learning. The cycle involves the collection of evidence about learning, the interpretation of that evidence in terms of progress towards the goals of the work, the identification of appropriate next steps and decisions about how to take them. In this and the next two chapters processes involved in this cycle of events are discussed and illustrated. This chapter makes a start by discussing the importance of having clear goals and a range of strategies for gathering evidence about the children's ideas and inquiry skills. How this evidence is interpreted to give information about progress in relation to the achievement of lesson goals, and used as feedback into teaching and learning, is the subject of Chapter 17, whilst the role of children in the process of using assessment for learning is taken up in Chapter 18.

Having clear goals in mind

Clarity of goals is a pivotal requirement for all assessment; the difficulty that this often presents to primary teachers, in science, accounts for a good deal of uncertain practice in assessment in this area. Sometimes the focus is so much on what the children will be *doing* that what they are intended to *learn* from it is left a little hazy. Teachers need to have a clear idea in mind of what ideas and skills the children should be developing before they can find out about what relevant ideas and skills they already have. But science learning goals can be expressed with different degrees of specificity and while 'attainment targets' or other ways of specifying intended learning in national curricula have helped to communicate overall goals, it is still up to the teacher to identify the specific lesson goals. These must be clear if assessment is to be used to help learning.

Broad aims such as 'ability to plan and conduct a scientific investigation' or 'understanding the diversity and adaptation of organisms' are too general to be achieved in a single lesson or even a set of lessons on a particular topic. The goals of a specific lesson might include the understanding of how the structure of particular plants or animals is suited to the places where they are found. This will contribute to a broader goal of understanding how living organisms in general are suited to their habitats, but achieving this understanding will depend on looking at a variety of organisms, which will be the subject of other lessons across the years with their own specific goals. Similarly, skills such as planning a scientific investigation are developed not in one lesson, but in different contexts through various lessons and topics.

Gaining access to children's ideas and inquiry skills

In Chapter 13 we mentioned the relevance of a positive learning environment that enables children to feel free to express their ideas and reasons for action without fear that what they say or do will be 'wrong' or will be dismissed as unworthy of attention. It is important to keep this in mind in this context since, if teachers are to gain access to children's ideas and skills as required for formative assessment, such a safe environment for expressing them is essential.

Against this general background of a supporting classroom climate, there are various strategies that teachers can use for eliciting students' ideas and finding out about their inquiry skills. These are listed in Box 16.1 and each is illustrated in the following sections. Some of these methods are useful for collecting information about skills and others about ideas. For instance, concept mapping has great potential for finding out children's ideas, whilst observing actions provides rich information about skills and attitudes. However, most are capable of providing information about both, and since inquiry-based learning will involve children in developing their understanding through using inquiry skills, it makes sense to consider what can be learned about both in the same situation where this applies.

Box 16.1 Strategies for gaining access to children's ideas and inquiry skills

- Questioning – using open and person-centred questions.
- Observing – focusing on significant indicators of development.
- Asking for writing or drawings that communicate what students think.
- Involving children in concept mapping.
- Initiating debate with concept cartoons.
- Engaging in discussion through puppets.
- Eavesdropping and discussing words.
- Using technology to discuss specific activities with children.
- … and hundreds more.

Questioning

We discussed the form and content of teachers' questions in Chapter 10. Here we are particularly interested in those questions that reveal children's ideas and inquiry skills. Consider, for instance, a situation in which a teacher has provided lots of home-made and other musical instruments for children to explore as a preliminary to more structured activities aimed at the idea that sound is caused by objects vibrating. To find out the ideas the children already have the teacher might ask questions such as:

1. What is happening when you pluck the string and hear the sound?
2. What causes the guitar to make a sound?
3. Why does the sound change when you shorten the string?
4. Explain why you are able to make the bottle make a sound by blowing across the top?

Or, the teacher might ask:

5. What do you think makes the sound when you pluck the string?
6. What are your ideas about how the guitar makes a sound?
7. What do you think is the reason for the bottle making a sound when you blow across the top?
8. What are your ideas about why you get different sounds when you shorten the string?

Or, perhaps:

9. What difference do you see in the drum when it makes a sound?
10. What do you think will happen if you make the string even shorter?
11. How can you show me what makes a difference to the note you get by blowing across the top of the bottle?
12. What could you do to find out if the way you pluck the string makes a difference?

In the first set (1–4) the questions are open ones (see Box 10.2), but they ask directly for *the* answer, not the children's ideas about what is happening. These are subject-centred questions (see Box 10.3) and do not specifically ask the children to express their ideas. By contrast, the questions in set 5–8 are expressed so as to ask for the children's own ideas, with no suggestion that there is a right answer. They are person-centred open questions. All the children should be able to answer the second set, while only those who feel that they can give the right answer will attempt to answer the first set. Thus the open, person-centred questions are preferred for eliciting children's ideas.

The questions in the third set (9–14) are also expressed as open, person-centred questions, but they are more likely to lead to action and to the use of inquiry skills. To answer them children have to use or describe how they would use inquiry skills – observation, prediction, planning. Although the actions taken would imply some ideas about the cause of the effects, these questions are more useful for finding out about children's ways of observing or investigating than for eliciting their ideas.

A further point about questioning that should be recalled in this context is the importance of giving children time to answer. The 'wait' time (see Box 10.6) is necessary not only to allow for the children to think and to formulate their answer but to convey the message that the teacher is really interested in their ideas and will listen to them carefully. It also slows down the discussion, giving the teacher time to phrase thoughtful questions and the children time to think before answering. The whole exchange is then more productive in terms of giving teachers access to children's real understanding and not just their first superficial thoughts.

Observing

There is a great deal of information to be gained, particularly about children's inquiry skills from observing how they go about their investigations or seek evidence from secondary sources. The main problem is one of logistics – how to observe each and every child in relation to a range of skills and attitudes. This is an impossible task and is not to be expected. It is made manageable by planning and focusing. Not all skills will be used in every inquiry and so the focus can be on the particular skills that are the goals of the lesson and the content of the activities will determine the specific ideas that will be being developed. Moreover, while in theory everything a child does can give some evidence of his or her thinking, some things are more useful than others. So it helps to be able to pick out the behaviours of most significance. This is where 'indicators' come in. Indicators describe aspects of behaviour that can be taken as evidence of certain skills and ideas being used. Indicators can be even more useful if they describe progression in development of the skills.

Identifying developmental indicators
The starting point in developing such indicators, say in relation to skills of observation, is to ask the question: *what kinds of actions would indicate that a child is using observation skills?* The first thought might be that the child seems to be paying attention to details, which might show through noticing similarities and differences between things, perhaps using senses other than sight. Then the question: *how would this be different for younger than for older children?* For the younger child the similarities and differences might be just the obvious ones, while for the older child we would expect more detail, more accuracy in observation, through using measurement and checking results. The differences would reflect the dimensions of developing inquiry skills set out in Chapter 12 (Box 12.1).

Given more information about the development of skill in observation, these statements could be refined into a list of indicators arranged as far as possible in the sequence of development. 'As far as possible' is a necessary qualification because there is not likely to be an exact and invariable sequence that is the same for all children, but it is helpful to have a rough idea. As a result of this kind of thinking, and using shared experience of how children's skills develop, a set of statements about how 'gathering evidence by observing' shows in what children do can be identified. For instance:

- Making use of several senses in exploring objects or materials.

- Identifying relevant differences of detail between objects or materials and identifying points of similarity between objects where differences are more obvious than similarities.

- Using their senses appropriately and extending the range of sight using a hand lens or microscope as necessary.

- Taking steps to ensure that the results obtained are as accurate as they can reasonably be by repeating observations where possible.

This is how the indicators given in Chapter 17 were created. Boxes 17.1–17.4 give the result of similar exercises for the groups of inquiry skills identified in Chapter 12. Boxes 17.5 and 17.6 refer to the scientific attitudes identified in Chapter 13. (The indicators serve both to focus observation to gather evidence and to interpret the evidence, which is why they are situated in Chapter 17.)

The progress in forming scientific ideas, discussed in Chapter 11, can similarly be expressed in general terms that can be applied to particular ideas being developed in an investigation. A child would show a good grasp of an idea by expressing it in a way that applies to a range of relevant events or phenomena and one that explains rather than merely describes. By contrast, at an early stage the idea is likely to refer only to a specific situation (a 'small' idea as compared with a 'bigger' one which explains more things). For example, in discussing how worms live in soil, reference to living things being adapted to their environment shows a more advanced understanding than simply referring to their shape. This approach leads to the generic indicators of development of scientific ideas in Box 17.8.

Using developmental indicators
Developmental indicators have two important roles:

- To focus attention on aspects of behaviour which signify skills, attitudes in action or the development of understanding. Knowing what to look for makes observing much easier.

- To help in interpreting evidence and deciding about next steps and how to take them.

The use of the indicators for the second purpose is considered in Chapter 17, where the lists of indicators can be found. Our focus here is the use in collecting evidence by observing children whilst they are involved in their activities, providing a rich source of evidence for use in helping their learning.

As noted earlier, almost everything that a child does could provide useful evidence for formative assessment, but paying attention to details of behaviour for all children is impossible. Some planning is necessary. In deciding when to observe and what to observe it helps to distinguish between those aspects of behaviour where there are frequent opportunities for observation and those where opportunities are infrequent. Many (most?) activities involve children in using inquiry skills; thus there are frequent events where these skills can be observed in action. By contrast, opportunities to gather evidence related to grasp of particular concepts are limited by the content of the activity – you cannot assess children's ideas about living things whilst they are engaged in exploring electric circuits. However, children's written work and other products can provide evidence of their understanding to supplement what teachers can find out through questioning and observing.

Since children are working in groups for most of the time, the question arises as to whether evidence is gathered about groups as a whole or about individuals. As noted in Harlen (2006a: 110), 'teachers generally have no difficulty in identifying the separate contributions of children even when they are combining their ideas and skills in a group enterprise'. Further, when the evidence is used for feedback into teaching (see Chapter 17), it is not always necessary to assess individual children. If the information is used to make decisions about the activities and help to be given to children as a group, then assessment of the group is all that is needed for this purpose. Evidence of the achievements of individuals can be found from the products of their work and discussion of these products.

Children's drawings

In the earlier discussion of questioning it was implicit that the questions and answers were oral. Alternatively, in some circumstances children may write or draw to express their ideas and inquiry skills. This can give the teacher a view of the full range of ideas in the class and a permanent record for each child which can be perused at a later time. The same points made about oral questions apply, however, to the form of the questions that the teacher asks in setting children's written work and drawings in order to find out their ideas and skills; open, person-centred questions are necessary.

Examples of children's drawings which reveal their ideas have been given in Chapter 5. It is not easy for anyone to draw abstract concepts such as ideas about melting, force or evaporation. The use of labels and annotation is necessary as a commentary on what is represented, but the drawing is essential for conveying the image that the child has in mind. For example, the drawing in Figure 16.1 by a 7 year old shows very clearly that the child considered the direct action of the sun to be important in causing the disappearance (by evaporation) of water from a tank.

In this example we see that the value for opening access to children's ideas depends on how the drawing task is set. Merely asking for a drawing to show the water levels in the tank would not necessarily be useful in this respect. A request for a drawing of 'what you think makes the water level change' is more fruitful.

Another kind of drawing that helps children to show their ideas is to create a 'strip cartoon' or a series of drawings across time, as in the example of the representation of the stages in the manufacture of a spoon in Figure 16.2. In this case the teacher asked the children to draw what they thought the object was like just before it was in its present form, then what it was like just before that and so on.

(Age 7 years)

"The sun is hot and the water is cold and the water sticks to the sun and then it goes down"

Figure 16.1 A 7 year old's ideas about evaporation of water (from Russell and Watt, 1990: 29)

what it is like	what it was like before that	and before that	and before that
It is shiny and it is a silvery colour. It has got a handle. You eat with it.	It is a liquid – it is melted. It is a silvery colour. It is very hot. This is put in a moulding shape and then it is left to cool.	This is being boiled down in a big pan. It is hot and sticky.	These are iron and metal. If they are mixed together they make steel. The iron is heavier than the metal.

Figure 16.2 A child's idea of the origin of a spoon (unpublished SPACE research

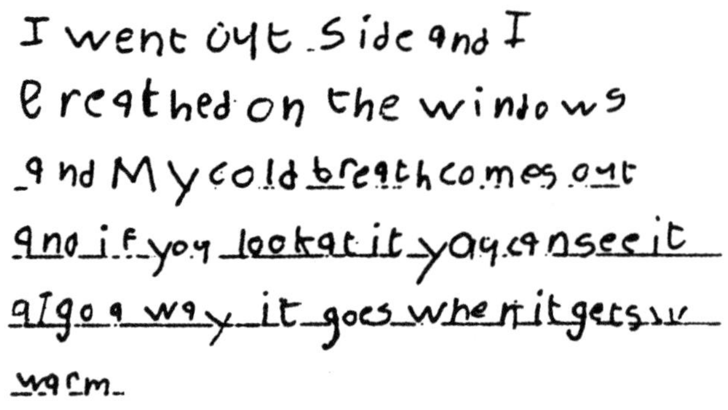

> I went out side and I
> e reathed on the windows
> and My cold breath comes out
> and if you look at it you can see it
> algo a way it goes when it gets v
> warm

Figure 16.3 A 6 year old's writing about condensation (from Russell and Watt, 1990)

> by putting a peice of glass
> covering it and it will last
> longer because it can't gas
> out.

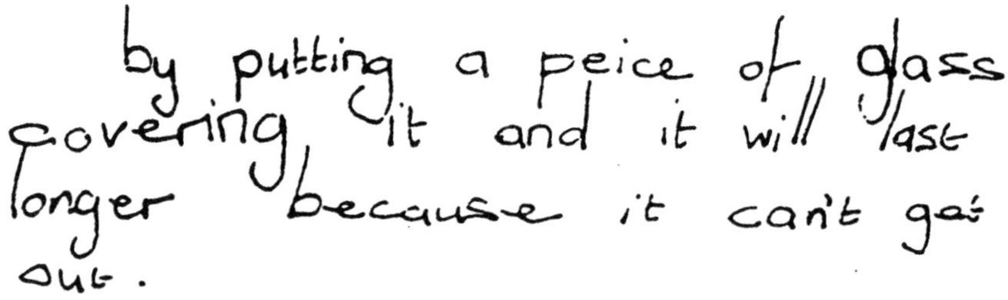

Figure 16.4 A 10 year old using ideas about evaporation to suggest how to prevent it (from Russell and Watt, 1990)

Children's writing

While drawings can usually be made by even the youngest children, writing is most helpful when children become at ease in doing it. Figure 16.3 was written by a 6 year old to explain why the condensation from her breath on a cold window went away. This shows, as does the 10 year old's answer to how to slow down evaporation of water from a tank (Figure 16.4), the value of not just asking for writing about what has been observed but posing questions that require ideas to be used.

Children's written work also provides information about their inquiry skills, particularly in the case of older children. Again, it is important for the task to be set so that the children are required to describe what they have done, or plan to do. The examples in Figures 16.5 to 16.7 illustrate the value of the products. They all come from Paterson (1987).

In Figure 16.5 two predictions are made, both of which can be tested by investigation. The first prediction is based on the everyday experience that it is easier to see things which are closer than when they are far away. However, the basis of the second prediction, about people wearing glasses, is less easy to follow and deserves discussion.

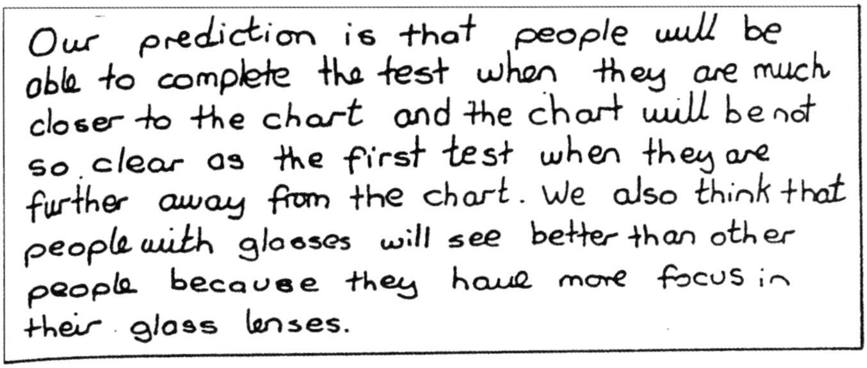

> Our prediction is that people will be able to complete the test when they are much closer to the chart and the chart will be not so clear as the first test when they are further away from the chart. We also think that people with glooses will see better than other people because they have more focus in their gloss lenses.

Figure 16.5 An 11 year old's prediction as part of planning an investigation

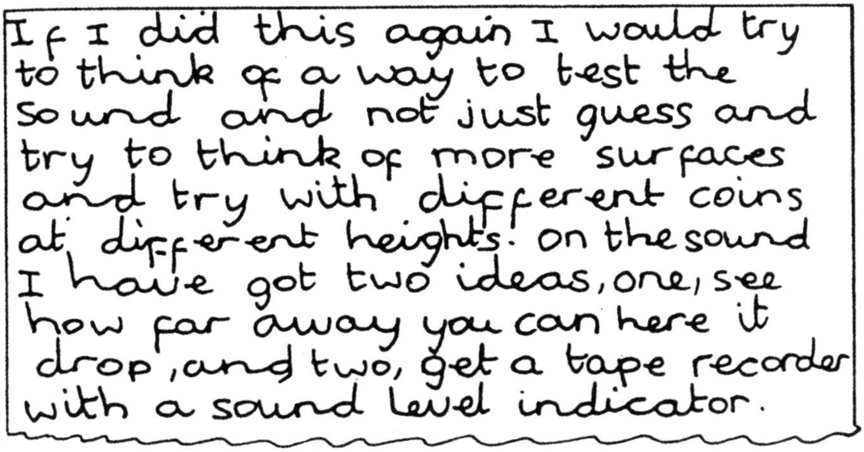

> If I did this again I would try to think of a way to test the sound and not just guess and try to think of more surfaces and try with different coins at different heights on the sound I have got two ideas, one, see how far away you can here it drop, and two, get a tape recorder with a sound level indicator.

Figure 16.6 A 9 year old's reflection after reporting her investigation

Figure 16.6 shows a child's reflection on an investigation of how far away the sound can be heard of a coin being dropped. Not only does she identify the deficiencies of the investigation carried out, but shows some aspects of planning, including the ingenious use of an instrument to measure the sound level.

Figure 16.7 shows very detailed observation, using four senses, carefully and vibrantly described so that the reader can almost share the experience.

Concept maps

A concept map is another kind of drawing that is particularly useful for finding children's ideas. Concept maps are diagrammatic ways of representing conceptual links between words. There are certain rules to apply which are very simple and readily grasped by children of 5 or 6. If we take the words 'ice' and 'water' we can relate them to each other as in Figure 16.8 by connecting them with an arrow to signify a relationship between them. If we write 'melts to give' on the arrow, we have a way of representing the proposition that ice melts to give water, but not vice versa. We can add to this by linking other words and so forming a map.

When we examined a lychee we found out that the skin or peel had tiny hairs on it. When we held it quite far away the whole fruit looked like a hard and over grown rasberry. When we tasted the peel it was like an advocardo. The peel was all either red or yellow as I just said the red tasted like an advocardo but the yellow was rearly dicusting this ment that the fruit is ripe when it is red or yellow. Then when we took the peel of totltaly we found that there was another skin but this was transparent. When we took that skin of we found that the juice was in some sort of segments like an orange. Then we tasted the flesh and it was lovely. After that we found a stone or seed in the middle so we cut it open and it went broun after a few seconds then we smelt it and it smelt like a conker.(or Horse Chessnut)

Figure 16.7 Observations recorded by two ten year olds

Asking children to draw their ideas about how things are linked up provides insight into the way they envisage how one thing causes another. The starting point is to list words about the topic the children are working on and then ask them to draw arrows and to write 'joining' words on them. Figure 16.9 shows the list and the map which 6-year-old Lennie drew after some activities about heat and its effect on various things. It is possible to spot from this that Lennie has not

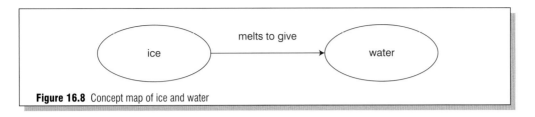

Figure 16.8 Concept map of ice and water

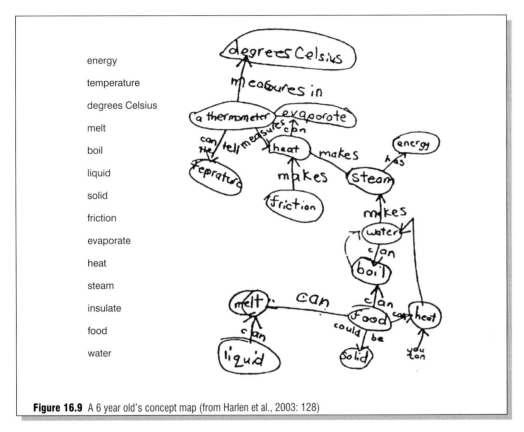

Figure 16.9 A 6 year old's concept map (from Harlen et al., 2003: 128)

yet distinguished heat from temperature but that he has some useful ideas about what heat can do. As with all diagrams, it is advisable to discuss them with the child to be sure of the intended meaning.

Concept cartoons

Concept cartoons were devised by Naylor and Keogh (2000). An example is given in Figure 16.10, but a wide range of cartoons have been published and used both with trainee teachers and primary children. Their key features include:

■ Representing scientific ideas in everyday situations wherever possible, so that connections are made between scientific ideas and everyday life.

■ Using minimal amount of text, in order to make the ideas accessible to learners with limited literacy skills.

Figure 16.10 Concept cartoons: ideas about germinating seeds (from Naylor and Keogh, 2000: 30)

- Using simple cartoon-style presentation which is visually appealing and which empowers teachers and learners to create their own concept cartoons.

- Using published research to identify common areas of misunderstanding, which then provide a focus for the concept cartoon.

(Keogh and Naylor, 1998: 14)

The applications of concept cartoons have been widely extended and their uses include assessment and research. For finding out children's ideas and skills, children discuss the ideas suggested by the cartoon characters either in small groups or as a whole class and talk about why they may agree or disagree with the suggestions, or give their own ideas. In many cases the situations have no 'right' answer and in all cases the discussion of pros and cons of the suggestions made requires some explanation of why one or another view could be supported. The situations and speech bubbles can refer to how to conduct an investigation, such as 'how are we going to find out if sunshine makes any different to how quickly these ice cubes melt?' with different suggested ways of doing this. Alternative ways of using this device include leaving the speech bubbles empty and asking children to complete them with their own ideas after discussion, or the teacher completing them after asking for children's ideas.

Using puppets

The use of puppets to represent the characters in concept cartoons brings life to situations presented in the cartoons in the same way that puppets can 'bring stories to life'. Keogh *et al.* (2006) researched the use of puppets in helping children across the whole primary school age range to engage in talk about situations involving scientific ideas and inquiries. The idea is that children talk to the puppets rather than the teacher. The approach works because it is easier for many children to respond to an idea from a puppet and to address their ideas to a puppet than to a teacher. It is also easier for the teacher to suggest, through a puppet, non-scientific ideas for the children to challenge than to express such ideas directly to children. The puppet can keep asking questions for explanations – 'I don't understand'; 'explain to me why you think that' – enabling the teacher to probe the children's thinking.

Eavesdropping and discussing words

Concept cartoons also provide a very useful way of setting up small group discussions that allow the teacher to listen in to the conversation without taking part. Setting groups to work on a combined concept map serves a similar purpose. Children-only discussions are valuable in freeing children to express their ideas in their own words. To quote Douglas Barnes:

> The teacher's absence removes from their work the usual source of authority; they cannot turn to him [sic] to solve dilemmas. Thus … the children not only formulate hypotheses, but are compelled to evaluate them for themselves. This they can do in only two ways: by testing them against their existing views of 'how things go in the world', and by going back to 'the evidence'.
>
> (Barnes, 1976: 29)

So 'listening in' can help the teacher to find out how children are reasoning and using evidence in their arguments as well as about the words they use. When the children are talking directly to each other they use words that they and their peers understand. These, as well as the explanations and reasons that they give to each other, can give clues as to their ideas. For example in their discussions of melting children often appear to confuse it with dissolving. Being alerted to this the teacher can take some action to find out whether the children have not distinguished between the processes of melting and dissolving or just not realised which is called melting and which is dissolving. In such cases it is important to explore the children's meaning for the words in order to know what their ideas are. It is useful to ask them to give an example of melting or to say how they would try, for instance, to make sugar melt. This would indicate whether melting is different in their mind from dissolving. (Other points about using scientific words are discussed in Chapter 7.)

Using technology to discuss specific activities with children

The ready availability of cameras in phones and i-pads has opened up a new set of opportunities for exploring children's thinking. The speed with which the photographs can be displayed on a computer screen or an interactive white board means that teachers can study images of children within a short time of the event, discuss with the children their thinking at the time or preserve the images for perusal later. An example was described by Lias and Thomas (2003), working with 8 year olds:

> During the activity (making a 'circuits game' for practising multiplication tables) we took several digital photographs of the children making and testing their circuits to display later. Because there was a PC, an LCD projector and an interactive whiteboard in the room, we decided to show the photographs to the children at the end of the activity. … The captured images of particular events helped children to recall what they were doing at a particular time and prevented confusion over which event was being discussed. They also helped to keep the children's minds focused and provided a visual scaffold to support their descriptions and explanations. Compared with previous occasions, the children answered questions far more confidently and fluently, needed far less prompting and support, and their responses were far more detailed and complete.
>
> (Lias and Thomas, 2003: 18)

… and hundreds more!

Many activities through which teachers engage children in learning science are at the same time opportunities for assessing their ideas and ability to investigate in a scientific manner, or can easily be adapted for this purpose by adding questions or challenges such as spotting (deliberate) mistakes in arguments. Naylor *et al.* (2004) have brought together an extensive collection of ideas for activities that provoke children to express their thinking. Some of these are similar to those discussed in this chapter, but there are many more. For example:

- Sorting cards: children are given cards with statements or pictures on them. They use this information to sort them into different groups and then explain their reasons, which indicate the ideas they have about the depicted objects or events.

- KWL grids: simple three-column grids in which children or teacher set out what the children think they Know, what they Want to know about a topic and then what they have Learned. They are used at the start and end of a topic and help both children and teacher to focus on what needs to be learned and what had been learned.

- Matching exercises: in which children make connections between two sets of information, one likely to be a list of names and the other descriptions, properties or functions. Useful for identifying ideas at the start of a topic.

- Generating questions: in which children are the ones who think up questions that it is useful to ask about a topic.

- Sequencing: where children are given a set of statement, pictures or ideas about a scientific process and are asked to arrange them in a logical sequence.

■ Thought experiments: where children make predictions about a situation which cannot be investigated in real life, perhaps because it is imaginary or inaccessible. Used to introduce a topic, their ideas indicate what they already know and how they can apply it in novel situations.

For each of the 32 strategies they describe, Naylor *et al.* (2004) give examples of their use with younger and older pupils.

Summary

This chapter has discussed ways of gathering information about children's scientific ideas and inquiry skills to use to help learning. All the methods are ones that teachers can use during regular science activities in the classroom or elsewhere. The main points have been:

■ It is important to be clear about the specific goals of the children's activities in order to focus the information gathering.

■ Also important is a classroom ethos in which children feel comfortable in expressing their ideas.

■ The main strategies that are useful in gathering information from regular activities are questioning, observation, writing or drawing tasks that reveal their ideas and skills, concept mapping, discussing concept cartoons, using puppets, eavesdropping and discussing words and using technology to reflect on particular activities.

■ Most useful questions for gaining access to children's ideas and skills are open and person-centred.

■ Observation needs to be planned and focused by knowing what behaviours are useful indictors of the development of skills, attitudes and conceptual understanding.

Further reading

Goldsworthy, A. (2003) *Raising Attainment in Primary Science: Assessment, Monitoring and Evaluation,* Oxford: GHPD

Keogh, B., Naylor, S., Downing, B., Maloney, J. and Simon, S. (2006) Puppets bringing stories to life in science, *Primary Science Review,* 92: 26–8.

Naylor, S. and Keogh, B. (2000) *Concept Cartoons in Science Education,* Sandbach: Millgate House Publishing.

Naylor, S., Keogh, B. with Goldsworthy, A. (2004) *Active Assessment: Thinking Learning and Assessment in Science,* London: David Fulton in Association with Millgate House Publishers.

Website

Puppets Project Resources from Millgate House Education Ltd: www.millgatehouse.co.uk

17

Interpreting evidence for feedback

Introduction

In Chapter 15 we described formative assessment as an ongoing cyclic process in which evidence is gathered and used by teacher and pupils to regulate teaching and learning and ensure children's active engagement in learning. In Chapter 16 we considered the importance of goals and ways of gathering evidence. In this chapter, continuing round the cycle, we consider the interpretation of the information, the decision about next steps and how to take them. In the first of three main sections, we propose the use of developmental indicators relating to science inquiry skills and attitudes in guiding decisions about next steps in children's learning. The second section proposes a similar approach that can be used for helping progress in scientific ideas. The third section concerns the use of feedback in adjusting teaching and ways of providing feedback to children that have a positive impact on their learning.

Interpreting evidence of children's inquiry skills and attitudes

The model of formative assessment (Figure 15.1) suggests that, in order to decide the next steps for children to take in learning, evidence of current skills and understanding is interpreted in terms of progress towards the goals of the activity. The idea of identifying indicators of development of inquiry skills and attitudes and using them for two purposes in formative assessment was introduced in Chapter 16. The first was in focusing the collection of evidence on aspects of behaviour signifying the development of certain skills and attitudes. The second, considered here, was in interpreting evidence to decide next steps. For this purpose the indicators of development of science inquiry skills and scientific attitudes in Boxes 17.1 to 17.6 were identified using the methods described in Chapter 16.

Within each of the boxes the attempt has been to list the indicators in a sequence in which they are most *likely* to be developed by children during the primary and middle school years. However, this will not necessarily be the case for every child. The progression here has elements of putting together the pieces of a jigsaw rather than climbing the steps of a ladder (Harlen, 2010b). In other words it will not be that each step necessarily follows on from the one before. Each piece of the jigsaw is needed and if it is not put in place earlier this will have to be done later. It should also be noted that there are no 'levels', grades or stages suggested. For formative assessment it is not necessary to tie indicators to grades or levels: all that is required is to see where children are and what further progress they can make. The statements are labelled (a) to (e) for convenience of reference.

Box 17.1 Things children do that indicate gathering evidence by observing and using information sources

(a) Make use of several senses in exploring objects or materials.

(b) Identify relevant differences of detail between objects or materials and identify points of similarity between objects where differences are more obvious than similarities.

(c) Use their senses appropriately and extend the range of sight using a hand lens or microscope as necessary.

(d) Take steps to ensure that the results obtained are as accurate as they can reasonably be by repeating observations where possible.

(e) Regularly and spontaneously use printed and electronic information sources to check or supplement their own observations.

Box 17.2 Things children do that indicate raising questions, predicting and planning investigations

(a) Readily ask a variety of questions and participate effectively in discussing how their questions can be answered.

(b) Attempt to make a prediction relating to a problem or question based on their ideas.

(c) Identify the variable that has to be changed and the things which should be kept the same for a fair test.

(d) Identify what to look for or measure to obtain a result in an investigation.

(e) Take an adequate series of observations to answer the question or test the prediction being investigated.

Box 17.3 Things children do that indicate skill in analysing, interpreting and explaining

(a) Discuss what they find in relation to their initial questions or compare their findings with their earlier predictions/expectations.

(b) Distinguish from many observations those which are relevant to the problem in hand and explain the reason.

(c) Use patterns in their observations or measurements to draw conclusions and attempt to explain them.

(d) Use scientific concepts in reaching and evaluating conclusions.

(e) Recognise that there may be more than one explanation which fits the evidence and that any conclusions are tentative and may have to be changed in the light of new evidence.

Box 17.4 Things children do that indicate skill in communicating, arguing and evaluating

(a) Talk freely about their activities and ideas giving evidence to support their findings.

(b) Listen to others' ideas and look at their results.

(c) Choose a form for recording or presenting results (drawings, writing, models, paintings, table and graphs, etc.) which is appropriate to the type of information and the audience.

(d) Use appropriate scientific language in reporting and show understanding of the terms used.

(e) Compare their actual procedures after the event with what was planned and make suggestions for improving their ways of investigating.

Box 17.5 Things children do that indicate the scientific attitude of willingness to consider evidence in relation to ideas

(a) Recognise when the evidence does not fit a conclusion based on expectations.

(b) Check parts of the evidence which do not fit an overall pattern or conclusion.

(c) Show willingness to consider alternative ideas which may fit the evidence.

(d) Spontaneously seek other ideas which may fit the evidence rather than accepting the first which seems to fit.

(e) Recognise that ideas can be changed by thinking and reflecting about different ways of making sense of the same evidence.

Box 17.6 Things children do that indicate the scientific attitude of sensitivity to living things and the environment

(a) Provide care for living things in the classroom or around the school with minimum supervision.

(b) Minimise the impact of their investigations on living things and the environment, by returning objects and organisms studied to their initial conditions.

(c) Show care for the local environment by behaviour which protects it from litter, damage and disturbance.

(d) Adhere to and/or take part in developing a code of care for the environment, with reasons for the actions identified.

(e) Help in ensuring that others know about and observe such a code of care.

Using the indicators to identify next steps

In this process, evidence gathered – perhaps in one of the ways suggested in Chapter 16 – during a range of activities, is scanned against the relevant indicators. An 'on balance' judgement is made about where the evidence matches the indicators. For the youngest children the first one or two indicators may be the appropriate ones to focus on. For older or more experienced children it will often be the case that what a child does meets these first indicators and attention is focused on those later in the list. Where there is evidence of an indicator not being met, this suggests a focus for 'next steps'. It is important to distinguish between 'no evidence', which does not allow a decision to be made, and evidence that the behaviour is not shown when there is opportunity to use it. If there are no opportunities for certain skills to be used across a range of activities, this should alert the teacher to the possible need to extend activities or to ensure that certain children are taking a full part in explorations and inquiries

In relation to skills and attitudes, what we are looking for is a pattern across various activities, not a judgement based on one activity. This will inevitably mean that 'sometimes it happens and sometimes it doesn't', in which case it is useful to consider the nature of situations where an indictor has, and has not, been met, since this leads to identifying the kind of help needed.

Since they are arranged in a rough sequence of progressive development, the indicators give guidance as to where a child has reached. To make progress the child is likely to need to consolidate these behaviours and begin to develop the ones later in the list.

Although it is not advisable to judge from one event, for the purpose of illustrating the approach we can use the example shown in Figure 17.1.

Figure 17.1 A 9 year old's account of her group's investigation

---

Box 17.7 Interpretation of information in Figure 17.1 using developmental indicators for inquiry skills

Inquiry skills	Interpretation of information using indicators
Gathering evidence by observing and using information sources (Box 17.1)	Some information in relation to statement (b): identifying differences … Apparently only one set of measurements taken (statement d) No information from this investigation in relation to statements (c) and (e). *Next steps:* Not enough information here to inform a decision.
Raising questions, predicting and planning (Box 17.2)	No prediction made (a); information that a useful approach taken and the variable to be changed was appropriately selected (c) (although not clear how much of the planning was the children's own); identified what to observe to find result (d). *Next steps:* give further opportunities for child to plan a fair test independently.
Analysing, interpreting, explaining (Box 17.3)	Results not interpreted in terms of initial question (a); no conclusion drawn or attempt to explain what was found *Next steps:* question child about relation between findings and question being investigated. Ensure reason for an investigation is understood.
Communicating, arguing, evaluating (Box 17.4)	For this exercise, assume (a) and (b) observed during the activity. Evidence of use of drawing to show what was done, but not findings (c). *Next steps:* Discuss with child how to make drawings more informative and how to structure reports of investigations.

The account gives a good idea of what the children did and we will assume that the teacher was able to observe the investigation as well as to read the account. How might this information be interpreted in relation to the child's inquiry skills? Box 17.7 suggests some interpretations and identification of next steps resulting from using the developmental indicators in Boxes 17.1 to 17.4.

The limited decisions that can be taken on the basis of one activity underline the importance of having indicators in mind so that evidence from several activities can be combined.

A similar approach can be used for attitudes, but this requires information to be brought together from a very wide range of activities; there is little evidence in just one event. Suggestions in Chapter 12 for helping the development of inquiry skills may be useful in deciding how to take the next steps.

Interpreting evidence of children's ideas

In principle it would be possible to use what is known from research about the development of children's scientific ideas to describe development in terms of indicators, as we have done for inquiry skills. It would require a very large number of lists, of course, and would be unmanageable. A more practical way is to consider the overall development of ideas as they grow from 'small' ones (which explain particular events or phenomena) to 'bigger' ones (relevant to a range of linked phenomena). In encouraging this development the aim is to help the children construct more widely applicable ideas that are shared by others in making sense of the world around them.

For each idea, then, we can think of a sequence in the ways it is used in giving explanations, reflecting the 'growth' from a 'small' to a 'bigger' idea. The generic indicators of development in Box 17.8 can be applied to particular ideas such as 'life processes', 'habitats', 'food chains', 'sources of sound,' 'the solar system', 'a simple electric circuit' and so on.

Suppose we apply the indicators in Box 17.8 to the children's work in Figures 5.7 and 5.8 (p. 82). There the children were giving their explanations of how the drum makes a sound and how we hear it. The two ideas that the teacher was probing were that 'sound is caused by vibration' and that 'we hear sound when the vibrations reach our ears'. We consider the evidence in relation to the first of these.

In Figure 5.7 the child claims to give an explanation but it is really just a description (the sound is very loud). From the evidence available (and the teacher would use more than this one piece of work) none of the indicators

---

Box 17.8 Generic indicators of development of scientific ideas

Things children do that indicate their ideas about ...
(a) Names a relevant idea but does not use it to explain a relevant event or phenomenon.
(b) Attempts to use a relevant idea in explaining the particular event or object being investigated.
(c) Applies a relevant idea to try to explain events or objects similar to ones already investigated.
(d) Expresses the idea in a way that applies to a range of related events or phenomena.
(e) Uses a relevant idea to predict what would happen in a situations not encountered.

apply so the next step is for some experience of the difference between a drum that is making a sound and one that is not. In Figure 5.8 the child uses the word 'vibration' directly in relation to the production of a sound. This child does more than simply name the cause (indicator a) but has used the idea about sound being caused by vibration in the situation given (b). We have no evidence that this can be applied in other situations (c). So the next step might be to give experience that enables the child to see if the idea explains other events where sound is produced. Further development of the idea about sound might be evident, for example, in explaining how a guitar and other musical instruments make sounds (d). A child who can predict that, if there wasn't any air around, we would not be able to hear anything, would show the understanding in indicator (e).

As in the case of inquiry skills, the purpose is identifying useful next steps so that there is progression in developing ideas. There is no need to pin down the children as working at a particular level. Suggestions in Chapter 11 may be helpful in deciding how to take the steps identified.

Taking a scientific approach to interpreting evidence

A good deal of information about children's ideas will come from their explanations of events, whether written, drawn or spoken. Writing and drawing will often be used because of the convenience of being able to study it after the event. But that brings with it the need to check the assumption that the evidence really reflects the conceptual understanding that is the goal of the activity. It means taking a scientific approach to interpretation, reinforcing the point that any conclusions that are drawn (about next steps) are tentative and subject to change in the light of further evidence.

For example, if as part of exploring light sources children are asked to draw things that they think give out light, and they include a mirror and the moon in their drawings, the *evidence* is what is in the drawings. The *interpretation* might be that the children do not distinguish between things that give out light and those that reflect it. Before deciding what action to take, it would be wise to check this interpretation. Is this really the problem, or did the children mistake 'things that are bright' for 'things that give out light?' Is there supporting evidence from other things the children have done or from what they say about the things they have drawn? If the interpretation is confirmed, the next step becomes clear – to provide opportunity for children to test their ideas by exploring what happens to a mirror in the dark, compared with a torch or other source of light, for example.

Similarly, if a child produces the drawing in Figure 17.2 of an electric circuit with two bulbs, it is necessary to make sure that the connection to the left-hand bulb is not just a mistake in drawing. If the child does not see anything wrong, then the next step might be to test the circuit in practice, following the diagram carefully.

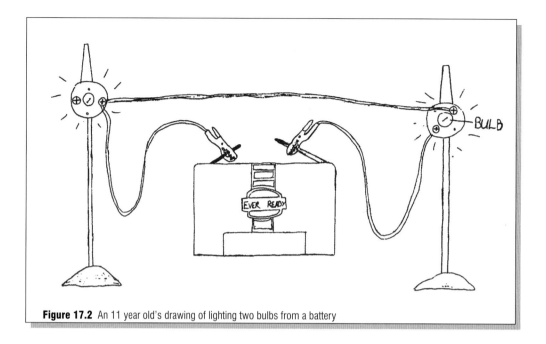

Figure 17.2 An 11 year old's drawing of lighting two bulbs from a battery

Feedback in the context of formative assessment

The essential feature that makes assessment formative is that information from the evidence gathered is used to help children take the next steps in learning. This requires information to be fed back into the teaching–learning process. How this is done and the role that it has in learning depends on how the process of learning is understood. Box 17.9 summarises the key points of three main groups of learning theories.

Swaffield (2008) suggests that there are three models of feedback which are related to these different models of learning. When learning is equated with 'being taught', feedback is one-way: from teacher to pupil. Learning viewed as being actively constructed by the learner means that information is needed about how new ideas are being understood in relation to previous ideas. So feedback is two-way, from pupil to teacher and teacher to pupil. In the third model of learning, the socio-cultural model, where learning is regarded as arising from interactions with others, feedback will also come through this interaction 'which is as likely to be initiated by pupils as by the teachers, and to which pupils contribute their expertise so that everyone learns, teacher included' (p. 60). Swaffield notes that this third model is not often found in classrooms.

Here we have to consider feedback to the teacher and feedback to the children. In both cases, of course, the teacher takes action. The difference lies in the focus of the action – to change what the teacher does or to change what the learner does.

Box 17.9 Theories of learning

There are various theories of learning which can be grouped into three kinds: 'behaviourist', 'cognitive constructivist' and 'socio-cultural constructivist'. A simple formulation of these terms, based on Watkins (2003), expresses their meaning as:

- Behaviourism: 'Learning is being taught.'

- Cognitive constructivism: 'Learning is individual sense-making.'

- Socio-cultural constructivism: 'Learning is building knowledge as part of doing things with others.'

Behaviourism describes a view of learning in which behaviours are formed by a system of rewards and punishments. The assumption is that behaviours that are rewarded will be reinforced and those that are punished will disappear. It implies that learning can be controlled externally.

Cognitive constructivist views describe the process as one in which learners construct their own understanding by developing mental models and that existing knowledge has an important role in this development. The aim is understanding, which is seen as occurring when new experience is incorporated into existing thinking through the active participation of learners.

In *socio-cultural constructivist* perspectives on learning there is also a focus on understanding but through 'making sense of new experience with others' rather than by working individually. In these situations the individual takes from a shared experience what is needed to help his or her understanding, then contributes the result as an input into the group discussion.

(Based on Harlen, 2013: 32)

Feedback into teaching

A good deal of children's responses to particular activities reflect decisions of the teacher made in planning the lesson. These may not always turn out be the best decisions and one of the great values of using formative assessment is the opportunity to revise and change teaching decisions. In so doing the teacher can adjust the challenge so that, in the words of the Plowden Report (CACE, 1967) quoted in Chapter 4, there is 'the right mixture of the familiar and the novel, the right match to the stage of learning the child has reached'. In Chapter 3 we have examples of the teachers changing their plans. Chris (p. 42) used the feedback from observing the difficulty her class were having in using the worksheet she had prepared in deciding to introduce a less demanding way for the children to record their findings. Lisa (p. 48) adjusted her goals in response to her pupils' difficulty in grasping relationships of bodies in the solar system. These are just two instances of a not uncommon event where the 'next step' is for the teacher rather than the children. The decision based on the children's reactions is to change the teacher's plans rather than leave these unaltered and risk a sense of failure in the children.

Older children can indicate more explicitly where they are having difficulty (see Chapter 17) and come to expect the teacher to respond to the feedback they give. Black *et al.* (2003: 67) cite the case of a class where pupils had become familiar with assessing their own work who, when taught by a teacher who was not emphasizing the formative use of assessment, complained to the teacher when their inability to understand appeared to be ignored.

Teachers also obtain feedback to use in their teaching through looking for evidence of their pupils using certain skills or ideas. If over a number of activities there is no evidence of, say, children planning investigations or raising their own questions, a teacher might well look at the whether the planned range of activities provides opportunities for using and developing these skills.

Feedback to children

There are different *ways* of feeding back to children about the next steps to take and different *kinds* of feedback to give. We have to consider both.

There has been a good deal of research into feeding back information to children through marking their work. It indicates that the form of the feedback has an impact on children's motivation as well as on their achievements. The importance of this is underlined by reflecting that motivation and enjoyment are as relevant to future learning as is information about how to correct errors. Thus the *way* in which feedback is given to children is as important as the focus of the feedback. Indeed research shows that feedback can have a negative impact on performance as well as a positive one. An extensive review by Kluger and DeNisi (1996) found a high proportion of feedback (two in every five cases) resulted in negative effects on performance. Further investigation suggested that what makes a difference is the extent to which the feedback focuses on the task or on the person. Feedback about weaknesses which is prefaced by praise for the person tends to focus the learner's attention on themselves rather than on how to correct weaknesses in the task.

There is a natural desire to provide positive feedback, but there is a key distinction to be made between positive comments on the work and positive comments on the person. It means that care has to be taken in using a formula such as 'two stars and a wish', to ensure that the 'stars' describe aspects of the work and do not divert attention from the points about how to improve. This is easier in face-to-face feedback than in written feedback (marking).

A study that has influenced thinking about the feedback that is most effective, which was highlighted in the review of Black and Wiliam (1998a), is summarised in Box 17.10. This study leads to the conclusion that children seize upon marks and ignore any comments that accompany them. They look to the marks for a judgement rather than help in further learning. When marks are absent they engage with what the teacher wants to bring to their attention. The comments then have a chance of improving learning as intended by the teacher. In order to do this, of course, the comments should be positive, non-judgemental and where possible identify next steps.

Box 17.10 Research into different kinds of feedback

In studies by Ruth Butler (1987 and 1988) the effect of different types of feedback by marking were compared. In a controlled experimental study she set up groups which were given feedback in different ways. One group of pupils was given only marks or grades; pupils in another group were given only comments on their work and the third group received both marks and comments on the work. These conditions were studied in relation to tasks which required divergent and convergent thinking. The result was that, for divergent thinking tasks, the pupils who received only comments made the greatest gain in their learning, significantly more than for the other two groups. The results were the same for high and low achieving pupils. For convergent tasks, the lower achieving pupils scored most highly after comments only, with the marks only group next above the marks plus comments group. For all tasks and pupils, comments only led to higher achievement.

Turning to the content of the feedback, the main point to emerge both from research studies and from experience of effective practice is a distinction between feedback that gives information and feedback that is judgemental. Feedback that gives information:

■ focuses on the task, not the person;

■ encourages children to think about the work, not about how 'good' they are;

■ suggests what to do next and gives ideas about how to do it.

Feedback that is judgemental:

■ is expressed in terms of how well the child has done rather than how well the work has been done;

■ gives a judgement that encourages children to label themselves;

■ provides a grade or mark that children use to compare themselves with each other or with what they want to achieve.

Interestingly, praise comes into the judgemental category; it makes children feel they are doing well but does not necessarily help them to do better. It is fine to acknowledge what is good about a piece of work, if this reinforces the goals, but praise in itself will not improve learning. Children are more motivated by comments and questions that help them think about their work and realise what they can do to improve it and which give them help in doing this, such as:

How did you decide which was the best ... ?

Is there another way of explaining this by thinking of what happened when ...?

Next time, imagine that someone else is going to use your drawing to set up the circuit and make sure that you show them clearly what to do.

Such questions and comments are part of learning and teachers should check that children understand them and have planned time to respond to them where this is required. Comments can also help children to realise what they have learned through a topic or activity and not just what is left to be learned.

Dos and don'ts of feedback through marking

Some very practical guidelines for marking, particularly applied to science, were proposed by Evans (2001). The 'dos' and don'ts' in Box 17.11 are derived from his list.

Feedback to children is more effective in improving learning when children realise the goals of their work and then begin to take part in the decisions about next steps. This takes us to the subject of pupils assessing their own work, which is discussed in the next chapter.

Box 17.11 Dos and don'ts of marking

Do

1. Plan the task with specific learning goals in mind.

2. Identify one or two aspects for comment and review which are related to the planned learning goals.

3. Comment first (and perhaps only) on aspects specific to *science* since the task was set to help learning in science.

4. Think carefully about whether or not any other comment is needed at all, for instance about neatness or effort, deserving though these may be. By all means acknowledge and encourage effort and progress, but not in a way that diverts attention from how to improve and move ahead.

5. Pinpoint weak aspects, e.g. misuse of a technical term (but don't be pedantic about the use of words), or assertions the children may have made that are not supported by their own evidence.

6. Indicate next steps.

7. Give children time to read, reflect on and, where appropriate, to respond to comments.

Don't

1. Give judgemental comments and above all scores or symbols (such as B+ or 7/10) since these divert children's attention from learning from what they have done.

2. Don't pose rhetorical questions ('Do you think so?' 'I wonder why?').

3. By all means pose questions, so long as the child understands that a response will be expected and will be read.

4. Don't waste precious time on evaluating tasks that are mainly about reinforcement. Concentrate on work that is really worth evaluating *for its science*. Any other work should be acknowledged by signature, not by the ubiquitous and ambiguous tick, which is often interpreted by children (not to mention parents and others) as commendation.

Summary

This chapter has continued the discussion of how to conduct formative assessment by considering the interpretation of evidence of children's learning in a way that enables next steps to be identified. It has considered how the resulting information can be used as feedback into teaching and learning. The main points have been as follows.

- Deciding next steps requires a clear view of the nature of progression.

- Developmental indicators for identifying next steps in inquiry skills and attitudes have been proposed.

- Identifying next steps in ideas can be helped by applying generic indicators to the particular ideas developed in a topic or set of activities.

- Learning is helped by providing feedback to children and to teachers who use it in adapting teaching.

- Feedback to children on their progress should be non-judgemental and give information about next steps and how to take them.

- Some suggestions have been given relating particularly to marking in primary science.

Further reading

Harrison, C. and Howard, S. (2009) *Inside the Primary Black Box,* London: GL Assessment.

Schofield, K. (2011) Formative feedback and self-assessment, in W. Harlen (ed.) *ASE Guide to Primary Science Education,* new edn, Hatfield: ASE, 85–93.

Swaffield, S. (2008) Feedback: the central process in assessment for learning, in S. Swaffield (ed.) *Unlocking Assessment,* London: David Fulton, 57–72.

18

Children's role in formative assessment

Introduction

Children always have a role in the assessment of their learning, of course, if only as passive objects of assessment and receivers of others' judgements. This chapter, however, is concerned with the active part they can take in assessment for learning. We begin by setting out reasons – from experience, research and ideas about how people learn – for giving children this active role in the assessment of their work. Children can have a role in all parts of the formative assessment cycle. By engaging in activities they provide evidence that is needed by them and their teacher to build their understanding through using inquiry skills. But involvement in the further stages of making decisions about their progress and next steps depends on children knowing what learning they are aiming for and hence on ways of communicating goals and standards of quality. We consider how to help children to reflect on their work with others as well as individually, and how to provide them with opportunities to decide their next steps and take greater responsibility for their learning.

Children's role in assessing their learning

Placing children at the centre of the formative assessment cycle (Figure 15.1) draws attention to their pivotal role in the way learning is conceived in this book. Learners are in any case responsible for learning, but whether they *take responsibility* for it depends on their participation in the decisions represented by the two-headed arrows in Figure 15.1. The inward pointing arrows indicate that the children are the subject of the teachers' decisions about goals, evidence, interpretation and so on. The outward pointing arrows indicate the children's role in all these decisions.

Although we loosely refer to this involvement as 'self-assessment', the focus should be on the actions and the work rather than the 'self' so it is more accurate to refer to children taking part in the formative assessment of their work. Expressed in this way it includes assessment of each other's work, which can have particular value, as we discuss later. So children's participation in assessment means reviewing their work, interpreting their progress in relation to the goals and taking part in deciding their next steps. A good deal of these processes depends, as it does for teachers, on knowing what to aim for, the learning goals of their activities. Helping children to understand what they are intended to learn is important, but not at all easy, particularly in science, as we see later. But first we look briefly at the reasons that make this effort worthwhile.

Why involve children in assessing their learning?

When asked this question a group of teachers came up with the list in Box 18.1 from their experience of encouraging self-assessment in work across the curriculum.

These points based on experience are backed up by evidence from research. Many of the studies reviewed by Black and Wiliam (1998a) highlight the central role of children in their own learning. The involvement of children in assessment of their own and each other's work was among the approaches that were most successful in raising achievement. In the studies reviewed, there were examples of successful strategies for involving children from the age of 5 upward in assessing their work.

Support for involving children in decisions about their learning also derives from theories of learning. The kind of learning we need to aim for, as discussed in Chapter 6, is not a matter of absorbing information and ready-made understandings. Instead, it involves the active participation of learners in using existing ideas to try to make sense of new experiences. Learning goes on inside children's heads and so they must be willing to undertake it and to make the necessary effort. This being so, the way to help learning is to give the children as much opportunity as possible (appropriate to their age and stages) to know what they are intended to learn and how to go about it. This may seem an obvious point but it is in fact quite uncommon for children to be able to articulate what the teacher intends them to learn from a particular activity, as opposed to what they are supposed to do.

Box 18.1 Some reasons for involving children in using assessment to help learning

- The children are the ones who ultimately have to take the actions that lead to learning.

- Knowing their goals puts any learners in a better position to achieve them.

- Taking part in assessment of their own and their peers' work means that children see assessment as something in which they have an active part.

- There is less need for feedback from the teacher if the children are involved in assessing their work and deciding next steps.

- Involvement in self-assessment facilitates ownership of their learning and enables children to be responsible for and accountable for their learning.

- It provides for independence and can lead to self-regulated learning.

- It raises children's self-esteem.

- It promotes higher order thinking since it requires children to think about how they learn (meta-cognitive thinking).

Communicating goals

When any of us tries to learn something or improve performance, whether it is a physical activity such as playing a sport, or a mental one such as learning another language, we like to be able to tell how we are doing. We can only assess our progress, though, if we have a clear notion of what we are aiming for. It is the same with children: they need to be aware of the goals of their learning. However, as just mentioned, often children do not have a clear notion of the purpose of their activities. Consequently, classroom activities appear to children as collections of disconnected and often meaningless exercises.

One way of giving activities meaning for the children is to set them in a real context – or at least one that simulates reality. The case studies in Chapter 3 all provided a purpose for the activities involved. For instance in the science week (p. 50) there was real interest in finding out whose fingerprints were on the ginger beer can. Similarly, finding a suitable ball for the dog motivated the children to think about what properties to test and how to do it. However, the solution to these problems was not the essence of what they were learning, or what the teachers hoped they would be learning. There was no great value in finding whose fingerprints were identified or which ball was most bouncy; the point of the activities was in the process of finding these things out. Similarly in many activities, such as the common one of finding which of certain different kinds of paper is strongest (see Box 18.2), the learning is not about paper but about how to make fair comparisons.

Box 18.2 Missing the point about testing the strength of paper

A group of 11-year-old boys spent three lessons finding out which of three kinds of paper was the strongest. After the lesson an observer interviewed the boys:

Interviewer What do you think you have learned from doing your investigations?
Robert ... that graph paper is strongest, that green one.
Interviewer Right, is that it?
Robert Um ...
Interviewer You spent three lessons doing that, seems a long time to spend finding out that graph paper is stronger
James Yeah, and we also found which ... papers is stronger. Not just the graph paper, all of them.

The boys appeared to be unaware of the process of investigation as a learning goal, in contrast with their teacher. It seems reasonable to assume that, had they been aware of this goal, they would have reflected more on the way they were investigating, found more satisfaction in the investigation and made more progress towards the goal that the teacher had in mind but kept to herself.

Giving reasons in terms of learning

To improve understanding of the purposes of activities, teachers need to find ways of conveying the goals. In practice this means communicating the intended learning, not just what they are to do and not just what outcomes are expected. Graham, in the case study about soils in Chapter 3 (p. 48), did this in setting up the soil investigations. Three of his instructions were about what to do, but the fourth gave a reason for doing it – so that the children could think about what makes a difference to how well plants will grow in the soils. Without this fourth part, the children would probably have investigated the soils, but if asked what they were learning would be likely to have answered 'about soils' or to have listed their findings without drawing conclusions from them. The reason for the investigations given by the teacher focused their observations on relevant differences and thus not only made them aware of why they were investigating the soils but made the intended learning more likely.

It is not helpful to be too mechanistic about how to share a learning goal with children, by insisting on it at the start of every lesson or on the use of a particular form of words to express what the children will be learning. Clarke (1998) introduced WALT (We Are Learning Today) and WILF (What I am Looking For) as devices for sharing goals and outcomes with children. When used mechanistically the value of this approach is diminished, but the idea has stimulated teachers to communicate in other ways – such as by using KWL grids (see p. 242) – what is the learning intention of an activity. Graham gives an example of a subtle approach by telling the children what to think *about* but not what to think, and at the same time avoids the pitfalls of giving the answer or using words that they would not understand.

In science activities there are both goals related to understanding (concept-based goals) and those related to inquiry skills (skill-based goals) to be communicated. Given that the aim of most activities is to help children think for themselves, telling children what to do is to be avoided in both cases. In communicating concept-based goals it is important also to avoid telling children what they will find. In the case of skill-based goals, the aim of working scientifically has to be made clear; otherwise the children will assume that the answers they get are the main aim rather than the way in which they go about finding the answers, as was illustrated in Box 18.2.

Here are some examples of different ways of expressing both kinds of goals in the context of an investigation of the heat-insulating properties of different materials by using them to prevent ice from melting.

Concept-based goals
Suppose that in this activity the teacher's concept-based goal is for pupils to understand that *materials differ in their heat-insulating properties* through investigations with ice. The goal cannot be shared with the children in this form. Instead some possible alternatives are:

a.   In this activity you are going to try wrapping ice cubes in different materials and see how long they take to melt.

b. This activity will show that how quickly the ice melts depends on the material you use to wrap it in.

c. In this activity you are going to find out about how well different materials keep ice from melting.

The first (a) tells the children what to do but not why. They are cued into timing and are likely to consider that the aim of the activity is to produce an estimate of time for each material. The second (b) tells them what they are intended to find and takes away the opportunity to think for themselves about the meaning of their results. It is (c) that gives the children a reason for the activity in terms of what they will learn but does not tell them 'the answer'.

Skill-based goals

In the same context of activities with the ice, one of the teacher's goals for the children might be: *To plan an investigation that will be a fair test of the insulating properties of their materials.* This might be best shared with the children in this way:

a. When you test these materials make sure that you do it in a way that the test is fair and you are quite sure any difference is because of the material used.

b. In this activity think about what you need to do to make sure that you test the materials fairly.

Here (a) focuses attention on the outcome, a fair comparison, whilst (b) is focused on the process of fair testing. The difference between these formulations is indeed subtle but makes a difference between focusing on the process and focusing on the outcomes. Harrison and Howard (2009) describe this in terms of the difference between 'Learning Outcomes' and 'Learning Intentions'. The first, as the title suggests, is concerned with products, which can help to make explicit what is expected. However, the second encourages more thinking about learning.

Reinforcing the goals

It is not enough, however, to talk about goals only at the beginning of an activity. The purpose of what they are doing needs to be reinforced during it and at the end. Ensuring that discussion of results picks up on these intentions will help to set the pattern of taking the purpose seriously and working towards the intended learning.

One teacher regularly asks the children to explain to others what they have learned, making explicit reference to what they hoped to do or find out. If, as often happens, there was some unplanned feature of the enquiry, she asks them 'what did you learn from that?' Sometimes she asks the children to think of questions to ask each other about what they have learned; she finds that these are often more probing and difficult than her own questions. All these things combine to reinforce the learning atmosphere and support learning as a shared endeavour.

> **Box 18.3** Communicating what is 'good work' to young children
>
> The process can begin usefully if children from about the age of 8 are encouraged to select their 'best' work and to put this in a folder or bag. Part of the time for 'bagging' should be set aside for the teacher to talk to each child about why certain pieces of work were selected. The criteria which the children are using will become clear and may have messages for the teacher. For example if work seems to be selected only on the basis of being 'tidy' and not in terms of content, then perhaps this aspect is being over-emphasised. At first the discussion should only be to clarify the criteria the children use. 'Tell me what you particularly liked about this piece of work.' Gradually it will be possible to suggest criteria without dictating what the children should be selecting. This can be done through comments on the work. 'That was a very good way of showing your results, I could see at a glance which was best.' 'I'm glad you think that was your best investigation because although you didn't get the result you expected, you did it very carefully and made sure that the result was fair.'
>
> Through such an approach children may begin to share the understanding of the goals of their work and become able to comment usefully on what they have achieved. It then becomes easier to be explicit about further targets and for the children to recognise when they have achieved them.

Communicating expectations of quality

In order to take part in assessing their work, children not only need to know the purpose of what they are doing but have some notion of the standard they should be aiming for, that is, what is 'good work' in a particular context. This is less easy in science than in an area such as language development, where children might be told that in a piece of writing they are to use a particular genre or make sure that the events in a story are in the correct sequence. The children then know what to look for in assessing their work. In science it is more difficult to make general statements that convey meaning to the children. Thus the required features are better conveyed through examples; over time the children come to share the teacher's criteria. Box 18.3 outlines an approach that can be used with young children.

Teachers of older children can share more explicitly with them the criteria they use both in assessing practical skills and marking written work. One science teacher, for example, did this by writing his own account of a class investigation and distributing copies for the children to mark, looking for particular features. It led to lively discussion and a keener understanding of what was expected in their accounts (Fairbrother, 1995).

Another approach is to use examples of other children's work, which could be collected for the purpose and made anonymous. Alternatively, the examples from the collections published or created in the school to help teachers assess work could be shared with the children. The discussion of these examples should lead to the children identifying the criteria for 'good work'. If they have done this for themselves, the teacher does not have to convince them of 'what is good'. Other ways in which teachers have helped children to recognise criteria of quality are outlined in Box 18.4 (based on Harlen, 2006b).

Box 18.4 Helping children to identify quality expectations

Using examples

One teacher of 10 year olds spent some time at the beginning of the year discussing with her class what made a 'good' report of a science investigation. She gave each group of children two anonymous examples of children's writing about an investigation from children in the same class in earlier years. One was a clear account, well set out so that the reader could understand what had been done, although the writing was uneven and there were some words not spelled correctly. There were diagrams to help the account, with labels. The results were in a table, and the writer had said what he or she thought they meant, admitting that the results didn't completely answer the initial question. There was a comment about how things could have been improved. The other account was tidy, attractive to look at (the diagrams were coloured in but not labelled), but contained none of the features in the content shown in the other piece.

The teacher asked the children to compare the pieces of work and list the good and poor features of each one. Then they were asked to say what were the most important things which made a report 'good'. She put all the ideas together and added some points of her own, to which the children agreed. She later made copies for all the children to keep in their science folders. But she also went on to explore with the children how to carry out an investigation in order to be able to write a good report. These points too were brought together in the children's words and printed out for them.

Brainstorming

A variation on the above is to brainstorm ideas about, for example, how to conduct a particular investigation so that the children can be sure of the result. The list of what to think about can be turned into questions (Did we keep everything the same except for …? Did we change …? Did we look for…? Did we check their results? etc.). Before finishing their investigation they check through their list, which becomes a self-assessment tool for that piece of work.

Involving children in deciding next steps

When children have a view of what they should be doing and how well they should be doing it, they are in a position to share in deciding the next steps to be taken. Using the word 'sharing' recognises that the responsibility for helping children's learning is ultimately the teacher's; we are in no way suggesting that children decide what they do and don't do. However, sharing means that the children understand why they are being asked to do certain things and have a firm grasp of what they should do. Moreover their involvement is likely to lead to greater motivation for the work.

Ways of involving children

In Box 18.5 a teacher of 9 and 10 year olds describes how she helps the children to decide what they need to do.

> **Box 18.5** An example of involving children in deciding next steps
>
> I make time to sit down with each group after an activity and talk about what they found difficult, what they thought they did well and what they could have done better. I ask them if they thought about particular aspects relating to the processes and then about how they explain their results. This is important for me because I won't have followed every step of their investigation and it helps me decide how much they have progressed from earlier work and whether they have taken the steps we agreed previously. I then ask questions that indicate my view of what they need to do, but by expressing this as questions, they actually identify what they are going to do. The questions are like: 'what can you do in your next investigation to be more sure of your results?' 'what sorts of notes could you make as you go along to give you all the information for preparing a report at the end?' 'where could you find out more information to explain what you found?'
>
> (personal communication)

Note that the teacher 'makes time' for this which, she reports, is time well spent. It saves time for teaching and learning in the end by obviating the need to repeat explanations of what children are to do and the children learn more quickly by thinking rather than from making mistakes. This teacher treats the group as a learning unit and encourages them to help each other. Since the purpose of the assessment is formative, and since they learn as a group, the decisions made together are important for their learning. However, she also looks at the work of each child individually and makes sure that they recognise their own next steps in learning.

Harrison and Howard (2009) recount how some teachers used a similar approach across the whole range of children's work. It involved changing their planning so that activities were planned for Monday up to Thursday lunchtime each week. Then the children and their teacher spent Thursday afternoon looking through their work for that week and discussing how well it had been done and where they needed to do further work. Then the teachers provided support and extension activities as needed to be carried out on Friday.

Various versions of the use of 'traffic lights' have been devised to enable children to think about the quality of their work, and to convey their judgements to the teacher. The idea is for the children to label their work according to their confidence in understanding: green for good, amber for partial and red for poor understanding. This can be shown by sticking a red, green or amber dot on written work or a coloured object placed on their table.

Other approaches in which children assess their work to identify next steps are encouraging reflection through questioning and peer-assessment.

Building on these approaches, children's reflection on their work and how it can be improved can be stimulated by questions such as:

What do you think you have done well?

Did you do what were you trying to do in this section?

Why did you do this, in this kind of way?

Do you think now that you could do it a better way?

Which bits are you unsure about?

What would you change if you did it again?

What could you add to strengthen this part?

In the same way as for the quality criteria, these questions can be provided to children in their notebooks or displayed on the classroom wall, to think about as a regular part of their work.

Peer-assessment by children

Some researchers have suggested that children assessing other children's work is a good way to develop skills of self-assessment. In the context of formative assessment, this peer-assessment means something quite different from marking each other's books. In essence it means children helping each other with their learning, by suggesting the next steps to take to improve the work.

Black *et al.* (2003) report several arguments in favour of encouraging learners to judge each other's work, some based on promoting better understanding of learning goals and criteria of quality. It is claimed that peer-assessment is more effective in this regard than self-assessment. More pragmatically, children are likely to pay attention to quality if they know that it is going to be read by a peer. One of the advantages of peer-assessment is that it requires less one-to-one attention from the teacher than some other approaches to involving children in formative assessment. Children can more frequently discuss their work with each other and help each other to improve. When they have confidence in gaining help from a structured exchange with a peer, children begin spontaneously to ask each other for their opinion. The recognition of being able to help themselves and each other enables learning to continue when the teacher is occupied with those who need extra help. But there are other more important reasons, summarised in Box 18.6.

Box 18.6 Advantages of peer-assessment

Saving on teacher time is not the only reason for encouraging peer assessment. Having children talk to each other in pairs about their work requires them to think through the work again and find words to describe it without the pressure that comes from the unequal relationship between the child (novice) and the teacher (expert). It is also consistent with the understanding of learning as being the development of ideas through social interaction as well as through interaction with materials (see Chapter 17). It can help children to respect each other's strengths, especially if pairs are changed on different occasions.

The skills needed both for self-assessment and peer-assessment have to be learned. Paired discussion needs to be structured, at least when it is new to the children. For example, the children can be asked to exchange work and then think about two of three questions about it, reflecting the criteria of quality. For instance if the work describes a conclusion from something that has been observed or found from an investigation the questions might be 'Can you tell what was found?' 'Does the conclusion help to answer the question that was being investigated?' 'What would help to make what happened clearer (a diagram or series of drawings)?' After such a discussion one child said about having her work assessed by another: 'She said it was hard to understand my investigation so I asked her what sort of thing I should have put to make her understand. Next time I will make sure that I describe things more clearly.'

But there is an important caveat. Peer-assessment clearly requires a class atmosphere where cooperation and collaboration, rather than competition, are encouraged. Unless used sensitively and with positive intent, the process can be demotivating for some children. Case studies by Crossouard of peer assessment by students aged 11 and 12, provide disturbing evidence of how gender, social class and students' attainment hierarchies are 'implicated in processes that are typically bathed in the supposed "neutrality" of assessment judgements' (Crossouard, 2012: 736). The benefits of peer-assessment were observed to be unequally spread, the practice supporting and extending some students whilst working 'oppressively' for others. Thus teachers may need help in recognising the issues of equity that are raised and in addressing the influence of social class, gender and general ability when practising peer-assessment.

Summary

This chapter has discussed the value of helping children to take part in the formative assessment of their work. The main points have been:

- There are important theoretical and practical reasons for involving children in assessing their own work.

- Acting on this means sharing learning goals with the children, conveying an operational meaning of quality and helping them to identify their next steps.

- Discussion of goals should help children to focus on the learning from an activity rather than the details of how to carry it out.

- Sharing goals means communicating to children a reason for their activities in terms of learning which is reinforced in discussion during and at the end of the activity.

- Helping children to judge the quality of the work requires the subtle communication of criteria of quality through discussion of examples.

- Children can be involved in deciding their next steps following a review of what they have done and how they have done it, and agreeing ways of improving or moving on from it.

- Children can take part in deciding their next steps through self- and peer-assessment, but care has to be taken that the children have the skills necessary and that the classroom climate is positive and supportive.

Further reading

Earl, L. and Katz, S. (2008) Getting to the core of learning: using assessment for self-monitoring and self-regulation, in S. Swaffield (ed.) *Unlocking Assessment, Understanding for Reflection and Application*, London: David Fulton, 90–104.

Harrison, C. and Howard, S. (2009) *Inside the Primary Black Box: Assessment for Learning in Primary and Early Years Classrooms*, London: GL Assessment.

Harrison, C. and Howard, S. (2011) Issues in primary assessment 2: assessment for learning: how and why it works in primary classrooms, *Primary Science*, 116: 5–7.

19

Summarising and reporting learning

Introduction

Following the discussion in the last three chapters of formative assessment, we turn here to the second of the two main purposes of assessment noted in Chapter 15 (p. 217). Summative assessment is probably the first thing that comes to mind for many people, including parents, when assessment is mentioned, since receiving reports is the most visible sign of assessment taking place. Although they tend to be seen as contrasting – formative as assessment *for* learning, summative as assessment *of* learning – both should help learning in different ways.

After briefly reviewing the properties that summative assessment in primary science needs in order to serve its purposes, the main sections discuss and illustrate three different approaches to assessing pupils' achievements at particular times. The first of these involves administering tests or special tasks at the time when a report on performance is required. Echoing some concerns expressed in Chapter 15 we set out some disadvantages of using tests for assessing the goals of primary science. The other two approaches – summarising at a particular time the evidence collected across a range of activities, and building a record over time – depend on teachers' judgements. We outline a set of procedures which enable the best work to be used in the assessment and includes formative assessment. Procedures for quality assurance of teacher-based assessment are discussed.

Information for summative assessment

The characteristics of formative and summative assessment (pp. 224, 227) indicate that formative is 'close to the learning', providing quick feedback into decisions about learning activities. Summative assessment is 'more distant from the learning' and less detailed but nevertheless its impact should be to help in decisions that improve children's learning opportunities, albeit through a much longer feedback loop.

To serve its purpose of giving information about children's achievement, summative assessment needs to be

- a summary of what has been achieved at a particular time in relation to the full range of goals, including social, emotional and physical as well as cognitive development;

- succinct, giving an overview of progress, preferably in the form of a short profile where main aspects of development are identified;

- expressed in terms of attainment of standards or criteria that have the same meaning for all children;

- as reliable as possible; ideally involving some procedures for quality assurance.

Ways of reporting achievement at a particular time

The main ways of providing a record of achievement at a particular time are:

- using tests or special tasks to determine what has been learned at a certain time;

- summarising at a certain time information gathered by teachers during their work with children;

- building a record over time.

We now consider each of these in turn, looking at what they entail and their suitability for assessing learning in science at the primary level. In doing so it is important to have in mind what is required for valid and reliable assessment of the understanding and skills which are the goals of primary science, and especially inquiry-based primary science activities.

Assessing understanding has to be distinguished from assessing factual knowledge. Although facts are needed, they are only as useful as the links that can be made between them, so the assessment has to be concerned with application of knowledge, not only recall. Thus the questions or tasks being undertaken should be novel – so that they cannot be answered from memory – and also meaningful and engaging. They should require pupils to give an explanation of an event or interpretation of data or a prediction involving application of some ideas of science.

In relation to *assessing inquiry skills*, clearly the tasks or questions have to require the use of the skills being assessed such as predicting, planning, carrying out an investigation or finding a pattern in given data. This need not mean only physical performance but it does require an authentic setting in which the skills need to be used (see the example in Figure 19.1 and later in Figure 19.2).

However, it is not possible to assess skills without involving some knowledge of the subject matter of its use. At the same time, tasks used for assessing understanding will require some use of skills (explaining, interpreting, predicting). Thus there will always be some aspects of understanding and skill required in *all* tasks, as indeed is the case in inquiry-based learning activities.

Using tests or tasks

The use of tests to find out what a pupil knows is a time-honoured approach to summative assessment. It is an attractive approach for certain purposes, particularly where pupils are in competition with each other, because each pupil can be given the same task or asked the same questions in the same conditions. This contrasts with using teachers' judgements of regular work where the evidence arises from situations which vary from pupil to pupil. However, it should be noted that giving them the same task does not necessarily provide the same opportunities for children to show what they can do.

Tests vary considerably in their form and the items they contain vary according to the nature of the task and the way of responding. So there are:

- performance (practical) items (where pupils have to manipulate equipment or conduct an investigation);
- multiple-choice items (where pupils choose between given answers);
- open-response items (where answers have to be supplied by writing or drawing);
- and various combinations of these.

Written tests

Written items are the most common and most convenient if a test is intended to be given to a large number of children. The qualities of good oral questions, discussed in Chapter 16, apply equally to written questions. That is, in order to gain access to pupils' thinking, it is useful to express questions in terms of what they think. So 'open' questions, asking for students to respond in their own words, are more likely to elicit information about what they know and understand than questions where they choose between given answers. Multiple-choice items are open to guessing and clues given by the words used in the options. However, open-response questions also have disadvantages, particularly for younger children who have greater difficulty in being specific in writing than in talking. Interpreting students' written answers can also be a problem. The item in Figure 19.1 avoids the need for writing and, by requiring a correct answer in each box, makes the chance of success by guessing very low. However, pupils have to read and understand the instructions for how to record their answer, otherwise there is risk of failure for reasons other than not having the skill that it is intended to assess.

Some problems with tests

In addition to the dependence on reading and writing skills and the possibility of other errors, such as in marking, there are some inherent problems in using tests for reporting the performance of individual pupils. Some of these were mentioned in Chapter 15 in relation to reliability and validity.

Emma and Anita were finding out <u>if the surface on which a ball is bounced makes a difference to how high it bounces.</u>

They found three different kinds of surface, which they called A, B and C.

They also had three different balls P, Q and R.

For a fair test what should they change in their trials and what should they keep the same?

Tick <u>Change</u> or <u>Not change</u> for each thing below:

	Change	Not change
The ball	☐	☐
The surface	☐	☐
The height it is dropped from	☐	☐

Figure 19.1 Item from a test for 11 year olds (APU Report, 4 (1985))

- First, because of the use made of summative assessment results, is the requirement for these results to be as reliable as possible. This influences the choice of items selected for the test, favouring those where answers can be unequivocally marked as correct or incorrect. This narrows the range of the test items and so reduces the validity of the test, which will not reflect the full range of goals but only those easily tested (see Box 15.3).

- Second, following on from this point, since what is tested is taken as an indication of what is to be learned and so what is taught, the narrowing of the range covered by the test will tend to dictate a narrowing of the range of the curriculum. This effect is greatly increased when the results are used for high stakes purposes (see Box 15.1).

- Third, if items are set in terms of problems in a real context, familiarity with the context might be expected to influence a pupil's response. For instance, would the identification of variables in Figure 19.1 be more difficult for some students if the context were about comparing the effect of changing the ingredients in making a cake, or the speed of toy cars down a slope? Would the ability to identify a pattern in data be affected by whether the data are presented pictorially or as numbers? Does the answering format affect students' performance? The answer to all these questions from research is that these features do matter and the context of an item is particularly important.

What an item seems to be about (even though knowledge of this may not be needed) affects pupils' ability and willingness to engage with it and thus to show what they can do.

There are, of course, many different contexts that could be used to assess a particular skill or concept and those included in a particular test are only a sample. If a different sample is chosen, some children would find some items easier that others might find more difficult. So a different selection would produce a different result, giving rise to what is described as the 'sampling error'.

The sampling error can be much larger than is generally realised. For example, Wiliam (2001) estimated that for national tests in England about 40 per cent of students are likely to be assigned the 'wrong' grade level, even though these levels each span roughly two years. A way of reducing this source of error would be to increase the number of contexts included for each competence assessed and thus the number of items used. But the length of a test cannot be greatly increased without incurring other forms of error (student fatigue, for instance) so more items per skill or concept would mean fewer skills and concepts included, thus reducing the range of what is assessed and so reducing the validity of the test.

Note that the sampling error is much less when tests are used for population surveys, where the total items used can be spread across several equivalent samples of children who take different groups of items. In these surveys, such as TIMSS and PISA and the national surveys in England, Wales and Northern Ireland conducted by the Assessment of Performance Unit (APU) in the 1980s, the results of individual children are not of interest, only the overall national, or regional, totals and how performance varies from year to year and for different learning goals.

The particular problems of testing in primary science

These points apply to some extent to tests in all subjects, but it is clear that they have a particularly large impact on the assessment of inquiry-based science and on the performance of primary children because of the nature and wide range of the goals. This was recognised by a group of expert primary science educators in a report to the Nuffield Foundation (2012), who argued that 'it is not possible for all the aims of primary science education to be validly assessed through external written tests, such as the national tests'. They point to the fact that this was acknowledged in the Bew Report (an Independent Review of Key Stage 2 Testing, Assessment and Accountability, 2011) and conclude that:

> These arguments lead to the conclusion that the situations in which children learn science provide the best opportunities for assessment of their learning. This point was accepted in the government's response to the Bew Report which expressed the view that teacher assessment is the most appropriate form of assessment for science at the end of Key Stage 2, so pupil and school level data should continue to be based on teacher assessment judgements.
>
> (Nuffield Foundation, 2012: 13)

Having considered the limitations of tests, we now look at the major alternative – of using teacher-based assessment – which is used in the other two approaches, but in different ways.

Summarising teacher-based assessment at a particular time

In this approach information gathered over time is brought together and judged at the time when reporting is required. Ideally the information will have been gathered in the context of formative assessment and used to help learning. However it not appropriate to rely on the interpretations made for formative purposes since these will have an ipsative element, that is, will take into account the individual child's progress and effort. Whilst this does not matter for formative assessment, where identifying the levels at which children are working or whether specific goals have been achieved is not necessary (see p. 222), things are different for summative assessment. In summative assessment the learning goals or levels of development are used as ways of communicating to others what children have achieved and so their work has to be judged against the same criteria for all children. Whilst the *evidence* used for the two purposes might be the same, the judgements in summative assessment are made differently. Where there are 'levels' specified, the evidence has to be reviewed against the broader criteria that define the levels. This is usually done by the 'best fit' method, recognising that there will never be a perfect match between the evidence and a specified achievement level.

The Early Years Foundation Stage (EYFS) Profile is an example of teacher/ practitioner observation being used to summarise children's attainment at a particular time. The Foundation Stage in England refers to the pre-school years, when children may be in nursery education or the reception year of a primary school. The first Foundation Stage Profile, introduced in 2002, was intended to have a formative as well as a summative function but it was considered to be unmanageable and, following a review (Tickell, 2011), was replaced by the EYFS Profile in 2012. This is a summative record of children's attainment, completed by early years practitioners in the final term of the year in which the child reaches the age of 5. Unlike its predecessor, it 'is not intended to be used for ongoing assessment or for entry level assessment for Early Years settings or reception classes' (STA, 2012: 5).

The profile records practitioners' judgements in relation to three primary areas, four specific areas of learning and three learning characteristics. The 'primary areas' are: communication and language; physical development; and personal, social and emotional development. The 'specific areas' of learning are: literacy; mathematics, understanding the world and expressive arts and design. Learning characteristics are: playing and exploring; active learning; and creating and thinking critically. The primary and specific areas of learning are subdivided into a total of 17 statutory Early Learning Goals (ELG), each with an explanatory note. The goal recognisably related to science, The World, is given in Box 19.1.

Box 19.1 The Early Learning Goal relating to exploring the world around

The world

Children know about similarities and differences in relation to places, objects, materials and living things. They talk about the features of their own immediate environment and how environments might vary from one to another. They make observations of animals and plants and explain why some things occur, and talk about changes.

Explanatory note

The child has a curiosity and interest about the immediate environment around them and recognises when things have similar or different features. Whilst exploring through play and real experiences, the child shows their learning and understanding of living things, materials and objects. The child investigates, notices changes and interacts with elements of their natural and manufactured environment. He or she communicates about what is happening and why.

A handbook (STA, 2012) provides information about the EYFS Profile, advice on completing it, exemplification, guidance on moderation and on use with children having special needs or English as an additional language. It also provides help for practitioners in judging a child's typical attainment at a particular time, through a process of 'best fit' between the child's behaviour and the Early Learning Goals.

Practitioners record each child's level of development in each of the 17 Early Learning Goals as:

■ emerging (not yet at the level of development expected at the end of the EYFS);

■ expected (meeting the description of the level of development expected at the end of the EYFS); or

■ exceeding (beyond the level of development expected at the end of the EYFS).

In making these decisions, practitioners are expected to refer to the exemplification material published on its website by the Department for Education. This material provides examples of observation notes made by practitioners, children's quoted words, children's pictures, photographs and in some case comments of parents, all of which illustrate a child's learning and development where it best fits the 'expected' category. There is currently no exemplification for the 'emerging' or 'exceeding' categories. A completed EYFS Profile consists of 20 items of information: the attainment of each child assessed in relation to the 17 Early Learning Goal descriptors, together with a short narrative describing the child's three learning characteristics.

As well as being used to inform parents and Year 1 teachers about individual children, the EYFS profiles are collected by the DfE for the purpose of monitoring 'changes in levels of children's development and their readiness for the next phase of their education both nationally and locally'. But it is not intended that results be published in performance tables.

Building a record over time

This approach differs from the one just discussed, in that the evidence that is judged at the reporting time reflects the child's best performance at that time, not a summary of all that has been done over the year or term. The evidence is accumulated gradually by retaining what is best at any time in a folder, or other form of portfolio, and replacing pieces with better evidence as it is produced. Whilst it is important to base the summative judgement on evidence from a range of activities and not judge from one task, there is no point in including work that no longer reflects what pupils are capable of producing. Moreover, such an approach enables children to have a role in their summative assessment by taking part in the selection of items in the folder or portfolio, a process for which they need some understanding of the broad goals and quality criteria by which their work will be judged.

The way in which this approach works is summarised in Box 19.2. Formative assessment is at its centre and it is important that time is set aside at regular intervals specifically for children to review their work. This gives them time not only to decide what to put in the 'best work folder' but also to consider what they can improve. The number of items in the folder grows from the start, but imposing a limit (of around 5 to 10 pieces) ensures that care is taken in decisions and that children really think about how they are judging their work.

It is not only the work in the folder that is gradually built up but also the teacher's judgement of the extent to which a child is achieving the expected learning. The teacher will use this information formatively, helping to ensure that expected learning is achieved. The folder provides the basis for writing the end of year reports. These are narrative reports describing what a child has been able to do and what is needed for further development or consolidation.

Box 19.2 Implementing the 'best work' approach to summative teacher-based assessment

- *At the beginning of the year,* after two or three weeks, the teacher introduces the idea of a 'best work folder' (BWF), shows the children an example and explains how it will be used.

- *During a topic* the teacher reserves time for children to think about their work, discusses what is 'good work' in relation to the activities.

- *At the end of a topic (or about half way through a term)* the teacher spends time (an afternoon) reviewing the topic and adding to or replacing work in the BWF, keeping the number of entries to an agreed maximum (e.g. 5 to 10). The teacher adds notes to the folders where appropriate.

- *At the end of the year* the teacher uses the work and notes in the folder to write a narrative report on each child's performance for parents and the child's next teacher.

- *At the end of the (key) stage* the teacher uses the BWF to judge whether, on balance, the statutory requirements for the stage have been achieved.

When it comes to the assessment at the end of the (key) stage, the teachers' ongoing assessment means that they have a very good idea of what the child can do and whether or not it meets the requirements of the Programme of Study (which now provide attainment targets) for the stage. All that is needed is to confirm and record the judgement.

The possibility of creating and using best work folders electronically is suggested in Box 19.3.

Box 19.3 A paperless approach to creating and using best work folders

The rapid spread of the use in primary classrooms of mini-laptop computers linked wirelessly to the teacher's computer, opens up the potential for assessment to be carried out without the need for a physical folder or portfolio. Such a process has been developed and trialled by Kimbell *et al.* (2009) in the E-scape (Electronic Solutions for Creative Assessment in Portfolio Environments), mainly for the assessment of technology projects. Pupils send their work, in the form of text, voice or video recordings, photographs or drawings, to the teacher as the work progresses as well as at the end of an activity. The uploaded work can be discussed with the pupil electronically or in person and the collection could be edited or changed as it is superseded by later work. The teacher stores the collection and uses it for end of year reporting, as in the case of a physical folder. Moderation of teachers' judgements for end of (key) stage records can be carried out using the electronic form. Davies *et al.* (2010: 21) describe its use with special assessment tasks but the approach can also be used in relation to other inquiries, offering, they suggest, 'a possible way forward in the contentious and tricky world of science teacher assessment'.

Whether in physical or electronic form, the range of entries has to match the range of the work during the year, as required by the curriculum. Taking the 2013 national curriculum as an example, the 10 entries might comprise for Year 1 and 2:

- four or five entries giving evidence of working scientifically: 'asking simple questions'; 'observing closely, using simple equipment'; etc.
- four or five entries giving evidence of conceptual understanding as specified in relation to plants, everyday materials, etc.
- one or two entries relating to science work beyond the requirements of the curriculum.

Making and recording judgements

In this approach the programme of study provides the criteria for judgement and there is no need for additional criteria, such as were provided by the APP (Assessing Pupils' Progress). Judgements are made by scanning across the final selection of items in the folder and deciding whether, on balance, they fit the description of what should be learned at the end of a key stage, as specified in the programme of study. The simplest form of judgement would be a decision as to whether the end of key stage goals were achieved, or were not yet achieved, for 'working scientifically' and for 'conceptual understanding' as in Box 19.4.

Box 19.4 A simple record of end of key stage achievement in science

Area of science curriculum	Key stage PoS requirements achieved	Key stage PoS requirements not yet achieved
Working scientifically		
Conceptual understanding		

Alternatively, work relating to particular aspects of the programme of study, for example, conceptual understanding related to living things, materials, forces and movement, could be judged and recorded separately, giving a profile of achievement.

This way of using the programme of study as attainment targets avoids the use of levels, as in the eight-level set of attainment targets in the 1999 National Curriculum. The use of levels of achievement for reporting has come under some severe criticism for reasons summarised in Box 19.5, which draws on the report of an influential expert group asked by the DfE in England to consider the framework for a revised National Curriculum.

Supplementing normal work with embedded tasks

The use of special tasks embedded in regular work provides the opportunity to set children a standard task without the anxiety of a formal test situation. This may be desirable even though evidence from regular activities is the main source of information if it has not been possible to collect some kinds of information in the course of normal work. One approach is to provide a bank of optional tasks to supplement teachers' assessment and of course there are commercial tests available. These generally take the form of 'stand-alone' items with well-defined 'right answers'. Such question formats are not well suited to assessing science, especially inquiry skills. An alternative is to embed questions in a theme, which is not only more interesting for the children but cuts down on the amount of reading the children have to do to establish a fresh context for each item.

Box 19.5 Problem with 'levels'

Experience of over 20 years of using levels to describe pupils' progress has revealed several unintended consequences, which can have impact on pupils' motivation and learning, particularly at the primary level. Some of the main points are:

■ When levels are seen as important, teachers, parents and students may use them inappropriately to label students.

■ Describing a pupil as having achieved a certain level does not convey anything about what this means the student can do.

■ Some pupils become more concerned for 'what level they are' than for the substance of what they know, can do and understand.

■ Assigning levels increases social differentiation rather than striving for secure learning of all pupils.

■ Students who are regarded as unable to reach target levels often have reduced opportunities for progress, increasing the performance gap between the more and less well achieving students.

■ As levels are well spaced (being about two years apart) the practice has grown of creating sub-levels in order to be able to show progress. However, these have little basis of evidence in cognitive development and serve only to prescribe the curriculum more closely.

An example of this approach is given in Schilling *et al.* (1990). Written questions assessing process skills were devised on the theme of the 'Walled Garden', which teachers could introduce as a topic or as a story. Questions were grouped into seven sections about different things found in the garden: water, walls, 'minibeasts', leaves, sun-dial, bark and wood. For each section there was a large poster giving additional information and activities and a booklet for children to write their answers. Children worked on the tasks over an extended period, with no time limit; they enjoyed the work which they saw as novel and interesting, in no way feeling that they were being tested. The examples in Figure 19.2, on pp. 280–281, are of the questions on 'minibeasts'. They can be used as guides to setting inquiry-based tasks in other contexts to suit the class activities.

Quality assurance of teachers' assessment

There are clear advantages in using teachers' judgements in terms of the validity of the results since teachers can collect information about a wider range of achievement and learning outcomes than formal testing allows. The whole curriculum can in theory be assessed, thus eliminating the narrowing effect of a special focus on those parts included in a test. Further, pupils are not subject to the anxiety that accompanies tests and which can affect the outcome. As we have seen, teacher-based assessment also enables pupils to have some role in the process through self-assessment.

However, there is a commonly held view that teachers' judgements provide unreliable results. This can be the case when no steps are taken to assure quality. The main causes of low reliability in this process are the inclusion of irrelevant information (such as neatness, when this is not a specific goal of the task), variation in interpretation of the criteria and the problem of relating performance in specific contexts to necessarily general statements in the programme of study used in judging achievement. There are several effective ways in which reliability can be improved to equal and even exceed that of tests. The main ones are using examples, group moderation and using a test or tasks as a check.

Using examples

There are many sources of examples of pupils' work or behaviours selected to illustrate particular achievement, such as are provided for the EYFS profile on the DfE website mentioned earlier. Some curriculum materials contain examples of children's actions, words, talk, writing or drawings annotated to highlight features which are significant in relation to the judgements to be made. The Nuffield Primary Science (1995) *Teachers' Guides* each contain a chapter on assessment giving examples and discussing aspects of the work which indicate whether certain key criteria have been met, illustrating the importance of excluding from consideration features which are not relevant.

Since teachers should be basing their judgements on a range of each pupil's work and not judging just from one piece, it is most useful to have exemplar material in the form of a portfolio of work from one child rather than single pieces of work. This helps teachers to apply the criteria in a holistic manner. Not every piece of work will fit the description, say, for 'working scientifically' and neither will each and every part of the programme of study for a stage be represented in the portfolio. This may seem rather a loose procedure, but assessment is not an exact matter and it is better to be aware of the uncertainty than to assume that we can describe children's learning more accurately than is the case.

Group moderation

This involves teachers meeting together to discuss examples of pupils' work. These meetings enable teachers to share their interpretations of the programme of study/attainment targets as well as to discuss their judgements of specific sets of work. Experience of group moderation suggests that it has benefits beyond the quality of assessment results. It has a well-established professional development function. Meeting to discuss the inferences that can be drawn from studying pupils' work provides teachers with insight into the nature of the assessment process which improves not only their summative assessment but also their formative use of assessment.

The rigour of the moderation process that is necessary depends on the use of the results. For internal school uses of summative assessment, such as reporting to parents and informing other teachers, within-school moderation meetings are adequate. However, inter-school meetings are advisable when the results are to be published on the school website and made available to inspectors.

Minibeasts

Dan and Tammy kept a note of all the 'minibeasts' they found in the Walled Garden. They drew the minibeasts as well as they could.

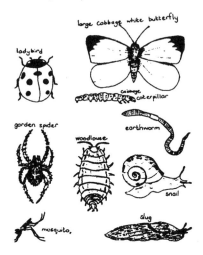

Read about 'minibeasts' in the project folder before you try to answer the questions.

Later, back at school, they used some books to get information about the minibeasts. They made a special chart, called a table, which showed the information, and put it in the Walled Garden project folder. Here is a copy of it.

Minibeast	legs	where eggs laid	eggs hatch into	sheds skin	adult feeds on
woodlouse	yes	under stones, logs	young woodlice	yes	dead animals and plants
snail	no	soil	young snails	no	dead and living plants
ladybird	yes	plants		yes	live greenfly
slug	no	soil	young slugs	no	dead and living plants
earthworm	no	soil	young worms	no	dead things in the soil
cabbage butterfly	yes	leaves	larva caterpillar	yes	plants
spider	yes	in cocoon on leaves	young spiders	yes	flies
mosquito	yes	on water		yes	

Figure 19.2 Examples of special tasks embedded in a theme (Schilling *et al.*, 1990)

1. Use the information in the table to answer these questions:

    a) What do ladybirds feed on? ....

    b) In the table all the minibeasts with legs have something else that is the same about them. Can you see what it is?

    ....

2. When they made the table they could not find all the information about the ladybird and the mosquito. Please fill in this information for them on their table:

    a) A ladybird's egg hatches into a LARVA.

    b) Adult mosquitos feed on ANIMALS and PLANTS.

3. Dan and Tammy's table shows that snails eat dead and living plants, but it doesn't say whether they like to eat some plants more than others.

    Suppose you have these foods that snails will eat:

    and as many snails as you want. Think about what you would do to find out which of these foods the snails liked best.

    a) Say what you would do to start with. (Draw a picture if it will help.)

    ....

    b) Say how you will make sure that each food has a fair chance of being chosen.

    ....

    c) What will you look for to decide which food was liked best?

    ....

4. What other things could you find out about snails by doing investigations with them? Write down as many things as you can think of to investigate.

    ....

5. Dan and Tammy went to visit their Aunt and looked for minibeasts in her garden. They found them all except for snails although they looked carefully for a long time.

    a) Write down any reasons you can think of to explain why there were no snails in their Aunt's garden.

    ....

    b) Their Aunt thought it could be because of the kind of soil where she lived; there was no chalk or limestone in it.

    What is the main difference between snails and other minibeasts which Dan and Tammy found?

    ....

    c) Why do you think snails only live where there is chalk or limestone in the soil?

    ....

Using tests or special tasks to check teachers' assessment

What is meant here is the use of special tasks or tests as a means of moderating or checking teachers' judgements but not as a separate measure of achievement. Tests are used in this way in the Scottish system for English and mathematics. Teachers decide on the basis of a range of evidence from everyday activities about whether a pupil has met the criteria at a particular level in the subject. Assessment against the level criteria is an ongoing process; a pupil may be judged to have reached a level at any time. When confirmed by moderation, this is recorded and then reported at the appropriate time. The moderation can be through taking part in collaborative moderation within and across schools or the use of tests, which are described as 'another way for teachers to check their judgements against national standards' (SEED, 2005). If they choose to use a test, although currently only for English and mathematics, teachers can use a test, drawn from an externally devised bank of items, which they mark themselves, and compare with the results of their own classroom assessment.

Uses of individual pupil achievement data

The main use of the results of assessing what individual pupils have achieved at a particular time, whether these results are produced by testing or teacher-based assessment, is to keep track of their achievement and feed into decisions about further learning. However, these results can also be used for other purposes if individual pupil results are aggregated to give class- or school-level results. The numbers or percentages of pupils achieving the learning outcomes (or reaching certain levels) at the end of each key stage are used by the senior management for internal school evaluation and fed back to classes to be used in reviewing and improving performance (see Chapter 25). The percentages of pupils achieving the learning outcomes at the end of the final primary year form a particularly important part of the account of the school's performance. It can be published in the school's annual report, where it is set in the context of factors which impact on performance (concerning, for example, the diversity of the pupil intake) and need to be taken into account in interpreting raw statistics.

There are many well documented reasons why schools should not be judged only on the achievement of pupils in their final year (Harrison and Howard, 2011; Harlen, 2013). Although there are various procedures that enable a school's result to be adjusted to take into account some of the factors that make it unfair to judge and compare schools on the basis of raw pupil achievement results, these do not remove the pressure to raise levels of achievement by a narrow interpretation of the criteria. The negative impacts can best be deterred by not collecting these results locally or nationally, as is the policy in Scotland. Whilst recognising that the creation of 'league tables' of schools cannot be entirely avoided when reports are in the public domain, presenting information in the context of the school's performance should encourage responsible use of the data.

For the purpose of national monitoring of performance, an entirely separate procedure from the assessment of individual pupils provides more valid data. This follows the design of national and international surveys, in which tests are administered to a sample of pupils. It is not necessary for all pupils in the sample to be given the same test, so a large number of items can be used, thus reducing the 'sampling error' mentioned earlier. The results are used, not only to monitor year-on-year performance, but in reporting trends in achievement in different skills and areas of knowledge and understanding, which all teachers can use to review and reflect on the balance in the science programmes.

Summary

This chapter has discussed some procedures and issues in using assessment for summative purposes. We have considered the use of teachers' judgements and of tests or special tasks. The main points have been:

- Summative assessment provides an account of what a child can do or understand at a certain time. Compared with formative assessment it has to be more succinct, strictly criterion-referenced and as reliable as possible.

- Summative assessment can be obtained by giving special tasks or tests that give a snapshot of what has been attained at a particular time, by teachers making judgements of evidence that has been gathered over time, or by building a record over time.

- Tests have considerable disadvantages for assessing individual pupils since they can assess only a restricted range of goals in addition to other limitations and have a potentially negative impact on pupils.

- Using teachers' judgements enables a wide range of different kinds of evidence to be collected and thus provides a more valid assessment of the goals of primary science.

- Procedures for identifying the best work that pupils can produce at a certain time can incorporate formative assessment processes.

- When teachers' judgements are used, criteria have to be applied uniformly so that comparable information is provided about each child. This requires some form of quality assurance.

- The use of the requirements of the programme of study as criteria for judging pupils' work obviates the need for reporting in terms of 'levels' and its associated disadvantages.

- Procedures for quality assurance of teachers' judgements include the provision of assessed examples, group moderation and the use of reference tests.

Further reading

Black, P., Harrison, C., Lee, C., Marshall, B. and Wiliam, D (2003) *Assessment for Learning: Putting it into Practice,* Maidenhead: Open University Press, ch. 4.

Davies, D. Collier, C., McMahon, K. and Howe, A. (2010) E-scape assessment, *Primary Science*, 115: 18–21.

Harrison, C. and Howard, S. (2011) Issues in primary assessment: assessment purposes, *Primary Science*, 115: 5–7

Nuffield Foundation (2012) *Developing Policy, Principles and Practice in Primary School Science Assessment,* London: Nuffield Foundation. Available for download from http://www.nuffieldfoundation.org/primary-science-assessment.

Planning for progression

20

School level planning

Introduction

In this chapter we discuss planning the school programme for science. The responsibility for planning at this level lies with the head teacher and senior management team – those with responsibility for subject areas or for year or stage programmes. The science subject leader or coordinator has a key role in developing an approach to implementing the science curriculum in a way consistent with the philosophy of the school. So we begin with a discussion of the role of the subject leader in terms of contributing to the strategic direction of the school, and in particular the school science policy. We then consider the aspect of the role concerned with the oversight of the effective use of people and resources to ensure high-quality science learning in the school. Two other key responsibilities – as the support for learning and teaching, and leadership and management of staff – are considered in Chapter 25. The second main part of this chapter considers some of the key topics that need to be addressed in planning at the school level and implemented in its programme.

Roles of the subject leader

School level planning requires consideration of a wide range of whole-school issues as well as those that fall more easily within a subject. Various management structures are used to address these issues. For example, some schools have teams of staff responsible for a subject or group of subjects or specific themes; in others there are teachers with responsibility for a year group, a phase (such as the Foundation Stage) or a key stage or phase. More commonly, for the core subjects of language, mathematics and science at least, there are coordinators or subject leaders with responsibility across the school. The science subject leader contributes to the strategic development of the subject in the school, securing and sustaining effective teaching, leading and managing staff and ensuring the most effective deployment of human and physical resources. This is achieved through:

- The development of a science policy that reflects the values of the school and is owned and understood by all those involved in supporting science learning.

- The effective management of resources including time, equipment and staff.

- The monitoring of learning and teaching that enables ongoing dialogue about ways to improve and enhance learning for pupils.

- The effective leadership of staff such that the subject leader can act as adviser, supporter, collaborator and, where necessary, champion of the subject.

These fall into two overlapping groups of activities. The first two relate to planning provision for science in the school and are considered here. The second two refer to subject leader's role in staff leadership and development, which are considered in Chapter 25. So we now look at what is entailed in the first two these aspects of the role, before turning to the planning of the whole-school programme in science.

Developing a whole-school science policy

National curricula set out what pupils should learn but not the lessons through which the intended outcomes can be achieved. It is up to schools to develop a philosophy and vision that will secure the desired high standards that national curricula are intended to achieve. Holding fast to a philosophy for the school and the individual areas within the curriculum is a challenge, which is why it is important for the school to develop a whole-school policy which should guide values and planning priorities. The example in Box 20.1 of an overall statement of values and beliefs about learning illustrates the role of the whole-school policy in setting the context for teaching and learning in different subject areas.

The science subject leader and others in the school with responsibility for an aspect of the curriculum need to spend time discussing school policies,

---

Box 20.1 A whole-school policy statement

From Year 1 to Year 6 the curriculum is planned using Contexts for Learning. Each year group has a different Context for Learning each term, apart from Year 6 who has one context which spans over two terms. Each Context has a broad title where a high value is placed on all subject disciplines. Each National Curriculum subject area has been rigorously planned into the contexts throughout the school to ensure the progression and entitlement to learning is provided for all pupils. The Contexts provide the opportunity for explicit links to be made across the subject areas ensuring an in-depth understanding of the learning. English and Maths are planned for separately but also within the Contexts to enrich the learning. The organisation of the Contexts for Learning provides the opportunities for children of all ability levels to access the learning creatively at an appropriate level and to be successful as learners. Research shows that children learn more effectively when there are explicit links and connections in their learning. Children don't learn in boxes- they learn most effectively when they, themselves can make links in their learning. They learn most effectively when their learning is motivating, exciting and connected.

(Policy statement of Ridgeway School, Croydon)

---

within a regular timetable of review. To do this well the science subject leader needs to understand the broader policies of the school, to know the capacity of the staff and school to achieve aspirations, to have a sound understanding of science and science teaching and to be up to date with current developments in the field. In addition, and most importantly, good communication with senior managers as well as colleagues is essential if a policy for science is to be developed collaboratively.

The science policy directs and guides staff, linking closely with the overall school policy and articulating within it a vision for science education. In the same vein our vision for science education is described in Chapter 1 of this book where we argue that 'If education is a preparation for life, it must prepare pupils for a life in a world in which science and its applications in technology have a key role. It follows that children need to develop some knowledge and understanding of aspects of the natural environment; a capacity to reason from evidence; an understanding of the nature of science and of how scientific knowledge and the key ideas that will help them make sensible decisions about how they live their lives and which affect the lives of others' (see p. 9).

The school science policy should provide a clear expression of values and aims and should inform teachers, governors, parents, children and the wider community about what the school sees as important in science teaching. The main the topics to be covered in a policy, proposed by CLEAPSS (2006) are:

- the aims of teaching science, reflecting the school aims;
- the philosophy of science teaching;
- the approach to science teaching;
- the approach to assessment;
- how equal opportunities are provided;
- how health and safety are assured;
- procedures for record keeping;
- cross-curricular links;
- outdoor education;
- the approach to planning;
- use of resources.

Box 20.2 illustrates some of these topics with statements drawn from a number of primary school science policies.

Management of resources

One of the roles that subject leaders have always recognised as important is that of resource manager. Primary science is demanding of resources. In Chapter 22 we discuss matters relating to resources in some details. However, it is important to note that the term resources can cover a multitude of things:

Box 20.2 Some examples of statements included in school policy documents

The science policy should include a statement of the …	Examples taken from a number of school science policies
… aims that reflect the school aims	Develop knowledge and understanding of important scientific ideas, processes and skills and relate these to everyday experiences. … Develop effective ways of thinking, finding out about and communicating scientific ideas and information. … Explore values and attitudes through science. Work with others, listening to their ideas and treating these with respect …
… philosophy of science teaching	We believe that children have a natural curiosity about their world and the enthusiasm to want to make sense of it. We aim to capitalise on this, using first-hand experiences so that our children come face to face with phenomena and learn directly about the ways things are, and why they behave as they do.
… approach to science teaching	Activities inspire the pupils to experiment and investigate the world around them and to help them raise their own questions such as 'Why … ?', 'How … ?' and 'What happens if … ?'.
… approach to assessment	Assessment is important in providing information about children's development that can be used to help teachers to help children. This can also be used to inform the planning of future work. Formative assessment will be ongoing during each unit of work and summative assessment will be used at the end of each unit of work.
… equal opportunities	All children are taught in their class groups, by the teacher, regardless of ability, race or gender. Lessons are differentiated to meet the needs of all class members, primarily by questioning at different levels and giving support during practical activities.
… health and safety	We aim to develop in children: ■ An appreciation of the need for safe action in scientific exploration and investigation. ■ The ability to handle materials and equipment with care. ■ An awareness of the need for safety and responsible behaviour in everyday life. Developing children's awareness of dangers and safety is planned into the schemes of work where appropriate. Safety must always be taken into account when planning science activities.

practical equipment, storage space, the time to carry out science activities and the knowledgeable teachers to support it, the information technology, books and posters that can enhance subject teaching, as well as visitors to the school and places for the school to visit.

Time is a major resource for science. Even when well planned, science is often squeezed out in implementing activities for several reasons, including the teachers' lack of confidence in teaching science or the special emphasis given to literacy and numeracy.

As well as the overall time for science, the timetabling of science activities is important. Where it is felt that science requires extended periods of time, this needs to be set against the demands of other curriculum areas. Getting the balance right when a cross-curricular approach is being taken is also something of a fine art. Where broadly based topic work is the predominant way of working, the timetable needs to allow this to take place for extended periods of time, interrupted only by the essential scheduling of activities where space, staff or equipment have to be shared, providing time for children to carry out investigations which would not fit into small time slots. In theory this could still be the case where the school organises the curriculum on a subject basis, with the time for each area designated. However, in this case there is a greater likelihood of time being chopped up into portions which restrict opportunities for children to try things out, discuss them, try other ideas while things are fresh in their minds and so derive maximum learning from their activities. Decisions about having a dedicated science week or the use or otherwise of subject specialist teachers can also restrict choice in terms of how science fits in the timetable.

Planning the school programme

As we have seen in Chapter 2, the national curricula or guidelines for each of the countries of the UK have diverged since the mid-2000s and now look very different from one another. Development in research and the greater globalisation of education have been reflected in a welter of new ideas and initiatives, some of which have been directly included in different ways in national curricula. However, although they differ in structure and detail, the curricula in all four countries of the UK share the aim of making science more relevant to children's lives and of reducing the prescription of content to allow more emphasis on the development of skills and working scientifically. This greater flexibility, particularly when set against the removal of end of key stage tests in England and Wales, gives schools and teachers more scope to plan curricula that will offer an exciting start to science education. At the same time this means that the planning at school or stage level has to take into account the wide range of issues involved in planning a programme that meets children's needs at the classroom level.

In particular, there was a worrying decline in the importance given to science in England after 2009, as revealed in a survey of teachers by the Wellcome Trust in 2011 (see Box 20.3).

Box 20.3 Some findings from the Primary Science Survey Report of the Wellcome Trust (2011: 20)

An online survey conducted by the Wellcome Trust during July 2011 asked primary school teachers for their views on the status of primary science, the opportunities available to their pupils and themselves as professionals, and how these things may have changed since the removal of SATs in 2009 in England. The survey was sent to all primary teachers on the National Science Learning Centre (NSLC) database, not a representative sample from across UK schools but those likely to be more engaged with the importance of primary science. From the 465 teachers responding there were 133 examples of negative changes and 48 examples of positive change.

The top examples of negative change cited by teachers were:

- less teaching time devoted to science
- change to the status of science
- science assessments not done
- reduced curriculum or coverage of the curriculum.

These examples are supported by the fact that 64 per cent of all respondents disagreed or strongly disagreed with the statement: 'Compared with other core subjects (mathematics and English) science currently has an equal or greater importance placed on it in our school'.

58 per cent of teachers who reported positive changes provided examples linked to a change to the aim of teaching science, from the need to pass tests to aiming to inspire their pupils instead. One wrote:

It has been a massive positive because we are not driven by a narrow test and have broadened the science curriculum making it far more practical. Our survey of the children two years ago rated science as the worst subject in the school, this year it was the most popular!

It is clear that the removal of science SATs had an impact on the teaching of science in many primary schools. Furthermore it seems worryingly likely that negative changes (e.g. reduced lesson time) are far more frequent than positive ones (e.g. reduced 'teaching to the test').

Issues in planning

We can think of planning at three main levels

- school level (long-term): planning at this level is bound closely to the school's overall policy for science, takes account of the school setting, the availability of staff and other resources, and the principles of learning that underpin the school's vision. This often results in a map or whole-school plan.
- programme level (medium-term): at this level the plan is designed to ensure continuity and progression in the subject, and that what is valued by the

school and community is woven into the curriculum opportunities. This means not only what is taught but how it is taught and learned.

- class level (short-term): this is where policy, values, content and approach come together and are translated into actual learning experiences for the children.

We discuss class level planning in Chapter 21 and here focus on the long and medium term.

There are some issues to be taken into account in planning a school curriculum that arise as a response to current concerns. For example, 'healthy eating' rose to prominence after reports of rising obesity levels in children; attention to thinking skills has been stimulated by a key research report; and 'sustainability' from the concern to promote environmental protection and understanding. To leave these matters aside is not to suggest that they are unimportant, but in a short chapter we have attempted to focus on the more perennial issues. These include cross-curricular themes, transfer and transition and parental involvement.

Cross-curricular themes and links

One of the major dilemmas facing teachers is to ensure that the whole required or advised curriculum content is included in the science programme. In some national curricula the emphasis has moved from single subjects to more cross-curricular or topic work, and indeed to themes such as 'The World Around Us' in Northern Ireland where the expectation is that teachers will integrate subjects. But there is a fine balance to be struck between meaningful learning opportunities and ensuring 'coverage' across a subject. A broadly positive report on the impact of the Scottish Curriculum for Excellence on science learning in 2012 raised this concern about primary science:

> In primary schools, learning in the sciences is too often predominantly or exclusively delivered through an interdisciplinary approach which is not planned sufficiently well to develop knowledge and skills in a progressive way. Often in these instances, there is insufficient science being experienced, resulting in gaps in learning. This is not providing a sound basis for progression to more advanced study. A few children in primary school, whose experience of the sciences was exclusively through an interdisciplinary approach, could not identify having studied any science.
>
> (Education Scotland, 2012: 16)

This does not mean that an interdisciplinary approach should be avoided, but rather that there is a need to be selective and clear about the value of the topic to science learning. One of the ways in which this tension can be overcome is to take advantage of any overlap between subjects and any reinforcement that learning in one area can offer to another by planning through topic rather than separate subjects. The advantages of such planning are not limited simply to efficiency, but where real overlaps or synergies arise the recognition of links between subject by children helps them to make sense of their world and to make connections more easily. Making 'connections' rather than collecting information is how we believe children learn and develop as learners. As we have noted elsewhere, facts are only as valuable as the links that are made between them.

A well-funded project initiated in Northern Ireland and extended into England and Scotland was based on the idea that artists and scientists are both searching for understanding and, like its namesake Leonardo, the aim was the synchronised integration of learning outcomes for art and science. Schools focused on the topic of flight during an eight-week programme of integrated activities in which children were encouraged to collaborate to explore an aspect of the topic. The planned activities involved children in information gathering, developing ideas, designing and creating a flying object or creature and some form of communication about their work through a storyboard, poster, video, etc. Teachers, pupils and parents have been overwhelmingly supportive, teachers noting that children with SEN and boys benefited and that all children 'were developing thinking skills and their ability to solve the problems they were facing' (Leonardo Project website). It is particularly interesting that this art and science project was seen to have had a significant impact on developing literacy skills as well as being seen by children as the best science they have done.

Although the importance placed on literacy and numeracy can often mean that there is a link made between science and these subjects, there is a risk that the science planning is less rigorous than for the other subjects. Teaching children to use science non-fiction texts in literacy work can provide good, authentic, opportunities to develop literacy skills, whilst supporting science learning. However, care needs to be taken if the intention is to teach science through literacy in this way. Newton *et al.* (2002) found, for example, that school science texts, like many schemes of work for primary science, do not show a concern for explanatory understanding. That is, they provide information on 'how 'and 'what' but not 'why'.

An interesting observation by Peacock and Weedon (2002) draws attention to the importance of helping children to interpret the non-verbal information in science books. They found that 9–10 year old pupils who had been taught the use of non-fiction texts did not use science texts well to gain information. This, they concluded, was because what is needed is the development of visual literacy. Most science books include more pictures, diagrams and symbols than they do words, it is therefore important that teachers actively teach children to use science information books, making links between labelled diagrams and text, and seeking to discuss the possible explanations for the phenomena being presented within the pages. The need for these skills is more and more important with the ever-increasing use of the internet which is even more likely to rely on visual images and demands the ability to read information in a range of presentational forms. What is important is to look for ways in which science learning can be enhanced or can contribute to literacy and numeracy learning. For example, data from science experiments can be used in numeracy lessons to construct graphs, diagrams and charts.

Transfer and transition

Concerns about the dip in measured attainment that tends to accompany the transfer of pupils from primary to secondary schools was highlighted and explored by Galton *et al.* (1999) who also commented on similar, if less extreme 'dips' in transitions from Year 3 to 4. In science, 'dips' in attainment and motivation have been identified, for example, by the AAP surveys in Scotland which showed a decline in the motivation of pupils towards science learning between Year 5 in primary schools and the second year of high school (SEED, 2003). The impact of curriculum changes since that date on transition from primary to secondary have not been the subject of significant research, although this remains an area of concern. As a result of continuing concern a number of initiatives, including some funded projects, have provided a wealth of materials that primary and secondary schools, working in partnership, can use.

The Wellcome Trust working with schools in Croydon developed a useful raft of transition activities as part of a wider project. These topics, designed by primary and secondary teachers, involve some 12 lessons, half before children move schools and half after. Materials for the topics are available on the website (see the end of this chapter). The success of the project is difficult to judge because children in London can transfer to so many schools.

In Wales, as part of a new project Get On With Science (GOWS), funded by the Welsh Government, several resources have been produced to encourage more young people, especially girls, to pursue science subjects. A resource on transition in science includes advice and ideas that have been found effective in promoting successful transition (see Box 20.4).

A key feature of all the projects is that they involve collaboration and communication among groups of primary schools and secondary schools. Often secondary schools have a teacher responsible for primary liaison. However, for these projects to become part of a school's practice, collaboration needs to be ongoing and the activities an integral part of the school's overall curriculum and written into the science programme or scheme of work and developed as a collaboration among teachers at each end of the transfer.

Similar collaborations are important wherever there is a transition for pupils from one class to another. Within the same school this can often be addressed through careful collaborative planning, where teachers develop a shared understanding about what it is they are trying to achieve in teaching science. The school science programme is not therefore a static entity but both a result of collaboration and discussion and the focal point for ongoing discussion, debate and development.

Involving parents

Parents are the first and most important educators of their children and yet often they can have little knowledge about, and even less opportunity to contribute to, their children's schooling. In recent years the notion has grown of schools as part of, and in some senses accountable to, the community they serve. A study by the

---

Box 20.4 Ideas to ease primary/secondary transfer from the Welsh GOWS project

- An after-school fun science club hosted by the secondary school for Year 6 pupils from nearby primary schools. Each session is run with secondary staff and pupils. Children from the primaries have a member of staff with them (e.g. teacher/teaching assistant); this helps to foster relationships between the staff.

- A girls' and boys' football, netball or other sports club (or a mixture) with science-related tasks built into the programme (e.g. sports science or biology).

- Lunchtime science clubs for primary schools in a rural area, supported by staff and teachers from the secondary school; these clubs continue in Year 7.

- A science workshop programme for Year 6 pupils for four weeks in the summer term, followed up with a week's summer school and a further four-week programme once the pupils transfer to the secondary school.

- The art of science – activities exploring how arts and science come together, finishing with a performance for family and friends from the primary and secondary schools.

- A network of science clubs with, and in, the village primary schools. The clubs are also for children from the local secondary school, and are staffed by all the schools involved.

- Family science days held at the secondary school, either after school or at a weekend. The days can involve Year 5 and 6 children and their families, as well as families of children at the secondary school.

- Performing science – groups of pupils put on mini-science shows/marvels to entertain Year 6 pupils and their parents at Year 6 open evenings.

- Science through cookery clubs – covering heat, change of state, solids, liquids, gases, etc.

(Chwarae Teg, 2012: 12)

Joseph Rowntree Foundation (Carter-Wall and Whitfield, 2012) concluded that there is a 'reasonable case' that parental involvement in their children's education has a causal influence on children's school readiness and subsequent attainment. They also argued that the closer to the classroom the parental support – such as study support – the more impact it is likely to have on pupil attainment, particularly for disadvantaged and lower achieving children. This increased emphasis on parental involvement has been enshrined in legislation in some countries, for example The Scottish Schools (Parental Involvement) Act 2006. To help put this into practice the Scottish Executive Education Department (SEED) produced a toolkit to provide parents and staff in education authorities and schools with a practical resource to support partnership with parents in all aspects of children's learning. It looks at the different ways parents and carers can be involved and includes advice and practical materials to support the arrangements introduced by the Act. The toolkit complements the Guidance to the Act published in September 2006.

Many schools are working actively to engage parents and guardians in their children's education. Schools need to decide on the nature of the relationship they want with parents or carers, along a continuum of involvement. At one end involvement can be simply keeping parents informed about their child's education, for example by sending out newsletters, or providing information about what their child will be covering in different subjects on the school website. Most schools have mechanisms to do this. Further along the continuum is the involvement of parents in school trips, helping with activities in class and helping with homework. But, with the increasing use of secure websites and VLEs (p. 203), parents can be offered more information, involvement and support. This can include, for example, reports on a child's progress or class activities in the form of video recordings of presentations.

With the help of parents, and with clear guidance, children's learning can more easily go beyond the confines of the classroom, taking advantage of out-of-school activities, homework, links to quizzes or film clips. Schools can choose to make blogs or discussion boards open to parents so that they can comment or post information, ideas or resources on websites for others to see and use. Schools have long relied on parents to join in school trips (as described in Chapter 9) and are increasingly invited to bring their specialist skills into school. Box 20.5 gives one example of a very successful project.

We are, perhaps, still a little way from a point where school professionals are able to work together with pupils and parents as co-designers of the curriculum but parental involvement is high on the government agenda.

Box 20.5 Using parents' expertise in creating a science week

At Meldrum Primary school an enthusiastic parent was co-opted to act as Science Week Parent Coordinator. The school wanted to provide opportunities for some really exciting science, but to go further by making links with the wider world and the world of work. The coordinator was able to make links with individuals and companies so that the week eventually included activities run by a deep sea diver, a chemist looking at colour, a visiting vet, a famous astronomer, a chocolatier, a geologist to help children to 'make fossils'. Involved parents persuaded other parents to come along, to offer workshops or to provide hands-on help. The school head teacher saw this project as a means of moving from parents helping on trips or with homework, to sharing in the teaching of their children. The children reported that they really enjoyed having real scientists teaching them about science and where these were also parents they gained insights into their working lives or interests that they would not otherwise have had.

(http://www.educationscotland.gov.uk/video/t/video_tcm4550158.asp?strReferring
Channel=educationscotland&strReferringPageID=tcm:4-615801-64)

Summary

Planning an effective science curriculum across the primary age range is a significant task with many issues that need to be taken into account. The subject leader ensures that there is a vision for science learning that fits with the wider school vision and which complies with national curriculum requirements or guidelines. We have identified the key roles of the science subject leader as follows.

- The development of a science policy that reflects the values of the school and is owned and understood by all those involved in supporting science learning.

- The effective management of resources including time, equipment and staff.

- The monitoring of learning and teaching that enables ongoing dialogue about ways to improve and enhance learning for pupils.

- The effective leadership of staff such that the subject leader can act as adviser, supporter, collaborator and, where necessary, champion of the subject.

The first two roles have been discussed in this chapter. The other two are discussed in Chapter 25.

The development of a whole-school plan for science that is consistent with the overall school policy and with national curricula involves many decisions at the school level. Three key aspects that have been discussed:

- how science is organised within the curriculum – in themes, science-based topics, cross-curricular topics, etc.;

- how continuity is ensured at points of transfer within the school and transition from primary to secondary school;

- how schools work with parents to maximise children's educational opportunities.

These are aspects of long-term and medium-term planning. For short-term planning, at the class level, we turn to the next chapter.

Further reading

Blacklock, K (2012) Science on a tight budget, *Primary Science,* 121: 5–7.

Hainsworth, M. (2012) Harnessing new technologies: a virtual world for science education? *Primary Science,* 122: 21–3.

Johnson, A. (2013) Is science lost in the world around us? *Primary Science,* 126: 8–10.

Lawrence, L. (2011) The science subject leader, in W. Harlen (ed.) *ASE Guide to Primary Science Education,* new edn, Hatfield: ASE, 133–40.

Peacock, A. and Weedon, H. (2002) Children working with text in science: disparities with 'literacy hour' practice, *Research in Science and Technological Education,* 20(2): 185–97.

Simon, D. (2011) School-level planning, in W. Harlen (ed.) *ASE Guide to Primary Science Education,* new edn, Hatfield: ASE, 126–32.

Smith, M., Howard, D. and Hoath, L. (2011) Head in the cloud, feet on the ground, *Primary Science,* 119: 21–3.

Websites

Wellcome Trust Croydon Schools project: http://blog.wellcome.ac.uk/2012/05/24/the-croydon-school-science-project.

The Leonardo Effect: http://www.leonardoeffect.com.

21

Class level planning

Introduction

In Chapter 20 we discussed planning at the school level, the development of a school policy and the roles of the science subject leader. In this chapter we consider the short-term planning that is needed to provide the activities and experiences that enable the long-term goals of the school programme to be achieved. We begin with an overview of lesson planning as a two-stage process. The first is concerned with the general shape of the lesson or several lessons on a topic, the activities to be included and aspects that may need advance preparation. The second is the more detailed decisions about setting the scene for each lesson, about questions to ask, and how to organise and manage the activities of all involved, pupils, teacher and any other adults in the activities. The last part concerns the aspects of planning that give the sparkle to lessons through creative teaching that encourages children's creativity.

Two-stage short-term planning

Planning at the class level is a process of gradually filling out the details of how to translate into practice the goals identified in the medium-term plans. The process starts with some overall general planning of a lesson relating to:

- the learning objectives;
- the children's activities and experiences;
- classroom organisation;
- equipment and materials needed by the teacher and pupils.

Then further detailed decisions are needed about

- starting points;
- questions to ask;
- key vocabulary;
- roles of the teacher, teaching assistant and any other adults involved;
- pupils' roles;
- assessment opportunities;
- timing.

General planning

Learning objectives

The teacher needs clear ideas about how lessons will contribute to the development of skills of working scientifically and of conceptual understanding. In a single lesson or sequence of lessons on a topic, the focus might be on particular inquiry skills which are used in the activities. For instance, planning skills are likely to feature in investigating the conditions which affect the evaporation of water, whilst observation and measuring skills may be more important in studying the weather. Different kinds of inquiries were mentioned in Chapter 6 and Turner *et al.* (2011) provides a number of examples of types of inquiry.

Ideas that can be achieved in a lesson will be 'small' ones (Chapter 2). As children's experiences are extended over a series of lessons, it becomes possible for them to link events which are explained in different ways to form 'bigger' ideas which have wider applications. Teachers need to have the big ideas in view even though the goals communicated directly and indirectly to the children will be the small ones specific to the lesson.

As well as the specific lesson objectives, the broader goals of science education have to be kept in mind. In Chapter 1 we set out some reasons for teaching science at the primary level. The importance of contributing to goals such as learning how to learn, being aware of how science can impact on daily life and the environment, becoming responsible citizens, being open-minded and considerate, are goals that should pervade all activities. These are not automatically achieved and are unlikely to be achieved if forgotten in planning at the level of children's everyday experiences.

Activities and experiences

There are multitudes of examples of children's activities and experiences available to teachers from a range of sources. The difficulty is not so much finding ideas for inquiries and investigations for children to undertake but choosing the most suitable ones. Possible activities need to be scrutinised in terms of the criteria suggested in Chapter 4 for effective learning experiences. It is useful to express these in terms of questions, as to whether the activities will:

- be interesting, relevant and appealing to the children?
- build on their previous experience and promote progress?
- involve the use of the senses, action, reflection and making meaning?
- encourage talk, dialogue and the representation and communication of ideas and events in various forms?
- help to develop scientific concepts, inquiry skills and attitudes of and towards science?
- provide opportunities for working cooperatively and sharing ideas with others?

Box 21.1 Some advantages and disadvantages of using published teaching materials

Advantages of using published teaching materials	Disadvantages of using published teaching materials
Helps to ensure content coverage	May limit the extent to which teachers
Saves planning time	use children's initial ideas as a starting
Helps to identify materials and	point
equipment	May reduce the use made of the
Can offer useful background knowledge	school's own environment and context
for teacher	May limit the opportunities for cross-
Can provide useful support as a teacher	curricular links
develops in confidence and knowledge	Less easy to cater for the differing needs
Curriculum materials can provide	of children
exciting resources for children and	Can become boring for the children (and
teachers to use.	the teacher)

The rich supply of classroom materials offers the opportunity for teachers to pick and choose; it is not suggested that a particular scheme be followed slavishly. If we believe that we need to start from children's ideas and interests, then no scheme can replace the teacher's insights into what will interest and excite the children, what approach is most likely to build on their ideas and help them to develop knowledge and understanding, skills and attitudes. However, there are significant advantages as well as disadvantages to using published schemes and curriculum materials, some of which are listed in Box 21.1

Class organisation

This involves making decisions about how best to organise the lesson; whether and when children will work in groups or as a whole class; whether other adults need to be involved if, for instance, the work involves taking children out of the classroom. Active learning – either through hands-on use of materials or discussion – means that for some of the time at least the children will be in groups. So questions arise as to what size of groups and how they are constituted. Feasey (2011: 48) recommends four as the optimum working group, since 'with larger groups the teacher runs the risk of having children who are off task'. She also suggests that for discussion, 'as with practical work, four is the optimum size where children can discuss in pairs and then share ideas within the foursome' (p. 49).

On the question of group composition, the work by Howe and colleagues in the early 1990s, comparing mixed-ability groups with groups selected on the basis of ability, is still relevant. Howe (1990) and Howe *et al.* (1992) undertook a study of group composition that convincingly demonstrated that, compared with groups where children had similar initial ideas, those where the ideas were more varied made most progress. Crucially the progress made by these mixed groups was more apparent six weeks after the group work than it was immediately after the lessons. Although other explanations for these differences were sought none was found.

In a later study, Howe and colleagues (2007) identified some key principles of group organisation in primary science. Their study was designed to draw together all the features that various research projects have identified as important in successful group work to explore their effects on attainment. Their findings revealed that classes where teachers supported group work effectively made greater progress than others. This was equally so in classes of mixed-age pupils. Their evidence showed the conditions in which pupils engaged in productive dialogue, including the sharing of ideas, discussing disagreements, sharing and explaining ideas. These behaviours were more likely to occur where teachers monitored groups, briefing children on the task in hand, ensuring good time management, encouraged the development of good group skills and modelled good interaction skills

Equipment and materials

The availability of necessary materials for children to use in practical inquiries and other equipment they may need are things to think about well in advance of a lesson. This includes ICT equipment, such as the use of an IWB, data-loggers, cameras, etc. that pupils might use. It is important to ensure that equipment is in working order and that materials are appropriate and in sufficient quantity. For example, Chris's lesson on melting ice, described in Chapter 3 (p. 42), required a large supply of ice cubes of different sizes. Her lesson plan, which includes some details as well as the overall framework, is given as an example in Figure 21.1.

Detailed plans

Detailed planning varies in the fineness of detail, depending on a teacher's experience and confidence in being able to make on-the-spot decisions. Such decisions will always be needed but are helped by having a well thought out structure for the lesson. Although planning takes place in the head, writing helps thinking and having written plans enables them to be shared and used by the teacher in reflection and evaluation of the lesson.

Starting points

One of the aims of inquiry-based science is for pupils to raise questions which they try to answer through investigation. In practice, this may happen during an extended activity but the starting point for the activity is set by the teacher, who sets up the lesson or topic in order to achieve certain learning objectives. However, achieving this learning is far more likely if children are engaged with and excited by the activity than if it seems of little relevance to them and is

Class	Date	Time	Staff
2W	8 Feb	30 mins am	Sally (am only)
Topic		1.10-3.15 pm	
Penguins and ice			

Subject focus	**Links to scheme**
am Science and literacy (see daily plan for literacy)	Grouping and changing materials
pm Science	**Cross-curricular links**
	Literacy

Objectives

- To develop words to describe ice and water (cold, wet, hard, melt, runny)
- To describe how ice feels
- To understand that ice is frozen water
- To make predictions
- To begin to understand 'fair testing'

Activities and Organisation

Iceberg ⟶ cold places ⟶ what do we know about ice?

'Look after this ice cube'

Penguin (big book) ⟶ equal chance, fair test

Insulation

Can we help penguins to keep ice for longer? Do you think ice cubes melt more or less quickly in a hot place or a cold place? How could we find out which is the best place to keep the penguins' ice cubes?

⟶ Big ice cube (fair test)

Investigation

What do we know about ice now? How can we get the ice back for the penguins?

Resources	**Desirable outcomes**
Bag of ice	Can describe ice (all), know that ice melts in warm (all)
Trays of ice cubes, one large ice cube	Understand idea of making a fair test (most)
Dishes – jug to collect melted ice in	Can make a prediction and say why (some)
Extra paper towels	Can record prediction on sheet (few).
Question sheet	
Prediction and results sheet	

Figure 21.1 An example of a lesson plan: Chris's lesson (see p. 42)

unconnected to their experience and interests. So a major aspect of the skill of the teacher is to catch the attention of the children so that they embrace the questions to be investigated as if it were their own. This involves finding a link to the children's experience or a 'hook' to engage their curiosity. Knowledge of the children is obviously needed but so is creativity on the part of the teacher. (We return to this later.) As Feasey (2011: 47) points out, it is not usually enough

> to begin lessons by asking children what they remember or what they know. Interestingly, this is often met with blank faces because young children find it difficult to recall prior knowledge if there is no context or practical activity to cue them into the area of learning.

Questions to ask

As we discussed in Chapter 10, the form and content of teachers' questions should match the purpose and the kind of thinking the teacher is seeking to encourage. It is therefore important to take the time to consider how key questions might be phrased, which generally means questions that are open and person-centred. It is particularly important to consider this aspect where classroom assistants are taking a group or the whole class, as without appropriate questions a well-planned lesson can become rather wooden and so result in far less learning. It is no simple matter to formulate the best questions for finding out children's ideas and for developing them. So some 'starting' questions need to be thought out. The questions will match the stages of the lesson. For instance:

- Questions to elicit the children's current knowledge and understanding will include questions such as 'have you noticed?' 'Do you remember when we … ?' These are followed by questions which ask for children's ideas about the phenomena, e.g. 'tell me what you think happens … ?'

- Questions to encourage exploration of materials will include attention-focusing questions, such as 'what do you notice about your ice cube now?'

- During investigations, questions will encourage the children to think about what they are trying to find out with the observations and measurements they are making, e.g. 'what does this tell you about how the sound gets from here to there?'

- In the reporting and discussing stage questions will help children to link their findings to what they were initially trying to discover, e.g. 'so what have we learned about the kind of soil that helps seedlings to grow best?'

- For reflecting on how the investigation was done: 'if you were describing to someone else how to do this investigation, what would you tell them are the important things to do?'

During the lesson more questions will arise, and it is not possible to anticipate exactly what ideas and questions the children will contribute. Indeed, being able to react to and work with children's responses to questions, and to the ideas and questions that they pose is much more likely when lessons are well planned. One teacher wrote 'Being open and flexible, and willing to allow the children to follow their own thinking was an integral part of my planning' (Boctor and Rowell, 2004).

Key vocabulary

Thinking through a lesson in planning identifies words that will be needed in discussions of their work with children and among children. Some words are ones that children may not understand or may use but misunderstand. Concept words related to the topic are the obvious ones: melting (which children can confuse with dissolving), reflection, vibration, temperature, etc. But words describing inquiry skills may also need to be introduced or clarified: prediction (not a guess), explanation, conclusion, and so on. Listing the words is the easy part. More challenging is deciding how to introduce or discuss them in the lesson. Some ideas on how to do this are given in Chapter 7 and 16.

Roles of the teacher, teaching assistant and other adults

When there is another teacher, teaching assistant or other adult present in the classroom with the teacher, the lesson plan should specify the roles of each. Preferably this is decided in joint planning beforehand so that everyone knows their role: who they will work with; what resources they will use; how they should interact with the children at different parts of the lesson. This latter point is particularly important, to avoid well-meaning helpers directing pupils' work too closely. Adults invited in to share their experience with the children should be briefed as to the level of ability and vocabulary and relevant past activities of the children. Those working with children with special educational needs should be those with necessary training.

As a lesson proceeds, whether the teacher is alone or helped by others, (s)he will take on different roles. At the start, the teacher is the energiser, capturing attention, creating the 'hooks' to engage children's interest and motivation. During group work the role is to support and encourage, to listen and to monitor, to question and provoke children to think about 'why' as well as 'what'. When children are reporting their work to each other, the teacher is the chairperson, ensuring each group has a fair hearing and modelling the role of constructive critic. Finally, in the whole-class discussion, the teacher is discussion leader, eliciting views about what has been learned and how it can be applied. At all times, of course, the teacher is both leader and collaborator in the learning, ensuring that the children take their roles in the activities and the thinking.

Pupils' roles

Our approach to teaching and learning in this book is based on the conviction that children learn best when actively involved, not passively receiving information. This means that they have to be both mentally and physically active and, also, that they engage in reflection about what they are learning. Even young children can take part in discussing *how* they are exploring and reasoning as well as what they are finding. Thus in planning teachers should ensure opportunities for children to take these roles in their learning:

■ engage in investigations and inquiry into events presented in the classroom and in the world around them;

■ become involved in developing ideas and skills that help them make sense of their environment;

■ reflect on how their ideas and skills have changed as a result of their activities;

■ begin to identify what they have learned from particular activities;

■ assess their work and take part in deciding how to improve it.

Assessment opportunities

Using assessment to help learning should be integral to every lesson. This is more likely to be the case if opportunities are thought out beforehand and some activities are organised so that children themselves identify where more help is needed, such as by the approaches mentioned in Chapter 18. It is useful to decide in planning the lesson what aspects of children's learning can be assessed and how this can be done by, for instance, scrutinising children's written work, drawings and concept maps, asking questions, observing, discussing findings.

The various phases of the lesson provide different opportunities for assessment. As noted earlier, asking children what they already know about a topic at the start of a lesson may not be productive, whilst asking what they would like to know may reveal the gaps that need to be filled. Group work provides the opportunity for the teacher to eavesdrop (see Chapter 16) on conversations, finding out how children are using words – 'skill' words as well as 'concept' words – and also observe how they go about their investigations and whether they need help, for instance, in dealing with variables in fair testing.

Opportunities for children to assess the quality of their work should also be identified, making sure that children know the criteria they should be using. This requires time during the lesson and draws attention to the need to consider timing and pace in planning the lesson.

Timing

When children are involved in hands-on activities it frequently happens that the 'doing' takes longer than anticipated and squeezes out the reporting and reflection and with it a lot of the 'thinking'. To avoid this happening, teachers' plans should indicate the time for each part of the lesson and, although there will always be good reasons for departing from this, the aim should be to keep to it. This need not curtail or cramp children's investigations if they are given an idea of the time they should spend and are helped to organise their work within it.

Some programmes use mnemonics to help teachers plan with a structure in mind. For example, the teaching units of the Australian project *Primary Connections*, widely used by schools in Australia and other English-speaking countries, are designed around a model based on 5Es: Engage, Explore, Explain, Elaborate, Evaluate. Teachers plan their lesson around this model, which helps them to ensure that all aspects are included. Another-five stage framework (Jones and Kirk, 1990) comprises: Focusing, Exploring, Reporting, Consolidating and Applying. Such aids to planning and remembering what point has been reached can be useful but, as with other approaches that try to do the thinking for the teacher, they can be constraining when followed mechanically. In particular they constrain teachers' creativity, which is our next subject.

'Creative learning requires creative teaching'

This heading is quoted from the report of the National Advisory Committee on Creative and Cultural Education (NACCCE), *All our Futures,* which defined creative activity as 'imaginative activity fashioned so as to produce outcomes that are both original and of value' (NACCCE, 1999: 6). Teachers must provide the conditions in which to maximise learning and among the conditions that do this are those that take children's emotional reactions into account. It is not difficult to realise that the affective response to science is as important as the cognitive learning during education. Those learners who find science boring or confusing or not relevant to their lives are unlikely to want to pursue it or put in the effort needed to develop their understanding. However, McCrory (2011: 94) notes that:

> Most teachers instinctively seem to recognise the need to interest their pupils in the classroom, yet they often complain that the short-term cognitive imperative of today's assessment-driven classrooms will always take precedence over the need for any longer-term affective outcomes.

He also points out that, in an age where children have instant access to entertainment, not only through television but also on their electronic mobile devices, school has a hard job competing for a positive emotional response. The satisfaction of learning is 'delayed gratification' and many pupils

> never sustain their engagement long enough to be able to stand on their achievements and survey the breath-taking way that science can unify seemingly diverse phenomena, or appreciate the awesome power of science to help explain and predict the everyday world around them.
>
> (McCrory, 2011: 95)

There are good reasons for teachers to take action to improve this situation since not only does teaching that leads to an emotional reaction engage children's attention, interest and enjoyment, but it leads to better learning. As we noted in Chapter 4, there is a close relationship between thinking and feeling.

Box 21.2 Young children thinking creatively in science

McFall and Macro (2004) report on some exciting work with nursery classes. They were inspired by a visit by the head teacher to the Reggio Emilia school, in Italy, where early years education is based on 'a respect for children's natural curiosity and creativity and their ability to produce powerful theories about the world and how it works (Thornton and Brunton, 2003). Having reviewed children's previous work the practitioners decided to focus on colour, camouflage and shadow. They wanted to develop the sense of wonder the children had shown when mixing colours as they painted model birds (after a visit to a local botanic garden) and noticed the shadows that were made.

The whole class sat on the carpet in front of an overhead projector and a blue shadow puppet. They were asked to predict what they would see on the screen when he was placed on the OHP. Most thought he would be blue, some made links with their experience of shadows and suggested grey or black. They tried this out, along with some stiff green foam in the shape of a tree, and one of a house (all part of the story they knew). The children began to modify their ideas as they noticed each time that the shadow was black. Then Mr Red was introduced. He had a shape but no eyes or mouth. The children were asked how these could be produced on the shadow. Initially many suggested drawing a face on the puppet, but this did not work. Finally, after lots of thought, some children suggested cutting out eye and mouth shapes. They were given plenty of time and appropriate equipment to try out their ideas. In this way they built up their ideas of light being blocked by a solid shape, and went on to observe that they could change the size and shape of the shadows by moving the puppets closer to and further away from the light. They then went on to explore coloured cellophane, experiencing with their own eyes how light passes through certain materials.

Creativity in teaching and learning in practice is illustrated by the lessons with young children in Box 21.2 and with older children in Box 21.3. Both fit well the NACCCE's definition of creativity.

In the example in Box 21.2 it is interesting that the teachers expressed their original intentions not as specific intended learning outcomes such as 'To know that light passes through some objects and not others' and 'that when light is blocked shadows form'. Rather they chose to express their intentions in terms of the broader goal of 'developing the sense of wonder the children had shown'. But it is not just a matter of 'going with the flow' of the children's ideas; it is also about knowing where the children are and finding interesting and imaginative ways to seize the opportunities provided by the children's emotional reactions to help them develop concepts, skills and attitudes. McCrory (2011) provides a number of techniques for emotional engagement that teachers can use. These include teachers referring to their own reactions, modelling emotions, creating suspense, generating surprise, using humour telling stories.

Box 21.3 Creating an imaginary science laboratory in the school grounds

Thirty Year 5 (9–10 year olds) explored the school grounds to think about ways in which the playground could be transformed into a laboratory or 'science garden'. Children played at being animals and plants in imaginary environments, wrote about and drew preferred animals or plant types and developed scientific languages through discussion. They imagined investigations that could take place in the school grounds and used sticks and bamboo to map out the shape of potential laboratories in the school landscape. Teams chose and worked on a focus – animals, archaeology, weather and plants. Collective decision-making challenged the children's social skills and emphasised the need for discussion, consideration of other people's ideas and cooperation. Children used photographs and notebooks to document their investigations and gave regular team presentations to their peers. They imagined the kind of work that a scientist of the future might engage in and designed costumes appropriate to the activity.

(Bianchi, 2005)

Summary

In this chapter we have outlined some of the key issues to be considered in planning science lessons. They have been considered in two groups: the matters needing decisions well in advance so that appropriate activities can be decided and resourced; and those concerning the details of how the various stages of the lesson will be managed. We have also underlined the importance of planning creative teaching that will enable children to think creatively and encourage positive emotional responses. The main points emphasised have been:

- Since there are very large numbers of activities available to teacher from websites and the STEM Centre e-library, criteria need to be applied in selecting the most appropriate.

- When there are other teachers or adults in the classroom with the teacher, the roles of each need to be agreed, including the kind of interaction with the children that is expected.

- To be flexible in meeting the needs of the children requires more careful advance preparation rather than less.

- Creativity in learning is essential and this requires creative teaching.

Further reading

Bianchi, L. (2005) Creative space, *Primary Science Review,* 90: 15–18.

Dabell, J., Keogh, B. and Naylor, S. (2006) 'Planning with goals in mind', in W. Harlen (ed.) *ASE Guide to Primary Science Education,* Hatfield: ASE, 135–41.

Feasey, R. (2011) Planning: elements of a effective lesson plan, in W. Harlen (ed.) *ASE Guide to Primary Science Education,* new edn, Hatfield: ASE, 44–52.

McCrory, P. (2011) Developing interest in science through emotional engagement, in W. Harlen (ed.) *ASE Guide to Primary Science Education,* new edn, Hatfield ASE, 94–101.

McFall, D. and Macro, C. (2004) Creativity and science in the nursery, *Primary Science Review,* 81: 17–19.

22

Sources and resources for practical inquiry

Introduction

For many years primary science has been seen as essentially a practical, hands-on endeavour where children learn by doing, feeling, touching and finding out 'what happens if … ?' However, in recent years our understanding of the role of practical, first-hand experience has become more sophisticated. The relationship between doing science and learning science is conceived as more complex than simply 'seeing is believing'. Clearly young children do need to experience the world, to see where apples grow, or where milk comes from, or how rivers flow to the sea, or to know what size a butterfly is, or to feel for themselves the effect of spinning on a roundabout. But learning science means going further than observing and in this chapter we begin by addressing two of the signature and related features of primary science: practical work and group work. In each case we consider the reasons for their importance and aspects of their implementation. Having considered these key elements of pedagogy we move on to the ways in which practical work is supported, first by looking at the selection, storage and maintenance of equipment and materials, and then at matters relating to safety. We end by listing sources of activities and materials available, often free, from the internet.

The value of practical work

It is notable that classroom resources for primary science, such as those that can be obtained from the sources in Box 22.6 at the end of this chapter, focus on supporting children's practical activities. Practical work alone is not sufficient for developing understanding, of course, and we have constantly referred to the importance of talk, discussion, dialogue and argument and to the value of reflection and reporting. However, these depend on having something to talk and write about; practical work remains at the heart of primary science, providing the 'hands-on' experience for 'minds-on' learning. The practical element of children's work in science remains quite challenging for many teachers, so it is useful to reiterate the reasons for its importance, what it means and how it is best managed in practice.

Why practical work?

Science goes beyond simple sensations; it attempts to explain the world and to make predictions about it. This requires more than experiencing phenomena; it involves exploring and testing out ideas by manipulating objects, asking questions of our world which are answered by investigating it. Scientific understanding needs individuals who possess the cognitive skills to engage with ideas and to explore them through the manipulation of objects and the opportunity to raise their own questions, plan how to obtain evidence, predict what might happen and think about how to capture and share their findings. This is the case for early learners as much as it is for research scientists. For young children to develop this complex set of skills for learning they need to go beyond being shown or told something. It is not sufficient to illustrate a point through practical work; practical *experience* is not the same as practical *inquiry*. Children need to learn how to explore and develop ideas through practical inquiry.

Evidence from a range of authorities in science education and from research studies is consistent in asserting the value of practical inquiry. The school inspection service in England, Ofsted (2004: 2), found that 'Teaching remains most effective where pupils are actively involved in thinking through and carrying out scientific inquiry'. Murphy *et al.* (2000) looked at classroom practitioners and concluded that the most effective in developing children's understanding were those teachers who promoted interaction, where classroom talk was a central feature of classroom inquiry. Bianchi (2003) found that teachers placed a high value on the provision of time for reflection during lessons, where children could think about what they were doing and discuss their ideas.

Evidence collected by Mant *et al.* (2007) in a study of cognitively challenging practical work showed that children enjoyed science lessons where the activities are challenging and encourage higher order thinking. This finding reflects an earlier study which concluded that pupils want to be challenged by new ideas and having to find things out for themselves (Braund and Driver, 2002). However, Mant *et al.* also found that performance by pupils on national tests increased significantly as a result of these challenging, exciting lessons. What most writers, inspectors and many teachers have suspected to be the case seems in fact to be so. The key then is to give sufficient time to practical science to make it worthwhile for the pupils, to give them real, quality learning time.

Features of effective practical work

Sufficient time

Looking back at the activity described in Box 7.2 (p. 106) gives us an illustration of the value of allowing time for pupils to explore and think about what they are finding may mean. The girls repeatedly put the eggs in the water in various ways, not randomly, but each time with an idea in mind that they wanted to test. It is also notable how the teacher encouraged this thinking by careful 'light touch' questioning so that the girls were required to provide evidence for their conclusions.

It is evident that practical inquiry takes time if children are to learn. 'Seeing for themselves' is important, especially for young children who, unlike adults, have not got a wealth of other experiences to fall back on when trying to make sense of events. Adults might be able to learn in more abstract ways but children need both physical and intellectual interaction with the world. The most effective teachers do not allow the pressure to move on to prevent them from allowing the children time to explore.

However, in this context, 'seeing for themselves' means more than watching; it implies a much more direct experience. This has implications for using teacher demonstrations as a substitute for children investigating for themselves. Indeed Ward (2008: 144) describes teacher demonstration with the support of a few chosen pupils as 'a worryingly common feature of primary science teaching'. Her reasons for this are quoted in Box 22.1.

Box 22.1 Pros and cons of teacher demonstrations

[In teacher demonstrations] there appears to be control over progression and behaviour, and little equipment is needed. Exciting and interesting experiments that learners could not undertake independently can be shown, although, in practice, demonstrations are often of everyday activities that learners are very capable of undertaking independently. The disadvantages of this method far outweigh any advantages, as demonstrations are 'hand off', 'minds off' experiences. Opportunities for differentiation are reduced to teacher questioning, which, when undertaken within a full class demonstration, often result in low quality recall. Opportunities for learners to develop skills are limited and gaining an insight into learners' attainment is a challenge. However, demonstrations are excellent when carried out by visiting science theatres and groups, as these are one-off exciting events that motivate and inspire.

(Ward, 2008: 144)

Being clear about the purpose

We noted in Chapter 18 that children's understanding of the purpose of a lesson can be quite different from the teacher's purpose. Box 18.2 gave an example of children missing the point that conducting an investigation of the strength of paper was intended to help them to plan a fair test. Goldsworthy *et al.* (2000) give another example, quoted in Box 22.2

It is clear that learning by seeing and doing is much more successful if the pupil knows the purpose of the activity and can therefore focus on what is important.

Set in a real context

In all the examples given in Chapter 3 – as indeed in other examples in this book – the teacher set the scene for children's practical activity by creating a 'real' context for it. Although mostly fictional, the contexts were 'real' enough to the children so that they were engaged and wanted to find an answer to

Box 22.2 What is the investigation about?

Interviewer:	Whilst Daryl is running around, tell me, what do you think you are learning in this investigation?
Robert:	How fast you can run.
Jody:	The length of your legs.
Interviewer:	What about the length of legs?
Jody:	Well, if there are bigger legs you can run faster and with shorter legs you can run a bit faster.
Interviewer:	And anything else you think you are learning?
Jody:	How much muscle it needs to go, how fast it can take.
Robert:	About forces.
Interviewer:	What about anything about doing investigations?
	(Interrupted by Daryl returning from running)
	Do you think you are learning anything about how to do an investigation?
Jody:	Yes
Interviewer:	What sort of things are you learning?
Jody:	Hot and cold and stuff
Robert:	Body

(Goldsworthy *et al.*, 2000: 1)

the question. The children in the school involved in science week for Year 6 (p. 50) who undertook the forensic science work were able to engage with very complex scientific ideas, undertake accurate tests and write well constructed articles for the school newsletter because the context they were operating in was realistic. This contextualisation provides a platform for authentic discussion and debate.

It is perhaps the lack of real contexts that results in less time being given to the consideration of evidence than planning and doing. In the example of Daryl and his friends given in Box 22.2, a much more lively discussion with more focus on how to investigate it might well have been achieved if the children were responding to, say, a suggestion by the head teacher that on school sports day pupils should be in teams of similar heights rather than in year or class groups. In this way pupils could get to exchange and challenge each other's ideas, to construct appropriate ways to investigate their ideas and to develop theories based on that evidence.

Part of establishing a real context for practical work is that the children do not already know the result. This may seem obvious but it is not uncommon for this to be the case. For example, most children already know from experience that the more times they turn the key of a clockwork toy, the further it will travel. The time and effort involved in practical work is justified if it requires children to think hard about a question they really want to answer.

In summary, the valuable contribution of practical work to learning science is most likely to be obtained when:

- Discussion among pupils and between teacher and pupils is seen as key to real learning with teachers modelling ways of asking questions and exploring ideas.

- The problem is set in a social, meaningful context such that there is a reason to puzzle over observations, to raise interesting questions, to take care when collecting the right sort of evidence and to make sense of that evidence in light of the original problem that was posed. Meaningful contexts also give a reason to communicate findings to others.

- Children feel challenged intellectually and in terms of the skills and processes they need to employ. Children enjoy thinking hard, employing a range of thinking skills and developing, through hands-on and minds-on experience, their ability to learn independently.

Organising group practical work

Why group work?

Almost invariably practical work needs to be undertaken in small groups. It is necessary for the efficient use of resources but most importantly for the opportunity it affords children to share ideas, to challenge each other's ideas and to reflect on their learning. In addition they need to learn how to work in groups and to plan together as a team. Group work done well, that is, where children are working as a group, not sitting in a group working individually, produces significant benefits to learning. A project funded by the Economic and Social Science Research Council as part of its Teaching Learning Research Programme studied large numbers of children in Scotland as their teachers implemented increased amounts of group work. The findings from this project were quite remarkable.

> Despite some views that group work is only beneficial for children's social development, we showed that group work can more positively influence academic progress than other forms of learning.

(TLRP, 2005)

Naylor *et al.* (2007) confirm a point made by Barnes (1976), and noted in Chapter 7, that argument and discussion are richest when the teacher is not present. Group work provides this opportunity since the teacher cannot be present in more than one group at a time. However, as the Scottish project cited above pointed out:

> It is well known that pupils need to have the skills to communicate effectively through listening, explaining and sharing ideas. But pupils also have to learn to trust and respect each other, and they need skills in how to plan, organise and evaluate their group work.

Develop good team working skills

In order to facilitate good group work children need to be taught how to work as part of a team. One way to do this is to allocate roles. Feasey (2011: 48) suggests that, in a group of four, the children can be assigned roles of: science resource manager; science fair tester; science measurer; science recorder. The children wear badges showing their roles, which are rotated so that the children have the chance to develop different skills. It is the teacher's role to ensure that some pupils, often boys, are deterred from laying claim to the equipment. Developing good team working skills is important for science learning and for life. Science lessons are the ideal opportunity for this.

Different starting points within the group

Research by Howe (1990) and Howe *et al.* (1992) mentioned in Chapter 21 showed that discussion among children is likely to be enhanced when the group comprises children with different ideas to put forward and defend. Later research by Howe *et al.* (2007) clearly indicates the importance of there being different ideas among the pupils at the start but also shows that mixed-age groups can be equally successful as more homogeneous groups. The point seems to be to ensure an equality of status within the group by encouraging the valuing and sharing of ideas. Hence group composition can be determined by a range of other factors based on a simple issue of expediency. Where a teacher feels the need to carefully target assistance, more homogeneous groups might be best, but on the whole ensuring a mix of ideas and a willingness to work together should guide decisions.

Opportunity to discuss and share ideas

Teachers can support good group work by modelling the kinds of thinking and discussion required for creating the atmosphere for productive reporting and discussion (Box 7.4, p. 111). The literature on 'argumentation' discussed in Chapter 7 provides a useful framework and a common language, with teachers playing a relatively 'hands-off' role while pupils 'propose and justify ideas to other group members' (Howe *et al.*, 2007: 561).

Different group activities

It is likely that, if all the pupils in the class are working on the same general problem but on different aspects, then the discussion among groups will be richer and the teacher will be able to draw together the ideas from different groups to create a really challenging discussion. However, the nature of the problem that is being looked at, and the availability of the equipment, will have a bearing on how the work is organised. What is probably most important is that the pupils and the teacher can see how and why the work is distributed as it is and how it contributes to the whole.

Providing a work-card or worksheet

A key message running through our discussion of children's science activities is that they should engage children's thinking and ideas. This may be incompatible with providing instructions in the form of a work-card or worksheet when, in the extreme case, children may be so occupied in making sense of the instructions that the overall plan and purpose escapes them. Following a recipe may achieve the intended result but not the intended learning. However, there are times when children will need written instructions of some sort. For instance, very occasionally, they may need to follow a set approach in setting up some equipment. In some cases pupils and their teacher may discuss as a class or group how to tackle an investigation and then agreed procedures can be written onto the computer and projected or printed off for each group.

Instructions can also help children to organise themselves and share ideas. For instance: 'Get one person to write down all the ideas in the group and then decide which you all agree with and which you don't' or 'Each write down your ideas on a *Post-it* and stick them on one piece. Make sure you understand all the ideas even if you don't agree with them.' It can also be useful to provide some form of simple writing frame to help the children structure their thinking and record outcomes. When the investigation is about fair testing, a planning board such as in Figure 12.1 (p. 171) may be useful, but whether this is appropriate depends on the goals of the activity. When the purpose is to give children experience of carrying through a complete investigation of their own, a work-card or sheet prepared in advance is unlikely to be appropriate. Guidance for inquiries based on children's own questions is best given in discussion with the teacher, when new ideas for procedures and explanations can be 'scaffolded' by the teacher. Key points from the discussion could be written down as an *aide-memoire*, ensuring that matters such as safety and care of equipment are not forgotten.

Equipment and resources

On the whole, the equipment and resources used in primary science are not complex, often everyday items are more appropriate than specialist science equipment. The important thing is that the resources the children need are readily available, well maintained and efficiently deployed.

Obtaining resources

Clearly the resources used in primary science are dictated by the planned activities, which are in turn guided by learning goals. Hence planning and resourcing are closely linked. Good published schemes tend to provide lists of resources needed, as do the materials that can be obtained from the websites listed later in Box 22.6.

A high proportion of practical activities of the kinds discussed in this book, such as floating and sinking, growing plants, dissolving materials, collecting woodlice or using string telephones, require only materials that can be described as 'everyday'. Some of these resources can be used over and over again, others, such as flour or pieces of wire, will be used up. Shortage of these things causes the greatest frustration because this is what many of the children's activities are all about; so some money needs to be set aside for their purchase throughout the year.

In addition to the 'everyday' items there are some more specialist items that can enhance learning without being so difficult to use that they act as a barrier to learning. Work on electricity is an obvious example, and measuring instruments such as stop clocks or light meters can provide clear and accurate recordings that would not otherwise be possible. Other equipment, such as data-loggers, tablets and digital cameras, have become common in schools with children, if not always adults, seeing them as 'everyday'. In addition there is now a wide range of software, internet resources, posters, models and of course books available to support learning as discussed in Chapters 8 and 14.

The lists in Box 22.3 are not comprehensive; the first column in particular could be much longer, including items brought in from the seashore, from visits to grandparents or objects brought in by the teacher. The list could be endless, but the storage space is not. Hence the imperative is to consider what needs to be in the collection of resources.

Box 22.3 Resources for science

Everyday objects and materials	Consumables	Specialist equipment	Support resources
Boxes, plastic bottles, other containers, string, scissors, rulers, paper clips, sticky tape, drawing pins, elastic bands, glues, card, plasticine, plant pots, spoons, straws, marbles, toy cars, rocks, pieces of fabric, ...	Flour, bicarbonate of soda, soap powder, plaster of Paris, mirror card, wood for hammering, batteries, wire for shaping, aluminium foil, fruits or flowers for cutting, seeds for planting, ...	Pooters for collecting insects, torches, mirrors, glass blocks, triangular prisms, hand lenses, measuring cylinders, spirit thermometers, data-loggers, tuning forks, stop clocks and watches, springs, bathroom scales, pulleys, filter paper, gardening and other tools, magnets, bulbs, wire, etc. ...	CD ROMs or a list of appropriate web sites containing resources that show events (e.g. volcano or plant growth), or that model phenomena (e.g. the solar system, or trajectories) Models (e.g. aprons of the digestive system, or a 3D eye), appropriate resources for use with the IWB, hardware such as posters and books and other paper resources, ...

In selecting equipment and materials, the key is to link resource needs to planning and so to the intended learning outcomes. Here the science coordinator or subject leader has a key role. It may, for example, not be value for money to buy something like a model of a human eye if it is only to be used by the oldest pupils once in a year. It may be better to arrange to borrow one from the local high school, FE College or regional Science Learning Centre.

Storing equipment and materials

Access is the key word in deciding a system of storage for equipment and materials. There are various possibilities and the advantages and disadvantages of each in a particular case will depend on the size, physical layout and curriculum planning of the school. We can do no more here than point out options.

Central or distributed storage
A decision has to be made about central storage versus distribution of the equipment among classes. Apart from availability of space for a central store, a major consideration is having someone to look after it. There are obvious advantages in sharing expensive items which are only infrequently used but some of these advantages are lost if the equipment is not kept in good order. Clearly the science subject leader, or coordinator, has to be willing and able – in the sense of having the time – to organise a central store and to check that items are not 'lost' by being put back in the wrong place or in an unsatisfactory condition. In schools where teaching assistants and other support are available it is helpful to put time aside for them to take on the role of maintaining resources. This is more easily achieved in a central store.

Giving children access
Another decision is whether children should have access to the equipment store as well as teachers. The problems of maintaining an orderly central store can be exacerbated by too many having access, yet the teacher will want children to help in the collection and return of equipment. The suggestion of appointing a few children to be 'monitors' or 'storekeepers' may be a solution. If the store is within each class the same considerations apply. If children are to have access then the labels used to classify the equipment should be ones that they will relate to and understand. There are considerable dividends for the initial investment of time when children are, perhaps, involved in drawing up lists of what equipment there is and creating rules for using the store.

Whether or not there is a central store, within a class the equipment for a certain session needs to be accessible to the children. The demands of providing group activities for all the children at once are of course considerable and require pre-planning and preparation. The materials and equipment needed for a set of activities can be anticipated and a suitable selection made available without limiting what the children will be able to do using their own ideas. It is handy to have these materials on a trolley if possible so that they can easily be put safely out of the way when not being used. When the equipment is being used the teacher should be able to depend on the help of the children to take responsibility for choosing, collecting and later returning it to its proper place. Building up a system for this is important in developing children's ability to take a part in facilitating their own learning, as well as for the teacher's sanity. It involves making sure that children know what is available, where, and how to look after it and keep it tidy.

Topic boxes
A third major decision point, which applies where a school or class organises science within topics, is whether equipment should be boxed by topic or stored as separate kinds of items. The topic box is a great convenience, but can tie up equipment which could be used for work outside the topic. This can lead to 'plundering' from the box, with the chance of the item not being there when that topic is being used. The effort put into developing topic boxes is also a disincentive to changing topics, when perhaps they have outlived their freshness. The device of temporary topic boxes is a useful compromise. The box exists for as long as the topic is being used and is dismantled when moving onto another topic.

Safety in and out of school

Despite the fact that science is now taught by most primary teachers and in all primary schools, it remains very safe. Teachers and others take sensible precautions and hence very few accidents are related to science activities. However, this situation should not lead to complacency. Part of the reason science is so safe is that there is a good deal of high-quality advice available to support science coordinators and teachers. The ASE produces and updates an essential guide called *Be Safe* (ASE, 2011) (see Box 22.4). There is also a *Be Safe INSET Pack* (ASE, 2002) which can be used with the fourth (2011) edition of *Be Safe*.

Box 22.4 Topics covered in *Be Safe*, 4th edn (ASE, 2011)

- Using tools, glues, sources of heat, chemicals and electricity
- Investigating 'Ourselves'
- Looking at the Sun
- Working out of the classroom including gardening and visits to farms, ponds and other field trips
- Keeping and studying animals and a list of those that should not be kept
- Using plants and a list of hazardous and poisonous plants
- Food hygiene, growing micro-organisms,
- Working with children under 5.

There are also sections on what is required by law, health and safety policies and advice on accidents and emergencies.

Ensuring safety in science is not achieved by simply reading booklets, no matter how good. It requires the application of common sense. Burrows (2003) comments that an activity that is safe for a group of children with high levels of literacy may be less so where many of the children are young newcomers with limited experience of English or formal schooling. Notes to this effect can be added to the school scheme of work, and to the policy for science, but staff training is essential to ensure that all know about and can apply safety procedures. This applies as much to support staff and parent helpers as it does to teachers.

Safety is not only a matter for the staff to consider, these considerations need to be shared with the pupils. Health and safety rules should not simply be presented to the children. Most curriculum guidelines require the explicit development by children of ideas relating (for example) to road use, mains electricity, and the health hazards of smoking or drug abuse. All these ideas need to be discussed with children in such a way as to encourage understanding and therefore self-discipline in terms of obedience to the rules. Rules and obedience to them are necessary where safety matters are concerned but the sooner compliance becomes voluntary the sooner the temptation to break them is eliminated. Hence the item in the school science policy presented in Box 22.5 where explicit mention is made of pupils undertaking their own risk analysis. The prime importance of safety should not be to curtail children's investigations but to ensure that the necessary precautions are taken and that children gradually come to understand the reasons for them. The same arguments apply to health and safety issues when taking children out of doors and on school trips.

Box 22.5 Safety matters within a school science policy document

Excerpts from the science policy of Hillside Primary School, Orpington

Learning and teaching
Children will be taught to make their own 'risk-assessment' before undertaking work.

Health and Safety

- Teachers should make themselves aware of any safety issues before undertaking work with children.

- In order to ensure the safe teaching of Science it is required that all staff read the A.S.E. 'Be Safe' booklet and read any safety bulletins which are circulated by the post-holder.

- There are also a number of CLEAPSS publications which deal with a wide range of safety issues – these and the 'Be Safe' booklet will always be available in the staff-room.

- If any safety issues are unclear the Science Co-ordinator will seek clarification from CLEAPSS.

Sources of activities and materials

In the 1990s and 2000s published materials and schemes of work, designed to match the requirements of national curricula, were a key source of activities and lesson plans. The best schemes provided ideas for activities, background knowledge for teachers, insights into progression, possibilities for assessment and often interesting materials for children and teachers. Since that time teachers have turned more often to the internet for teaching materials and ideas. Resources no longer in publication can be accessed freely through the extensive and growing e-library of the National STEM centre. For instance, the Nuffield Primary Science (SPACE) teachers' guides and pupils' books can be downloaded from the e-library site (http://www.nationalstemcentre.org.uk/elibrary/search?te rm=Nuffield+Primary+Science+Teachers%27+Guides&order=score).

Box 22.6 lists some of the many websites that provide access to classroom resources and science activities for primary schools.

Box 22.6 Useful website sources of activities and classroom materials

British Science Association (BSA)
The BSA runs the CREST Star award scheme designed to enrich activities for 5–11 year olds. It provides teaching resources and case studies.
http://www.britishscienceassociation.org/node/578/www.britishscienceassociation.org/creststar

CLEAPSS (no longer an acronym, just a name, but originating as the Consortium of Local Education Authorities for the Provision of Science Services)
A membership organisation providing guides on selecting and using equipment and chemicals safely and on keeping plants and animals. Runs an annual primary science competition and publishes a newsletter three times a year. Supports a telephone helpline on matters related to practical science.
http://www.cleapss.org.uk/primary/primary-resources

National STEM Centre
The National STEM Centre in York is building the largest collections of resources for teachers of science, technology, engineering and mathematics in the UK. The collection, which is constantly being enlarged, is easily searchable and open to all users.
http://www.nationalstemcentre.org.uk/elibrary/

The Primary Science Teaching Trust (PSTT)
PSTT has an extensive website providing a rich range of classroom activities, guides for science curriculum leaders, a CPD Unit on running a science club, examples of activities and sources of ideas and help, exemplar materials for the Primary Science Quality Mark (see Chapter 25) and a number of useful links to other sources and websites.
http://www.pstt.org.uk/resources/continuing-professional-development/enrich-science-learning.aspx

continued ...

Box 22.6 continued

Planet Science

For children: regularly changed set of activities, answers to questions, games and ideas of things to do, addressed directly at children:

http://www.planet-science.com/categories/under-11s/what-do-you-know-about.aspx

For teachers: information and the latest news about science education.
http://www.planet-science.com/categories/parentsteachers.aspx

RSPB (Royal Society for the Protection of Birds)

Offers free posters of birds
http://www.rspb.org.uk/Images/form_tcm9-172648.pdf

SSERC (Scottish Schools Education Research Centre)

A service providing support, mainly in science and technology education, to all Scottish Local Authorities; health and safety advice, guidance on practical work, a quarterly bulletin, professional development programmes and web-based materials.
http://www.sserc.org.uk

TES (Times Educational Supplement)

This website provides a huge range of free worksheets, lesson plans and teaching ideas for primary schools.
www.tes.co.uk/primary-resources/

Wellcome Trust

The Wellcome Trust produces several resources for primary children and teachers. These include *Okido* (an art and science magazine for children aged 2–7), *The Great Plant Hunt* (a series of Darwin-inspired activities for primary schools), a free kit of activities *In the Zone* (providing scientific equipment, teaching resources and experiments inspired by the London 2012 Olympic Games to help teach the science behind sport and activity for pupils aged 4–19).
http://www.wellcome.ac.uk/Education-resources/Education-and-learning/Resources/Primary/index.htm

Woodland Trust

Offers free activity sheets and resources for teachers in and out of the classroom.
http://www.woodlandtrust.org.uk/en/learning-kids/Pages/children.aspx

Summary

This chapter has concerned questions of why and how relating to practical work in primary science, including its rationale, organisation, equipment and safety precautions and sources of classroom activities. The main points have been

- The value of practical work in primary science is not simply 'learning by doing', but rather providing children with real experiences and the opportunity to explore, discuss and test their ideas, to construct their own knowledge and understanding about the physical world and the nature of science.

- For practical work to be successful sufficient time needs to be set aside.

- Children need to see the purpose of their investigations and for that purpose to be meaningful, in this way they will develop their skills as scientists.

- Working in groups provides children with the opportunity for discussion and argumentation, best supported by developing team working skills and an atmosphere that encourages pupils to express their ideas.

- When selecting materials and equipment for use in primary science it is important to keep in mind the centrality of first-hand experience. Children learn best when they explore things around them, therefore simple, familiar utensils are to be preferred over more complex laboratory apparatus.

- When building up a stock of resources it is essential to consider the curriculum and the activities planned and to ensure that consumables are available as appropriate. The responsibility for maintaining resources must be clear and care taken to maintain and store equipment and materials in good condition. Children should be involved in keeping all the things in good order.

- Understanding and following safety codes minimises any risks involved in certain activities without inhibiting children's experience. Helping children to understand reasons for safety codes has to be seen as an important part of learning in science.

- A wide range of ideas for practical activities can be obtained from websites, supplementing or replacing published programmes of activities.

Further reading

Burrows, P. (2003) Managing health and safety in primary science, *Primary Science Review*, 79: 18–20.

Mant, J., Wilson. H. and Coates, D. (2007) The effect of increasing conceptual challenge in primary science lessons on pupils' achievement and engagement, *International Journal of Science Education*, 29(14): 1707–19.

Naylor, S., Keogh, B. and Downing, B. (2007) Argumentation in primary science, *Research in Science Education*, 37: 177–89

Formative evaluation of practice

23

Evaluating provision for science at the class level

Introduction

This is the first of two chapters about the evaluation of provision for children's learning in science. As we noted at the beginning of Chapter 15, the term 'evaluation' is used in education in relation to educational programmes, systems, or effectiveness of the provision for learning at school and classroom levels. This distinguishes it from 'assessment', which is a similar process but used in relation to pupils' performance and achievement of learning goals. Both terms refer to a process of generating and interpreting evidence in order to make judgements for a particular purpose. In both cases the purpose can be formative – helping to improve teaching in the case of formative assessment, or to improve learning opportunities in the case of formative evaluation – or summative, in providing summative judgements of achievement. Also common to both is that they require criteria or standards against which the evidence is compared.

In this chapter we are concerned with the formative evaluation of the opportunities for learning science provided at the classroom level. We begin by considering the kinds of evidence that are needed in evaluating provision for learning and the standards used to make judgements about the evidence. We look at how pupil progress can be recorded and analysed by computer programs and the use of more 'home-made' records of activities in ensuring that all pupils have opportunities for learning. Not all aspects of provision can be, or need to be, evaluated at a particular time. We provide an example of an evaluation focused specifically on children's opportunities for inquiry-based learning, using an evaluation tool which can be adapted for evaluation by an observer or self-evaluation by the teacher. In Chapter 24 we look at the evaluation of provision at the school level, to which the data for each class contribute.

Evaluation at the class level

The purpose of evaluation at the class level is to improve provision for children's learning. It requires the collection of evidence about the opportunities provided in the class activities and the extent to which these meet expected standards and enable children to make progress in their learning. Some of the evidence will be about the progress that children have made over a period of time; some will be about the content and topics experienced by the children during that time; and some will be at the more detailed level of the kinds of learning processes they have used, particularly those relating to inquiry.

In the process of evaluation, relevant evidence from these kinds of records will be compared with what is regarded as 'good practice' or standards to be aimed for. Box 23.1 suggests some standards of practice for teachers which incorporate aspects of good teaching, such as formative assessment procedures, discussion and time for reflection. These may be used in regular reviews of the activities of a class but also kept in mind at other times. Ideally teachers collaborate in collecting information to conduct this evaluation. Observing each others' lessons with the standards in mind is a valuable experience for both the observer and the observed. However, where this is not possible, the standards may help personal reflection. Later (p. 335) we consider more focused evaluation of opportunities for children to learn through inquiry.

Box 23.1 Standards for classroom practice

Teachers should:

- Use a range of methods suited to the achievement of the various goals of learning science.

- Provide simple materials and equipment for children to use in first-hand exploration and inquiry of scientific phenomena in their environment.

- Regularly ask questions which invite children to express their ideas.

- Know where children are in the development of ideas and inquiry skills and use this information to provide opportunities and support (scaffolding) for progress.

- Include in lesson plans what children are intended to learn as well as what they will do.

- Provide comments that help progress in oral or written feedback on children's work.

- Ensure that children regularly have chance to raise questions and that these are addressed.

- Ensure that children always know the purpose of their investigations and other science activities.

- Provide opportunities for children to discuss observations, plans, findings and conclusions in small groups and as a whole class.

- Provide opportunity for children to obtain information from books, the internet, visits out of school and visiting experts.

- Discuss with children the qualities of good work so that they can assess and improve their own and each others' work.

- Provide time and encouragement for children to reflect on how and what they have learned.

- Keep records of children's progress based on questioning, observation, discussion and study of products relevant to the learning goals.

Records to keep

Records of pupils' progress

Schools are required to keep certain records of the curricular experiences and progress of each child. The law in England requires schools to 'disclose these records to parents and pupils, report at least annually to all parents on their child's progress and attainment and transfer pupil information and educational records as a pupil changes school. The head teacher's report must take in a wide range of curricular information, together with a more general summary of progress' (DfE website).

The use of ICT for management purposes in schools has transformed the keeping of records of pupils' progress and their use in monitoring the progress of individuals and groups of children. Many teachers have used the Pupil Achievement Tracker but, since the closure of the QCDA, this is now only available from The National Archives website (see Further reading section). Instead, schools can subscribe to any of a number of commercial enterprises providing software and some supporting services for tracking pupil progress, bringing together all the records for an individual pupil. Examples include Target Tracker, Classroom Monitor, Edudata UK. Essentially they comprise spreadsheets which can contain all the information about pupils' personal details, educational history and performance levels at various dates. The use of the software comes at a price – generally an annual licence fee of about £500.

In order to track progress, teachers enter attainment data at chosen times. Progress through the year is automatically computed, using the end of the previous school year as the baseline. The progress of an individual child can be compared with the average for the year group or with a particular group, and within or across subject areas. These computations depend on there being a quantitative measure of attainment so that progress can be calculated as the difference between two measures. Attainment is generally recorded in terms of levels or sub-levels of attainment identified in national curricula. There are some concerns about tracking progress on the basis of sub-levels, given the shortcomings that we noted in Chapter 19 (see Box 19.4): that there is generally little basis for the distinctions made between them and that there are likely to be variations in how they are interpreted by teachers. So it is important to note in relation to tracking using performance data that:

- the information gained from tracking in this type of analysis is only as good as the data on which it is based;

- the outcome of the analysis will, at best, draw attention to problems of poor progress; it cannot suggest action that might improve progress;

- the tracking is of 'coarse' data, relating to overall performance rather than the finer detail that is needed to support learning of particular skills or areas of knowledge and understanding.

Records of individual children's activities

Individual children's experiences are likely to vary from group to group, and even within groups, if children follow up questions that arise during activities. Unless all the children in a class always work on the same activities as each other, there is a need for a system which records what individuals have actually done. Even if the activities were the same for all it would be no guarantee that their *experiences* would be identical, since children attend selectively to different parts of the work, extend some and give scant attention to others.

It is not always possible, or appropriate, for every child to undertake every activity. For example, in the case studies in Chapter 3, in Graham's class the groups of children each conducted different investigations. However the different activities were intended to address the same ideas and develop similar skills and the children presented their findings to the rest of the class. In this case there was no need for them all to do each investigation, but what each group did should be recorded.

A record of science-based experiences is particularly needed when work is undertaken through cross-curricular topics. Box 23.2 describes one such example.

Experiences directed to the same objectives as in Box 23.2 were planned for the next week in another topic on the gingerbread man. This gave them opportunity to investigate ways to keep a gingerbread man dry and, in baking, would look at a variety of materials using their senses. Figure 23.1 indicates the kind of record kept of the activities undertaken by each pupil.

Certain activities will probably be regarded as equivalent to each other, while in other cases it may be that the context is so different that repetition is desirable. Taking these things into account, the teacher will use the record to keep an

---

Box 23.2 Science in a topic at the foundation stage

A reception class was undertaking a week-long topic 'Our New School' in which they considered a wide variety of aspects of the Foundation Stage curriculum, including knowledge and understanding of the world. A new school building was being erected in the grounds of their very old school. The children talked to parents who had attended the school as children, discussed old photographs and considered how people felt about their old school being knocked down. Within the Foundation Stage 'Understanding the World' the focus in science was to 'know about similarities and differences in relation to places, objects, materials and living' (DfE, 2012). The children explored building materials and thought about how to build a stable wall. Within the topic there were many opportunities to develop understanding. For example, an activity table of various play bricks was used to encourage building and testing the strength of a wall. The children were also able to test the properties of different materials (squashy, breaks easily, goes runny when wet) to see which might be good to build with. By the end of the week teachers wanted to be sure that all children had experienced each of these activities. They kept a chart for each activity table, so that children could record their visit to the table (using laminated name labels to stick on a wall chart). At the end of the week gaps could be easily spotted and recorded.

Class .... Term				
Topic	Our New School (Week 4)		The Gingerbread Man (Week 6)	
Activity	Build a wall	Explore building materials	Baking	Rain cape for Gingerbread	Judge the best Gingerbread man
Goals	Prediction Describes what they did	Investigates using senses Appropriate language	Uses senses to explore Appropriate language	Investigates materials Prediction Describes what they did	Describes simple features Compares features
Ali					
Sam					
Charlene					
etc					

Figure 23.1 Record of science activities undertaken within topics

eye on the gaps in the activities of individual children and act on this, either in planning the next term's work or having one or two sessions in which children are directed to activities which they have missed. This should avoid children missing out on all experiences relating to materials for any reason such as absence or lack of engagement with an activity.

Tailor-made records

Teachers vary as to how much information they can carry in their head and how much they like to write down and this may be one of the factors which leads to a preference for a check-list, or for a more detailed pro forma which gives opportunity for comments, caveats and explanations. However, systems for recording, whether on paper or computer, need to be simple and, in most cases, understandable by others. This is particularly important in cases where a classroom assistant or other adult takes part in assessing what has been learned. The class teacher and her assistants in the reception class described in Box 23.2 used a simple record for each topic, as shown in Figure 23.2. These records formed the basis of discussions between the class teacher and her assistants and in turn contributed to the individual records for each child (looking down the columns) and helped to identify aspects to focus on in forthcoming topics (looking across the rows).

Nursery – Mrs Cole and Mrs Kahn – Week 4

Building a new school –

Knowledge and Understanding of the world

Objective	Ali	Sam	Charlene	Kylie 1	David	Liam	Leanne	Kylie 2	India
Tests Strength of materials	✓	✓	✓	✓	✓	✓	✓	O	✓
Able to make prediction	✓	✗	✓	✓	✓	✗	✗	O	✓
Describes what he/she did	✗	✓	✓	✓	✓	✓	✓	O	✓
Investigates objects/materials using all senses	✓	✓	✓	✓	✓	✗	✓	✓	✓
Uses appropriate language to describe objects/materials	✗	✓	✓	✓	✓	✓	✓	✓	✓
Comment	Facial expression etc. but not speaking					Needs to slow down too rushed		Did not do wall.	

Smelly, Squashy hard, cold etc.

Figure 23.2 Simple topic record sheet

Records that children keep

The reception class children in Box 23.2 recorded the completion of particular activities by posting their name on a chart. The next logical step is for children to keep their own records of their achievements when the children are a little older and are able to reflect on their learning. This is quite different from the record they make of their investigations; it involves self-assessment of the learning achieved as a result of these investigations.

A number of approaches have been adopted to focus pupils' thinking on the learning. We noted in Chapter 22 (Box 22.2) the importance of children understanding the purpose of their activities and various ways of going about communicating goals were noted in Chapter 18. Clearly it is necessary for children to be conscious of and committed to goals before they can be expected to be able to consider whether they have been achieved. The use of KWL grids (see Chapter 16) helps to develop this thinking, particularly the third part, where the children record what they think they have learned (L).

Figure 23.3 is an example of a class record adapted from Nimmons (2003) of records for a Year 5 class having studied the unit on changing state. Children are asked to indicate with smiley (or otherwise) faces, ticks or comments, or 'traffic lights' (Harrison and Howard, 2009), as to how far they feel they have achieved the goals. Teachers can then moderate this judgement as they make their own records. Individual records of the same kinds could be created for children to keep in their folders with the unit work or kept on a computer.

	Names of children							
I have experimented to find out about some of the difference between ice, water and steam								
I know what happens when water 'disappears'!!								
I have found out about the evaporation of other liquids								
I have investigated different conditions that can affect the rate of evaporation								
I have found out how to evaporate water and change it back to water again								
I have found out about the water cycle!!								
I know the boiling temperature and freezing temperature of water								
I know how to change water into ice and make it melt again								
I can use a temperature sensor and create a graph on the computer								
I can suggest what might happen and explain why								
I can write clear accounts and explain my results using my scientific knowledge								

Figure 23.3 An end of unit record sheet completed by children

Focused evaluation: learning through inquiry

In this section we consider evaluation focused on learning through inquiry. This focus is selected for two reasons: first, on account of the particular value of inquiry-based learning for children's development of scientific literacy and the skills needed for continued learning (see Chapter 1); second, because inquiry is a term that can be rather loosely applied. In particular it is often equated with 'hands-on' activities or 'practical work'. This is far too limited a view. A key characteristic of inquiry is the use of evidence and this may be found in a range of ways beyond direct action on objects, and may come from secondary sources, the media and the internet. A related mistaken view is that inquiry means that students have to 'discover' everything for themselves and should not be given information by the teacher or use other sources. Again, as we discussed in Chapter 6, it is often the case that children's own ideas may not provide a useful explanation and an alternative idea has to be sought, which may be suggested by other children, the teacher or provided from other sources. The close specification of what inquiry in science that is entailed in the evaluation means can help to improve provision and practice.

An evaluation tool

To find out how well the children's learning matches the processes of learning through inquiry requires relevant evidence to be collected. A useful approach has been developed as part of an EU project designed to develop and disseminate practice in inquiry-based science education and inquiry-based mathematics education – the Fibonacci project (www.fibonacci-project.eu). One strand of this project developed a tool for evaluation of children's activities in science and a related tool for evaluation of teachers' activities, specifically focused on inquiry-based activities. To sharpen this focus, the tools did not deal with prerequisites such as the provision of equipment and materials, class organisation, etc., which are part of good practice

	Yes	No	NA
Did children work on questions which they identified as their own, even though introduced by the teacher?			
Did children make predictions based on their ideas?			
Did children take part in planning an investigation?			
Did children include 'fair testing' in their plan if appropriate?			
Did children carry out an investigation themselves?			
Did children gather data using methods and sources appropriate to the inquiry question?			
Did the data gathered enable children to test their predictions?			
Did children consider their results in relation to the inquiry question?			
Did children propose explanations for their results?			
Did children collaborate with others during group work?			
Did children engage in class or group discussions of their investigations and explanations?			
Did children listen to each other during reporting?			
Did children respond to each other during reporting?			

Figure 23.4 Tool for evaluation of children's learning through inquiry (adapted from a resource developed by the Fibonacci project)

but not specific to inquiry learning. Part of the tool for evaluating pupils' learning activities is given in Figure 23.4. The indicators of inquiry learning are expressed as questions for teachers (or observers) to answer with a simple judgement of 'Yes' or 'No' or 'NA' (not applicable). In the full version of the tool each question is expanded with examples of what it can mean in terms of good inquiry-based activity.

To use the tool, teachers first become familiar with the questions, then choose a series of lessons during which inquiry-based activity is planned. There are various ways of gathering information. Some teachers make a point of discussing with groups of pupils, or listening into their discussion, to find out about their ideas and what they feel about their activities. Others prefer to tape-record group discussions or pupils' reports to the whole class. When the children are working in groups the teacher observes each group as (s)he moves from group to group. Since the purpose is to evaluate the learning opportunities and experiences, not the performance of individual children, it does not matter that evidence from different groups will be collected at different points in the lesson(s). After the lesson or sequence of lessons, teachers then review the pupils' written records, their own notes and the recalled or recorded events and use this information to reflect on the lesson and answer the questions.

The purpose of the tool is to highlight aspects of inquiry learning which may not have been experienced by the children. Since the items are chosen to reflect inquiry-based learning, answering 'Yes' to as many questions as possible indicates involvement in inquiry. This will not happen for every sequence of activities, as some items may not be relevant. However, when a question is considered to be 'Not Applicable', it is important to ask 'why not?' There may be good reasons, perhaps related to the subject matter, or it may be that opportunities for using and developing inquiry skills were missed.

In order to fulfil a formative purpose, reasons for 'No' and 'NA' answers need to be sought. The actions of the teacher are likely to lead to possible reasons. This suggests an important role for teachers' self-evaluation, whereby they ask themselves: "Am I providing the opportunities for children to do these things?" For many items in the tool in Figure 23.4, there is a potential item for evaluating the teacher's activity. For instance teachers could ask themselves:

- Did I encourage children to ask questions?
- Did I ask them to make predictions?
- Did I involve them in planning investigations?
- Etc.

It is also easy to see how the questions can be worded so that the tools can be used by observers in the classroom rather than the teacher. Indeed such versions are included in the Fibonacci publication (2012) as a means to diagnose teachers' professional development needs. If teachers are able to observe each other, and discuss their lessons, this gives them a concrete basis for sharing ideas about how to improve practice. Since they know what their teaching partner is looking for, there is no mystery or anxiety about the process.

This procedure is not intended to be carried out frequently. It is an occasional activity to help teachers review their practice, particularly when new aspects are being attempted. Thorough analysis of a record made occasionally is more important than more frequent records considered only superficially. More head teachers are making such opportunities available in recognition of their value as professional development and spreading better practice.

Summary

In this chapter we have considered how evaluation at the class level can be used formatively to improve provision for children's learning in science. The main points have been:

- It is important to identify an agreed set of standards against which provision for learning in science can be judged.
- Teachers can use computer programs to monitor children's progress but they also need to keep records of individual children's activities and experiences.
- Children can take part in recording their activities and, when they have a grasp of the goals of their work, in indicating the extent of their learning.
- There are several advantages to using tools for observing pupils' and teachers' actions in the classroom, as in the example of inquiry-based learning:
  - finding the gaps in children's experiences and possible reasons for them;
  - diagnosing teachers' need for professional development;
  - making explicit the meaning of inquiry-based learning in terms of what pupils and teachers do.

Further reading

Fibonacci (2012) *Tools for Enhancing Inquiry in Science Education*. Available for free download from http://www.fibonacci-project.eu.

Harlen, W. (2007) Holding up a mirror to classroom practice, *Primary Science Review*, 100: 29–31.

Harrison, C. and Howard, S. (2009) *Inside the Primary Black Box: Assessment for Learning in Primary and Early Years Classrooms*, London: GL assessment.

Website

The National Archives website (Pupil Achievement Tracker) http://webarchive.nationalarchives.gov.uk/20060829080949/standards.dfes.gov.uk/performance/pat.

Evaluating provision at the school level

Introduction

In this chapter we discuss the action that schools can take to review, evaluate and improve the provision they make for children's learning. It falls into two main parts. The first describes some self-evaluation frameworks supplied by various agencies in the UK to help schools conduct evaluation of their performance. These documents provide criteria that schools can use in judging their performance across a wide range of their activities. Although of value in schools' preparation for an inspection, their more important function is to help a school to keep its work under regular review. In the second part of the chapter we look particularly at how primary schools can review their provision for science. This requires a view of good practice and of standards to aim for at the school level. The chapter ends with a case study of effective school self-evaluation, emphasising the importance of involving all staff and keeping the process manageable by focusing on what has relevance for children's learning.

Quality assurance at the school level

In many countries, since the late 1980s, the responsibility for ensuring quality in a school's provision for learning has shifted from external agencies to schools themselves. Schools have been given more responsibility for maintaining and improving standards, in recognition that too much external regulation impedes schools' freedom to take action appropriate to their pupils' particular needs and circumstances. Consequently schools in many countries have been given more autonomy both in relation to their budget and how to meet external requirements. In England, Ofsted and the National Curriculum set external requirements and schools' autonomy is restricted to how to meet them. This contrasts with countries such as the Netherlands and Flanders (Belgium) where 'schools can use instruments developed by researchers or companies and the framework may differ, ranging from school inspectorate factors to important factors found in school effectiveness research' (Schildkamp et al., 2012: 125). Although school evaluations by inspectors in England and other countries of the UK are partly based on school self-evaluations, these are created using frameworks developed by government agencies.

However, the value of self-evaluation is not merely to contribute to the judgement of the school by inspectors. It is a process that is essential to professional activity involving the constant review of what the school is doing and the use of this information to find the best way to help pupils' learning.

> Self-evaluation is forward looking. It is about change and improvement, whether gradual or transformational, and it based on professional reflection, challenge and support. It involves taking considered decisions about actions which result in clear benefits for young people.
>
> (HMIe, 2007: 6)

It is important that self-evaluation is seen in this way – as useful and indeed essential for ensuring the effectiveness of the school. If, instead, it is regarded as an obligation that is externally imposed, rather than a tool for improvement, then it is unlikely to be seen as a meaningful activity. Research (Vanhoof *et al.,* 2009) shows that head teachers have a more positive attitude towards self-evaluation than do class teachers. It seems that this difference is likely to be found where the process is controlled from the top and not shared by the whole school – staff, pupils and parents – as it is in the case study at the end of this chapter (Box 24.4).

Frameworks for self-evaluation

Whether or not a school is expecting an inspection, self-evaluation should be a regular part of its activities, having a formative role in helping to inform decisions about all aspects of the functioning of the school. Just as formative assessment of children's learning involves finding where children are in their learning and how to help them take next steps, so school self-evaluation involves asking questions about 'where we are now' in relation to achieving the school's aims and realising its vision. But, as in the case of formative assessment, it will only be as useful as the action taken to move forward, usually set out in a development plan.

Schools can find various frameworks for identifying information to be collected for self-evaluation and criteria that can be used in identifying strengths and weaknesses. Only a few years ago self-evaluation frameworks were provided mainly by government agencies, now many organisations, authorities and publishers have produced self-evaluation forms and schemes.

Early Years Foundation Stage Self-Evaluation Form

Although Ofsted no longer provides the Self Evaluation Form (SEF) for schools, it continues to provide a form for Early Years Foundation Stage (EYFS) providers (see Box 24.1), which can now be completed online. Use of this particular form is optional and EYFS providers can use another form if they wish, but are expected either provide the information to Ofsted or to have it available at the time of an inspection.

Box 24.1 The Early Years On-line Self-Evaluation Form (SEF)

The EYFS SEF is in two parts:

Part A. Setting details and views of those who use the setting

In section 1, providers describe the main characteristics of their setting and the culture and backgrounds of the children who attend.

In section 2, providers record the views of the children who attend the setting and those of their parents and the views of any professionals who work with the setting, especially the local authority, local children's centre or any health professionals.

Part B. The quality and standards of the early years provision

The four sections of this part concern:

- How well the early years provision meets the needs of the range of children who attend.

- The contribution of the early years provision to children's wellbeing.

- The leadership and management of the early years provision.

- The overall quality and standards of the early years provision.

For the first three of these aspects, providers give their evaluation of the performance of the setting and a statement of the 'priorities for improvement'. They also give a judgement of their performance in each aspect in terms of a four-point scale: Outstanding, Good, Satisfactory, Inadequate. In the final section the provider makes a judgement of the overall quality and standards of early years provision of the setting.

The aspects covered and criteria used in making judgements in Part B are the same as those used by inspectors and explained in the guidance that is available on the use of the SEF.

RAISEonline

Ofsted and the DfE provide an online tool for schools to use to analyse performance data of their pupils: Reporting and Analysis for Improvement through School Self-Evaluation (RAISEonline). It aims are to

- Enable schools to analyse performance data in greater depth as part of the self-evaluation process.

- Provide a common set of analyses for schools, local authorities, inspectors and governors.

- Better support teaching and learning.

(www.raiseonline.org/about.aspx)

Using information about a school and its results for end of key stage data, RAISEonline provides analyses which show how the school's performance compares with schools nationally and with those with comparable characteristics. It also helps schools to analyse the performance of various groups of pupils, for example: how the performance of boys and girls compares at different ages;

how children in minority ethnic groups are making progress; how children with special needs groups are doing compared with special needs performance criteria; where the gap between high and low achievers is greatest. If schools use the optional tests for Years 3, 4 and 5 in English and mathematics, they can obtain analyses at the question level to investigate the performance of pupils in specific curriculum areas and track progress over time using the optional test progress charts. The reports and graphs can be used to support teaching and learning and to help schools provide evidence for their judgements. However this does not apply to science where, since 2010, there have been no tests and results are only available for the end of Key Stage 2, based on teacher-based assessment of levels.

How good is our school

The Scottish inspectorate has for many years provided schools with a framework for self-evaluation so that schools can judge their performance using the same categories and criteria as used by inspectors. The framework, entitled *How Good is Our School: the journey to excellence Part 3*, identified nine key areas of the school functioning:

1. Key performance outcomes
2. Impact on learners, parents and families
3. Impact on staff
4. Impact on the community
5. Delivery of education
6. Policy decisions and planning
7. Management and support of staff
8. Partnership and resources
9. Leadership

In most cases there are several subsections within a key area and the document provides indicators of each. Schools judge their performance on each subsection on a six-point scale (1 = unsatisfactory; 6 = excellent) and examples are given for level 2 and level 5. Schools are advised to review key areas 1 to 4 and some aspects of area 5 every year. The results of this review help to identify which other aspects of area 5 and 6 to 9 should become the focus of review at a particular time.

The HMIe publication *The Child at the Centre* provides a similar structure for self-evaluation in the early years, with indicators and criteria appropriate to early years education (see Further reading section).

Other sources related to inspections

The inspectorate in Wales (Estyn) publishes *Guidance for the Inspection of Primary Schools* which helps schools prepare for inspections, describing the criteria employed, which can also be used by schools in self-evaluation. Similarly, the Northern Ireland inspection service provides guidance for schools in the document: *Short Inspection of Primary Schools – Self-Evaluation Proforma*. This is designed to assist schools to conduct an audit of the work of the school and a summary evaluation on the quality and range of provision. The outcome also provides the inspection team with an overview of the work of the school.

Evaluating the provision for science

The procedures for self-evaluation outlined above have concerned the general functioning of the school, concerning specific subjects only in relation to student attainment levels. We now consider what schools can do, in addition to reviewing their overall performance, to evaluate their provision in science. Teachers and schools can use evaluation formatively to improve provision by comparing their practice with standards of quality, derived from 'best practice'. (We use the word 'standards' here to mean something to aim for, not what has been achieved.)

Standards for school provision for science

Box 24.2 suggests some indicators for use by the school's science subject leader or senior management in evaluating provision for science at the school level. It is important for all the school staff to agree to the standards to aim for and to participate in evaluating progress towards them. The standards can be used as indicators in much the same way as indicators of pupils' achievement at a particular time. Evidence relevant to each standard will come from a range of documents, records, observation, lists of resources, review of pupils' work, discussion with advisers, parents and more besides. The intention is not to judge the provision as 'good' or 'poor' but to draw attention to areas where practice falls short of aspirations and so focus action to develop and maintain agreed standards of practice.

It is useful to note here that there is some overlap between the indicators in Box 24.2 and the criteria used in the Primary Science Quality Mark (PSQM) programme. Since the PSQM requires the school to take action and to undertake professional development, it is discussed in Chapter 25.

Good teaching in science

At a more detailed level, the Ofsted report *Successful Science* (Jan. 2011) brings together the findings from inspectors' reports of science in 94 primary schools during the period 2007–10. Schools can use these as indicators of what to aim for and take steps to find out their progress towards them.

In relation to teaching, the report finds that this was judged to be 'good' or 'very good' when teachers:

Box 24.2 Standards for school provision for science

The school should:

- Have a school policy for science which reflects the above standards for classroom work consistently across the school.

- Regularly enable teachers to discuss the policy and update it as necessary.

- Expect teachers to use the agreed standards in their lesson planning, teaching and self-evaluation.

- Provide regular opportunity for teachers to plan and, where possible, to teach science lessons collaboratively.

- Have effective procedures for the provision and maintenance of equipment and materials to support inquiry-based activities and sources of information for children and teachers.

- Keep records of individual children's progress in science based on annual or bi-annual summaries of teachers' records.

- Ensure that parents and carers are aware of the school science policy and of how they may be able to support their children's learning in science.

- Enable teachers to upgrade their science teaching skills and knowledge through regular professional development.

- had a clear understanding of what knowledge, understanding and skills were to be developed;

- understood how development in scientific inquiry promotes effective learning;

- understood the relationship between concepts and the cognitive demand they make;

- and were clear about what pupils already knew, understood and could do.

The impact of good teaching on pupils was evident when pupils:

- understood clearly the standards they had achieved;

- knew what they needed to do to improve and were involved in peer and self-evaluation;

- took part in decision-making, discussion, research and scientific inquiry;

- and were engaged in science that had relevance to their lives.

Good curriculum provision

Ofsted found that the curriculum in the effective primary schools engaged pupils' interest and enthusiasm and promoted good progress in knowledge, understanding and skills in science. This was achieved best through collaboration among teachers on planning for science and the effective sharing of good practice. The report commented that there was less good practice in relation to the curriculum in primary schools than in secondary schools. It was also noted that the removal of the requirement for statutory tests in science at the end of Key Stages 2 and 3 helped schools to avoid an undue concentration on revision in Years 6 and 9 and freed teachers to be innovative in planning their teaching and in enriching the science curriculum. As testing ceased only in 2010, for most of the time covered by the report, primary schools were under the constraints resulting from high stakes testing at the end of Key Stage 2.

As a result of the review the report recommended that primary schools should

- ensure that pupils are engaged in scientific inquiry, including practical work, and are developing inquiry skills;
- be providing a balanced programme of science education for all year groups that develops science knowledge and understanding and has a significant focus on developing skills;
- make provision for effective continuing professional development to support and extend teachers' knowledge, understanding and skills in science and their confidence in teaching it;
- invest in developing the role of the science coordinator to provide effective, sustained leadership in the subject and promote improvements in teaching and learning.

Gathering data for school self-evaluation

For self-evaluation to be seriously undertaken and used effectively all those involved should agree on the standards to be applied, that is, on the vision of good practice that is the aim. The standards in Box 24.2, the indicators in the various self-assessment frameworks and the Ofsted report provide starting points, but the eventual list should be the one that has the support of the school. Then the data relevant to the agreed standards can be collected.

The data will concern a range of aspects of provision, the main ones being:

- curriculum documents and teachers' medium-term plans;
- teachers' short-term lesson plans;
- teachers' records of activities and pupil performance;
- teacher actions and talk;
- pupil actions and interactions;
- pupil–teacher interactions;
- pupils' written records and other products.

Methods of collecting evidence about these aspects include classroom observation, interview or discussion with the teacher, teaching assistants and pupils, analysis of documents and scrutiny of pupils' written work. The evidence is collected with the help of the science subject leader, by teachers themselves or by teachers and

---

Box 24.3 The evidence from children's work in science

Looking through a collection of work also gives a good idea as to whether the pace of lessons is appropriate. A lot of unfinished work may indicate a mismatch between tasks and the pupils' interest and abilities, particularly for the lower attaining pupils. Are the children putting enough effort into it so that it reflects care and pride in their work? In some science activities, such as observing seeds, drawings are probably more important than words. Are drawings and diagrams large enough, neat enough and correctly labelled? Do they show what they are supposed to show?

... Without scrutinising work, it can be quite difficult to get an accurate idea of the balance of recording methods used across the school. There is nothing wrong with worksheets, but if every lesson is recorded on them, have the children enough opportunity to express their own thoughts and ideas fully? Sometimes older children record science as dictation, copying from the boards or as a cloze procedure. Again, is there enough chance for the children to describe and explain their own developing science ideas? The scrutiny will provide a check that in each class children have the maximum opportunity to learn by using an increasingly wide range of appropriate recording techniques. These should reflect not only what they know and understand, but also how their science skills are developing. Is there clear evidence of investigative activities?

(Wright, 2003: 9)

---

helpers working together. Classroom observations always seem to be the most valid way of collecting evidence – and so they are in many respects, particularly in relation to pupil–teacher interactions, teacher actions such as allowing 'wait' time after asking a question and obtaining a general impression of pupils' activity and enjoyment. However, even if it is possible for the head teacher, science subject leader or another teacher to observe in other teachers' classrooms, as may be feasible in a large primary school, at most one or two lessons can be observed and these are hardly likely to be entirely typical of all lessons. For the older primary classes, the pupils' written work provides an easily accessible source of evidence, as pointed out by Wright (2003) in Box 24.3.

This seems a good deal of work and the time has to be justified by the value to children's learning. It is not necessary for every aspect of the school's provision to be reviewed and evaluated at the same time. The focus should be on those aspects where there is some concern and where it is possible for the school to take action. It is also useful to note a tip from the head of Eliot Bank Primary School whose good practice is summarised in Box 24.4:

> not to waste time on things that aren't going to make a difference to the children in the classroom, so not a moment or conversation is wasted. We constantly ask 'what is the impact on the children?' If there is no impact then it is of no value.

Box 24.4 Case study of good practice in school self-evaluation

Eliot Bank Primary School in Lewisham serves an ethnically diverse community. It has an above average proportion of pupils with England as an additional language and of pupils with special needs. It has been an outstanding school for a number of years, praised particularly for the way in which it uses systems for monitoring and evaluation to narrow the attainment gap for those pupils at risk of not attaining the levels expected for their age.

The continuous process

Monitoring and evaluation are a continuous process that is carefully planned through a calendar of activities. The process begins at the end of the school year. Information about the year's performance is collected from teachers, pupils, parents, governors and support staff. The analysis of this information is used at the beginning of the next school year, in September, in two staff development days, resulting in decisions about:

- improvement priorities
- how they will be developed
- the contributions of different teams and individuals to achieving the whole-school priorities
- allocation of resources.

For evaluating teaching, a schedule of activities including lesson observation, work scrutiny and reviewing teachers' planning is agreed. The involvement of all staff means that, in the words of one team leader, 'we all know why we are doing what we are doing. But we also know why others are doing what they are doing. Nothing comes as a shock because we have been involved.'

For evaluating learning, assessment weeks take place towards the end of each term when outcomes are moderated and entered on the school's data tracker. In the first week of every term, pupil progress meetings identify individuals and groups of pupils who are underachieving, and agree actions to ensure that they make the progress they should.

Pupils takes part in regular reviews of learning. One of the many approaches used is to hold school council meetings for half a day every half-term. The focus of each meeting is linked specifically to the key school priorities.

Key features of the process

- having high expectations of staff and pupils and communicating this message consistently;
- involving all staff in the process, so that they feel ownership and accountability;
- involving, pupils, parents, carers and governors and acting on their feedback;
- being confident about what information, data and approaches to use;
- monitoring and evaluating in teams to develop skills and moderate outcomes;
- challenging each other in teams, across teams and at different levels of leadership;
- analysing and using information, but knowing when to stop and take action;
- acknowledging the outcomes and acting on them quickly;
- allowing time for actions to have an impact;
- customising the approach so that it is fit for purpose.

This example of good practice is adapted from the Ofsted website. Using the links, more information can be accessed about how the procedures and uses of the information (http://www.ofsted.gov.uk/resources/good-practice-resource-systematic-approach-effective-school-self-evaluation-eliot-bank-primary-schoo).

Summary

This chapter has been concerned with the process of school self-evaluation, which schools can use to identify strengths and weaknesses as a basis for improving provision for children's learning. The main points have been:

■ It is important for all staff to be involved and to agree the aspects of their performance to be evaluated and the criteria used in the process.

■ School self-evaluation should be a continuous part of schools' activity, not just conducted in preparation for an inspection.

■ In relation to science, the standards against which schools evaluate their provision should reflect effective practice in science education relating to pupils' engagement in science inquiry and development of skills, the provision of professional development for teachers and the role of the science subject leader.

Further reading

Harlen, W. (2007) Holding up a mirror to classroom practice, *Primary Science Review*, 100: 29–31.

Richardson, I. (2006) What is good science education? in W. Harlen (ed.) *ASE Guide to Primary Science Education*, Hatfield: ASE, 16–23.

Wright, L. (2006) School self-evaluation of teaching and learning science, in W. Harlen (ed.) *ASE Guide to Primary Science Education,* Hatfield: ASE, 73–9.

Websites

How Good is Our School, The Journey to Excellence, part 3:
http://www.educationscotland.gov.uk/Images/HowgoodisourschoolJtEpart3_tcm4-684258.pdf

The Child at the Centre – Self-evaluation in the early years
http://www.journeytoexcellence.org.uk/Images/hgios3bEarlyYears_tcm4-489372.pdf

Guidance for the inspection of primary schools (Wales)
http://www.estyn.gov.uk/english/search/?keywords=Guidance+for+the+Inspection+of+primary+schools

Northern Ireland Inspection Service guidance for primary schools
http://www.etini.gov.uk/index/support-material/support-material-primary/short-inspection-of-primary-schools-self-evaluation-proforma.htm

25

Enhancing provision for children's learning in science

Introduction

Having looked at ways of evaluating provision at class and school level – which inevitably reveal aspects that could be improved – in this chapter we turn attention to action to enhance provision. As we noted in Chapter 20, part of the science subject leader's role is enhancing provision through monitoring learning and teaching in the school and providing for staff development. So in the first part of this chapter we review what the subject leader can do to identify – and help their colleagues to identify for themselves through a dialogue about teaching and learning – aspects of teaching which can be improved. The second part discusses some issues relating to primary teachers' science subject knowledge. We then turn in the third and fourth parts to sources and providers of professional development. A number of these depend centrally on the science subject leader, particularly activities such as working toward one of the awards of the Primary Science Quality Mark project. But professional development is also a personal matter and we consider several avenues for individual teachers to upgrade their qualifications, or simply satisfy the urge to keep abreast of new ways of enhancing pupils' learning. So we also recognise that teachers may undertake CPD not on account of any inadequacy but to increase their knowledge and skill.

Continuing improvement: the subject leader's role

The subject leader helps to support teachers and other educators within the school to provide the best possible science education for children. This means ensuring that teachers understand the science policy and science curriculum and feel able to plan and teach creatively in a way that suits their own pupils. This is no small challenge. Aiming for continuing improvement means that the subject has to be monitored and evaluated. In a sense the aim here is to ensure that there is a continuing dialogue among staff about science teaching. This can be approached through the scrutiny of teachers' planning, the review of pupils' work and the observation of teaching. We have touched upon all of these as part of evaluation at the class and school levels and now consider them briefly as key activities for the science subject leader in identifying priorities for staff development.

Undertaking these monitoring tasks makes heavy demands on leadership skills in finding the balance between ensuring rigour and encouraging open discussion and debate. Schools where teachers agree together how this 'continuing dialogue' will be approached will find that balance easier to achieve. For example, each subject leader might have a plan for developing their subject and maintaining a file of information and data, structured to an agreed format, that can be drawn upon for school self-assessment or inspections and, importantly, for annual review and school curriculum planning.

Scrutiny of teachers' planning

At the level of medium-term planning this should involve asking questions such as: do the plans reflect the overall school curriculum in terms of topics, coverage and approach? Is there a good balance of coverage of different areas of the curriculum? Is there a good range of different approaches being planned (working outside, use of ICT, group and individual work)? Is there good integration of investigative work across the term?

In relation to the activities in a lesson or group of lessons the questions can be drawn from those given in Chapter 4 and referred to again in Chapter 21 on lesson planning. For example:

- Are the activities likely to be interesting and relevant to the children?
- Do the activities build on previous experience and promote progression?
- Will the children be able to use a range of senses and learn actively?
- Will the children talk and represent their ideas in different ways?
- Will the children be able to develop scientific ideas, use inquiry skills and demonstrate scientific attitudes?

Review of pupils' work

Pupils' notebooks should provide a record of some of the children's work in science, reflecting teachers' medium- and short-term plans. So it is useful to refer back to teachers' plans when looking at children's work. We noted the value of reviewing children's work in Chapter 24 (Box 24.3). In addition, some crucial questions relating to inquiry were suggested by the AKSIS project, and quoted by CLEAPSS (2006). These include:

- Whose inquiry is it? The answer should be clearly the child, or group of children, rather than the teacher.
- What is its context?
- What questions are the children trying to answer?
- Have children drawn conclusions? How good is their evidence?

- Has the teacher's marking helped, for instance by indicating what is good about the work, what could be improved or by raising questions for the child to consider?

Of course not all the work produced is presented in books. It is also useful to look at the product of collaborative work, for example a big book from a class topic, or displays on classroom and corridor walls. Wall displays can give an impression of the profile of science in the school, the emphasis that is being placed on inquiry, and the extent to which children themselves are involved in the whole process. The work displayed should be something that children themselves feel is worth showing to others. Often wall displays can be used to inform, excite and motivate children and visitors to the classroom. This last point ensures that parents are informed about ongoing science work in school.

Observation of teaching

A really useful way to encourage dialogue among staff is for them to be able to observe each other teach. Science subject leaders are often in this fortunate position. However, it is also helpful for others to either observe each other teach, or to team teach. Observation has to be seen as positive and conducted sensitively, recognising that some people find it difficult both to be observed and to act as observer. A discussion before the lesson between the teacher and observer should identify what is planned for the lesson. More detailed information about individual pupils, for instance, will help the observer to understand what is happening and why. The teacher being observed should be fully aware of what the observer will be looking for and, for the process to be of most use, should help to decide the focus. This may be on certain parts of a lesson that a teacher wants to improve, for example, plenary discussions, or ways to organise practical work. Teachers might want to consider particularly successful strategies that might be shared with others.

The subject leader's file

The subject leader's file might include vision and aims statements, policy documents and information about subject audits, as well as long- and medium-term plans. It should also be a working document with ongoing information on monitoring and evaluation and records of scrutiny of plans across the school, lesson observations and examples of children's work. Samples of work help to articulate the expectations of children's achievement throughout their primary school career and can be used to support discussions amongst staff when moderating children's work (see Chapter 19). The subject leader also needs to keep information about resources, finances and health and safety issues and a record of, and plans for, staff development. The account of science education in the school given in this information should be regularly scrutinised against the statements in the school policy for science.

Where schools use a VLE (see Table 14.1) all this information can be made readily available to teachers and, selectively, to parents, governors and others as appropriate. A section could also be developed to provide well-targeted background information for teachers, put together as suggested in Box 25.4.

Supporting and advising colleagues: the subject leader's role

Science subject leaders need to provide information, advice and guidance for colleagues in such a way as to enable the whole school to move forward. This can involve providing support in relation to approaches to teaching and subject knowledge as well as issues such as health and safety. In addition, the subject leader needs to be a champion ensuring that science is afforded appropriate resources, including time within the timetable and sufficient funding for resources and travel to external sites.

Developing teachers' confidence

In a study of primary teachers' confidence in teaching science in England, Scotland, Wales and Northern Ireland (Murphy *et al.*, 2007), teachers rated their confidence to teach science higher than for teaching history, geography and information and communication technology (ICT), but lower than that for teaching English and mathematics. This was an improvement on the findings of study ten years earlier undertaken by Harlen *et al.* (1995), where confidence in teaching science was lower than most other subjects.

One of the enduring sources of low confidence – teachers' own subject knowledge – has shown some improvement. In the 1990s, research into the effect of teachers' own understanding of science on the science activities of their pupils (e.g. Harlen *et al.*, 1995) led to a demand on initial teacher training courses to increase the focus on science and in particular on science subject knowledge. This, coupled with the compulsory study of science up to the age of 16 in UK schools for many years, means that recently qualified teachers are likely to have a better grounding in the subject. This was borne out in the Ofsted report of January 2011, which found that: 'In all the primary schools visited, teachers' subject knowledge was at least satisfactory'. They noted that teachers had more concerns about their knowledge of physical sciences than of living things and that 'Limited expertise and confidence restricted the level of challenge that some teachers could provide for more academically able pupils' (Ofsted, 2011a: 15, para. 25).

The question of the extent to which a primary teacher who is a generalist has the knowledge to provide learning activities of the necessary challenge for children throughout the primary school remains a contentious issue. The arguments are clouded by reducing the concept of 'teachers' knowledge' to 'knowledge of the subject matter', with little regard for other kinds of knowledge which are involved in teaching. These, as notably identified by Shulman (1987), are:

- Content knowledge – about science and of science;

- General pedagogical knowledge – about classroom management and organisation, non-subject-specific;

- Curriculum knowledge – guidelines, national requirements, materials available;

- Pedagogical content knowledge – about how to teach the subject matter, including useful illustrations, powerful analogies and examples;

- Knowledge of learners and their characteristics;

- Knowledge of educational contexts;

- Knowledge of educational goals, values and purposes, including the history and philosophy of education.

It is significant that Shulman puts content knowledge first in this list, since several of the subsequent items depend on it. But what he emphasises is not so much the mastery of each and every aspect of a subject, as an understanding of what it is that identifies science; how the discipline of science differs from other disciplines; what are its boundaries, its limitations and the different ways in which it can be conceived. With this grasp teachers can develop pedagogical content knowledge (often referred to a PCK).

Given the current view of the aims of science education and the importance of inquiry-based learning in advancing towards them, the development of PCK would appear to be the priority. Newton and Newton (2001) suggest that teachers who have some science knowledge are more likely to develop the pedagogical skills to support pupils' learning. The emphasis is not on facts but on the broad principles which, as adults with much existing relevant experience to bring together, teachers very quickly grasp, and, most importantly, on the understanding of what it is to be scientific.

The support now available online, through guidance books on subject knowledge and initial teacher training courses, as well as published schemes of work, have increased confidence in teaching science. In turn, the added confidence and support should enable primary teachers to continue to teach science to their own classes rather than separate it from other work by using specialist teachers. As the debate continues, schools need to make decisions about how to support staff in developing their science knowledge and understanding and how to deploy staff. The subject leader has a key role here in identifying the strengths and weaknesses of teachers and in supporting staff whilst making maximum use of their expertise. One practical way of doing this and then providing the support that is needed is described in Box 25.1.

Sources of continuing professional development

Continuing professional development (CPD) is the means by which members of a profession maintain, improve and broaden their knowledge and skills, throughout their career. It is increasingly recognised that all educators should have access to good-quality opportunities for professional development. In the past this might

---

Box 25.1 The subject leader as subject knowledge support

Caroline has a BEd science degree; she teaches 7–8 year olds and has been science coordinator for three years. There is no specialist science teaching in this two-form-entry school which is housed in a new building. The classrooms for each year group are semi open-plan and linked by a shared work area. The year teachers develop their medium- and short-term plans together, with the member of the pair who is most confident in a subject taking the lead.

The school's long-term plan is based on, but is not the same as, the QCA scheme of work. Each section of the plan is supplemented by a series of notes developed over the years by Caroline. The notes focus on subject knowledge, with advice on additional sources, websites and books. Each year she makes a note of questions teachers ask her and the research she has done in order to answer the questions. In developing the long-term plan for the following year she reviews her file of notes and ideas and uses this to inform the development of the next plan. In this way she has built up a file of useful supplementary information and ideas for teachers that is organised in units according to the school plan. Teachers may access this through the school's VLE and then use it in their medium- and short-term planning.

---

have meant simply 'going on a course' or attending a workshop. However, our understanding of the range of opportunities for CPD has broadened considerably. In part, this is because research has shown that attendance at a short course, off site, with little or no follow-up, often has a limited impact in improving teaching. Effective teachers are 'continually learning on the job, because their work entails engagement with a succession of cases, problems or projects which they have to learn about' (Eraut, 1994: 16). Eraut emphasises the point that, in order to make the most of these learning opportunities professionals must have time to reflect on them either individually or with others. Thus the wider interpretation of CPD is recognised in this definition from the Professional Standards for Teachers of 2007:

> Reflective activity designed to improve an individual's attributes, knowledge, understanding and skills. It supports individual needs and improves practice.
> (TDA, 2007, archived at http://webarchive.nationalarchives.gov.uk)

The 2012 Teachers' Standards indicate that CPD is an obligation:

> As their careers progress, teachers will be expected to extend the depth and breadth of knowledge, skills and understanding that they demonstrate in meeting the standards.
> (DfE, 2012: 4, para. 14)

Teachers can develop their professional practice through a variety of activities including:

■ Reflecting on their practice, action research or in discussion with others.

■ Mentoring or coaching by a more experienced colleague or adviser.

- Attending accredited or non-accredited courses.
- Membership of professional associations.
- Attending conferences and workshops.
- Independent study through TV or online courses and sources of information.

Since primary teachers generally have to consider extending their expertise in a range of subjects, it is perhaps not surprising that the uptake of science-specific continuing professional development was reported as being low by Ofsted in their January 2011 report. They note that:

> While much of the professional development they received overall was relevant to science, it was often generic, for example being focused on improving teaching and learning or assessment generally. In just under two thirds of the primary schools where science-specific continuing professional development was evaluated, it was no better than satisfactory.
>
> (Ofsted, 2011a: 5)

Other evidence points to the same problem. Johnson (2013), for example, notes that very few primary teachers reported receiving training in teaching the elements of science in the 'World Around Us' theme of the Northern Ireland Curriculum as part of their CPD for the revised curriculum.

Sharp and Hopkin (2008) in a survey of English primary teachers in 2007 found that 60 per cent of respondents had received no science-focused training either within school or outside over the previous three years. Considering that the subject specialism of the respondents was skewed in favour of science subject leaders, and that science subject leaders had undertaken significantly more training than other colleagues, the situation is not encouraging. In particular the lack of professional development within schools suggests that science subject leaders have not had the opportunity to provide this essential support for staff. This is a particularly important gap, especially with the increase in support staff and in the level of responsibility for teaching and assessment that they can have in some schools.

CPD needs analysis

The key to making the most of the opportunities is to identify needs as clearly as possible. Indeed, selecting the best route for acquiring CPD starts with identifying needs and then looking to ways in which these needs can be met. This can be done through systems of performance management, or appraisal, and through staff self-assessment of needs using a questionnaire set against what is required in the school development plan. Specific subject focused needs analysis can be conducted by subject leaders using the methods suggested earlier for scrutiny of plans, review of children's work and observation of teaching as means to establishing non-threatening dialogue about learning. The science subject leader can help individuals to identify needs that could be addressed through mentoring and coaching, through working with others, course attendance or a combination of these. The audit of provision for science required by the Primary Science Quality Mark project (see below) provides a model for identifying needs for teacher development – and also for taking action.

Providers of continuing professional development

In many respects improving provision is best tackled at the whole-school level so that children can be provided with a consistent and progressive education in all areas of learning. In the context of science this is recognised in programmes of CPD which work through the subject leader and aim to influence the whole staff. However, not all schools are able to take part in these programmes and it is important for individual teachers to be able to access CPD provision. Below we discuss the following main providers:

- Primary Science Quality Mark;
- Science Learning Centres;
- The Association for Science Education;
- The Primary Science Teaching Trust (PSTT);
- Universities;
- Teachers' TV.

Primary Science Quality Mark scheme

The Primary Science Quality Mark (PSQM) is an award scheme to enable primary schools across the UK to evaluate, strengthen and celebrate their science provision. Schools can achieve bronze, silver and gold awards. The project aims to:

- raise the profile of science in primary schools;
- provide schools with a framework and professional support for developing science leadership, teaching and learning;
- celebrate excellence in primary science;
- work with existing and facilitate new networks across the UK and wider to provide local support for primary science;
- assemble and make accessible to the wider science education community a rich database of current practice in primary science. (PSQM website)

PSQM has identified criteria at three levels (bronze, silver and gold) relating to all aspects of a school's science programme under the broad headings of: subject management; teachers and teaching, pupils and learning; broader opportunities (links to organisations and agencies outside the school). Box 25.2 gives an example of the indicators for a subsection of 'subject management' relating to the science subject leader's knowledge of science teaching across the school. In

---

Box 25.2 PSQM indicators relating to the subject leader's knowledge of science across the school

Bronze award indicator
The science subject leader works with, or monitors, the work of a colleague. School-wide work book scrutiny takes place.

Silver award indicator
Peer-assessment and team teaching of science takes place across the school. School-wide workbook scrutiny takes place.

Gold award indicator
There is a robust process of monitoring science teaching and learning in place. Outcomes are shared with the staff and actions taken when issues are identified. Regular discussions take place between coordinator and senior management teacher about science in the school.

---

each case there are examples of the kind of evidence which can be used to decide whether or not practice meets the criteria.

When a school registers for the PSQM scheme, staff take part in an initial training session which prepares them for auditing practice against the PSQM indicators. This will enable the school to decide which level of award to aim for. The next step is to devise an action plan for changes necessary to reach the chosen award level within a year. When this is agreed it is uploaded to the PSQM website. During the next nine or so months schools have access to a mentor and a second training session as they implement the plan and collect evidence of changes. At the end of that time they submit a report and evidence of changes made. A certificate is presented at an award ceremony to celebrate the achievement.

Since it was piloted in 2008 and 2009 the scheme has grown and is now firmly established as a project within the University of Hertfordshire with funding from the Primary Science Teaching Trust (PSTT). It aims to increase recruitment of schools to about 1,200 each year. The PSTT website provides exemplar materials of how schools have met the criteria for the PSQM awards http://www.pstt.org.uk/resources/continuing-professional-development/enrich-science-learning.aspx

Science Learning Centres

The national network of Science Learning Centres provides science Continuing Professional Development for those working with pupils aged 5 to 19, including: primary teachers, secondary school teachers of science, design and technology and psychology, teaching assistants, technicians and Further Education lecturers. The aims of the network are to support teachers and technicians in enhancing their professional skills and to:

inspire pupils by providing them with a more exciting, intellectually stimulating and relevant science education, enabling them to gain the knowledge and the understanding they need – both as the citizens and as the scientists of the future.

(SLC website)

More information about the network and its role in providing for primary teachers is given in Box 25.3. The national centre is run by the White Rose Consortium of universities and all the regional centres are based at universities and in some cases run in partnership with local authority education services and private companies.

Steps have been taken to alleviate the difficulty that some primary schools find in making use of the courses on account of their cost and their location. All teachers, tutors, lecturers and technicians involved in science education at state-funded schools and colleges in England may be eligible for an Impact Award to help them cover the cost of attending certain courses at the Regional Science Learning Centres. For residential courses at the National Centre there are ENTHUSE Awards to help cover the costs of course fees, travel, supply cover and accommodation and food (see Further reading section). To make courses more easily accessible most regional centres offer courses at satellite centres as well as at the universities at which they are based, and will also provide bespoke courses in schools.

Box 25.3 Science Learning Centres

The National Network of 6 Science Learning Centres (5 regional centres in England and the residential National Centre based in York which covers the whole of the UK) opened its doors in 2004, following the recommendations of the Roberts report into science education (Roberts, 2002). Jointly funded by the Department for Education and the Wellcome Trust, the network provides high-quality, short and longer-term professional development for teachers of science, including technicians and teaching assistants, in all phases of education. The main aims of the network are to improve science education and to bring contemporary science into the classroom.

The network works closely with a wide number of stakeholders across the science education and STEM communities, plus Local Authorities, to coordinate develop and deliver CPD. Over 26,600 SLC training days were delivered in 2012–13 with both primary and secondary teachers reporting very positively about the impact of the CPD on their practice. However as a result of the additional funding for secondary teachers and the relatively higher profile of science in the secondary education agenda, take up for CPD from secondary teachers has been considerably higher than that of primary teachers and it is of concern to the network that large numbers of primary teachers still have not heard of the Science Learning Centres (Sharp and Hopkin, 2008). The network is working with stakeholders at all levels to raise awareness of the significant value of and increasing need for high quality science CPD for primary teachers, children and schools, and thereby increase demand and potential impact. [Figures updated]

(Turner, 2011: 144)

The Association for Science Education

In 2013 the Association for Science Education (ASE) celebrated 50 years of supporting science education. As soon as it was established (from the amalgamation of the Science Masters' Association and the Association of Women Science) it established a primary science sub-committee. Since then the membership and services provided for primary teachers have gradually increased. As well as publishing *Primary Science* five times a year and the online *Journal of Emergent Science* (concerned with research in science education for 3 to 8 year olds), it also produces publications specifically to share good practice in primary science. These include various editions of the *ASE Guide to Primary School Science* and the popular *Be Safe* (see Box 22.4). These publications contribute to professional development but it is perhaps the regional and national conferences that provide the richest opportunities for teachers to learn about and try out new materials resources and ideas. The conferences include whole and half-day workshops, talks and extensive exhibitions of children's work and equipment, all highly valued by participants, especially on the 'Primary Days'.

Each year the ASE organises the competition for the PSTT Primary Science Teacher of the Year awards. The awards, presented at the national conference, recognise and promote excellence in primary science teaching. The winners are enrolled in the PSTT Primary Science Teacher College, receive a sum of money for their school and for themselves, a certificate and ASE membership for one year.

The ASE recognises expertise in science teaching through the award of CSciTeach for both primary and secondary teachers. This award is open to members who meet strict criteria relating to academic qualifications and experience in science teaching, who undertake an academic review of professional knowledge and practice and make an annual commitment to continuing professional development. The first awards were made in 2007 and since then many members involved in primary teaching and the support of primary teachers have gained the award. (In 2012 the ASE began to award Registered Scientist (RSci) and Registered Science Technician (RSciTech) for those eligible.)

In Scotland the Standard for Chartered Teacher comprises part of the national framework for teachers' continuing professional development. Although the Chartered Teacher scheme, which is open to all teachers at the top of the main scale, is not subject-specific, it involves teachers either taking a number of study modules with recognised providers in order to develop the evidence base needed, or gaining some exemption through the provision of a portfolio of evidence.

The Primary Science Teaching Trust

In 1997 AstraZeneca set up a Trust, the AZSTT, specifically to provide financial assistance to help improve science in lower secondary and primary schools in the UK. Now renamed the Primary Science Teaching Trust (PSTT), it continues to do this through funding projects, providing CPD resources, lesson plans and activities, reflecting its philosophy that the most effective way to improve teaching is to support teacher development. Through CPD units and other dissemination tools it provides a platform of resources across primary science and into lower secondary classes to support science teaching in the UK.

In 2010 the Trust established the Primary Science Teacher College. This virtual college draws together past winners of the PSTT Primary Science Teacher Award and all new winners are automatically members of this college. The college has its own annual conference, web area and most importantly its own funding. The Trust invests £50,000 a year into the college to allow these excellent teachers to develop new projects, undertake professional development and to disseminate best practice from their own teaching and that from the Trust-funded work.

The PSTT website (www.pstt.org.uk) is a key resource for primary teachers providing a comprehensive list of links to other organisations, curriculum materials, a database of Trust-funded projects, research publications related to particular themes and exemplary materials relating to the PSQM indicators.

Universities

The traditional approach to CPD has been to undertake a master's course at a local university, or as a distance learning programme. However, there are very few master's programmes that focus specifically on science education, and even fewer where the focus is primary science, although it is possible to select individual modules and to relate assignments for more general modules to science. What such courses can provide is an opportunity to take a step back and to reflect on practice, which is seen as important in developing the extended professional. A full master's programme is a major undertaking which may not always be the appropriate route. Indeed, if we are to see CPD as lifelong learning, one would expect to continue learning beyond the award of the degree.

Increasingly, universities are offering programmes that are more integrated with the teachers' own professional setting, making links not just by encouraging school-based research to provide the material for assignments, but by extending this into schools. This is in response to the mounting research evidence that effective CPD constitutes

> use of peer support and specialist expertise; use of observation and feedback; teachers experimenting in applying the new skills in classroom teaching; consultation with teachers during the CPD process; and a significant in-school component to CPD.
>
> (Cordingley *et al.*, 2005)

It appears, however, that the idea, once mooted by the Training and Development Agency before it was absorbed into the DfE, that graduate teacher programmes could be accredited towards a master's level qualification gained over a longer period, has not been pursued.

Teachers' TV

Teachers' TV, which we have mentioned several times in this book, is an excellent source of CPD, providing very useful reviews of resources as well as short (15-minute) videos which are broadcast on television and can be downloaded from the internet. These can be used by teachers individually, or to provide the basis of group work where the ideas can be discussed and ideas shared.

Of course the internet itself is a powerful source of information and so can be invaluable for teachers who identify a need, whether this is in terms of gaps in subject knowledge, or to develop pedagogy.

Summary

The teaching profession is, by its very nature, a learning profession. The pace of change over the last 20 years has meant that keeping up with developments and continuing to learn has become more of a challenge. It is not simply new technology that has changed or that science itself has moved on apace, but also the frequency of appearance of new ideas about learning and teaching. In this chapter we have discussed ways of enhancing schools' provision for children's learning in science through monitoring and meeting needs for continuing professional development. The main points have been as follows.

- Continuing professional development is both a right and a responsibility for teachers who need time and space to reflect on and engage in dialogue about their practice.

- Science subject leaders have a key role in supporting colleagues individually and in school-wide improvement programmes.

- Although there are many forms of CPD available, uptake of science-specific courses is reported as being low.

- Bursaries are available to help schools and teachers to meet the cost of courses at the national and regional science learning centres.

- Schools can raise the standard of their science education by auditing their provision and taking action with the help of mentors in the Primary Science Quality Mark scheme.

- There are sources of CPD that individual teachers can access at a distance through TV and the internet.

Further reading

Bishop, K. and Feasey, R. (2006) Supporting in-school opportunities for professional development, *Primary Science Review,* 95: 37–8.

Turner, J. (2011) Continuing professional development and the role of Science Learning Centres, in W. Harlen (ed.) *ASE Guide to Primary Science Education,* new edn, Hatfield: ASE.

Websites

Association for Science Education: www.ase.org.uk/

Chartered Teacher: http://www.charteredteacher.co.uk/

Enthuse Charitable Trust: https://www.sciencelearningcentres.org.uk/centres/national/awards-and-bursaries/enthuse-award

National Science Learning Centres: https://www.sciencelearningcentres.org.uk/

PSQM: www.PSQM.org.uk/

PSQM exemplar materials: http://www.azteachscience.co.uk/science-teaching/primary-science-quality-mark/exemplar-materials.aspx

The Primary Science Teaching Trust (PSTT) http://www.pstt.org.uk/resources/continuing-professional-development/enrich-science-learning.aspx

References

Abelson, R.P. (1988) Beliefs are like possessions, *Journal for the Theory of Social Behavior,* 16: 223–50.

Adams, J. (2006) Starting out in your own backyard, *Primary Science Review,* 91: 7–10.

Adey, P. and Shayer, M. (1994) *Really Raising Standards: Cognitive Intervention and Academic Achievement,* London: Routledge.

Alexander, R. (1995) *Versions of Primary Education,* London: Routledge.

Alexander, R. (2008) *Towards Dialogic Teaching,* York: Dialogos.

Alexander, R (2010) *Children, their World, their Education: Final Report and Recommendations of the Cambridge Primary Review,* London: Routledge.

American Association for the Advancement of Science (AAAS) (2001) *Atlas of Science Literacy*, Washington, DC: AAAS.

ARG (Assessment Reform Group) (2002) *Assessment for Learning: 10 Principles*, London: ARG.

Asoko, H. and DeBoo, M. (2001) *Analogies and Illustrations: Representing Ideas in Primary Science*, Hatfield: Association for Science Education.

Asoko, H. and Scott, P. (2006) Talk in science classrooms, in W. Harlen (ed.) A*SE Guide to Primary Science Education*, Hatfield: Association for Science Education, 158–66.

Association for Science Education (ASE) (1999) *Science and the Literacy Hour,* Hatfield: Association for Science Education.

Association for Science Education (ASE) (2002) *BE Safe!* INSET pack, 2nd edn, Hatfield: Association for Science Education.

Association for Science Education (ASE) (2011) *Be Safe*, 4th edn, Hatfield: ASE.

Atkin, M. and Black, P. (in press) The central role of assessment in pedagogy, *Handbook of Research on Science Education,* London: Routledge, ch. 38.

Bamberger, Y. and Tal, T. (2007) Learning in a personal context: levels of choice in a free choice learning environment in science and natural history museums, *Science Education,* 91(1): 75–95.

Banks, J. and Smyth, E. (2011) *Continuous Professional Development among Primary Teachers in Ireland: A Report Compiled by the ESRI on Behalf of The Teaching Council,* Dublin: ESRI.

Barker, S. and Buckle, S. (2002) Bringing birds into the classroom, *Primary Science Review,* 75: 8–10.

Barnes, D. (1976) *From Communication to Curriculum,* Harmondsworth: Penguin.

Barnes, D. (2008) Exploratory talk for learning, in N.Mercer and S. Hodkinson (eds) *Exploring Talk in School,* London: Sage, 1–15.

Barnes, D. and Todd, F. (1995) *Communication and Learning Revisited,* London: Heinemann.

Battro, A.M. (2000) *Half a Brain is Enough: The Story of Nico,* Cambridge: Cambridge University Press.

BECTA/ORC (2010) *Harnessing Technology School Survey 2010:* http://dera.ioe.ac.uk/1545/1/htss_survey_technical_appendix.pdf.

Bew, P. (Lord Bew) (2011) *Independent Review of Key Stage 2 Testing, Assessment and Accountability. Final Report. June 2011.* Available for download from www.education.gov.uk

Bianchi, L. (2003) Better learners, *Primary Science Review*, 80: 22–4.

Bianchi, L. (2005) Creative space, *Primary Science Review,* 90: 15–18.

Bird, S. and Saunders, L (2007) *RATIONal Food,* Sandbach: Millgate House Publishers.

Bishop, K. and Feasey, R. (2006) Supporting in-school opportunities for professional development, *Primary Science Review,* 95: 37–8.

Black, P. and Wiliam, D. (1998a) Assessment and classroom learning, *Assessment in Education,* 5(1): 7–74.

Black, P. and Wiliam, D. (1998b) *Inside the Black Box,* London: School of Education, King's College London.

Black, P., Harrison, C., Lee, C., Marshall, B. and Wiliam, D. (2003) *Assessment for Learning, Putting it into Practice,* Maidenhead: Open University Press.

Blacklock, K. (2012) Science on a tight budget, *Primary Science,* 121: 5–7.

Boctor, S. and Rowell, P. (2004) Why do bees sting? Reflecting on talk in science lessons, *Primary Science Review,* 82: 15–17.

Bowker, R. (2004) Children's perceptions of plants following their visit to the Eden Project, *Research in Science and Technology Education,* 22(2): 227–43.

Bowker, R. and Jasper, A. (2007) Don't forget your leech socks! Children's learning during an Eden education officers' workshop, *Research in Science and Technology Education,* 25(1): 135–50.

Boyers P. (1967) *Report to the Department of Education and Science on an Enquiry into the Formation of Scientific Concepts in Children 5–13,* Oxford: University of Oxford Institute of Education.

Braund, M. and Driver, M. (2002) Moving to the big school: what do pupils think about science practical work pre- and post-transfer? Paper presented at the Annual Conference of the British Educational Research Association, University of Exeter, 12–14 Sept.

Budd-Rowe, M. (1974) Relation of wait-time and rewards to the development of language, logic and fate control: part II, *Journal of Research in Science Teaching,* 11(4): 291–308.

Burrows, P (2003) Managing health and safety in primary science, *Primary Science Review,* 79: 18–20.

Butler, R. (1987) Task-involving and ego-involving properties of evaluation: effects of different feedback conditions on motivational perceptions, interest and performance, *Journal of Educational Psychology,* 79(4): 472–82.

Butler, R. (1988) Enhancing and undermining intrinsic motivation: the effects of task-involving and ego-involving evaluation on interest and performance, *British Journal of Educational Psychology,* 58: 1–14.

Byrne, J. and Sharp, J. (2002) *Using ICT in Primary Science Teaching,* Exeter: Learning Matters.

CACE (1967) *Children and their Primary Schools* (Plowden Report), London: HMSO.

Carter-Wall, C. and Whitfield, G. (2012) *The Role of Aspirations, Attitudes and Behaviour in Closing the Educational Attainment Gap,* York: Joseph Rowntree Foundation.

CCEA (Council for the Curriculum, Examinations and Assessment) (2007) *The Northern Ireland Curriculum: Primary,* Belfast; CCEA: http://www.nicurriculum. org.uk/docs/key_stages_1_and_2/northern_ireland_curriculum_primary.pdf.

Centre for Research and Innovation in Learning and Teaching (CRILT) (2009*) Digital Literacy in Primary Schools (DLPS),* Dublin: National College of Ireland.

Charpak, G., Léna, P. and Quéré, Y. (2005) *L'enfant et la science*, Paris: O. Jacob.

Chippindall, J. (2012) Using free on-line survey software in your teaching, *Primary Science,* 121: 16–19.

Chwarae Teg (2012) *Moving On: Supporting Transitions through Science,* produced by Chwarae Teg for the Welsh Government as part of the Get On With Science (GOWS) project. http://chwaraeteg.com/get-on-with-science/

Clarke, S. (1998) *Targeting Assessment in the Primary Classroom,* London: Hodder & Stoughton.

Claxton, G (2007). Expanding young people's capacity to learn, *British Journal of Educational Studies*, 55(2): 115–34.

CLEAPSS (2006) *A Guide for Primary Science Coordinators* (L265), place: Brunel University.

Cordingley, P., Bell, M., Evans, D. and Firth, A. (2005) The impact of collaborative CPD on classroom teaching and learning. Review: What do teacher impact data tell us about collaborative CPD? *Research Evidence in Education Library*, London: EPPI-Centre, Social Science Research Unit, Institute of Education, University of London.

Crompton, Z. and Davies, E. (2012) Models and analogies: making movies, *Primary Science*, 123: 8–9.

Crossouard, B. (2012) Absent presences: the recognition of social class and gender dimensions within peer assessment interactions, *British Educational Research Journal*, 38(5): 731–48.

Davids, S. (2008) Growing faster than their sunflowers, *Primary Science,* 101: 5–8.

Davies, D., Collier, C., McMahon, K. and Howe, A. (2010) E-scape assessment, *Primary Science*, 115: 18–21.

Davis, J. (2012) The Ripple Primary School experience (of the Great Bug Hunt), *Primary Science,* 123: 24–5.

Dabell, J., Keogh, B. and Naylor, S. (2006) Planning with goals in mind, in W. Harlen (ed.) *ASE Guide to Primary Science Education,* Hatfield: ASE: 135–41.

Dawes, L. (2004) Talk and reasoning in classroom science, *International Journal of Science Education*, 26(6): 677–95.

Dela Sala, S. and Anderson, M. (eds) (2012) *Neuroscience in Education: The Good the Bad and the Ugly, Oxford:* Oxford University Press.

DCELLS (2008) *Science in the National Curriculum for Wales,* Cardiff: DCELLS: http://new.wales.gov.uk/topics/educationandskills/curriculum_and_assessment/arevisedcurriculumforwales/nationalcurriculum/sciencenc/?lang=en.

DCSF (Department for Children, Schools and Families) (2009) *Independent Review of the Primary Curriculum: Final Report,* Nottingham: DCSF.

DfEE and QCA (Department for Education and Employment and Qualifications and Curriculum Authority) (1999) *National Curriculum for England,* London: DfEE and QCA.

DfE (Department for Education) (2012) *National Curriculum for Science Key Stages 1 and 2: Draft:* http://media.education.gov.uk/assets/files/pdf/d/draft%20national%20 curriculum%20for%20science%20key%20stages%201%202.pdf.

DfE (2012) *Teachers' Standards,* London: DfE.

DfE (Department for Education) (2013) *National Curriculum for England Key Stages 1 and 2* Framework Document, https://www.gov.uk/government/uploads/system/ uploads/attachment_data/file/244223/PRIMARY_national_curriculum3.pdf.

DfES (Department for Education and Skills) (2006) *Learning Outside the Classroom Manifesto,* London: HMSO: http://www.teachernet.gov.uk/teachingandlearning/ resourcematerials/outsideclassroom.

DfES (2004) *Every Child Matters: Change for Children,* London: HMSO.

DES and WO (Department of Education and Science and Welsh Office) (1985) *Science 5–16: A Statement of Policy,* London: HMSO.

DES/DENI/WO (1985) *APU Science in School Age 11: Report no. 4,* London: HMSO.

DES (Department of Education and Science) (1989) *Aspects of Primary Education: The Teaching and Learning of Science,* London: HMSO.

DeWitt, J. and Osborne, J. (2007) Supporting teachers on science focused school trips: towards an integrated framework of theory and practice, *International Journal of Science Education,* 29(6): 685–710.

Dillon, J., Morris, M., O'Donnell, L., Rickinson, M. and Scott, M. (2005) *Engaging and Learning with the Outdoors: The Final Report of the Outdoor Classroom in a Rural Context Action Research Project*, Slough: NFER.

Dixon-Watmough, R. and Rapley, M. (2012) The Great Bug Hunt is back! *Primary Science,* 123: 24–6.

Dweck, C. S. (2000) *Self-Theories: Their Role in Motivation, Personality and Development,* Philadelphia: Psychology Press.

Earl, L. and Katz, S. (2008) Getting to the core of learning: using assessment for self-monitoring and self-regulation, in S. Swaffield (ed.) *Unlocking Assessment: Understanding for Reflection and Application*, London: David Fulton, 90–104.

Eccles, D. and Taylor, S (2011) Promoting understanding through dialogue, in W. Harlen (ed.) *ASE Guide to Primary Science Education,* new edn, Hatfield: ASE, 77–84.

Edmonds, J. (2002) Inclusive science: supporting the EAL child, *Primary Science Review,* 74: 4–6.

Education Development Center (1966) *Elementary Science Study (ESS)* New York: McGraw Hill.

Education Scotland (2012) *Sciences 3–18 Curriculum Impact Report,* Glasgow: Education Scotland.

Elstgeest, J. (2001) The right question at the right time, in W. Harlen (ed.) *Primary Science: Taking the Plunge,* 2nd edn, Portsmouth, NH: Heinemann, 25–35.

Eraut, M. (1994) *Developing Professional Knowledge and Competence,* London: Taylor & Francis.

Evans, N. (2001) Thoughts on assessment and marking, *Primary Science Review,* 68: 24–6.

Fairbrother, R. (1995) Pupils as learners, in R. Fairbrother, P. Black and P. Gill (eds) *Teachers Assessing Pupils,* Hatfield: Association for Science Education, 105–24.

Feasey, R. (1999) *Primary Science and Literacy*, Hatfield: ASE.

Feasey, R. (2011) Planning: elements of an effective lesson plan, in W. Harlen (ed.) *ASE Guide to Primary Science Education*, new edn, Hatfield: ASE, 44–52.

Fibonacci Project (2012) *Tools for Enhancing Inquiry in Science Education*: www.fibonacci-project.eu.

Fisher, J.A. (2001). The demise of fieldwork as an integral part of science education in schools: a victim of cultural change and political pressure, *Pedagogy, Culture and Society*, 9(1): 75–96.

Fitzgerald, A. (2012) *Science in Primary Schools: Examining the Practices of Effective Primary Science Teachers,* Rotterdam: Sense.

Foxman, D., Hutchinson, D. and Bloomfield, B. (1991) *The APU Experience, 1977–1990,* London: Schools Examination and Assessment Council.

Fradley, C. (2006) Welly walks for science learning, *Primary Science Review,* 91: 14–16.

Frand, J. (2000) The information-age mindset: changes in students and implications for higher education, *Educause Review,* 15–24: http://connect.educause.edu/Library/EDUCAUSE+Review/TheInformationAgeMindsetC/40216?time=1204296604.

Futurelab (2010) *Digital Literacy across the Curriculum: A Futurelab Handbook,* Bristol: Futurelab: www.futurelab.org.uk.

Galton, M.J., Simon, B. and Croll, P. (1980) *Inside the Primary Classroom,* London: Routledge & Kegan Paul.

Galton, M.J., Hargreaves, L., Comber, C., Wall, D. and Pell, T. (1999) Changes in patterns of teacher interaction in the primary classroom: 1976–96, *British Educational Research Journal*, 25(1): 23–37.

Galton, M., Gray, J. and Ruddock, J. (1999) *The Impact of School Transition and Transfer on Pupil Progress and Attainment,* Research Reports, RR131, London: DfEE.

Gardner, J. (ed.) (2012) *Assessment and Learning,* 2nd edn, London: Sage.

Get On With Science (GOWS) Project (2012) *Moving on: Supporting Transition through Science*, Cardiff: Welsh Government: http://chwaraeteg.com/downloads/Moving_On_Supporting_transition_through_science.pdf.

Gipps, C.V. (1994) *Beyond Testing,* London: Falmer.

Goldsworthy, A. (2011) Effective questions, in W. Harlen (ed.) *ASE Guide to Primary Science Education,* new edn, Hatfield: Association for Science Education, 69–76.

Goldsworthy, A., Watson, R. and Wood-Robinson, V. (2000) *Investigations: Developing Understanding,* Hatfield: Association for Science Education.

Goldsworthy, A. (2003) *Raising Attainment in Primary Science: Assessment, Monitoring and Evaluation,* Oxford: GHPD.

Gopnik, A., Meltzoff, A. and Kuhl, P. (1999) *The Scientist in the Crib,* New York: William Morrow.

Goswami, U. (2012) Principles of learning, implications for teaching? Cognitive neuroscience and the classroom, in S. Dela Sala and M. Anderson (eds) *Neuroscience in Education: The Good, the Bad, and the Ugly,* Oxford: Oxford University Press, pp. 47–59.

Goswami, U. and Bryant, P. (2007) *Children's Cognitive Development and Learning,* Primary Review Research Survey 2/1a: www.primaryreview.org.uk. Cambridge: Cambridge Primary Review.

Graham, B. (2012) Visit a farm – surely not! *Primary Science,* 122: 15–17.

Greenfield, S. (1997) *The Human Brain: A Guided Tour,* London: Phoenix.

Guichard, J. (1995) Designing tools to develop conceptions of learners, *International Journal of Science Education,* 17(1): 243–53.

Guichard, F. (2007) *Comment devient-on scientifique? Enquête sur la naissance d'une vocation,* Paris: EDP Sciences.

Hague, C. and Payton, S. (2010) *Digital Literacy across the Curriculum: A Futurelab Handbook,* Bristol: Futurelab: www.futurelab.org.uk.

Hainsworth, M. (2012) Harnessing new technologies: a virtual world for science education? *Primary Science,* 122: 21–3.

Hall, I. and Higgins, S. (2007) Primary pupils' perceptions of interactive whiteboards, *Journal of Computer Assisted Learning,* 21: 102–17.

Hall, J. (2005) *Neuroscience and Education: What Can Brain Science Contribute to Teaching and Learning?* Spotlight 92, Glasgow: SCRE Centre, University of Glasgow.

Harlen, W. (1993) Science and technology north of the border, *Primary Science Review*, 27: 16–18.

Harlen, W. (2001a) The rise and fall of peripatetic demonstrators, *Primary Science Review,* 67: 9–10.

Harlen, W. (ed.) (2001b) *Primary Science: Taking the Plunge,* 2nd edn, Portsmouth, NH: Heinemann.

Harlen, W. (2005) Teachers' summative practices and assessment for learning: tensions and synergies, *Curriculum Journal*, 16(2): 207–23.

Harlen, W. (2006a) On the relationship between assessment for formative and summative purposes, in J. Gardner (ed.) *Assessment and Learning,* London: Sage, 87–102.

Harlen, W. (2006b) *Teaching, Learning and Assessing Science 5–12,* 4th edn, London: Sage.

Harlen, W. (2007) *Assessment of Learning,* London: Sage

Harlen, W. (ed.) (2010a) *Principles and Big Ideas of Science Education,* Hatfield: ASE. Available for free download from http://www.ase.org.uk/documents/principles-and-big-ideas-of-science-education.

Harlen, W. (2010b) What is quality teacher assessment? in J. Gardner, W. Harlen, L. Hayward and G. Stobart, with M. Montgomery, *Developing Teacher Assessment,* Maidenhead: Open University Press, 29–52.

Harlen, W. (2013) *Assessment and Inquiry-Based Science Education.* Trieste: IAP-SEP. Available free from www.interacademies.net/activities/projects/12250.aspx.

Harlen, W. and Jarvis, T. (2011) What happens in other countries? in W. Harlen (ed.) *ASE Guide to Primary Science Education,* new edn, Hatfield: ASE, 195–203.

Harlen, W., Holroyd, C. and Byrne, M. (1995) *Confidence and Understanding in Teaching Science and Technology in Primary Schools,* Research Report, Edinburgh: SCRE.

Harlen, W., Macro, C., Reed, K. and Schilling, M. (2003) *Making Progress in Primary Science: Study Book*, London: Routledge Falmer

Harrison, C. and Howard, S. (2009) *Inside the Primary Black Box,* London: GL Assessment.

Harrison, C. and Howard, S. (2011) Issues in primary assessment 2, assessment for learning: how and why it works in primary classrooms, *Primary Science*, 116: 5–7.

Hawking, S. W. (1988) *A Brief History of Time,* London: Bantam Press.

Haworth, C., Dale, P. and Plomin, R. (2008) A twin study into the genetic and environmental influences on academic performance in science in nine-year-old boys and girls, *International Journal of Science Education*, 30(8): 1003–25.

HM Inspectorate of Education (HMIe) (2007) *How Good is Our School? The Journey to Excellence Part 3.* Livingston: HMIe.

Hoban, G. and Nielsen, W. (2010). The 5 Rs: a new teaching approach to encourage slowmations (student generated animations) of science concepts, *Teaching Science,* 56(3): 33–8.

Hodson, D. (1993) Re-thinking old ways: towards a more critical approach to practical work in school science, *Studies in Science Education,* 22: 85–142.

Hodson, D. (1998) *Teaching and Learning Science,* Buckingham: Open University Press.

House of Commons Education and Skills Select Committee (2007) *Creative Partnerships and the Curriculum.* London: House of Commons. http://www.publications.parliament.uk/pa/cm200607/cmselect/cmeduski/1034/103402.htm

Howard-Jones, P., Pollard, A., Blakemore, S.-J., Rogers, P. Goswami, U., Butterworkth, B., Taylor, E., Williamon, A., Morton, J. and Kaufmann, L. (2007) *Neuroscience and Education: Issues and Opportunities*, London: TLRP/ESRC.

Howe, C. (1990) Grouping children for effective learning in science, *Primary Science Review,* 13: 26–7.

Howe, C., Rodgers, C. and Tolmie, A. (1992) The acquisition of conceptual understanding of science in primary school children: group interaction and the understanding of motion down an incline, *British Journal of Developmental Psychology,* 10: 113–30.

Howe, C., Tolmie, A., Thurston, A., Topping, K. Christie, D., Livingston, K., Jessiman, E. and Donaldson, C. (2007) Group work in elementary science: towards organisational principles for supporting pupil learning, *Learning and Instruction,* 17: 549–63.

Hurley, S. and Chater, E (eds) (2005) *Perspectives on Imitation: From Neuroscience to Social Science*, vol. 2, Cambridge, MA: MIT Press.

IAP (Global Network of Science Academies) (2006) *Report of the Working Group on International Collaboration in the Evaluation of Inquiry-Based Science Education (IBSE) Programs*, Santiago, Chile: University of Chile, Faculty of Medicine.

IAP (Global Network of Science Academies) (2012) *Taking Inquiry-Based Science Education into Secondary Education: Report of a Global Conference:* http://www.sazu.si/files/file-147.pdf.

Isaacs, N. (1962) The case for bringing science into the primary school, in *The Place of Science in Primary Education,* London: British Association for the Advancement of Science, 4–22.

Jabin, Z. and Smith, R. (1994) Using analogies of electricity flow in circuits to improve understanding, *Primary Science Review,* 35: 23–6.

James, M., McCormick R., Black, P., Carmichael, P., Drummond, M.-J., Fox, A., MacBeath, J., Marshall, B., Pedder, D., Proctor, R., Swaffield, S., Swann, J. and Wiliam, D. (2007) *Improving Learning: How to Learn,* London: Routledge.

Jannikos, M. (1995) Are the stereotyped views of scientists being brought into the 90s? *Primary Science Review,* 37: 27–9.

Jarvis, T. and Pell, A. (2005) Factors influencing elementary school children's attitude towards science before, during and after a visit to the UK National Space Centre, *Journal of Research in Science Teaching,* 42(1): 53–83.

Jelly, S.J. (2001) Helping children to raise questions – and answering them, in W. Harlen (ed.) *Primary Science: Taking the Plunge,* 2nd edn, Portsmouth, NH: Heinemann, 36–47.

Johnson, A. (2013) Is science lost in the world around us? *Primary Science,* 126: 8–10.

Johnston, J. (2005) *Early Explorations in Science,* Maidenhead: Open University Press.

Jones, A.T. and Kirk, C.M. (1990) Introducing technological applications into the physics classroom: help or hindrance to learning? *International Journal of Science Education,* 12: 481–90.

Kelly, A.V. (2009) *The Curriculum: Theory and Practice,* 6th edn, London: Sage.

Keogh, B. and Naylor, S. (1998) Teaching and learning in science using concept cartoons, *Primary Science Review,* 51: 14–16.

Keogh, B. and Naylor, S. (2000) *Concept Cartoons in Science Education*, Sandbach: Millgate House Publishers.

Keogh, B and Naylor, S (2004) Children's ideas, children's feeling, *Primary Science Review*, 82: 18–20.

Keogh, B. and Naylor, S. (2006) Access and engagement for all, in W. Harlen (ed.) *ASE Guide to Primary Science Education,* Hatfield: ASE, 151–157.

Keogh, B. and Naylor, S. (2011) Creativity in teaching science, in W. Harlen (ed.) *ASE Guide to Primary Science Education,* new edn, Hatfield: ASE, 102–10.

Keogh, B., Naylor, S., Downing, B., Maloney, J. and Simon S. (2006) Puppets bringing stories to life in science, *Primary Science Review,* 92: 26–8.

Kershner, R., Mercer, N., Warwick, P. and Kleine, J. Staarman (2010) Can the interactive whiteboard support young children's collaborative communication and thinking in classroom science activities? *Computer-Supported Collaborative Learning,* 5: 359–83.

Kimbell, R., Wheeler, A., Miller, S. and Pollit, A. (2009) *E-scape Portfolio Assessment Phase 3 Report,* London: Dept of Education, Goldsmiths, University of London: http://www.gold.ac.uk/teru/projectinfo/projecttitle,5882,en.php.

Kiseil, J.F. (2007) Examining teacher choices for science museum worksheets, *Journal of Science Teacher Education,* 18: 29–43.

Kluger, A.N. and DeNisi, A. (1996) The effects of feedback interventions on performance: a historical review, a meta-analysis, and a preliminary intervention theory, *Psychological Bulletin,* 119: 254–84.

Kohn, A. (1993) *Punished by Rewards*, Boston, MA: Houghton Mifflin.

Lawrence, L. (2011) The science subject leader, in W. Harlen (ed.) *ASE Guide to Primary Science Education,* new edn. Hatfield: ASE, 133–40.

Lias, S. and Thomas, C. (2003) Using digital photographs to improve learning in science, *Primary Science Review*, 76: 17–19.

Loi, C.K., Zhang, B., Chen, W., Seow, P., Chia, G., Norris, C. and Soloway, E. (2011) Mobile inquiry learning experience for primary science students: a study of learning effectiveness, *Journal of Computer Assisted Learning,* 27: 269–87.

McCrory, P. (2011) Developing interest in science through emotional engagement, in W. Harlen (ed.), *ASE Guide to Primary Science Education*, new edn, Hatfield: ASE, 94–101.

McCullagh, J. (2009) *DREAMS (Digitally Resourced, Engaging and Motivating Science) project: Final Report*, http://www.stran.ac.uk/media/media,181303,en.pdf.

McFall, D. and Macro, C. (2004) Creativity and science in the nursery, *Primary Science Review,* 81: 7–10.

McGuinness, C. (2000) ACTS (Activating Children's Thinking Skills): a methodology for enhancing thinking skills across the curriculum, paper presented at the ESRC TLRP conference, Nov.

McMeniman, M. (1989) Motivation to learn, in P. Langford (ed.) *Educational Psychology: An Australian Perspective*, Melbourne: Longman Cheshire, 215–239.

Maloney, J. and Curtis, S. (2012) Using models to promote children's scientific understanding, *Primary Science* 123: 5–7.

Mant, J., Wilson, H. and Coates, D. (2007) The effect of increasing conceptual challenge in primary science lessons on pupils' achievement and engagement, *International Journal of Science Education,* 29(14): 1707–19.

Mercer, N. (2000) *Words and Minds: How we Use Language to Think Together,* London: Routledge.

Millar, R. and Osborne, J. (1998) *Beyond 2000, Science Education for the Future,* London: King's College London, School of Education.

Morgan, M. (ed.) (n.d.) *Art in the First Years of Schooling,* Ipswich: Suffolk County Council.

Morris, R. (1990*) Science Education Worldwide,* Paris: UNESCO.

Murphy, C. and Beggs, J. (2003) Children's perceptions of school science, *School Science Review,* 84(308): 109–16.

Murphy, C., Neil, P. and Beggs, J (2007) Primary science teacher confidence revisited: ten years on, *Educational Research,* 49(4): 415–30.

Murphy, P., Davidson, M., Qualter, A., Simon, S. and Watt, D. (2000) *Effective Practice in Primary Science,* unpublished report of an exploratory study funded by the Nuffield Curriculum Projects Centre.

NACCCE (National Advisory Committee on Creative and Cultural Education) (1999) *All our Futures: Creativity, Culture and Education,* London: DfEE: www.artscampaigne.org.uk/campaigns/education/report.html.

Naylor, S. and Keogh, B. (2000) *Concept Cartoons in Science Education,* Sandbach: Millgate House Publishing.

Naylor, S., Keogh, B. and Goldsworthy, A. (2004) *Active Assessment: Thinking Learning and Assessment in Science,* London: David Fulton in Association with Millgate House Publishers.

Naylor, S., Keogh, B. and Downing, B. (2007) Argumentation in primary science, *Research in Science Education,* 37: 177–89.

Newton, D.P. and Newton, L.D. (2001) Subject content knowledge and teacher talk in the primary science classroom, *European Journal of Teacher Education,* 24(3): 369–79.

Newton, L.D., Newton, D.P., Blake, A. and Brown, K. (2002) Do primary school science books for children show a concern for explanatory understanding? *Research in Science and Technological Education,* 20(2): 228–39.

Ng, W. (2010) Why digital literacy is important for science teaching and learning, *Curriculum Leadership* (online journal) 10(10): http://www.curriculum.edu.au/leader/why_digital_literacy_is_important_for_science_teac,34913.html?issueID=12610.

Nimmons, F. (2003) Tracking pupils' progress. *Primary Science Review* 80: 13–15

Nuffield Foundation (2012) *Developing Policy, Principles and Practice in Primary School,* London: Nuffield Foundation: http://www.nuffieldfoundation.org/primary-science-assessment.

Nuffield Junior Science Project (1967) *Teachers' Guide,* London: Collins.

Nuffield Primary Science Teachers' Guides (1995) Various topics, London: Collins Educational.

Nuffield Primary Science (SPACE) (1995a) *The Earth in Space Ages 7–12 Teachers' Guide,* London: Collins Educational.

Nuffield Primary Science (SPACE) (1995b) *The Earth in Space Ages 5–7 Teachers' Guide,* London: Collins Educational.

Nusche, D., Laveault, D., MacBeath, J. and Santiago, P. (2012) *OECD Reviews of Evaluation and Assessment in Education: New Zealand 2011,* Paris: OECD Publishing.

Nystrand, M., Gamorgan, A., Kachy, R. and Prendergast, C. (1997) *Opening Dialogue: Understanding the Dynamics of Language and Learning in the English Classroom,* New York: Teachers' College Press.

O'Brien, L. and Murray, R. (2007) Forest School and its impact on young children: case studies in Britain, *Urban Forestry and Urban Greening*, 6: 249–65.

OECD (Organization for Economic Cooperation and Development) (1999) *Measuring Student Knowledge and Skills: A New Framework for Assessment*, Paris: OECD.

OECD (2006) *Assessing Scientific, Reading and Mathematical Literacy: A Framework for PISA 2006*, Paris: OECD.

OECD (2007) *Understanding the Brain: The Birth of a Learning Science*, Paris: OECD.

OECD (2009) *PISA 2009 Assessment Framework: key competencies in reading, mathematics and science*. Paris : OECD

OECD (2013) *Synergies for Better Learning: An International Perspective on Evaluation and Assessment, Summary*, Paris: OECD Publishing.

Ofsted (2004) *Ofsted Science Subject Reports 2002/3: Science in the Primary School*, London: DfEE.

Ofsted (2011a) Successful Science: an evaluation of science education in England 2007-2010. Manchester: Ofsted, Jan.: www.ofsted.gov.uk/publications/100034.

Ofsted (2011b) *ICT in Schools 2008–11: An Evaluation of Information Communication Technology Education in Schools in England*, London: HMSO, Dec.

Ormerod, M.B. and Duckworth, D. (1975) *Pupils' Attitudes to Science*, Windsor: NFER.

Osborne, J. Erduran, S. and Simon, S. (2004) Enhancing the quality of argumentation in school science, *Journal of Research in Science Teaching*, 41(10): 994–1020.

Osborne, J., Wadsworth, P. and Black, P. (1992) *Processes of Life*, SPACE project Research Report, Liverpool: Liverpool University Press.

Osborne, R. and Freyberg, P. (1985) *Learning Science: The Implications of 'Children's Science'*, Auckland: Heinemann.

Owen, D., Baskerville, S., and Evans, W. (2008) From source to sea, *Primary Science*, 101: 25–7.

Paterson, V. (1987) What might be learnt from children's writing in primary science? *Primary Science Review*, 4: 17–20.

Peacock, A. (2006a) Editorial, *Primary Science Review*, 91: 2–3.

Peacock, A. (2006b) *Changing Minds: The Lasting Impact of School Trips. A Study of the Long Term Impact of Sustained Relationships between Schools and the National Trust via the Guardianship Scheme*: http://www.nationaltrust.org.uk/main/w-schools-guardianships-changing_minds.pdf.

Peacock, A. and Weedon, H. (2002) Children working with text in science: disparities with 'literacy hour' practice, *Research in Science and Technological Education*, 20(2): 185–97.

Plowman, L., Stephenson, O., Stephen, C. and McPake, J (2012) Preschool children's learning with technology at home, *Computers and Education*, 59(1): 30–7.

Popper, K.R. (1968) *The Logic of Scientific Discovery*, London: Hutchinson.

Reid, C. and Anderson, M. (2012) Left-brain, right-brain, brain games and beanbags: neuromyths in education, in P. Adey and J. Dillon (eds) *Bad Education*, Maidenhead: Open University Press, 179–98.

Reimann, P. and Goodyear, P. (2004) *ICT and Pedagogy Stimulus Paper*: http://lrnlab.edfac.usyd.edu.au/Members/preimann/ICTintped/ICT-Pedagogies-v33.pdf.

Richard W. Riley College of Education and Leadership (2010) *Educators, Technology and 21st Century Skills: Dispelling Five Myths*, Place: Walden University, Walden University Press.

Roberts, G. (2002) *SET for Success: The Supply of People with Science, Technology, Engineering and Mathematical Skills*, London: HM Treasury.

Robertson, A. (2004) Let's think! Two years on! *Primary Science Review,* 82: 4–7.

Rose, J. (2009) *The Independent Review of the Primary Curriculum: Final Report,* London: DCSF.

Royal Society (2006) *Taking a Leading Role,* London: The Royal Society.

Royal Society (2010) *Science and Mathematics Education 5–14,* London: The Royal Society.

Rudd, T. (2007) *Futurelab Whiteboards Report*: http://www.futurelab.org.uk/resources/documents/other/whiteboards_report.pdf.

Russell, T. (2011) Progression in learning science, in W. Harlen (ed.) *ASE Guide to Primary Science Education,* new edn, Hatfield: ASE, 17–24.

Russell, T. and Watt, D. (1990) *Primary SPACE Project Report: Growth,* Liverpool: Liverpool University Press.

Russell, T., Longden, K. and McGuigan, L. (1991) *Primary SPACE Project Report: Materials,* Liverpool: Liverpool University Press.

Sandford, R., Ulicsak, M., Facer, K., and Rudd, T (2006) *Teaching with Games: Using Commercial Off-the-Shelf Computer Games in Formal Education,* Bristol: Futurelab.

Schildkamp, K., Vanhoof, J., van Petegem, P. and Visscher, A. (2012) The use of school self-evaluation results in the Netherlands and Flanders, *British Journal of Educational Research,* 38(1): 125–52.

Schilling, M., Hargreaves, L., Harlen, W. and Russell, T. (1990) *Assessing Science in the Primary Classroom: Written Tasks*, London: Paul Chapman Publishing.

Schofield, K. (2011) Formative feedback and self-assessment, in W. Harlen (ed.) *ASE Guide to Primary Science Education,* new edn, Hatfield: ASE, 85–93.

Science – A Process Approach (SAPA) (1966–76) Rank Xerox Services. Washington, DC: American Association for the Advancement of Science.

Science Curriculum Improvement Study (SCIS) (1970–4) Lawrence Hall of Science, Berkeley, CA.

SEED (Scottish Executive Education Department) (2003) *Assessment of Achievement Programme: Report of the 6th AAP Survey of Science,* Edinburgh: SEED.

SEED (2005) *Circular 02,* Edinburgh: SEED, June.

SEED (2006) *Parents as Partners in their Children's Learning Toolkit,* Edinburgh: Scottish Executive: available at www.scotland.gov.uk/Resource/Doc/147410/0038822.pd.

Serret, N. (2004) Leaping into the unknown: developing thinking in the primary science classroom, *Primary Science Review,* 82: 8–11.

Shulman, L.S. (1987) Knowledge and teaching: foundations of the new reform, *Harvard Educational Review,* 7, 1–22.

Sharp, J.G. and Hopkin, R.C. (2008) *National Primary Science Survey (England): In-Service Training Audit; A Report Prepared for the Wellcome Trust,* Lincoln: Bishop Grosseteste University College Lincoln and the Wellcome Trust.

Simon, D. (2011) School-level planning, in W. Harlen (ed.) *ASE Guide to Primary Science Education,* new edn, Hatfield: ASE, 126–32.

Simon, S., Naylor, S., Keogh, B., Maloney, J. and Downing, B. (2008) Puppets promoting engagements and talk in science, *International Journal of Science Education*, 309: 1229–48.

Skinner, B.F. (1974) *About Behaviourism,* New York: Alfred A. Knopf.

Smith, C., diSessa, A. and Roschelle J (1993) Misconceptions reconceived: a constructivist analysis of knowledge in transition, *Journal of Learning Sciences,* 3: 111–63.

Smith, F., Hardman, F. and Higgins, S. (2006) The impact of interactive whiteboards on teacher-pupil interaction in the National Literacy and Numeracy Strategies, *British Educational Research Journal,* 32(3): 443–57.

Smith, M., Howard, D., and Hoath, L. (2011) Head in the cloud, feet on the ground, *Primary Science,* 119: 21–3.

SPACE (Science Processes and Concepts Exploration) Research Reports (1990–8) various titles, Liverpool: University of Liverpool Press.

STA (Standards and Testing Agency) (2012) *2013 Early Years Foundation Stage Profile Handbook,* London: STA.

Starkey, L. (2010) Teachers' pedagogical reasoning and action in the digital age, *Teachers and Teaching: Theory and Practice,* 16(2): 233–44.

Sutherland, R., Armstrong, V., Barnes, S., Brawn, R., Breeze, N., Gall, M., Matthewson, S., Olivero, F., Taylor, A., Triggs, P., Wishart, J. and John, P. (2004) Transforming teaching and learning: embedding ICT into everyday classroom practices, *Journal of Computer Assisted Learning,* 20: 413–25.

Swaffield, S. (2008) Feedback: the central process in assessment for learning, in S. Swaffield (ed.) *Unlocking Assessment,* London: David Fulton, 57–72.

Tamim, R., Bernard, R., Borokhovski, E., Abrami, P. and Schmid, R. (2011) What forty years of research says about the impact of technology on learning: a second-order meta-analysis and validation study, *Review of Educational Research,* 81(1): 4–28.

Teaching and Learning Research Programme (TLRP) (2005) *Briefing No. 11: Improving Pupil Group Work in Classrooms. A New Approach to Increasing Engagement in Everyday Classroom Settings at Key Stages 1, 2 and 3*, London: TLRP: http://www.groupworkscotland.org.

Tickell, C. (2011) *The Early Years: Foundations for Life, Health and Learning. An Independent Report on the Early Years Foundation Stage to Her Majesty's Government,* London: DfE.

Thornton, L. and Brunton, P. (2003) All about the Reggio approach, *Nursery World* (Jan.): 15.

Tunnicliffe, S.D. (2001) Talking about plants: comments of primary school groups looking at plants exhibits in a botanical garden, *Journal of Biological Education,* 36(1): 27–34.

Tunnicliffe, S.D. and Litson, S. (2002) Observation or imagination, *Primary Science Review,* 71: 25–7.

Turner, J. (2011) Continuing professional development and the role of science learning centres, in W. Harlen (ed.) *ASE Guide to Primary Science Education,* new edn, Hatfield: ASE, 141–8.

Turner, J., Keogh, B., Naylor, S. and Lawrence, L. (2011) *It's Not Fair – or is it?* Sandbach: Millgate House Education and ASE.

UNESCO (1982) *New Trends in Primary Schools Science Education.* Paris: UNESCO

Vanhoof, J., van Petegem, P. and de Maeyer, S. (2009) Attitudes towards school self-evaluation, *Studies in Educational Evaluation,* 35(1): 21–8.

Villard, E. (2009) Le Cahier de sciences au cours préparatoire de l'école primaire en France, PhD dissertation, Université Louis-Lumière, Lyon.

Vosniadou, S. (1997) On the development of the understanding of abstract ideas, in K. Harnqvist and A. Burgen (eds) *Growing up with Science,* London: Jessica Kingsley, 41–57.

Vygotsky, L. (1978) Interaction between learning and development, in *Mind and Society,* Cambridge, MA: Harvard University Press, 79–91.

Ward, H. (2008) Organisational issues, in H. Ward, J. Roden, C. Hewlett and J. Foreman, *Teaching Science in the Primary Classroom,* 2nd edn, London: Sage, pp. 138–152.

Watkins, C. (2003) *Learning: A Sense-Maker's Guide,* London: Association of Teachers and Lecturers.

Webb, M. (2005) Affordances of ICT in Science Learning: Implications for an Integrated Pedagogy, *International Journal of Science Education,* 27(6): 705–35.

Wegerif, R. and Dawes, L. (2004) *Thinking and Learning with ICT: Raising Achievement in Primary Classrooms,* London: Routledge.

Wellcome Trust (2005) *Primary Horizons: Starting out in Science,* London: Wellcome: www.wellcome.ac.uk/primaryhorizons.

Wellcome Trust (2011) *Primary Science Survey Report*, London: Wellcome: http://www.wellcome.ac.uk/About-us/Publications/Reports/Education.

Wellcome Trust (2013) *Inside the Brain: Big Picture*, 17 (spring): http://www.wellcome.ac.uk/Education-resources/Education-and-learning/Big-Picture/All-issues/Inside-the-brain/index.htm.

Wiliam, D. (2001) Reliability, validity and all that jazz, *Education 3–13*, 29(3): 17–21.

Wiliam, D. (2008) Quality in assessment, in S. Swaffield (ed.) *Unlocking Assessment,* London: David Fulton, 123–37.

Williamson, B. (2006) Elephants can't jump: creativity, new technology and concept exploration in primary science, in P. Warwick, E. Wilson and M. Winterbottom (eds) *Teaching and Learning Primary Science with ICT,* Maidenhead: Open University Press, 70–92.

Winnie W.M. So (2012) Creating a framework of a resource-based e-learning environment for science learning in primary classrooms, *Technology, Pedagogy and Education,* 21(3): 317–35.

Wright, L. (2003) Science under scrutiny, *Primary Science Review,* 79, 8–10.

Wright, L. (2006) School self-evaluation of teaching and learning science, in W. Harlen (ed.) *ASE Guide to Primary Science Education,* Hatfield: ASE, 73–9.

Zull, J.E. (2004) The art of changing the brain, *Educational Leadership*, 62(1): 68–72.

Websites

Askabout Ireland http://www.askaboutireland.ie/learning-zone/primary-students

Association for Science Education http://www.ase.org.uk/home/

BBC Bitesize http://www.bbc.co.uk/bitesize/ks2/science/

BBC Learning Zone http://www.bbc.co.uk/learningzone/

DREAMS project: http://www.stran.ac.uk/informationabout/research/dreamsproject/

Eire on line curriculum planning tool
http://www.curriculumonline.ie/en/Primary_School_Curriculum/Curriculum_Planning_Tool/

Futurelab www.futurelab.org.uk

Hertfordshire Development Centre
http://www.thegrid.org.uk/learning/ict/technologies/index.html

The Leonardo Effect
http://www.leonardoeffect.com/connecting_learning_to_hard_to_reach_children.html

National Science Learning Centre
https://www.sciencelearningcentres.org.uk/centres/national

Primary Science quality Mark
https://www.sciencelearningcentres.org.uk/centres/west-midlands/primary-science-quality-mark

The Primary Science Teaching Trust (PSTT)
  http://www.pstt.org.uk/resources/continuing-professional-development/enrich-science-learning.aspx
RSPB birdwatch http://www.rspb.org.uk/birdwatch/
RSPB schoolswatch http://www.rspb.org.uk/schoolswatch/
Scottish Primary Curriculum Planning Tool
  http://www.curriculum-for-excellence.co.uk/planning-tool/
South East Grid for Learning http://birdbox.segfl.org.uk
Wellcome Trust Croydon Schools project
  http://blog.wellcome.ac.uk/2012/05/24/the-croydon-school-science-project/

Index